Louis Armstrong, in His Own Words

Louis Armstrong, in His Own Words

Selected Writings

Louis Armstrong

EDITED AND WITH AN INTRODUCTION AND APPENDIX
BY THOMAS BROTHERS

ANNOTATED INDEX
BY CHARLES KINZER

OXFORD
UNIVERSITY PRESS

Oxford New York
Athens Auckland Bangkok Bogotá Buenos Aires Calcutta
Cape Town Chennai Dar es Salaam Delhi Florence Hong Kong Istanbul
Karachi Kuala Lumpur Madrid Melbourne Mexico City Mumbai
Nairobi Paris São Paulo Shanghai Singapore Taipei Tokyo Toronto Warsaw

and associated companies in
Berlin Ibadan

First published by Oxford University Press, Inc., 1999
198 Madison Avenue, New York, New York 10016

First issued as an Oxford University Press paperback, 2001

Library of Congress Cataloging-in-Publication Data
Armstrong, Louis, 1901–1971.
Louis Armstrong, in his own words: selected writings / Louis Armstrong
edited by Thomas Brothers ; annotated index by Charles Kinzer.
p. cm.
Includes bibliographical references (p.) and index.
ISBN 0-19-511958-4 (Cloth.)
ISBN 0-19-514046-X (Pbk.)
1. Armstrong, Louis, 1901–1971. 2. Jazz musicians—United States—
Biography. 3. Jazz—History and criticism. I. Brothers,
Thomas David. II. Title.
ML419.A75A3 1999
781.65'092—dc21
99-17040

Design: Adam B. Bohannon

10 9 8 7 6 5 4 3 2 1

Printed in the United States of America
on acid-free paper

CONTENTS

"Swing a Lot of Type Writing":
An Introduction to Louis Armstrong's Writings, vii
Editorial Policy, xxv
Acknowledgments, xxvii

I. "Home Sweet Home":
Childhood and Apprenticeship in New Orleans, 1

1 "Louis Armstrong + the Jewish Family in New Orleans, La., the Year of 1907" (March 31, 1969–1970), 3
2 "Joe Oliver Is Still King" (1950), 37
3 "Bunk Didn't Teach Me" (1950), 40
4 Letter to Isidore Barbarin (September 1, 1922), 42

II. "Some Kind of a God":
Chicago, New York, and California, 1922-1931, 45

5 "The Armstrong Story" (1954), 47
6 Letters to Robert Goffin (May 7 and July 19, 1944), 77
7 The "Goffin Notebooks" (ca. 1944), 82
8 "The Satchmo Story" (early 1959), 111
9 "Jazz on a High Note" (1951), 127

III. "Book Anywhere--Anytime":
Life on the Road during the 1940s and 1950s, 137

10 Early Years with Lucille (ca. 1970), 139
11 Letter to Leonard Feather (September 18, 1941), 145
12 Letter to Betty Jane Holder (February 9, 1952), 150
13 Letter to Joe Glaser (August 2, 1955), 157
14 "Lombardo Grooves Louis!" (1949), 164

IV. "Music Has No Age": Late Years in Corona, New York, 167

15 Letter to L/Cpl. Villec (1967), 169
16 "Scanning the History of Jazz" (1960), 173
17 "Our Neighborhood" (ca. 1970), 176
18 Open Letter to Fans (June 1, 1970), 179
19 "Goodbye to All of You" (1969), 189

Appendix, 191
Bibliography of Writings by Louis Armstrong, 221
Works Cited, 225
Annotated Index of Proper Names, Places, Songs, and Shows, 229

"SWING A LOT OF TYPE WRITING"

AN INTRODUCTION TO LOUIS ARMSTRONG'S WRITINGS

> Am sorry that I have to write this letter with a pen, but, on arriving at the air port in Las Vegas yesterday, My typewriter fell from on top of all, that luggage that was on the truck, And the "Jolt" Sprung' everything. Tch, Tch, isn't it A Drag? And I wanted so badly to swing a lot of Type Writing, "Gappings" on ya"
>
> —Louis Armstrong, Letter to Joe Glaser

Armstrong the Writer

The present collection of writings is like no other, for the simple reason that no jazz musician of Louis Armstrong's stature matched his sustained interest in writing. Some jazz musicians did write autobiographies, though more produced autobiographies in "as-told-to" collaborations. With the exception of two or three items, Armstrong alone wrote the words in this book with pen, pencil, and typewriter. In addition to the two autobiographies that were published during his lifetime, he wrote memoirs, essays, magazine articles, book reviews, and letters. It would be difficult to come up with a long list of major twentieth-century musicians working in any genre, not just in jazz, who produced a comparable body of written work. Armstrong's written legacy is a treasure for jazz history, for the history of African-American culture, and, indeed, for the cultural history of the United States.

The documents published in this book have been arranged to lead the reader through four main periods of Armstrong's life—early life in New Orleans, the spectacular rise of his career in Chicago and New York during the 1920s, touring life during the 1940s and 1950s, and his final years in

Corona, New York. The main documents have never been published before. "Louis Armstrong + the Jewish Family in New Orleans, the Year of 1907" is a poignant account of Armstrong's youth, differing in tone and content from previously published accounts. "The Armstrong Story" is material that was cut from the end of the 1954 autobiography *Satchmo: My Life in New Orleans*. Also unpublished until now is "The Satchmo Story," which Armstrong conceived as a sequel to *Satchmo: My Life in New Orleans*. The sequel never came to fruition, perhaps because its beginning is dominated by Armstrong's thoughts on the benefits of marijuana—"This whole second book might be about nothing but gage," he says. The "Goffin Notebooks" is a colorful narrative of the 1920s that Armstrong wrote for Robert Goffin to use in his biography of Armstrong. Also unpublished until now are essays written during the last years of Armstrong's life (Chapters 11, 18, and 19), as well as the letters to Betty Jane Holder, Joe Glaser, and L/Cpl. Villec.

It is important to bear in mind the different purposes for which Armstrong wrote. One motivation was simply to stay in touch with distant friends and admirers. His 1922 "Letter to Isidore Barbarin," written from Chicago to Barbarin in New Orleans, is the earliest known document written by him. For Armstrong, as for thousands of African Americans who moved from the South to the North during the first big wave of the Great Migration, the warmth of a letter from home was welcome indeed. Armstrong continued to write letters as he settled into the life of a touring musician during the 1930s, '40s and '50s. The 1967 "Letter to L/Cpl. Villec," a soldier stationed in Vietnam, is a good example of his ability to open up to a stranger in a letter. Someday—especially after more of Armstrong's letters have found their way into archives—we may enjoy a substantial edition devoted exclusively to his letters. The total number of surviving letters is likely to be astonishing, probably in the thousands.

A very different reason for Armstrong to write was to supply professional writers with material that they could use for publicity purposes. Armstrong learned to cultivate strategic relationships that were beneficial to both parties. In the "Letter to Joe Glaser," his manager for several decades, he candidly recalls some advice given him by a childhood mentor before his departure from New Orleans:

> [Black Benny] said (to me) "*Dipper*, As long as you live, no matter where you may be—always have a White Man (who like you) and can

> + will put his Hand on your shoulder and say—*"This is "My" Nigger"* and, Can't Nobody Harm' Ya."

In telling this story to Glaser, who was the main White Man who had his arm on Armstrong's shoulder, Armstrong reveals its direct truth, the core of which carries over to his relationships with Leonard Feather and Robert Goffin, two important writers on jazz. There is no reason to doubt the sincerity of Armstrong's friendships with these men, but he was obviously aware that writers served as intermediaries between black musicians and white audiences, just as a manager did. He happily supplied Goffin with autobiographical material (The "Goffin Notebooks") for use in the biography *Horn of Plenty.* "Lombardo Grooves Louis!" is Armstrong's contribution to an article by Feather in *Metronome.* In an ongoing correspondence, Feather posed questions that Armstrong would answer, all with publication in mind; "Letter to Leonard Feather" is one of Armstrong's replies. When these and other writers asked, Armstrong freely "greased their mitts"—his way of describing his dispensation of cash handouts, which seems equally applicable to his dispensation of information. (In "Letter to Robert Goffin," May 7, 1944, Armstrong expresses irritation at Feather's apparent ingratitude for the material he has provided—"I've done ever' so much for him and didn't even charge him one nickel.") Unlike Armstrong's gifts of cash, however, these written handouts held the promise of a return in the form of free publicity.

Some magazines were interested in presenting Armstrong's own words directly to their readers. This book includes excerpts from two articles written for the fiftieth-birthday celebration given in his honor by *The Record Changer* ("Joe Oliver Is Still King" and "Bunk Didn't Teach Me"), two articles written for *Esquire* ("Jazz on a High Note" and "Goodbye to All of You"), and one for the *Jazz Review* ("Scanning the History of Jazz"). Publicity was one motivation for these articles, but it would be unfair to suggest that it was the sole motivation. Armstrong had a great urge, especially during his last years, to set the historical record straight. He cherished any opportunity to communicate with his fans, and in this sense publication provided him with another kind of public stage.

Which brings us to the most important motivation underlying Armstrong's written work: Armstrong writes because he sees himself as a writer. His writing became a hobby: "Of course I am not so bad myself at 'Swimming.— In fact it's one of my' famous 'Hobbies, outside of "Typing."— I loves that also." This hobby was well suited for passing time in a dressing room or hotel. His portable typewriter became his off-stage passion, though visitors sometimes made it difficult for him to find the time to write.[1] Eventually, the hobby became part of his identity. The following exchange, from a radio interview that was transcribed by Armstrong's management and entered into a publicity booklet from the late 1940s ("Publicity Manual," held at the Institute of Jazz Studies, Rutgers University), is revealing:

ANNOUNCER: Well, you've certainly come a long way along the comeback trail if we may call it that. What do you think helped you the most during this period, Louie?

LOUIS: Well, phonograph records, of course. They are important to any band, and especially to one like mine, which doesn't get as much radio time as a lot of the others, although we did have a commercial once. And then, the motion pictures, with Bing Crosby and the other stars. That helped a lot to let the public know what we were trying to do.

ANNOUNCER: I remember you distinctly in that one picture "Pennies From Heaven," with Bing, when you sang "The Skeleton in the Closet." That was a killer, old man.

LOUIS: You sound like you were hep to the jive?

ANNOUNCER: That's a mistake. The script writer merely wrote that line in for me. But they tell me that you are one of the original "jive" artists, Louie, and that's why they call you "Pops"?

LOUIS: I could always fall in the righteous groove with the rest of the cats, and either dig the jive or beef on back with the Duke, the Cab, the Coop or the other killer-dillers. But all that comes natural, and what I'm really proud of is my ability to speak and write straight English.

ANNOUNCER: You are a writer, too, Louie?

LOUIS: Man, I'm a two-fingered blip on my portable typewriter.

ANNOUNCER: That reminds me, you did write a book once, didn't you Louie, without the assistance of a ghost writer or press agent, they tell me?

LOUIS: That's right! We called it "Swing That Music" and it might not have been a literary masterpiece, but every word of it was my own, so I can read it and understand it.

ANNOUNCER: That's more than a lot of celebrities can say about the books they are supposed to have written, Louie. I've been told that you

> carry a dictionary and a book of synonyms and antonyms in your brief case wherever you go, is that true?
> LOUIS: Certainly is. I learned to use them when I was writing the book, and I keep 'em handy now for my letter writing. Then when one of those hard words jumps up, I've got the answer in the bag. I didn't get much education when I was young, you know, so I'm still learning.

There is a bit of comedy here, with the announcer hiding behind his script while Armstrong spins circles of jive talk. There is also some important information, not least being the flat assertion that Armstrong wrote "every word" of *Swing That Music*.[2] Armstrong insists that the book was not "ghost written," and given what we know about him as a writer we should believe him. Also interesting is Armstrong's placement of the autobiography alongside recordings, radio shows, and movies. The multimedia approach of presenting entertainers to the public was coming into full bloom during the 1940s, and Armstrong's writing hobby gave him an additional advantage.

More personal is the information that Armstrong carries with him a dictionary and a book of synonyms and antonyms, which educate him in "straight English."[3] "Jive talk," on the other hand, comes naturally. Signaled is a certain pride in verbal ability, along with pride in achievement against the odds of early poverty and limited formal education. Also signaled is a two-fold social orientation that is a familiar theme in African-American literature. This theme is articulated with reference to both music and words by bell hooks (1980: 11), who relates the musical dimension to Armstrong:

> In part, attending all-black segregated schools with black teachers meant that I had come to understand black poets as being capable of speaking in many voices, that the Dunbar of a poem written in dialect was no more or less authentic than the Dunbar writing a sonnet. Yet it was listening to black musicians like Duke Ellington, Louis Armstrong, and later John Coltrane that impressed upon our consciousness a sense of versatility—they played all kinds of music, had multiple voices. So it was with poetry. The black poet, as exemplified by Gwendolyn Brooks and later Amiri Baraka, had many voices—with no single voice being identified as more or less authentic. The insistence on finding one voice, one definitive style of writing and reading one's poetry, fit all too neatly

> with a static notion of self and identity that was pervasive in university settings. It seemed that many black students found our situations problematic precisely because our sense of self, and by definition our voice, was not unilateral, monologist, or static but rather multi-dimensional. We were as at home in dialect as we were in standard English. . . .

Armstrong's goal is to be as fluent in straight English as he is in jive talk, which may be defined as an African-American dialect cultivated especially by jazz musicians. Following hooks, we may view his two-fold orientations, musical and verbal, analogously. The requirement of mastering several musical styles was demanded of any African-American musician of Armstrong's generation working in the popular sphere; the goal to master straight English as well as jive talk is an aspiration of Armstrong the writer. In fact the adjectives "jive" and "straight" were commonly used by jazz musicians to refer to verbal as well as musical styles that could be identified with black and white cultural communities, respectively.[4]

Writers love words, and Armstrong's credentials in this regard are firm. Baby Dodds (Dodds 1992: 25) and others credited him with innovative usage of "cats," "Pops," "jive," and "scat." Two discussions of highly charged topics (both from "The Satchmo Story") indicate his sensitivity to nuances that attach to common usage:

> What is it telling a kid the life of the musicians who played there—and give them a phony name such as Storyville, which has never registered with me, like the magic word—redlight district . . . It sounds more musical to say the real thing.
>
> That's one thing that I personally found out about Gage, or Marijuana, Narcotic, P.S. Maybe that's why that it is put on the Narcotic list—those two names does sound real bad. Marijuana—Narcotic . . . Sometimes names—just the sounds can cause one, grief of somewhat . . . Such as big stars . . . Just a change in the names sometimes, bring them big successes, fortunes, and stuff like that . . . Maybe someday—some big Authority on things—anything, just as long as he's a big man and has convincing words . . . Then he can probably someday have 'Marijuana name changed to 'Gage—'Muta—'Pot—or some of that *good shit* . . .

He enjoys semantic play. For example, the word "gappings," which dictionaries of African-American dialect define as "salary," is used both in this conventional sense and in an idiosyncratic sense, as an onomatopoetic reference to the action of typing (as in the quotation placed at the beginning of this introduction).

Armstrong brought to the invention of words the same package of creativity, intelligence, nuance, and charm that he brought to the invention of music. The reader will quickly learn to recognize his prose style, which combines jive talk and straight English in a personal and very fluent way. He is not bound by the conventions of either dialect; rather, his personal approach to combining them seems to open up a field of creativity. The style is forthright and crisp. It features vivid descriptions that give the reader a sense of place, of mood, of interpersonal relations. Visceral topics—sex, food, defecation, laughter, illness, music—are presented directly, without self-consciousness. Through years of practicing his hobby, he acquired a prose voice that is every bit as distinctive as his musical voice.

Most distinctive of all about Armstrong's prose is his idiosyncratic use of visual symbols. His usage is consistent enough that we may speak of an orthographic style. Most of Armstrong's previous editors have tended to "correct" these idiosyncrasies, giving the prose a more conventional appearance. From the beginning of the present project it was clear that Armstrong's orthography is an integral part of his writing and that it must be respected. Here we may identify a few general tendencies and suggest an approach for interpretation.

For punctuation, Armstrong uses all of the standard symbols, but with only a few of them (period, question mark, exclamation mark, semicolon, and colon) does he limit himself to conventional practice. Ellipses, dash, parentheses, comma, apostrophe, and double apostrophe are all used inventively. For example, sometimes he abandons the period as an indicator of a full stop while ellipses (in typed documents) and dashes (in handwritten documents) take over. In a thoughtful analysis of Armstrong's punctuation, William Kenney (1991) observes the use of the apostrophe independently of syntactical function and the vast number of unconventional capitalizations. The reader may have noticed these in passages already quoted:

> *This is ''My'' Nigger''* and, Can't Nobody Harm' Ya.
> And the ''Jolt Sprung' everything.
> Then he can probably someday have 'Marijuana name changed to 'Gage—'Muta—'Pot—or some of that *good shit* . . .

But I just wouldn't let it 'Bug me.
I had just come up from the South, where there weren't anything near as beautiful as that 'happening.
a certain 'Spoon for this and a certain 'fork for that

Kenney suggests that ellipses, apostrophes, and capitalizations "indicate a distance from the meanings of words." When unconventional marks are eliminated by an editor, Armstrong's intended meaning may be reversed: irony is destroyed and the sentence stands as a literal statement of fact. In this way, the two autobiographies published during Armstrong's lifetime were severely distorted, according to Kenney.

We owe Kenney thanks for taking Armstrong's orthography seriously, yet I would argue that he has strongly overstated the case for reading these marks ironically. It is possible that Armstrong occasionally uses ellipses, apostrophes, and capitalization in this way.[5] But from the randomly selected passages just quoted the reader can see how the apostrophe and capitalization are used more simply, as a way to convey emphasis. For example, in the second quotation, the closed double apostrophe gives primary emphasis to "Jolt" while the single apostrophe gives secondary emphasis to "Sprung." Capitalization also conveys emphasis, often in combination with apostrophes and underlining (everything underlined by Armstrong has been converted to italic font in this book). These devices are part of Armstrong's routine, sentence-by-sentence style. The occasional example where unconventional marks suggest irony must be factored into the big picture, the thousands of words Armstrong wrote with no apparent trace of irony. It is attractive to think of jazz musicians as masters of irony, and for Armstrong especially, with his problematically shifting relationships to black audiences and to white audiences, there is great incentive to nurture this perspective; there is an incentive, that is, to think of him as sending double messages, one message for the commercial crowd and one for the more knowing crowd. Yet, I find it highly unlikely that his writings are saturated with irony, and there may be a more persuasive way to analyze the general trends that mark his idiosyncratic orthography.

The interpretation that seems to hold most consistently is that Armstrong is interested in depicting an oral rendition of his prose; he offers not just written prose but his version of how to hear it. He is especially attentive to emphasis and pace. Given who he was as a musician, this interest is not surprising, for he was a great master of melodic nuance and rhythm. The improvising musician controls time completely; that is the challenge and envy of his profession, since his abilities in performance and composition combine duties that are typically relegated to separate people in Euro-centric musical traditions. The jazz musician, more than any other kind of improviser, makes his reputation through this ability to control time, from the smallest nuance to the most complicated syntactical structure. In the blues tradition that Armstrong learned as a child, mastery of pitch inflection was also highly valued. Armstrong later brought this mastery to performance of all kinds of music.

These African-derived musical practices surface also in the improvisatory traditions of African-American verbal performance. Armstrong's creative step is to bring these improvisatory—or *performative*—techniques to his writing hobby. The varied lengths of his ellipses, from standard three (sometimes two are used) to as many as fifteen, imply varied durations of pause. Commas and apostrophes clarify syntax, but they are also used to convey emphasis or to mark off the pace of a sentence. Armstrong has available a large array of symbols for marking degrees of emphasis, including capitalization of the initial letter or an entire word and, as we have seen, single and double apostrophes marking the beginning of a word, the end, or both. In the following sentence, dashes emphasize "stopped," and both the comma and underlining emphasize "health":[6]

> But—very few of them—stopped—once to consider that, *health* plays the most important part of it all.

Thus, the symbols do not create a sense of distance—just the opposite. They personalize the text. They attempt to add Armstrong's *voice* to his words. L/Cpl. Villec, stationed in Vietnam, probably sensed this, and we can too:

> Dear L/Cpl, Villec″
>
> I'd like to 'step in there for a 'Minute or 'so' to ″tell you how much—I 'feel to know that 'you are a 'Jazz *fan*, and 'Dig' 'that 'Jive—the 'same as *'we* 'do, ″yeah.″ ″*Man*—I carry an 'Album, 'loaded with *Records*—'Long playing 'that is. And when I am *'Shaving* or 'Sitting on the 'Throne with *'Swiss Kriss'* in me—*That* Music 'sure 'brings out those 'Riffs 'Right Along with 'Swiss Kriss, which I 'take 'every night or when

> I *go* to bed. '*Yeah.* I give myself a 'Concert with those 'records. 'Music is 'life it'self. What would this 'world be without 'good music? No matter 'what kind it is.

Armstrong's attempt to convey a personal, oral rendering of his text resembles, in some ways, the scholar's attempt to convey in notation the improvised nuances of a jazz solo. Neither task is easy. Armstrong has an advantage in that he is composing the text and depicting its rendering at the same time. Again, the parallel between verbal and musical practices is strong. Though Armstrong was musically literate, the distinctive features of his style were rooted in an aural, performative conception of musical practice.[7] Similarly, though he was verbally literate and took pride in his writing, his literature has been touched by an aural, performative conception of verbal practice. As far as I know, he never became interested in finding ways to capture the performative subtleties of his musical style in notation. We are fortunate that the idea of capturing the performative subtleties of his verbal style through writing caught his imagination and became part of his hobby.

I do not wish to promote the idea that Armstrong is completely systematic in his use of symbols, that we can read every mark as conforming to some overarching premise. His practice is flexible. Capitalizations are sometimes used in a loose syntactical sense, to mark off the beginnings of clauses within a sentence (that is, the word that follows a dash or comma is capitalized).[8] Parentheses are used in several personal ways.[9] Commas are used both syntactically and to lend a sense of pace. The apostrophe appears frequently as a lighter form of pause, as well as for emphasis. Sometimes the inventive orthography communicates humor, as in the "Letter to Joe Glaser":

> "I— Just, Love, Your, Checks, in, My POCKETS—"OH" They look so *pretty*, until, I hate like hell to cash them.

Armstrong draws on the conventions and symbols of standard English as they suit him. A similar process was at work historically in the formation of jazz, where techniques that arose in the literate practice of European America—mainly harmony—were used by jazz musicians in a fresh way, according to a conception of musical style that arose through aurality. Armstrong the writer thus helps us to understand Armstrong the musician—and vice versa.

Armstrong and History

"As I've said, all through this story, that I have always been a great observer."

The most immediate value in reading Armstrong lies in the ability of his prose to draw the reader closer to his life, his personality, and his music. One may also value these documents for their usefulness in advancing interpretation along a range of historical issues. Consider, for example, a few themes related to the Great Migration, an event of great importance for Armstrong and for the history of African-American culture generally during the first half of this century.

In a striking passage from "The Armstrong Story" Armstrong describes his experience of a "trance," through which he becomes fully aware of the dramatic changes caused by his move to Chicago. From his first days in Chicago, Armstrong was surrounded by friends from New Orleans. But he was also beginning to step out of this cozy circle to form a relationship with Lil Hardin, his future wife. Though not originally from Chicago, Lil must have represented so much of what was new, exciting, and sophisticated about the place. Armstrong experiences his trance while the two of them are looking for an apartment for his mother, May-Ann, just arrived from New Orleans for an unexpected visit. He places this daydream in the context of his eagerness to repay his mother, who had helped him through difficult times with a woman named Nootsy. We may read a broader significance into these thoughts and this moment. For the daydream seems to gain meaning through the confluence of personalities and places, the sophistication of Armstrong's present and the relative lack of sophistication of his past:

> While Lil and the Realtor talked, I wandered back to the old days. I was going around with an old gal and I mean an old gal, named Nootsy. [. . .] I went with this chick for a long time—one night she wanted me to spend the night with her. I wasn't going for that jive. When I started out of the house she stuck me in the back with a *chib* (knife). I *cut* out on the *double*. When I got home May-Ann saw the blood on me and she took me back to the chick's house and grabbed her in the collar and gave her the whipping of her life. Every time she saw the blood on me

> she gave her another blow. That taught me a lesson. I have never been in any other cutting scrape since. That is when I was directly involved. There she was fighting my battle. She was always in my corner. So there was nothing too good for my mother and sister.
>
> Lil and the Realtor continued to talk—I came out of my trance and joined them.

The contrast between Nootsy and Lil is powerful enough to give trance-like pause; the unexpected arrival of May-Ann brings the contrast into focus.[10] Lil was college-educated and full of ambition. Nootsy wielded a chib, while Lil groomed Armstrong in table manners—"a certain 'Spoon for this and a certain 'fork for that." The difference between Nootsy and Lil is emblematic of the differences between Armstrong's New Orleans and his Chicago. It is the kind of cultural dynamic that was central to the Great Migration.

Armstrong describes Lil as a "Big High-powered 'Chick." With her education and refinement, she was so different that, initially, he simply "couldn't conceive of the Idea" of a romance. When his first wife Daisy, who was similar to Nootsy in some ways, traveled from New Orleans to Chicago in hopes of a reunion, Armstrong rebuked her: "I was a changed man since I came to Chicago and married Lil. No more 'Boisterous, 'Barrel house 'stuff. Am trying to 'Cultivate Myself." At one point Armstrong refers to Lil as the "master mind of the two," contrasting her prowess with his own "schooling from the old masters from those old good 'coal cart days." Lil's cultivation of Armstrong extended well beyond table manners. The master mind would "Run over some of the finest Classics, etc. on that Bran-new Baby Grand Piano I Bought for her . . . in our 'Parlor' Evenings After Supper." In due course, she prodded Armstrong to break away from his comfortable though restrictive position with Joe Oliver and to accept a position as soloist with Feltcher Henderson in New York City.

Armstrong attributed the eventual breakup of his marriage with Lil to differences in social class.[11] Similar tensions would arise in his last and longest-lasting marriage, to Lucille, though they were handled more successfully. Like Lil, Lucille worked in the entertainment business and she was socially ambitious—she had "a sense of *"Aires'*." This kind of social juxtaposition and the tension that went along with it made the mature Armstrong who he was. Had he stayed in New Orleans with Nootsy (or Daisy or even, perhaps, in Chicago with his third wife, Alpha) there would have been less tension of this kind, and one may imagine that there would also have been less achievement.

In "The Armstrong Story" Armstrong writes: "As I've said, all through this story, that I have always been a great observer." Armstrong the observer may be read as a central witness to the Great Migration. In Chicago he is marked as a "country boy"—even though he had rarely visited the country in Louisiana—by his manners, his clothing, and his naiveté. He is awed by the tall buildings, by an "all-colored" auto race, by the high level of respect afforded musicians, and by the heady flow of money. Thus, the line between New Orleans and Chicago is full of significance. It is easy to understand why Armstrong often turns back to his New Orleanian youth in his writings. He does so not simply out of nostalgia, but because of the dramatic boundary between youth and adulthood, apprenticeship and maturity, poverty and wealth, old musical style—represented, first and foremost, by his mentor, Joe Oliver—and new musical style, forged primarily by Armstrong himself. The break was mediated by the tethered departure from New Orleans via employment on Mississippi riverboats, where Armstrong was tutored in musical notation while he learned to play in a broader range of styles. He then found in Chicago a situation that embraced his distinctively New Orleanian abilities, giving him ample time to absorb the dazzling new trends in African-American entertainment that also flourished there.

African-American Chicago offered an array of musical sophistication, including renditions of the "Classics" by Lil Hardin, the song and dance routines of Ollie Powers and May Alix, Carroll Dickerson's polished orchestra, the "Symphonic music" of Erskine Tate, and the inspiration of dancer, mime, and comedian Bill "Bojangles" Robinson. Alongside this flourishing diversity of African-American entertainment there was a degree of racial mixing that was also new to Armstrong. He describes a "beautiful picture" from the Fiume Cafe:

> The *Fiume* was a Black + Tan place, which means Colored (of course) and they had an *all white* Dixieland Combo playing there' Nightly. Which was Something (at that time) very rare. Of course, there wasn't no particular reason why that I was a *little bit* surprised to see White Boys, playing music on the South Side of Chicago. It's just that I had never seen such a beautiful picture before. I had just come up from

> the South, where there weren't anything near as beautiful as that 'happening. *White* musicians, playing all of that good 'Jump' music—making those Colored people (mostly colored) *Swing like Mad.*

Thus went the nightly Northern display that Armstrong, along with thousands of others from the South, eagerly soaked up.

In sum, not only is Armstrong a witness to the cultural dynamics of the Great Migration, his musical achievement can be understood only as a *product* of this phenomenon. His personal journey from New Orleans to Chicago, from Nootsy to Lil, is the journey that produced the epoch-making break, out from the collective style of New Orleans and into a virtuoso solo style that belongs very much to the Northern 1920s. Though he had no desire to go back, Armstrong never forgot where he came from, musically and otherwise. Just as he mastered straight English without abandoning jive talk, so was he able to master the show styles and even classical styles of the North, successfully folding this mastery back into his emerging personal style. Reading him closely we learn about the core musical lessons from New Orleans—mastery of the blues and of "hot music," the ability to "invent," and an unyielding commitment to beautiful melody. Equally important are the personal lessons from his youth: the tough lessons of surviving poverty with optimism, the strong, communal bonds that fostered a gregarious spirit, techniques for coping with racism, relations with women, and the maintenance of daily health. And when, in 1922, he leaves his childhood and New Orleans behind, Armstrong's life unfolds in counterpoint to dramatic changes in both music and society. This keen observer did indeed live in interesting times, and there is much to learn from him not only about jazz but about social and cultural history, all seen through the eyes of one of America's most beloved entertainers.

Notes

1 As Armstrong explained in a letter to Leonard Feather, December 5, 1946, held by the Institute of Jazz Studies, Rutgers University:

> "'Man—I've been trying so hard to write you a letter—but owing to the fact that they have been bouncing us around so fast one would swear that we were a bunch of adagio dancers, etc. . . . Ha ha . . But I just wouldn't let it 'Bug me. . . . I intend writing you at the Golden

Gate Theater in San Francisco California. . . . Huh. . . . My dressing room was so crowded all the times, until every time I made an attempt to write a paragraph they'd look at me so wistful until I'd stop writing automatically. . . . You know how my disciples are . . . Tee Hee."

Another account of Armstrong's dressing room comes from Danny Barker (as quoted in Collier 1983: 314): "He be sittin' down in his underwear with a towel around his lap, one around his shoulders an' that white handkerchief on his head, and he'd put that grease around his lips. Look like a minstrel man, ya know . . . an' laughin' you know natural the way he is. And in the room ya see, maybe two nuns. You see a street walker dressed all up in flaming clothes. You see maybe a guy come out of a penitentiary. Ya see maybe a blind man sitting there. You see a rabbi, ya see a priest, see. Liable to see maybe two policemen or detectives, see. You see a judge. All of 'em different levels of society in the dressin' room and he's talking to all of 'em. 'Sister So and So, do you know Slick Sam over there? This is Slick Sam, an ole friend of mine.' Now the nun's going to meet Slick Sam. Old Notorious, been in nine penitentiaries. 'Slick Sam, meet Rabbi Goldstein over there, he's a friend of mine, rabbi good man, religious man. Sister Margaret, do you know Rabbi Goldstein? Amelia, this is Rosie, good time Rosie, girl used to work in a show with me years ago. Good girl, she's great performer. Never got the breaks.' Always a word of encouragement, see. And there'd be some kids there, white and colored. All the diverse people of different social levels . . . an' everybody's lookin'. Got their eyes dead on him, jus' like they was lookin' at a diamond."

2 I comment on the authority of *Swing That Music* in the Chapter 5 section of the Appendix. I should mention here my opinion that for none of the documents published in this book is there any question about Armstrong's authorship. For handwritten documents, the question of authority does not arise. For typewritten documents, there is usually such a strong presence of Armstrong's prose style and orthographic style that there can be little doubt about his authority. Magazine articles that have been edited in such a way as to diminish Armstrong's distinctive voice usually carry enough of that voice to identify his authorship—and given the fact of such a large body of firmly authenticated writings, Armstrong's authority usually seems unchallengable. The question arises only once in this vol-

ume, and that is in respect to the typescript for the initial part of "The Armstrong Story." There is some possibility that parts of this document (and parts of the overlapping typescript that formed the basis for *Satchmo: My Life in New Orleans*) were dictated by Armstrong to a secretary; see the discussion in the Chapter 5 section of the Appendix.

3 From "Louis Armstrong + the Jewish Family in New Orleans, the Year of 1907" we learn the following about Armstrong's early education in "straight English": "Helping on the Coal and Junk wagons every day with those *fine* Jewish Boys was great schooling for me. If I would say a *word* such as *Dat*—they the whole family would say ″no Louis, *that*, and not *Dat*″—Something on that order." In letters, Armstrong sometimes makes a joke out of his use of words that were apparently not part of his everyday vocabulary and may signal his use of a thesaurus. To Joe Glaser (undated letter, held at the Library of Congress): "I *personally* think that it is *imperative* that you do it. . . . . Damn. . . . That's a *big ass woid*." And in a letter to William Russell (Oct. 3, 1939; held at the Historic New Orleans Collection): "Say′ ′Gate′—concerning the Trumpet for my boy Bunk—I haven′t forgotten it at all . . . I just hadn′t had the time to go over to Rudy Muck′s place, and ′Intercede . . . ′Ump—′ ′Diddat Come Outa Mee? . . . Ha . . Ha . . . That′s a $5.00 ′Word isn′t it?" He also translates jive talk, occasionally, with parenthetical explanations. This happens particularly in the notebooks written for the Belgian Goffin, but it happens when Armstrong writes to others as well. For example, from The "Goffin Notebooks": "spade (that′s colored folks)," and "a lot of ′Ice′ (meaning) they treated us rather cool."

4 Armstrong wrote a weekly column (that ran for at least two issues, copies of which are held at the Institute for Jazz Studies) titled "Jive Talk" in the obscure *Harlem Tattler* during 1940.

5 Here is an example (from "The Armstrong Story") of ellipses used in an ironic context:

"There were so many I wanted to know all about, all of my old (white boys) childhood pals, the ones I played cowboys and Indians with in our good old school days. . . . . (We were the Indians.)"

6 In this passage, the dash after "But" exemplifies Armstrong's frequent

habit of inserting a dash or comma after an initial "And," "However," "But," "After all," "Anyway," "For instance," "Shucks," etc.

7 On this, see Brothers 1997.

8 I will leave for others the task of analyzing Armstrong's syntax and his use of African-American dialect. But I would like to suggest that there is something similar about the flow of many jazz solos, in which phrases may routinely lack a firm ending point, and the verbal flow that Armstrong cultivates with his dashes and ellipses. It would be interesting to look for literary antecedents that Armstrong may have known. The dash is occasionally used in combination with comma and with period, forming what Nicholson Baker dubs "dash-hybrids" in a discussion of nineteenth-century styles of punctuation (Baker 1994: 82).

9 Sometimes parentheses are used to qualify: "This was the time I met Louis Panico who was the ace Trumpeter (white) at that time." Sometimes a single word is bracketed in a place that would conventionally be bracketed more extensively: "She said in a sad voice, ″Son I don't think I like it up North with all of these new fangled gadget,″ (meaning) all the modern things they had in Chicago, which they didn′t have in New Orleans." Numbers are sometimes bracketed, perhaps as an alternative to the double apostrophe: "He would go to a place right down there in one of the neighborhoods, called (25)."

10 At the end of this story, as Armstrong tells it, his mother, delighted with her new apartment, "thanked Lil, with a big kiss, and wished that she′d someday be my wife . . ."

11 From The "Goffin Notebooks": "Alpha was a fine gal. She was a poor girl—not near as Fortunate as ′Lil was when I First met her—Maybe the one reason why Lil + I didn′t make a good go of married life together—"; and "But still with all of that swell Home, Lil, and I had—There was not happiness there. We were always Fussing and threatening to ′Break up if I ′sat on the ′Bed after it was ′made up."

EDITORIAL POLICY

Editorial policy for this book has been designed to serve two goals: to make Armstrong's writings accessible to the general reader and to preserve the unique features of his style. I have preserved the vast majority of Armstrong's idiosyncrasies, but I have not attempted a literal transcription of every mark, no matter how obscure, misleading, or whimsical. Thus, the policy is not one of documentary editing but general editing, such as any author routinely expects.

Spelling has been corrected, as a rule. I agree with Gary Giddins (1988) that Armstrong, who carried a dictionary with him while touring, would not have regarded misspellings as colorful. Exceptions to this policy are intentional misspellings that represent colloquial speech, humor, or emphasis (for example, "somphn" for "something," "wattcha" for "what are you," "hongry" for "hungry," "keed" for "kid"). Grammar has not been corrected. Though he aimed to master standard English, Armstrong was also a master of jive talk. I do not attempt to translate from one to the other.

Errors of omission or repetition have been corrected without comment. Like any writer, Armstrong occasionally leaves out a word or phrase that obviously needs to be there. When, as happens in a few places, the editorial insertion is not obvious, I have placed it in brackets, which identify it as editorial. (Armstrong never uses brackets.)

Spacing has been made regular; this includes paragraph indentations, space between words, space between sentences, and space between paragraphs. When every sentence is punctuated with ellipses and the number of dots varies slightly from sentence to sentence (usually between two and four), I have standardized to three dots. When there seems to be some point to variable numbers of dots in ellipses, I have transcribed those numbers precisely.

Run-on sentences have been broken up into shorter sentences when it is difficult to gloss the sentence. In some handwritten documents Armstrong does not use paragraph breaks, which I have added according to the sense of the prose.

Armstrong frequently goes back to his manuscript and glosses what he has written, inserting comments in the margins or between sentences. When the glosses are corrections, I make the correction without comment; when they are qualifications, I enter the remark in parentheses. Incomplete parentheses have been completed and double parentheses have been eliminated. I have punctuated all direct dialogue with quotation marks, which are also used to indicate titles of songs.

Matters of emphasis and punctuation are the most difficult areas to deal with editorially. Underlining (whether single, double, or triple) is always represented as italicization. Unconventional capitalization is followed, generally, though occasionally I have made this consistent (for example, if two words in a three-word series are capitalized by Armstrong, I have capitalized the third word, as well). In handwritten documents, there can be many subtle differences in letter size that cannot possibly be communicated in print. In such cases, I have been conservative about unconventional capitalization. For clarity I have occasionally added a comma, dash, or period, or changed one mark to the other. I have uniformly added appropriate punctuation (period or question mark) to sentence endings when (rarely) necessary.

Because Armstrong often uses quotation marks unconventionally, I have presented his own applications in the traditional format available on a typewriter (″), rather than in the format one would normally expect to see in material that has been typeset (“ ”).

Armstrong wrote these documents over a period of many years, and with shifts in memory. Documents previously unpublished have been left intact, but when a previously published document carries redundant material carried elsewhere, I have deleted the redundancy, as indicated by ellipses placed in brackets.

ACKNOWLEDGMENTS

My main thanks go to my two collaborators, Charles Kinzer and Maribeth Anderson Payne. Professor Kinzer's annotated index of proper names, places, songs, and shows is, in addition to being a guide to this book, a reference tool that will be useful to the student of jazz at any level. Maribeth Payne at Oxford University Press far exceeded the expected duties of an editor. Without her diligence in working out an unbelievably complicated series of permissions, this volume would not have been possible. Two friends of Armstrong's, Dan Morgenstern of the Institute of Jazz Studies and Phoebe Jacobs of the Louis Armstrong Educational Foundation, helped get the volume going during the difficult early stages. So did Scott DeVeaux, Gary Giddins, and Lawrence Gushee. Michael Cogswell at the Louis Armstrong House and Archives at Queens College/CUNY; Bruce Boyd Raeburn at the Hogan Jazz Archive, Tulane University; Wayne Shirley at the Library of Congress; and Dan Morgenstern at the Institute of Jazz Studies, Rutgers University, were all helpful in bringing forth the valuable documents over which they keep good watch. I am also grateful to Michael Cogswell for clarifying some obscurities in the text and for supplying superb photographs; to Richard Hadlock, who permitted partial publication of articles from *The Record Changer*; to *Esquire*, a longtime friend of jazz; to Bryan Gilliam, whose generous advice improved this book immensely; and to Ruth Bardon, who, at a party, listened to my story about publishing the writings of Louis Armstrong and exclaimed, "I have a letter written by Louis Armstrong!" She has graciously allowed publication of this important letter, which may serve as a tribute to the late John C. Browning, a devoted collector of materials documenting the history of African American music.

I. “Home Sweet Home”:

Childhood and Apprenticeship in New Orleans

“After blowing the tin horn–so long–I wondered how would I do blowing a real horn,–a cornet was what I had in mind. Sure enough, I saw a little cornet in a pawn shop window–Five dollars–my luck was just right. With the Karnofskys loaning me on my Salary–I saved 50 cents a week and bought the horn. All dirty–but was soon pretty to me. After blowing into it a while I realized that I could play "Home Sweet Home"–then here come the Blues. From then on, I was a mess and Tootin away.”

I

"LOUIS ARMSTRONG + THE JEWISH FAMILY IN NEW ORLEANS, LA., THE YEAR OF 1907"

(MARCH 31, 1969–1970)

Armstrong refers to this extraordinary document as a "book," clearly signaling his desire that it be published. He began writing it while recovering from a life-threatening illness at New York's Beth Israel Hospital, inspired, apparently, by his doctor Gary Zucker, who had just sung a Russian lullaby that Armstrong recognized from childhood. Armstrong first learned the lullaby from a Jewish family for whom he worked. He dedicates his book to his longtime manager Joe Glaser, another Jew who figured prominently in his life. Thus, the document provides a poignant flashback to the author's positive experiences with Jews in childhood, through his career, and now at the end of his life. Catalyzing his memory is a song. Armstrong copies the song's lyrics four times over the course of the document, testifying to its importance.

The writing is extraordinary not only because of these circumstances but also in its frankness about racial issues. Armstrong speaks bluntly and somewhat bitterly about racially conditioned attitudes among whites, blacks, Creoles, and Jews. He suggests that African Americans can learn from the Jewish example of how to succeed in the face of racial hostility. This comparison becomes a point of departure for generalized criticism of African Americans. As we watch Armstrong become caught up in the emotions of this line of thought, it is important to remember the special context in which the document was written. Gary Giddins (1988: 20) appropriately describes it as an "obsessive *cri du coeur.*" Laurence Bergreen (1997: 76) characterizes Armstrong's writings generally as "a series of moral lessons." Nowhere is this description more applicable than to this document, where African Americans are urged toward values of thrift, family and group loyalty, honesty, and good work habits.

Stray remarks indicate some of the causes of Armstrong's bitterness. Certainly old age and physical suffering are factors. (Signs of advanced age in this document include the faulty recollection of stories that are more accurately told elsewhere; in fact, the entire chronology is open to question, as I suggest in the Appendix.) It is clear that Armstrong has been stung by criticism. He cites the 1957 controversy when he spoke out against government passivity in the integration of schools at Little Rock, Arkansas. There are references to "*over Educated fools*" who condemn the "*White* Folks *Nigger*." To them, Armstrong sharply retorts: "Believe it—the White Folks did *everything that's decent* for *me*. I wish that I can *boast* these *same* words for *"Niggers*. I think that I have always done *great* things about *uplifting* my *race* (the Negroes, *of course*) but *wasn't appreciated*." The document may be read, in part, as a commentary on the change in audience that sectionalizes Armstrong's long career: During his apprenticeship in New Orleans and during the first great peak of his career, in the 1920s in Chicago, he played almost exclusively for blacks; the last decades of his career found him playing almost exclusively for whites, while many African Americans resented the cultural role in which he seemed to thrive (see, for example, Early 1989).

The candor in this document should sufficiently challenge the one-dimensionality of the cheerful, even obsequious public image that Armstrong could project so well. It should warn the reader that there was more to Armstrong than the entertainer's mask that he wears in some of his writings. In 1950, Armstrong reviewed Alan Lomax's book *Mr. Jelly Roll* for the *New York Times*. He expressed general praise and only the lightest criticism of Jelly Roll Morton, who was disliked by many musicians. He mentioned that Morton had a diamond in his tooth and that, due to his light complexion, he could win jobs in Storyville that were denied to darker-skinned pianists. In the present document, he explains that Morton claimed that he "was from an Indian or Spanish race," with no "cullud" ancestry, and that there were many darker-skinned pianists who could outplay him. And he recalls, with a sense of justice: "No matter how much his Diamond Sparkled he still had to eat in the *Kitchen*, the same as *we* Blacks."

Musically, Armstrong claims (perhaps inaccurately; see the Appendix) that his first instrument was a tin horn that he blew on the junk wagon he ran with the Karnofsky family. He first learned to play "Home Sweet Home" and blues—an auspicious combination for the career that would follow. The Karnofsky family is credited with advancing money to their child laborer for his first cornet, with recognition of his excellent intonation and encouragement to sing, and with instilling in him the value of "singing from the heart." Armstrong also speaks about the importance of Storyville for jazz history, about the unfortunate consequences of most musicians having to take day jobs in addition to their musical jobs, and about Freddie Keppard's inability to "play the cornet seriously at any time. Just Clowned all the way. Good for those Idiots' fans' who did not care whether he played correct, or they did not know good music, or cared less." Here Armstrong seems to say that similar criticism directed toward himself is off the mark, since he always played good music, correctly and seriously. The document ends with Armstrong "calling the names" of the New Orleanian greats from his younger years, and with expressed admiration for contemporary White New Orleanians, with whom he can now enjoy a friendship in the North, far from the "Disgustingly Segregated and Prejudiced" world of his birth place.

"Louis Armstrong + the Jewish Family in New Orleans, La., the Year of 1907"

Written by Louis Armstrong—Ill in his bed at the Beth Israel Hospital
March 31st, 1969
New York City, N.Y.

A Real life story and experiences at the age of seven years old with the Karnofsky (Jewish) Family, the year of 1907.

All Scenes happened in New Orleans, La., where Armstrong was Born, the year 1900.

The neighborhood was consisted of Negroes, Jewish people and lots of Chinese. But the Jewish people in those early days were having problems of their own—Along with hard times from the other *white* folks *nationalities* who felt that they were better than the *Jewish* Race. And they *took* advantage of every chance that they had to prove it. Of course the Jewish folks had a better break than the Negroes. Because they were *white* people. That's what was so puzzling to me. Just the same they had hard times for a long time. The Karnofskys' papa and mama came from Russia—before I was born.

The Chinese finally moved into a little section of their own and called it

Used by permission of Louis Armstrong House and Archives at Queens College/CUNY.

China Town, with a few little *beat* up restaurants serving *soul* food on the same *menu* of their Chinese dishes. I used to hear the Negroes braggin about their *Lead Beans* and *Lice*. That's the way a Chinese waiter would order it for you. *Lead* Beans + Lice *wasn't* bad at all. Of course the Colored people cook the best *Red* Beans + Rice. But for a change and something different—My Mother + my *Step* Father used to take *me* + *Mama* Lucy (my sister) down in China Town + have a Chinese meal for a change. A kind of *special* occasion. And the *Bill* in those days were real cheap. And we felt as though we were having something Big. We would also order Fried Rice and *Liver Gravy* with our Red Beans. And *ooh, God*—you would *lick* your *fingers'* it would taste *so* good.

I dedicate this book
to my manager and pal
Mr. Joe Glaser
The best Friend
That I've ever had
May the Lord Bless Him
Watch over him always.

His boy + disciple who *loved* him *dearly*.
Louis
Satchmo
Armstrong

Russian Lullaby Song'
Donated by Dr. Gary Zucker M.D. (my doctor—He *saved* my Life at the *Beth* Israel Hospital, N.Y. Dr. Zucker took me out of *Intensive care "Twice. Yea.*)
Beth Israel Hospital
New York, N.Y.
Russian Lullaby—Chorus
Every night you'll hear her Croon
A Russian Lullaby
Just a little Plaintive Tune
When Baby Starts to Cry
Rock a bye my Baby

Some where there may be
A Land, that's Free
For you and Me
And a Russian Lullaby.

This is the song that I sang when I was *Seven* years old—with the *Karnofsky* family when I was working for them, every night at their house when Mother Karnofsky would rock the Baby David to Sleep. Then I would go home—across the track, cross town to *May-Ann* and *Mama Lucy*, my mother and sister.

Negro Neighborhood

Louis Armstrong, who was born July 4th 1900, in the Back O' Town section (Jane Alley) in New Orleans. Mary Ann, the Mother of Two Children who she had Raised and Supported All by herself. We did not have a Father. They must have separated soon after we were born. Mama Lucy (my sister) nor *I* can recall *seeing* him. Anyway—*May Ann* (that's what everybody called her), she worked hard to see that we had food and a place to sleep.

We moved from Back O' Town (the rear of N.O.—Jane Alley) into the city, into the *Third Ward*, located at *Franklin* and *Perdido Streets*, where the *Honky* Tonks were located. A row of Negroes of *all* kind of *characters* were living in *rooms* which they 'rented and *fixed* up the best way that they could. We were *all* poor. The *privies* (the toilets) was out into a *big yard*—*one* side for the *men* and *one* side for the *women*. They were pretty good size *privies* (toilets, with wooden seats). Also, a *yard* of a *big* size. The folks, *young* and *old*, would go out into the *yard* and *sit*, etc., or *lay* around, or the *Old* Folks would *sit* in their *Rockin* Chairs, *etc*. out in the Sun until—*out house* time (go to the toilet). Oh' *everything* happened in the *Brick Row*. That was the *famous* name for the *Row* of *houses* which was made of all *Bricks*. *Everything* went on in that yard. I remember one *moonlight* night a *woman hollered* out—into the yard to her *Daughter*—she said (*real* loud)—"*You Marandy*, *you'd* better come into this *house*—you *laying* out there with *nothing on top* of *you* but that *Thin* Nigger." Marandy Said—"Yassum."

My mother May Ann (Mary Ann)—*Young* with a *nice smile*, a little on the *chubby* side. *Beatrice*, which was *Mama Lucy* (nickname), was *Two* years *younger* than *me*. We had a *few Step Fathers* through the years Since we *never* did see our *real* Father, whose name was *Willie* Armstrong. A *Tall Nice* looking Guy, Brown Skinned. With holes in his face—indications of healed small pox. He was a *Freak* for being the *Grand Marshal* for the *Odd* Fellows Lodge parade. Especially when they had Funerals (or the 10th of May celebration). Then he would go on the *hard* working job that he had. He was working for a big *Turpentine* company keeping *fire* in those big furnaces, for a very *small* pay. He also had other *children* by *another woman* who lived into the *Uptown* Section of New Orleans. I had two step brothers, a step sister and Step Mother named Gertrude.

I had a long time admiration for the Jewish People. Especially with their long time of courage, taking So Much Abuse for so long. I was only *Seven* years old but I could easily see the *ungodly treatment* that the White Folks were handing the poor *Jewish* family whom I worked for. It dawned on me, how drastically. Even *'my race,'* the Negroes, the way that I saw it, they were having a little *better* Break than the *Jewish* people, with jobs a plenty around. Of course we can understand all the situations and handicaps that was going on, but to me we were better off than the Jewish people. But we didn't do anything about it. We were lazy and *still* are. We never did try to get together, and to show the younger Negroes such as myself to try and even to show that he has ambitions, and with just a little encouragement—I could have really done something worthwhile. But *Instead*, we did nothing but let the young *up* starts know that they were young and simple, and *that* was *that*. N*ever* a warm word of doing anything important came to their minds. My nationality (Negroes) took advantage of my mother (May Ann) because they thought they were over smart, meaning May Ann gave birth to Mama Lucy and me (so what) and she had to struggle with us, until we both grew up. After grabbing a little schooling, and a *job* at a very young age, I myself will never forget. I'll try to forgive. But they were in an alley or in the street corner shooting dice for nickels and dimes, etc. (mere pittances) trying to win the little money from his Soul Brothers who might be gambling off the money he should take home to feed their starving children or pay their small rents, or very important needs, etc.

Mama Lucy + I used to go out to *Front of Town* when we were very young—among those *produce* places—where they used to throw away spoiled potatoes and onions into a big barrel. And she + I among other kids used to raid those barrels, cut off the spoiled parts and sell them to *restaurants*. There was a Baker Shop which sold *two* loaves of stale (the day after baked) bread for a *nickel*. They would do that to help the poor children. They could always get filled up at least on bread. Mama Lucy and me, we had to do it lots of times. Many Kids *suffered* with *hunger* because their Fathers could have done some honest work for a change. *No*, they would *not* do that. It would be *too* much like *Right*. They'd rather lazy around + gamble, etc. If it wasn't for the nice *Jewish* people, we would have *starved many* a time. I will love the *Jewish* people, *all* of my life. The *Negroes* always wanted *pity*. They did that in places of going to work, Instead of *gambling*, *shooting* and *Cutting* up *one* another so much. But real *Meek* when just *one* white man—chase a *hundred Negroes*, just like *Rats*.

The Negroes always hated the Jewish people who never *harmed* anybody, but they stuck together. And by doing that, they *had* to have *success*. Negroes *never* did stick together and they *never* will. They hold too much *malice*—*Jealousy* deep down in their heart for the *few* Negroes who *tries*. But the odds were (are) *against* them. Of course, we are all well aware of the *Congo* Square—*Slavery*—*Lynchings* and *all* of that *stuff*. Maybe the Jewish people did not go through' *All* of those *things*, but they went through *just* as *much*. *Still* they *stuck together*. Most of the Negroes who went through some of those *tortures*, they *asked* for it. *Those* days were like some of these *Modern* days—*one* Negro who has *no* ambitions, or any intention of doing the *right* things, will bring sufferings to a *whole* Flock of *Negroes* that is at least trying to live like *Human* Beings. Because they know within themselves that they're doing the wrong things, but expects *everybody* just because he is a *Negro* to give up everything he has *struggled* for in life such as a *decent* family—a *living*, a *plain* life—the *respect*. This Trifling *Negro* expects him to *give* up everything just because of his *Ignorant*, *Lazy Moves*. *Personally* I think that it is *not fair*. And the *Negro* who *can't see* these *foolish* moves from some *over Educated fools' moves*—then *right* away he is *called* a *White* Folks *Nigger*. Believe it—the White Folks did *everything that's decent* for *me*. I wish that I can *boast* these *same* words for "*Niggers*.

I think that I have always done *great* things about *uplifting* my *race* (the Negroes, *of course*) but *wasn't appreciated*. I am just a *musician* and *still* remember the time, as a *American* Citizen I *Spoke* up for my people during a *big* Integration *Riot* in Little Rock (Remember?). I wrote Eisenhower. My *first comment*, or compliment, whatever you would call it, came from a *Negro Boy* from my *hometown*, New Orleans. The first words that he said to me after reading what I had said in the papers concerning the Little Rock deal—he said as we were sitting down at a table to have a *drink*. He *looked straight* at me and *said—"Nigger—you* better *stop* talking about them *White* People *like you did." Hmm.* I was trying to stop that unnecessary *Head whippings* at the time—that's all.

He's the type of Negro who will *pan* the *White* Man behind *closed* doors—and the minute he *leaves* you, he will *slip* over to some *white* man and *tell* everything that was said against him, get your *head whipped*. And he will be the *first* Negro who will *Rape* a *white* woman. It happened in *Slavery* days. The *Negroes* has always *connived* against each other' and they *still* do. They never will be like the *Jewish* people. I should *say* not. Half of these young Negroes just don't know what they are getting *upset* about. If they'd consult the old generation of their families who really witnessed *hard* times and 'maybe they will *study* a little more *and* do *things* the *right* way. *Force* and *Brute strength* is *no* good—not even *love* and *sex*.

There isn't *anything nicer* to know and feel deep down in your heart that you have something—*anything*—that you've *worked* and *strived* for honestly—rather than to do a *lot* of *ungodly things* to get it. *Yes*—you *appreciate* it better.

The Negroes will *pan* another *Negro* because he is *trying* to have a little *something half* way *decent*. They'll go as far as to *pan* you for *at least trying*.

They would rather *Lazy Away* their time doing *Nothing*. Or *feel* because they have Diplomas which some of them *shouldn't* have *received* in the *first* place, They feel that the world *owes* them something because of it. And some of them can't even *spell cat correctly*. Just a *waste* of money to some of the *Hep Cats* who *Graduated*. I went only to *Fifth* Grade because I had to *work* along with my *schooling*. I wasn't *fortunate* to have *parents* with enough *money* to *pay*, like some of these *Idiots* whom I see making these *big Soap Box Speeches, etc.* I had to work and help *May Ann,*—put *bread* on the *table*, since it was just the three of us living in this one *big room*, which was *all* that we could afford. But we were *happy*. My mother had *one* thing that *no* matter *how* much *schooling anyone has*—and that was *Good Common Sense* (and respect for human beings). *Yea. That's My Diploma*—All through my *life* I *remembered it*. To me, *no college* in this *whole world* can *top* it, as *far* as I am concerned.

I may not profess to be the *smartest Negro* in the *world.* But I was *taught* to *Respect* a *man* or *woman* until they *prove* in my *estimation* that they *don't* deserve it. I came up the *Hard* way, the same as lots' of people. But I always *help* the *other* fellow if *there's Anyways'* possible. And I *Still say* my *prayers every* night when I go to bed. And I say the *Blessing* when I *eat my food.*

White Audiences from all over the world *picked* up on my *music*, from the *first note* that I ever *Blown.* And until *these* days they are *still with* me. And they seem to *love all* the *Negroes* that has *Music* in their *Souls—Operas, Spirituals, etc.* I am very proud to *realize that.* They never *let* us down with their *Attendances* and their *Appreciations.* I was real relaxed *Singing* the *song* called "Russian Lullaby" with the *Karnofsky* family when Mother Karnofsky would have her little *Baby* Boy in her arms, *Rocking* him to sleep. We all sang together until the little baby would doze off.

The Jewish people has such wonderful souls. I always enjoyed *everything* they sang and *Still* do. Of course I *sang* the Lullaby Song with the *family*—I did not go through every song they sang. But I was a good listener. *Still* am. That was a *long* time ago. And I *Still* remember their *Phrases.* When Mrs. *Karnofsky* would start singing these words to "Russian Lullaby" we all would get our *places* and sing it. So *soft* and *sweet.* Then *bid* each other *good* night. They were *always warm* and *kind* to *me*, which was very *noticeable* to me—*just* a *kid* who could *use* a little *word* of *kindness*, something that a kid could use at *Seven*, and just starting out in the *world.* My first Jewish meal was at the age of seven. I liked their *Jewish food* very much. Every time we would come in *late* on the little *wagon'* from *buying* old *Rags* and *Bones*, when they would be having *'Supper'* they would *fix* a *plate* of *food* for *me*, *saying*—you've *worked*, might as well eat here with us. It is too *late*, and by the time you get home, it will be *way too late* for your supper. I was *glad* because I fell in *love* with their *food* from those days *until now.* I *still eat their* foods (matzos). My wife *Lucille* keeps them in her *Bread* Box so I can *Nibble* on them any time that I want to eat late at night. At the Beth Israel Hospital, N.Y., I enjoyed All of my Jewish meals. So Tasty—Deelicious."

When I would be on the *Junk* wagon with *Alex* Karnofsky (one of their sons), I had a little *Tin Horn*—the kind the people *celebrates* with.— I would *blow* this long tin *horn* without the *Top* on it, *Just*—hold my *fingers close* together. Blow it, as a *Call* for old Rags—*Bones*—*Bottles* or *Anything* that the people and kids had to *sell.* The *kids* would bring *bottles* and receive *pennies* from *Alex.* The *Kids loved* the *sounds* of my tin horn. The Karnofskys lived on the corner of *Girod* and *Franklin* Streets. *One Block* away from the *Girod* Street *Cemetery.* In the colored section, we used to call it the *Girod Street Grave* yard.

We kids used to *Clean* the *graves* on *Decoration* Days, For the *families* of the *Dead.* We used to make a *nice* little *Taste* (tips). I had a *lot* of *Lucky Moments* with the Karnofskys. After *blowing* the *tin* horn—*so* long—I *wondered* how would I do *blowing* a *real horn,*—a *cornet* was what I had in *mind.* Sure enough, I saw a little *cornet* in a *pawn* shop *window*—*Five dollars*—my *luck* was *just* right. With the *Karnofskys loaning* me on my *Salary*—I *saved* 50 cents a *week* and *bought* the *horn. All dirty*—but was soon *pretty* to me.

After *blowing* into it a while I realized that I could play *"Home* Sweet Home"—then *here* come the *Blues.* From *then* on, I was a *mess* and *Tootin* away. I *kept* that *horn* for a *long* time. I *played* it *all through* the *days* of the *Honky* Tonk. People thought that my *first horn* was *given* to me at the *Colored Waifs' Home* for *Boys* (the orphanage). But it *wasn't.*

Things were getting pretty *rough* for *May Ann, me* and *Mama* Lucy—especially without a *Father.* But we *managed* beautifully. With the Karnofskys in my corner, and May Ann had her little hustle in the white folks yard (Mama Lou didn't work). The Karnofsky family came to *America* from somewhere in Russia a long time before I was born. They came to New Orleans as poor as *Job's Turkey.* They settled in a neighborhood of Niggers which was nothing but a gang of Old *Run* down houses with the *Privies* (toilets) out in the *back* yard. If they *rented* the house or *bought* it, I did not *know* for sure. It wasn't *My* Business *Anyway.* The house was *old,* but since *things* were so *Tough* for them at that time, they made the *best* of it and *fixed* it up *real* nice. They put their *Shoulders* together and did a fine job *fixing* up that *house.* They had a *pretty* good size *yard.* So they started a little *business* in *no* time at all. *That's* where *I came* in. With the *little* money that they had, they *Bought Two Small Horses*—*Two Small Wagons*—*Harness* for the *Horses.* Their *two* sons, their ages *19* or *20* years old—went into *business.* I *alternated* with the *two sons. One* went out in the street, buying Old *Rags*—*Bones*—*Iron*—*Bottles*—*Any* kind of Old *Junk.* Go *back* to the *house* with the *big* yard—*empty* the *wagon*—*pile* up the old *Rags* in *one* place, the *bottles*—*Bones* and the *rest* of the *Junk,* all in *separate places.*

Soon there would be *big* piles of *everything*. There was enough *Room* for piles of *Stone coal* which the *older* son Morris *sold* in the *streets* also. *Especially* in the *Red Light District—mostly* in the *evenings—way* into the *nights*. He sold it for *Five* Cents a *Water* Bucket, to *lots* of the *Sporting (Prostitutes) Women*, *standing* in the *doorways*. *Alex* would go out *early* in the *mornings* on his *Junk* wagon—stay out *all* day. *Me—right alongside* of him. Then I would help *Morris* at night. The *first* job that I ever had. So I was very *glad* over it.

Alex would get *good* money for his *Junk* when he had *saved* up enough to *sell*. And *pile* up the *yard* again, going to the *Bank* every week. *Both* Brother did the *same* thing with their *profits*. Being a *helper* for those boys made me very *proud* and *happy*. I began to feel, like I had a *future* and *"It's A Wonderful World"* after all.

They couldn't pay me much *money*. But at *my* age and as times were *so* hard, I was *glad* just to be *working* and very happy so I could *help* my *Mother* and' *Sister*. She had a *Job* at a *beat* up *paper* place where they *bundled* up old *newspapers* and make *Bales* with them and *sell* them to some other *company*. She was paid 50 cents a day and with my little 50 cents from each *Brother* we managed *pretty* good. We at least had *lots* to *eat*, and a *roof* over our *heads*. And *May Ann* could *really Cook'* good. *Ooh* she could *Cook*. On *Small Money*. Mama Lucy was *five* years old. *Too* young to work, so we gave her the job of house "keeper"—or, the *"one" room* where we *lived keeper."* She did a *Good* job and was *very Proud*. One thing that I couldn't help but notice about the Karnofskys, as poor as they were they weren't 'Lazy' people.

Morris had the coal route in the Red Light District. We *used* the *term—Stone Coal*, but I think you will understand *better* when we say—*Hard Coal*—which the young white prostitutes used in their Cribs 'one room, to keep warm. They would keep the fire burning in their *Grates*, by throwing a couple of pieces of hard *coal* on and *dim* it down to a mellow burn, so they could stand at the doors of their cribs and work and work, in their Silk Teddies (underwear—Lingerie), calling in the Tricks, as they were called in those days. *"Stone* coal *Lady'* a *Nickel* a *Water Bucket"* (coming *Morris + I* on the little wagon, *Morris* on *One side* of the wagon and *me* on the *other*). I *only* could get a *quick peep* at the girls *while* they were *standing* there at the door *almost naked*.

Since the *Red* Light District were *Strictly All White*—we *Negroes* were not *Allowed* to *buy Anything Sexy*. Some of those *Girls* who were Standing in the *doorway* of those *Cribs*, they looked *just* like a bunch of *Girls* who had just *finished High* School, or just *received* their Diplomas from *College*, they looked *so* young. They *all* had *pimps* to give their *money* to. As long as I was *working* for the *white* man—I could witness all of this. Even the *tough* cops didn't bother me. And believe me they were *really Tough*. They were known to *whip* heads *so* fast until *one* would *think* that they had an *Electric* Stick. The *whores* had to have *heat*. So that's where *I* came in, and was *safe* and *nobody bothered* me. In fact they began to know me personally, from seeing me on the little coal wagon every night, helping Morris Karnofsky Deliver those buckets of *Stone Coal* to them. Even when I got *good* enough on my *Cornet'* they rooted for me to keep it up. I *still stayed* with the Karnofskys, playing around with my horn in my spare time. And *Second* Line in the Bands and the Funerals, following behind my *Idol* Joe King Oliver when or where ever he played. Whether it was a parade—Funeral or *Funky Butt Hall*. As long as he was blowing that was who' I wanted to hear at any chance that I'd get.

Speaking of my job with the Karnofsky Family the profit from either Hustle from both wagons wasn't Such a *big* deal, but the Jewish people always managed to put away their Nickels and Dimes, Profits in which they *knew* would Accumulate into a *Nice* little Bundle some day. And from the way that *I* saw it, the Negroes which were handling *more* money than *those* people' didn't do *anything* but *shoot* craps—played cards all night and all day until they would wind up *broke*—hungry—dirty and funky-smelling just like *first one thing* then *another*. And on top of that—most of them would go to their homes—that is, if they still have one left—and find their landlord who is tired of their *ignorant explanations'* waiting to throw them out into the streets. Most of them had *Kids* depending on their Support.

The Karnofsky Boys were all fine young men, wonderful dispositions. The *whole* family had that *fine warmth* for all of their Negro help. Morris was the sharp one and wore' *plain* nice good clothes. I loved to see him in his *fine* vines (clothes). The Karnofskys would start getting ready for work' at five o'clock in the morning' And *me''* I was *right* there along with them. Morris and I had the Red Light District sewed up selling Stone Coal a Nickel a water bucket. I turned out to be a *good* helper to him. Morris served on *one* side of the street and me on the other. People had to buy this coal in order to keep warm those *chilly* nights.

They would buy a bucket or two to put into their fire *grates*, which only needed *two* or *three* pieces at a time. Each room had small grates. Most of the *Customers* would get their orders in before Morris would sell out. It was *very* important in those days to keep supplied—because when nights were real *Chilly*, *especially* in the *wee* hours of the Mornings, the *Girls* cannot work—not *comfortably*' anyway.

When I helped Alex Karnofsky on the wagon, we used to run across a lot of *bottles*. They came from *either* by *Drunks* or a *fight*. Maybe *two* women—fighting over the *same pimp*. It was quite a few *pimps* who had *Stables*. And their chicks used to fight like mad. A *Stable* means that *one pimp* has several girls in one house, hustling for him.

Another thing which caused a lot of trouble, even *killing* scrapes—where the *same whore* will have *two* Suckers' giving her their money at the *same* time, which when *each* other should meet and *find* out what was *going* on it could turn out to be an awful *Killing Scrape*, and most time it did. Or a *hell* of a *fist* fight or a *cutting scrape*, with *knives*, razors, etc. Some of those Tough women—Can stand—*Joe* to *Joe* and *Cut* one *Another* Just like men. They *all* stayed in *good shape* at *all* times. I *pitied* they *guy* who went to *bed* with those *whores*, and tried to get away without *paying* them for their service. *Ooh God.*

Another thing—if you should have one of those gals that's giving you money (her hard earned money as she called it)—you must make *lots* of *love* to *them*—and no fooling around. And no excuses when there is *love* time, or she just might get suspicious—and Brother you are in trouble and that's for sure.

The Karnofsky Family kept reminding me that I had Talent—perfect Tonation when I would Sing. One day when I was on the wagon with Morris Karnofsky—we were on Rampart and Perdido Streets and we passed a Pawn Shop which had in it's Window—an old tarnished beat up' "B" Flat Cornet. It only cost *Five* Dollars. Morris advanced me Two Dollars on my Salary. Then I put aside Fifty Cents each week from my small pay—finally the Cornet was Paid for in full. Boy was *I* a happy Kid.

The little Cornet was real dirty and had turned real black. Morris cleaned my little cornet with some Brass Polish and poured some Insurance Oil all through it, which Sterilized the inside. He requested me to play a Tune on it. Although I could not play a good tune Morris applauded me just the same, which made me feel very good. As a Young Boy coming up, the people whom I worked for were very much concerned about my future in music. They could see that I had music in my Soul. They really wanted me to be Something in life. And music was it. Appreciating my every effort.

Working for these fine people, I learned to be an *early* riser just like them. I noticed they believed in being on the move. Up Early every morning, making Hay while the Sun Shined. In Soulville where *I* lived on the other side of Town, the Negroes were just the opposite. Stay up all night in some Funky Honky Tonk, or an After hour Joint until day break—get so full of that bad whisky—when daybreak come he is so *Juiced*. He will Blow his Job and Sleep all day instead.

I used to love to help *Alex* Karnofsky Hustle up Old Rags + Bones etc. during the day. Get out into that good sunshine. Alex bought for me a Tin Horn. To blow and blow, the kind of a Tin Horn they use at Parties to make noises, while celebrating. The Children loved it. One day—I took the wooden top off of the horn, and surprisingly I held my *two* fingers close together where the wooden mouthpiece used to be, and I could play a tune of some kind. Oh′ the kids really enjoyed that. Better than the first time.

They used to bring their bottles, Alex would give them a few pennies, and they would stand around the wagon while I would entertain them. Alex and I enjoyed the Concerts′ ourselves. Alex always managed to get better *things* from the *White* Folks—they could afford to throw away better clothings. Sometimes I could find some real *fancy* things among the White Folks′ *throw aways* (they called it). Sometimes we would find real *valuable* things while assorting out those Rags and bones in the Karnofsky yard—drying out the damp Rags just before they go to some place and *weigh* up.

My Mother May Ann and my Uncle *Ike* Miles used to tell us about Slavery Times. They said—Slavery wasn′t half as bad as some of the History books, would like for you to believe. May Ann and Uncle Ike had a little touch of Slavery. Because their Relatives before them came up′ right in it. They said the Slaves, Acted *Dumb* and Ignorant, kept Malice and Hate among themselves so the White took Advantage of it. Especially when they were full of their Mint Juleps.

They couldn′t keep a secret among themselves. They would make plans among themselves and *one* Negro would double cross them by sneaking back and tell the white man everything they had planned to do. Quite naturally that would make him the Head Nigger. At least for the time being anyway. That's why' all the *Head* whippings was originated—from our own people. Malice, Jealousy and Hate. The same as of today. That's where that old phrase *Master* or *Marster* came from. From *conniving Lazy Niggers. Slavery* was just like Anything else. B.S.

The Jewish People never betrayed their own people. Stick together' yes. I watched the Jewish people take a lot of Abuse in New Orleans' ever since I was *seven* years old. I felt very lucky to get a job working for them. We suffered Agony right along with them. Only worst. They did not *Lynch* them, but us Negroes, *any*time they got ready'.

The other White Nationalities kept the Jewish people with fear constantly. As far as *us* Negroes, well, I don't have to explain anything. *Am* sure—you already know. At *ten* years old I could see—the Bluffings that those Old *Fat Belly Stinking* very *Smelly Dirty* White Folks were *putting Down*. It seemed as though the only thing they *cared* about was their Shot Guns or those Old time *Shot* Guns which they had strapped around them. So they get full of their *Mint Julep* or that *bad* whisky, the poor white Trash were Guzzling down, like water, then when they get so *Damn* Drunk until they'd go out of their minds—then it's Nigger Hunting time. *Any* Nigger.

They wouldn't give up until they would find one. From then on, Lord have mercy on the poor *Darkie*. Then they would Torture the poor Darkie, as innocent as he may be. They would get their usual Ignorant *Chess Cat* laughs before they would shoot him down—like a Dog. *My my my, those* were the days.

Speaking of the wonderful Karnofsky *family*. Just before I began to grow up and Singing with Papa and Mama Karnofsky, Morris and Alex—we all would sing this special tune, while Mama Karnofsky would have the baby in her arms—Rocking him until he would go to sleep:

Russian Lullaby
Every Night you'll hear me Croon
A Russian Lullaby
Just a little plaintive tune
When Baby Starts to Cry
Rock a bye my Baby
Some where there may be

A Land that's free
For you and Me
And a Russian Lullaby

When I reached the age of Eleven I began to realize that it was the Jewish family who instilled in me Singing from the heart. They encourage me to carry on.

These people finally saved enough money and bought a beautiful home in the white people section. Gave up the *Junk* and Stone Coal business and went into a bigger and higher classed one.

They saved plenty money. Nobody could stop them. They saved enough money to buy property any place in the City that they should desire. They bought property all through the South. Nothing but the best. *Oh* I was very happy for them. They deserved it. They Suffered so badly in their early days in New Orleans. I shall always love them. I learned a lot from them as to how to live—real life and determination. God bless them. Whatever they *Accomplished* they certainly deserve it.

Their food was always pure—the best. I noticed whenever I ate with them I would even sleep better. Much different from the heavy foods May Ann, Mama Lucy and *me* had to eat. I had the Stomach Ache All the time. Mama Lucy suffered with some kind of *fits*. One of those big names they called it. She Damn near died.

May Ann told Mama Lucy and me, since we have to eat this heavy kind of food because we couldn't do any better, too poor, we will just have to make the best of it. The food that you all eat today you must take a good *Purge* and Clean your little Stomachs out thoroughly. That will keep the Germs away. We both gave May Ann our word that we will stay Purge (physic) minded for the rest of our lives. May Ann would take a *purge* right along with us, every night before going to bed. It worked out fine. Every Morning when we would go to the *toilet* we would *all* have a Cleaned Stomach. P.S. I am *sure* you *know* what a Good *Purge* is.

The people stayed only *one* block from the *Girod* Street *Cemetery*, about six blocks long, a very popular one, with vaults above the ground. The front entrance was facing *Girod* street, at Liberty Street. Every Decoration Day we kids used to make lots of extra money for cleaning the Graves, for the people who were visiting their Folk's Grave and they didn't want to get themselves dirty and muddy, *etc.* I used to make a nice little *Taste* in Bucks to take home to May Ann and Mama Lucy, which wasn't bad' for a kid's' day's' Hustle. At least we could have a nice meal the same as the people whom I work for—*fixed.* They would give me the day off so I could do it and I sure appreciated it. Oh' they were so nice. Helping on the Coal and Junk wagons every day with those *fine* Jewish Boys was a great schooling for me. If I would say a *word* such as *Dat*—they the whole family would say "no Louis, *that*, and not *Dat*"—Something on that order. Even the little *Tin Horn* which only *Cost'* me a *Dime* turned out to be a great asset to the *Junk* wagon. I even learned to play popular tunes on it.

Alex would applaud me every time. He told me—"What a beautiful tone that you made, come out of a tin play horn. Just think—if you could play a real *Horn* as well." Funny thing, he did not mention any special Horn. Kids every*where* enjoyed it.

After a day's work in the Hot Sun, buying everything that we could buy—that evening we would finish up—unhitch the *horse* and wagon, pile the Rags + Bones in one corner to dry—Freshen up—have a good Jewish meal—relax for the night Route through the Red Light District selling Stone Coal a *Nickel* a Water Bucket. 1907 in the New Orleans Red Light District was in its Blazing Glory. Although I was just a young kid the police did not bother me. As long as a Negro had a reason to be in there. I was working for a white man. So that was reason enough. Helping to deliver buckets of Stone Coal to the Sporting girls—in their Cribs. I was O.K.

Everybody knew me by my right name. I managed to go to school through it all. Of course, not like I had wanted to. But I did a pretty good job pertaining to my Studies. I had to help *May Ann* with the Rent and our foods, *etc.* Mama Lucy was too young to work. So she kept our *one room* looking nice all the time.

I was Always *Quick* to *Catch* on to *Anything*. Had a *good memory*. Also had a little Talent. The Jewish people made every thing very easy for me. Gave me opportunities to learn. They could see that I was ambitious and I was always willing and *not* by all means Lazy. In those early days the Jewish people were catching *hell.* But they did not *Squawk*, such as a bunch of Negroes, Sing the *Blues* all the time. I being so young at the time—I've often wondered—how a White Man with the same skin as the other whites could be and were treated so badly. I didn't ask about it. I just *wondered.* Of course, May Ann knew a little about everything. We did not Question her about it.

The Negroes could do a much better job protecting themselves. And show no fear but they were actually afraid. They would not stick together and fight. But they would fight among themselves, at the drop of a hat. Guns—Razors and all, they were Lazy and would not pull together. It seemed as they were Jealous of each other, especially if one Negro had a little more than the other, no matter how hard he saved and got it. They always wanted somebody to give them something but *too* Lazy to work for it.

It has always been this way in the South. A White Man—may not care about *All* Negroes, but they all had a Negro he liked and Respected. The man who May Ann told us was our Father left us the day we were born. The next time we heard of him—he had gone into an uptown neighborhood and made several other children by another woman. Whether he married the other woman, we're not sure. *One thing*—he did not marry May Ann. She had to struggle all by herself, bringing us up. Mama Lucy + I were bastards from the Start. May Ann found a good Job working for a nice White family. She was very much relieved over it. The White family was very nice to us, whenever we had to go to Mama's job. These people had a couple of kids. We would play Hide and go seek, while May Ann do her days Washing and Ironing. Had a good time—every time.

The Lord kept his Arms around us all the time. He could see that, all we wanted to do in life is to *live* and at least be *contented.* Respect people and be respected.

New Orleans always was a town where Nick Names Originates. Even in my young days I accumulated several Nick Names, Given by your little pals and people who likes you. Of course that goes double. Because I have Originated Several Names for my playmates, and others as I grew up through the years. And they're *all* in good Faith. In fact—some of those names strikes me *funny*. And they live with you all through the years. Most of them anyway.

Of course "Satchmo" is here to stay. According to my Fans, all over the world. And I love it. Sort of a trade mark. Of course, in the early days when I branched out in the musical game and got to know—all of the Musical Greats as well as played with them. And they liked me and my cornet playing. Boy every time I looked around, somebody in some band had *laid* a new name on me. The *Dipper Mouth* is still around whenever I go to New Orleans and Run into some of the Old timers. Brings back real pleasant memories of the good old days.

Here's some Nick Names that very few fans, I doubt ever heard of. Such as—*Boat Nose*—Hammock Face—*Rhythm Jaws*—Satchelmouth—like a Dr's valise. In fact, I think that's how the name *Satchmo* was Originated. An Englishman who met me at the 'Boat in 1932, when I first went to England (we landed in Plymouth)—he shook my hand Saying "Hello *Satchmo*"—*Man* I flipped. That was *my* first time hearing this name. I shook his hand saying *whatcha* say *Gate*? And the first chance that I had to talk to my Trombone player who came from Paris to join my Band in England—I said to him, "The Editor of the Melody Maker Magazine just Shook my hand and called me *Satchmo* when my name was *Satchelmouth* before I came over here, why?" I asked my Trombone man. He said to me, "Because the man *thinks* you've got *Mo Mouth.*" *Hmm.* So *that's* how it happened. And I've been *Satchmo* ever since. You see how one can acquire a name that sticks. By the time I arrived in San Francisco California—this Colored Boy read about my new name—all he did was Shake my hand Saying "Hello *Sacra face.*"

Of course, I am not saying this to be funny, but it strike me as funny—since the Jewish people stuck together and *made* it—now they can stand on their own and no more struggling' because they kept their shoulders together. Now they've *got* it made—seems' like I am running into more *Cullud* Jews than the *Law Allows. Cats* who I used to *eat Hamhocks* and *Cabbage* with during those days when we used to play the *Apollo Theater*—good old days. Now *All* of a *Sudden* they have *turned Jewish.* I was *surprised* the other day when I ran across one of those *Jewish Jigs*—and he did not know how to *spell "Ka Fil Ta Fish"* [gefilte fish]. Hmm.

I still thank the Jewish family for my little job working for them. It was a *God send*, as we *phrases* it. They took a liking to me. And as for me to them—Ditto.

My first Sincere Applause came from the people whom I was working for. They enjoyed anything that I did musically. When Morris and I were delivering Stone Coal, a Nickel a Water Bucket in the District at night while the girls were working and call to us for a Bucket or Two of Coal, which ever they needed for the evening—I used to sing for my Boss, Some of those good *Ol* good songs. And he would enjoy them so well—he would applaud for me, so *earnestly* until I would feel just like I had just finished a cornet solo in the *French* Opera House—a place where Negroes were not allowed. Funny thing about it, I did not have or play a cornet at the time.

I would always look forward to Singing the Russian Lullaby with them while putting the baby to Sleep. The Right note, phrases, *etc.* The family always sang good and beautiful.

I enjoyed everybody who was Serious about their Music. Once I found *Seven* dollars in a pile of Junk. May Ann let me keep all of them. I gave Mama Lucy a Quarter. She bought a bag of candy called *All day* Sucker. It was just the *three* of us, since we had no Father. May Ann wasn't the *only* young woman who had no children without no *Father.* We had a step Father named *Tom.* He was very nice to May Ann, and treated Mama Lucy and me very nice. He and May Ann were both young. Mama Lucy and I were happy for them.

Although we all slept in that one big room we had a great understanding. Especially at sex time between May Ann and Tom. Mama Lucy and I slept on a *Pallet* on the floor nicely Padded. That gave May Ann and *Tom* the whole bed for themselves. We both had gotten old enough to know when May Ann and Tom were getting a little *Nookie. After all* we both had *ears.* And the room was dark, so there was nothing for Mama Lucy and I to see. We played asleep. *Hmmm.* Oh' those *Grunts.* Sometimes I wondered if they were angry with each other—silly boy. We said our prayers every night before bed time. Also said our Blessings before every meal. My Step Father worked at a big First Classed Hotel downtown in New Orleans. He was a Chef Cook. When Mama Lucy and I were going to School—many times he would bring home a lunch wrapped real good for Mama Lucy and I to take to School for our lunch at School each day. You can imagine how popular we both were with our school mates, when we would *open up* or *unwrap* our lunches, and those kids would *Dig* our lunches. *Hmm.* Filet Mignon Steak Sandwiches, Lamb Chops, Something different, different days. We both were very popular indeed. Sometimes we would give them a little pinch off our *Sandwiches.* Oh, they'd *love* that. May Ann *sure* could *cook* good also. I loved the way she used to cook those *Cat Heads*—P.S. *Biscuits. Yum yum.* Biscuits and *molasses* (syrups) were *Dee*licious. *Yea*—make you *Lick* your *Fingers.*

Mama Lucy—At Five years old was the *Cutest little Gal.*" She would tickle me when she was sweeping the floor. That was her job—keeping our room cleaned. She did a *good* Job. Tom—May Ann and me—we all had Jobs. So things weren't so bad with us. Yes—we were a *happy four*. P.S.—Much more happy when May Ann + Tom *rented* a house with Two Bed Rooms. Goody Goody no more Dreams—*wet ones* anyway. Mary Ann could always find a job. Every White family She worked for, whether they were Rich or Poor, they all were Satisfied with her work and gave her good Recommendations. She kept them very much contented. She also did *Days* work for different neighbors.

Everyday when I went to do my Days work for this Fine Jewish Family I felt great. I felt just like a young man trying to accomplish something in life. Some sort of a future. The Day's pay, the little Horses and Wagons to *Hitch up*—would give me something interesting to look forward to.

Although May Ann fixed a little lunch bucket for me every day, the Jewish boy which ever *one whom* I was working with would always offer me some lunch out of their Bucket. Oh' my young days I think were very nice. I never did wish for the impossible things. Until this day in my old age I am still the same. Just plain wishing is nowheres.

As I came into twelve years old I became a little large for the Job with the Jewish people. Anyway—they came into larger businesses. They had *Invested* their *Saved* Earnings, And before one realized it, they had New Orleans all *Sewed* up. I was so happy for them and still admired the whole Family. They will Always' stay in my heart. Just think, in their kind ways' etc., what they did for me. We never forgotten each other.

I got *Good* on my *Cornet*. Everywhere that I *played* and they (the public—Karnofskys) could attend, they would be there, rooting for me as usual. Always asking me—if I needed *Anything*. But, by that time, I was pretty *High High* on the *Horse* myself. I had reached the *Top* in music, I was considered one of the popular cornet players of that area. And I was making *nice money*. David the youngest of the family had grown into a fine young man and had a big business of his own. And was a real success. Everywhere that I played, even in New York—David, who turned out to be the biggest + best tailor *in New Orleans*—he'd *visit* me—with that big broad smile (the same as our present president of 'Associated Booking Corporation—Mr. Oscar Cohen—the smiles are the same, great).

For White People Only

The Negroes were only allowed to work in the Red Light District. As far as to *buy* a little *Trim*—that was absolutely out of the Question. Most of the help was Negroes. They were paid good Salaries and had a long time Job. The pay was swell, no matter what your vocation was. Musicians—Singers and all kinds of Entertainers were always *welcomed* and *enjoyed*. Just *stay* in you *place* where you belonged. No *Mixing* at the *Guests Tables* at *no time*. Everybody understood Everything and there weren't ever any mix ups, *etc.*

Most of the Musicians were mostly married people anyway. At any time—a young new *Jerk* would come into the *District* and get out of line, the *Musicians* would Straighten him out before he would go too far, and get into a whole lot of trouble. He would thank us later. Yes, he would get the message. That's where we all made a living and not to Glamorize.

The District never closed. There were *Actions* going on at all times—*Somewhere* or other. *Just think*—during the twenty-four hours, you could hear most of the top notch musicians, such as—Jelly Roll Morton, a great jazz piano man in those *days*—or should we use the phrase a *good time* pianist, or piano player. Anyway Jelly Roll was the piano player who had the best Job of them all. He played alone in the Leading *Whore* House called Lulu White, where some of the Richest men of all of Louisiana used to spend many nights and many dollars. Lulu White's was the biggest sporting house in the district, where the rich farmers went. All White. One bottle of beer cost $50 [50¢?].

Jelly Roll with lighter skin than the average piano players, got the job because they did not want a Black piano player for the job. He claimed—he was from an Indian or Spanish race. No Cullud at all. He was a big Bragadossa. Lots of big talk. They had lots of players in the District that could play lots better than Jelly, but their dark Color kept them from getting the job. Jelly Roll made so much money in tips that he had a Diamond inserted in one of his *teeth*. No matter how much his Diamond Sparkled he still had to eat in the *Kitchen*, the same as *we* Blacks. Jelly Roll made some very *fine* Recordings just before he died. He recorded them for the *Library* of Congress. Very good.

If it wasn't for those good musicians and the Entertainers who appeared nightly in the Red Light District—Clubs, etc.—the District wouldn't have been anything. Music lovers from all parts of the city came to hear them play Genuine Jazz. Speaking of some of the Musicians during those real beautiful days in different places in the District *way* back from 1910 to 1917, when they closed it down. One could hear real good jazz' telling it—like it was. Any place you should go in the District, whether it was a Cafe—Cabaret or Saloon—or if you should just stop in some place for a few drinks and listen—you heard the best in Jazz.

As a youngster in New Orleans in those Musical Days coming up and ambitious, I saw and listened to everybody' who was supposed to have been Somebody. To the good old musicians, most of them were fading out—some of them were still pretty good, but nothing like when they were in their *hey days*. Maybe it was because most of them worked too hard doing other hard jobs' such as Long Shoreman work—on the Docks all day *unloading* Ships, and lots of other hard Labor which kept them too tired to even look at their instrument let alone play it, which makes them *Rusty*.

New Styles and everything made them dated—in that case, they just threw the whole thing out of their minds into *Oblivion*. Of course there were still a few good musicians around—during the years of *1915* until the early *Twenties*. After *that* they commenced to getting fewer + fewer. Here's' some names whom I personally thought still held their own, as far as 1917—the year that they closed the District down for good. (The Government closed it down when a sailor got killed.)

As a youngster, I witnessed from lot of the old time *good* old good musicians who were fading out of the scenes had turned to drinking on and off their Jobs, trying to prove to themselves that they were still as good as they once were. But they couldn't make it. Freddie Keppard slipped out of the Scene into Oblivion. A Heavy Drinker.

His Ego when he was a young man and Clowning that he did must have been rather amusing for laughs, to get the recognition he achieved. But he sure did not play the cornet seriously at any time. Just Clowned all the way. Good for those Idiots' fans' who did not care whether he played correct, or they did not know good music, or cared less.

The first time I heard Freddie Keppard at an After Hour Joint, was on the South Side of Chicago. He did not move me at all. He played a lot of *almost* high drunken notes. Disgusting. Maybe his tone might have been a little better than Joe "King" Oliver's. He did not prove it that night—or any nights I'm thinking.

Like a sad piano player who was in that Band that night, who made the remark, as a piano player who did not know jazz—who had the nerve to accept the title as a piano player. And at the same time sitting in bands, with the most famous Jazz men in the world. How she got the job—*that* I can't figure out until this day. She admits the whole time she was in the band—she never understood *anything* (musically) that they ever played. Read music—yes. As an improviser—*Hmm*—terrible. At the same time musicians from all over the world *packed* the place every night just to hear *Joe King Oliver* and his Creole Jazz Band fresh from New Orleans. *Hmm.* Just to hear these *warm up* was *thrilling* to the *King's* Fans.

This Chick admits, all she was *interested* in was the pay days, more money than she's *ever* made, am *sure*. She hasn't made *near* that much salary since the band broke up. Because music is much more modern nowadays, and she was *corny* then. Guess who? [Lil Hardin Armstrong—ed.]

Speaking of Honore Dutrey. To me he was one of the *finest* Trombone players who left New Orleans and went to Chicago. I had the pleasure of working with him at the Sunset Cafe in Chicago in Carroll Dickerson's big band. Dutrey was in the *Navy* in his early days. He was accidentally *locked* up in some sort of Magazine on the Ship. It left him with shortness of the breath. The Navy Dr. gave him some medicine to Spray into his Nostrils and he played his horn with ease just the same. He used to play the Cello parts, beautifully. And tone + all so pretty—I've never heard anyone else yet do that on a Trombone. Dutrey had a brother in New Orleans by the name of Sam Dutrey, another wonderful musician. He played the Clarinet. A born genius, *yessir.*

Here is a short rundown of my idea of the choice musicians in my young days in New Orleans. Also, the Cream of the Crop at that time. Some of these names are still remembered in our History of Jazz. All of them pioneers—they could read music on sight, they might read a Fly Speck, if it get in the way. As *follows*.

Henry Kimball Bass Violin. Manuel Perez Cornet—Manuel and Joe *King* Oliver played together in the *Onward* Brass Band, really something to listen to when they played for Parades and Funerals. They had *Twelve* musicians in their Brass Band. Eddie Jackson used to really Swing the Tuba when the band played Marches. They sounded like a forty piece brass swing band.

The Second Line is a bunch of *Guys* who follows the parade. They're not the members of the Lodge or the Club. Anybody can be a Second Liner, whether they are *Raggedy* or dressed up. They seemed to have more fun than anybody. (They will start a free for all fight any minute—with broom handles, baseball bats, pistols, knives, razors, brickbats, etc.) The Onward Brass Band, Broke up a Baseball game, over in Algiers, La, when they passed by the game playing—"When the Saints Go Marching In." The Game Stopped *immediately* and followed the parade. (It happened in Algiers, La. Everybody were so busy "Swingin" + Dancing' they almost missed their ferry boat back to N.O.) Henry Zeno was a popular drummer during the days of the Red Light District. He was also a pretty good card player, well liked by people in every walks' of life. When he died he had people of *All* Races at his Funeral.

My life has always been music. Bill Bojangles Robinson's life was the Stage and Benefits. He never refused. Always willing. Of course there were greats on the *Stage* before my time. So it's impossible for me to speak of anyone who I knows' nothing about. It so happened that (Bojangles) Bill Robinson was passing through New Orleans on his way to open up at a Theater in Denver Colorado. We all know how serious he was about Benefits and Funerals, *etc.* Bo heard about this old actor who was Seriously *Ill.* Bill had time to go out and view the body of the actor who had died and been layed out in his coffin at home. Bill Robinson, who was a Southern Boy himself (he was born in Richmond, VA.), knew all about the *Wakes* where everyone can Review the Body. People who lined up for the last look at the Dead Body, had their different comments. When Bojangles reached in the coffin, touched the man's *forehead*, he immediately went into the *kitchen* where the *Dead* man's *wife* was *Crying*. Bill Robinson *said* to his *wife*, he *said* to *her*, "I *touched* your *Husband's Forehead* and he seemed a little *warm* to *me*." His wife *raised* up from her crying and said to Bojangles—"*Hot* or *Cold*—he *goes out* of *here tomorrow*."—Take's *only Bill* Robinson to tell that one. To me he was the greatest comedian + dancer in my race. He didn't need black face—to be *funny*. Better than Bert Williams.

I personally Admired Bill Robinson because he was *immaculately dressed*—you could see the Quality in his Clothes even from the *stage*. *Stopped every show*. He did not wear old *Raggedy Top Hat* and *Tails* with the *Pants cut* off—*Black Cork* with *thick white lips*, etc. But the Audiences *loved* him very much. He was *funny* from the first time he *opened* his *mouth* til he finished. So to *me* that's what *counted*. His *material* is what *counted*. I don't think that there will ever be a Bojangles Bill Robinson again. They might try to Duplicate him, but I doubt it. May the Lord bless his soul. I am very proud to say that I shared the stage with the great Bill Bojangles Robinson' many times for many years. *Yessir.*

Speaking of the Trumpet again, there was a good one named Arnold Metoyer. A very good first Sight Reader with a very beautiful tone. Arnold was a Negro but had White Folks features. It was hard to tell the difference—He played with the White Bands most of the times in N.O. He was a good Triple Tonguer. I played with him in Chicago. Enjoyed it. If he is still playing the Trumpet, where ever it is—you can bet, Golden Notes are dropping from his Horn.

Henry Martin was a fine Drummer. I should mention here' A perfect beat—A beautiful roll on his *snare drum*, the Bass Drum with a double beat at the same time. Henry would pull his pants legs *way* up to his Garters, when he starts to Swing. Better than anyone that I know. He used to kill me, watching him do it. A big cigar hanging from his mouth while he played in Kid Ory's early string band. Kid Ory's band would Cut All of the bands, during his Tail Gate Advertising. The Crowd would Roar and Applaud when Kid Ory would blow a few bars on his trombone, as his wagon was leaving, of a tune called "Kiss My Ass."

(This is the year of 1970)

Kid Ory is still a good man on his Trombone. Every time he is a guest and my band plays at Disneyland, he still has the old *power* and *tone* that made him *Famous* in New Orleans. When I played with Kid Ory's Band as a youngster in New Orleans (1918–19–20), I always felt like I was playing with the Cream of the Crops. And I *was*. *Yea* I was a proud young man, playing in Kid Ory's band.

Kid Ory had a trumpet player who played in his band, in the early days—way before my time. Mutt Carey. I enjoyed him every time that I could listen to him. Of course Joe Oliver joined the *Kid* later. That's who I replaced when Joe, went to Chicago. (Joe Oliver was my 'idol and my only love on the trumpet until the day that he died. No one has replaced him as yet in my heart, trumpetly.) Eddie Garland was a popular Bass Player at all times. I don't remember hearing him before he left New Orleans for Chicago. I heard him in California in the later years. Joe Oliver used to tell me about the double beat Garland had, when I joined his band at the Lincoln Gardens in Chicago, 1922. Still the old master on the *Bass* violin.

Erskine Tate's Symphony Orchestra, Chicago, Ill. In 1925 in Chicago I had the pleasure of playing with Erskine Tate's Symphony Orchestra, which was my greatest experience of them all. I had never played Symphonic music before with all of those different Tempos. Erskine Tate was a great leader. And he knew what he was doing at all times. We played for *Silent* pictures and all of the Pathe News, *etc.* At the end of each picture we would play one of those long Overtures, *etc.*

Before the Curtain would go back down and the whole Theater Darkened again I would be featured in a Jazz number with the entire Orchestra. Boy, did we Rock that theater. An Indian Reservation came up on the Screen during the Pathe News during their war dance. We faked the music to it *and* how. Imagine' five Scenes later' the Audience were *still* applauding for that same scene and the same music. I hadn't ever seen anything like it. Eddie Atkins (N.O. boy') played the Trombone in that Orchestra.

Erskine Tate's Symphony Orchestra in Chicago' made several recordings' while I was with them. Two of them were called, "Static Strut"—"Stomp Off Let's Go." I had feature solos in those tunes. I admired Teddy Weatherford's fine piano playing very much. Here's another Trombone Man who was very good, playing nightly in the Red Light District—his name is *Zoo Robinson* [probably Alvin "Zue" Robertson]. Every musician had 'great respects for *Zoo*. He was also a *highly* Educated Man. But *One* wouldn't know it. He was such a *plain* man in real life. He blew his trombone with no effort at all—no facial expressions, etc.

As I said before, I must have been born with *talent*. All that I needed was a little Encouragement to bring it out of me. And they *did thank God*. I was just a *Kid* trying to find' out which way to *turn*. So that *May Ann* and Mama Lucy could feel proud of their Louis. Not trying to be too much, just a good ordinary Horn Blower. The Jewish people sure did turn me out in *many* ways.

I will always remember how the Jewish people living in the Negro neighborhood Advanced and did *so much*, *right under* their *noses*. Boy—if the Negroes could stick together half that much. *Hmm* look where we would be today. But I doubt that it would ever happen. Too Much *Malice* and *Hate* Among us. And for no reason at all. Honest—these Jewish people accepted hard times far more better than my own people did.

Of course there would be the accepted few Negroes who seemed to see life the way I am trying to explain it. But as this world famous musician (D.E.) [probably Duke Ellington] so truly explain it—we just *ain't ready* yet. And *never* will be. How true. I was So proud and relaxed at all times to work for the Jewish people—They so warm, and made a little Negro boy such as me feel, like a Human Being. Never bored to have me around. I still say the Jewish people *deserve every*thing that they accomplished.

I thrilled *every* night—Singing with them when putting little David to sleep in Mama Karnofsky's arm, *Russian Lullaby*. Every night I would look forward to *joining* in Singing with Mama and Papa with the baby in her Arms—these words, real tenderly and softly—

Every night you'll hear her Croon
A Russian Lullaby
Just a little plaintive tune
When Baby starts to Cry
Rock a bye my baby
Somewhere—there may be
A land—that's free
For you and me
And a Russian Lullaby

A soft good night by every one. Everybody at my house would wait up until I got home Because I had already had my supper with the Jewish Bosses. Then my Step Father Tom, May Ann, Mama Lucy and me will go to bed. Look forward to the next day' on my job. Some nights we would see a moving picture at the Iroquois Theater—10 cents each for May Ann + Tom, 5 cents for Mama Lucy + me. (I won an amateur contest—dip face in flower.) [*recte* flour?—ed.]

I also looked forward to every night in the Red Light District, when I was delivering Stone Coal to the girls working in those Cribs. I could hear these wonderful jazz musicians playing music the way that it should be played. Paul Barbarin (he just died), one of the youngest drummers in those days, turned out to be a master on the instrument. He was always welcomed and sought after by other leaders. And here are some more of the great pioneers whom I shall call their names for you. As follows—

Alphonso Picou Clarinet. The one whom the jazz world still recognizes as the one who took the tune "High Society" and *transposed* the piccolo part for the clarinet. The tune is well known, also the clarinet part with a variations, *etc.* It was a very difficult part. And very few Clarinetists could play that particular chorus, correctly. I've heard Barney Bigard play it note for *note.* Since Picou died—Barney—is in a class by his lil *ol* self—still' great. I went to the *Lyric Theater* quite often. Located downtown on Iberville and Burgundy streets. Robichaux orchestra was always the best. They all read music. John Robichaux. They used to play for the stage shows. Andrew Kimball was the cornetist in the band (my choice). Speaking of a young cornetist around New Orleans in my younger days, there was Buddy Petit. I thought Buddy was very good. He had a little style all his own. He blew from the side + his jaw poked on one side. I did not hear Buddy as much as I wanted to. Our hours were the same. There were quite a few *Gigs*—and *Gig* Bands in those days. In my days there were *126* Gig bands. And they were all booked up every night in the week. Even when Buddy Petit's band and my band would be on the *Tail Gate* Advertising for different *dances* or advertising for a *fight*—*Gun* Boat Smith or Harry Wills (good fighters)—we both would meet on a corner, play our tune or a couple of tunes and we would cut out into different directions and give a big wave, playing our *cornets* with Admirations of each other's *Blowing*, which was really *Something* to hear. That alone cheered both of us up. We met several times since then, and after that, poor Buddy Died. Broke everybody's heart.

When the day came for the Burial of Poor Buddy I was in a Small Town not far from New Orleans. I went to the Funeral, was one of the Pall Bearers. Now Negroes will make *Jokes* out of *Anything*. They Buried Buddy at the St. Louis Cemetery, which have vaults to put coffins into, instead of six feet in the ground, Such as most cemeteries have. They call them Grave Yards.

Everybody were there at the Cemetery—Musicians, Hustlers, people of all walks of life. Friends of course, *etc.* When they shoved Buddy's coffin into the Vault, They *said* that *I said* as I looked at Buddy's *Coffin*—*I said O' you Dawg. Hmm"* Ain't *Dat somphn?*

The Excelsior Brass Band, a good one—Something in the same order as the *Onward* Brass Band. Had a Tall Fantastic Drummer named *Cottrell* [Louis Cottrell, Sr.]. He would come on the streets in each parade with a *Brand* new *Snare Drum*, which would Break it up. Black Benny the Bass Drummer Beats a whole lot of Bass Drum. And will fight at the Drop of the Hat. He would whip anybody's head if they molested us youngsters, who was following the parade. If Black Benny would get mad at a *Cat* during the parade, he would not take time to take his Bass Drum off of his Chest—he would take the Mallet which he beat the Bass Drum with and give him a good whipping across his head and chops. And return to the parade just as if nothing happened. The Ambulance will come and get this *Cat* and take him to the Charity Hospital. And that was that.

Most of the musicians were Creoles. Most of them could pass for white easily—They mostly lived in the Down Town part of New Orleans, called the Creole Section. Most of them were also good Sight Readers. They had Small Bands. The same as we call Combos' today. They went a lot of places with ease, because of their light skin. Places we Dark Skinned *Cats* wouldn't Dare to peep in. Most of the Service people of different jobs had permits, working cards. Negro Entertainers went through the same routine. It was worth it. The District had the best jobs, and paid more money.

In the District, Musicians-Entertainers had some cheaper places to buy drinks, such as Saloons, Small Restaurants to buy themselves a cheap or a quick meal, maybe a poor boy sandwich for their Lunch Break or between Shows or during the Shows. A poor boy sandwich is more bread than anything else. The Ham and Cheese is cut very thin, but you will get half a loaf of bread. Way back in those days, they didn't cost but a *nickel*. They must cost much more nowadays. They were good with a cold glass of Beer. Since there were no mingling with the Guests, the Musicians and the Entertainers had fun Chatting among themselves. Absolutely no mixing. After Intermission everybody would return to their *posts* and finish out the *night*. Most of them went to *After Hour* Joints.

Am happy to have traveled all over the world and have loads of fans—all Nationalities to enjoy my music. Am looking forward to another *world tour*. I get *requests* from all over the world to return. I played Kansas City on a *one nighter*. We finished late. I had to Catch an early train for St. Louis. I grab a cab and on the way to the Railroad Station the Cab Driver and I had a *conversation* talking about *any*thing in general. I noticed that the *Cab* Driver's *voice* was *Low*, just like Mine. When we reached the Station and as I was paying him my fare, I said to him, "Your *Voice* is *Low*—just like mine." He said, "I was *Shell Shocked* in the *war*."

Every Night you'll hear her Croon
A Russian Lullaby
Just a little plaintive tune
When Baby starts to cry
Rock a Bye my Baby
Somewhere there may be
A land that's free
For you—and me
And a Russian Lullaby

Speaking of the Red Light District and its Musicians, I was lucky to have heard all of them who played there. The White Boys were also Blowing up a Storm. There weren't as many White Bands as the Negro Bands in the District, but the ones who played there sure was good. I also heard them in the Rex (the *King*) in the Mardi Gras *Parades* and they played a whole lot of *Rag*time music. We called it—Dixie—Jazz, in the later years. I did not get to know any of the White Musicians personally, because New Orleans was so Disgustingly Segregated and Prejudiced at the time—it didn't even run across our minds. But I was fortunate to have the opportunity to meet some of them' up North in *1922* when I went to Chicago to play Second Cornet for Joe *Oliver*. He and Jimmie Noone the great (Creole) Clarinet man first went to Chicago in 1918. And I replaced Joe Oliver in Kid Ory's band. Joe Oliver was crowned *King* during those years in Chicago.

So when I joined him he was called King Oliver the rest of his life. The first White Boy Musician that I met was a Cornet Player by the name of *Wingy Manone*. He was always good on his horn. Still is. A wonderful Sense of Humor. He still knocks me out. And everybody else. All of the Musicians just loves him. He lives in Las Vegas Nevada. Wingy has a son who is *Superb* on the drums. He feels what he plays, just like his father.

The next fine bunch of Whites whom I met in Chicago were the New Orleans Rhythm Kings with Paul Mares and Rappolo—Oh *what* a band *they* had. They were the first ones who I heard play the "Tin Roof Blues." If I am not mistaken, they wrote it. I bought all of Larry Shields Original

Dixieland Recordings while I was in New Orleans—*before* I went to Chicago. They were all good and pioneers of the Jazz Records. Then, I heard other greats from New Orleans, later on through the years. The White Greats began leaving home for the North one after the other. It's very difficult to know exactly who left first, but they all made big hits and became very popular through the years. Louis Prima, a youngster who left New Orleans and went up North, especially New York, and did a wonderful job with cornet and singing. Became very famous. He kept 52nd' Street Blazing. Later—he changed his Small Combo into a Big Band—his own stage show, made a lot of Italian Recordings with *horn* and *vocals*, they were and still are sensational. Prima lives' in Las Vegas. And still doing *great*. Prima is still a big man in music. His Headquarters is Las Vegas, where he can always be seen and heard in *some* big Hotel there—Lake Tahoe' and Reno.

Al Hirt, another *Home Town boy* who left New Orleans and made a big hit up North everywhere he blew his *cornet*. He is one of the youngest to leave N.O. I enjoyed Al, everywhere that I could dig him. Powerful and that good New Orleans Soul pouring out of his horn. He have a wonderful band, they are all stars, good musicians and comedians to boot. Little Shorty his clarinet man *kills* me, when he does something musically with Al Hirt. In fact they are all a Swinging bunch of Cats.

Al Hirt—not only is he a *fine cornet* man, but he is an *Actor*. I've seen him on some of the biggest T.V. shows with some of the greatest stars, and *believe* me he held his *own*. He can be as funny as any of them when he want to. Of course his musical numbers as soloist on that horn and *Singing* is something that will always be appreciated. Held Down the replacement on the Jackie Gleason Show real beautiful. Just like an *ol pro*—I waited for the theme song "Do You Know What it Means to Miss New Orleans." That would *Hang me man*, every time. Al Hirt has a fine night club down in New Orleans, *Land*slide Business. A wonder *guy* that Al.

Another New Orleans White Boy who came up North and made a wonderful reputation for himself—Pete Fountain. I've just heard one of his Recordings on the air coming over my new *stereo set*, sure was pretty. I used to *dig* Pete when he was blowing with *Lawrence Welk* T.V. programs. Sounded so pretty. He used to really Swing those Cats. Now he has his own combo and doing a lot of fine recordings. I hear Pete *quite a bit*, coming from the Patterson New Jersey station. *Clarinet sounds* so beautiful and *smooth*. I can see New Orleans in every note and riff. Pete also has a swell night club in New Orleans, also doing *beeg* business. I like *all* of my White Boys from New Orleans. They are so warm and glad to see you all the time that we should meet anywhere. It's so *sad* to think how long it had taken for this fine friendship, and meetings between the White boys and the Negroes who has had admiration for each other. And had to meet at another place, outside our hometown (up North) to do it.

The Dukes of the Dixieland whom I think was the youngest Group to leave New Orleans was the first White Band whom me and my band played on the same stage with, which was a great thrill to me. It was the N.O. Auditorium. We played for a big concert there. I did not see the Dukes again until they came up North. I set in with them when they played at a night club in Chicago—in New York I made quite a few fine Albums with them. They also were sensational from the first day that they left New Orleans. I did T.V. shows with them, played at Walt Disney's, played Disneyland, etc. They are *still* going strong. So you can see how happy I am to know that I finally had a chance to *blow* with White Boys *at last* in my home town New Orleans (about time—*huh?*). So to me, the Dukes of Dixieland broke the Ice. One of the men said to me while we're *on stage—"Satch'* today they've got New Orleans Jazz—in *Black* and *White."*

My wife Lucille started me to taking Swiss Kriss. I came home one night as she was reading a book written by Dr. *Gaylord Hauser*, who introduced *Swiss Kriss*. Then when we were on our way to bed, she reached and open up her box of Swiss Kriss, took a *tea*spoonful, put it on her tongue dry, rinsed it down with water, settled into bed for the night, and went right off to sleep.

Now I *dugged* her for a couple of nights. So the next day I went out and bought a box for myself. She took a *tea*spoonful. But with all the heavy food that I eat—I must take a little more than Lucille takes. So I took a *table*spoonful of Swiss Kriss, rinsed it down off my tongue the same as *Ceily* (Lucille) did. It's so easy to take' I forgot that I had even taken it. It's nothing but *Herbs*. It said Herbal Laxative on the box anyway. I figured what she had takened *had* to be better than the *mild* Laxative that I've been taking which was pretty *good* but not strong enough for all of those *Ham* Hocks and Beans, Mustard Greens and Rice I had for Supper. It only made me *sput* like a Motor Boat. So I *slept* real peaceful with Swiss Kriss, *well say'* about *five* or *six hours*, which was *fine*. Then I *awaken* to a *little rumble* in my stomach, which was a warning—*let's* walk to the *John. Hmm*, I paid it no mind, and went back to Sleep, *that* is for a *few minutes* then a little *Larger* rumble saying—"Swiss Kriss time, *don't walk*—*Trot.*" And don't *Stumble* please. I was lucky though—I *made* it to the *Throne* in time. And All of a *Sudden*, music came—Riffs—*Arpeggios*—*Biff notes*—*etc.* Sounded just like ("Applause") Sousa's Band playing "Stars and Stripes Forever," returning to the *Channel* of the Song—*Three Times*. Wonderful. I felt a little weak' So I *Crawled back* to *bed* on my *hands* and *knees*. *Slept* about an hour and felt fine the rest of the day. And ate like a Horse.

2

"JOE OLIVER IS STILL KING"

(1950)

Armstrong never tired of recounting his debt to Joe Oliver. In this article, abridged from *The Record Changer*, he makes the case succinctly. Some biographers have suggested that this debt was more personal than musical, that Oliver provided a fatherly presence otherwise lacking during Armstrong's teenage years. In his recordings from the 1920s, Oliver's range is narrow, in contrast to Armstrong's exploitation of a wide range, and Oliver specialized in the use of plungers and mutes to achieve vocal effects on his cornet—techniques that hardly interested Armstrong. But Armstrong makes clear that Oliver was his main musical mentor. He explains that in even the first recordings from 1923, Oliver was much weaker than he had been in New Orleans, where he was an exciting high-note player. Armstrong's main musical debt to Oliver must have been in details of improvisational style, especially in up-tempo "ragtime." "[Bunk] didn't have the get-up-and-go that Oliver did; he didn't create a phrase that stays with you." These attributes that Armstrong credits to Oliver would also sum up Armstrong's own special stylistic qualities. Most of all, Armstrong admires Oliver's inventiveness, in which he would surpass not only his mentor but all other players from the 1920s.

Joe Oliver has always been my inspiration and my idol. No trumpet player ever had the fire that Oliver had. Man, he really could *punch* a number.

From *The Record Changer*, July-August 1950. Courtesy Richard Hadlock, *The Record Changer*.

Some might have had a better tone, but I've never seen *nothing* have the fire, and no one created as much as Joe.

The way I see it, the greatest musical creations came from his horn—and I've heard a lot of them play. I think he was better than Bolden, better than Bunk Johnson. Buddy blew too hard—he actually did blow his brains out. Even Bunk didn't offer nothing but tone. He didn't have the get-up-and-go that Oliver did; he didn't create a phrase that stays with you. But Joe Oliver *created* things—and they weren't skullbusters, either. There's your "Dippermouth"; all your trumpet players just aren't going to sound good unless they put that solo of his in it. And things that five-part brass sections play today, his horn played first—even if they don't give him the credit.

I was very young when I first heard Joe Oliver. He was in the Onward Band, a brass band they had down there in New Orleans—a good brass band. About twelve pieces: with three trumpets and three cornets. Joe was playing cornet at the time. Two of them would play lead; there was Joe and Manny Perez. I used to second line behind them. When Joe would get through playing I'd carry his horn. I guess I was about 14. Joe gave me cornet lessons, and when I was a kid I ran errands for his wife.

I could stay at the parade and listen to them blow all day. They just knocked me out. They'd come along with blue serge coats, white pants, and band hats—Joe would have cream-colored pants. I remember those hot days, and the hot sun. Joe would have a handkerchief on his head, and put his cap on top of it, with the handkerchief covering the back of his neck to keep the sun off him while he's blowing. All the cats would be blowing, even the second line. They'd play "Panama," or something like that, and the second line would applaud, and Joe was really blowing—he'd go way up there, you know, like on that last chorus of "High Society." If you've ever heard us play it, that's Joe Oliver up and down, note for note. I wouldn't change that solo; I see to it that I hit those same notes in my mind, because that's the way he'd end up those brass band solos.

Joe led the Magnolia Band at one time. And he and Kid Ory got together and made a grand band. With this brass band, that kept him in two bands—he really was King there. Bunk was as big a name as Joe then and I guess Bunk had a better tone than Joe but there never was a trumpet playing in New Orleans that had the fire that Joe Oliver had. Fire—that's the life of music, that's the way it should be. I joined Joe's band in Chicago in 1922. [. . .] We played around Chicago and made tours to various towns. I remember I used to do a little comedy dance then; I'd slide and fall, like I was going to hurt myself—I don't dance any more, not for years. [. . .] When we made those "Gennett" records Joe wasn't in his prime, like he was before he sent for me. To show you how much stronger I was than Joe: those were acoustical records, with those big horns; Joe would be right in the horn blowing and I would be standing back in the door playing second trumpet.

3
"BUNK DIDN'T TEACH ME"
(1950)

Bunk Johnson sprang unexpectedly from obscurity in 1939, when scholars began to take a keen interest in the early New Orleanian period. Johnson made many claims about his historic role that were later shown to be false. He put himself forward as Armstrong's main mentor, and though Armstrong supported Johnson (see the Appendix), he also made clear in this article and elsewhere that he got very little from Johnson, musically or otherwise. Since Johnson's contrary claims have continued to appear in biographies (as recently as 1997), it is worth reprinting Armstrong's clear statement, which appeared in an article titled "Bunk Didn't Teach Me," with byline "as told by Louis Armstrong," from *The Record Changer* in 1950. Reprinted here are passages identified as Armstrong's words by quotation marks in the original article.

Bunk didn't actually teach me anything; he didn't show me *one* thing.

You can sum it up this way. There was a honky-tonk at Gravier and Franklin Streets. That was my neighborhood up in that area; I lived somewhere in around there. At night I'd put on long pants—I was about 17—and I'd hang around this honky-tonk where Bunk was playing.

There's Bunk sitting up there drinking this port wine and playing all that pretty horn, and I am right in front of him. But "how would this phrase go?"—Joe taught me those things and the things that go with that. Bunk

From *The Record Changer*, July-August 1950. Courtesy Richard Hadlock, *The Record Changer.*

didn't show me nothing. He didn't even know me. In the days of the honkytonks I was just a little old kid and Bunk didn't know me. But I would sit in front of that horn and the port wine was coming out of that bell. But I'd stay there and them notes were prettier than that wine.

You can do that right now—there's somebody you want to hear, so you go pay and hear them. But, still, he *did not* teach me.

So you don't need to give the credit to Bunk, other than the tone. I mean, there could be similarity of tone, but that's all.

4

LETTER TO ISIDORE BARBARIN

(SEPTEMBER 1, 1922)

This is the earliest known document written by Armstrong. Armstrong wrote it a few weeks after having arrived in Chicago from New Orleans. Isidore Barbarin (cornet and mellophone) started playing before the turn of the century in marching bands, including the Onward Brass Band and the Excelsior Brass Band, two of the best in the city. Armstrong probably played with him in the Tuxedo Brass Band just before leaving New Orleans for Chicago. The "Celestin" referred to would be Oscar "Papa" Celestin, who founded the Tuxedo Brass Band in 1911. Ernest "Ninesse" Trepagnier played in this band from 1916 until 1928. In *Satchmo: My Life in New Orleans* (p. 143), Armstrong describes this band: "Several times later [the Robichaux band] asked us to join their band, but I had already given Celestin . . . my consent to join him. . . . Personally I thought Celestin's Tuxedo Band was the hottest in town since the days of the Onward Brass Band with Emmanuel Perez and Joe Oliver holding down the cornet section . . . So after Joe Oliver went to Chicago, the Tuxedo Brass Band got all the funerals and parades."

Armstrong's friendship with Barbarin is significant in that it reveals how much the downtown, Creole musicians and the uptown, darker-skinned musicians had integrated by the time of Armstrong's musical maturity (see the Appendix). Armstrong refers to Isidore's son Paul Barbarin, a drummer who was then in Chicago. By 1922, Armstrong's typing hobby was in full swing, and it seems that his friends were having trouble keeping up with him.

Chicago Ill.
Sept. 1, 1922

Mr. Barbarin,
Dear Friend,

Yours of this afternoon has been received. And I take Great pleasure In letting you know that I was glad to hear from you. I'm well as usual and also doing fine as usual. Hoping you and Family are well. Pops I just had started to wondering what was the matter with you. You taken so long to answer. Well I know just how It Is When A fellow Is playing with A Red Hot Brass Band And they have all the work he don't have time to be bothered with writing no letters.

Well I understand that pops. I heard all about you all having all those Funerals down there. I'm sorry that I ain't down there to make some of them with you all. The boys give me H . . . all the Time because forever talking about the Brass Band And how I youster like to make those Parades. They say I don't see how A man can Be crazy about those hard Parades. I told them that they don't go hard with you when you are playing with A good Band. Joe Oliver Is Here In my room now and He sends you his best regards. Also all the boys. I heard that Celestin lost his Sister. Well that's too bad. I feel sorry for the poor fellow. I will tell Paul what you said when I see him again. The next time you meet Nenest [probably Ernest "Ninesse" Trepagnier] ask him what Is the matter with him he don't answer my letter. Ask him do he needs any writing paper—stamps—to let me know at once and I'll send him some at once . . . Ha . . . Ha . . . Well old pal I tell you the news some other time. I have to go to work now. Good knight.,

All From Louis Armstrong. 459 East 31, St. Chicago Ill.

Courtesy Hogan Jazz Archive, Tulane University.

II. "Some Kind of a God":

Chicago, New York, and California, 1922–1931

"A musician in Chicago in the early twenties were treated and respected just like–some kind of a God."

5
"THE ARMSTRONG STORY"
(1954)

This document, now housed in the Louis Armstrong House and Archives at Queens College/CUNY, overlaps slightly with the conclusion of Armstrong's published autobiography of 1954, *Satchmo: My Life in New Orleans*. The present document begins and ends in mid-sentence; it is published here in its entirety. In the Appendix, I describe the relationships between *Satchmo: My Life in New Orleans*, the complete typescript for that book (a copy of which is now at the Institute of Jazz Studies, Rutgers University), and the present document. The present document covers Armstrong's experiences in Chicago, from his arrival in August 1922 through 1924, including his marriage to Lil Hardin, which took place February 5, 1924. There are also digressions to earlier events in New Orleans and on the Streckfus riverboat.

Satchmo: My Life in New Orleans concludes with Armstrong's first performance with Joe Oliver's band in Chicago. The beginning of the present document correlates with the middle of page 235 of that book, and the two documents run in parallel for the remaining few pages of *Satchmo: My Life in New Orleans*. Armstrong has just arrived in Chicago, and he is staying at a boarding house run by a woman named Filo, a friend of Oliver's from New Orleans. Comparison of the overlap between *Satchmo: My Life in New Orleans* and the present document will reveal the kind of editing that shaped the former. For example, Armstrong describes a skit that was adapted to a performance of "Eccentric," one of Joe Oliver's specialty numbers. In the skit, Oliver imitated two babies on his horn. To Oliver's "white baby," Bill Johnson responded with "Don't Cry Little Baby." Then, when Oliver imitated a "colored baby," Johnson responded with "Shut up you lil so and soooooo." The "whole house would thunder with laughs and applauses" in reaction to this bit of racially charged vaudeville. But when Armstrong's account was edited for *Satchmo: My Life in New Orleans*, the story included only one baby, lacking racial designation. As William Kenney (1991) has observed, the editors of *Satchmo: My Life in New Orleans* "removed many of the author's explicit references to the racial dimensions of his career." Perhaps one day there will be a new edition of that much-loved book, one more closely based on the typescript now at the Institute of Jazz Studies.

Since he usually writes for a general audience, Armstrong rarely includes technical details about music. Yet there are some valuable observations here about New Orleanian practice. Lil Hardin was tutored directly by the New Orleanian greats, thus accounting for her command of "that good ol' New Orleans 4 Beat," and Baby Dodds roused enthusiasm by beating on the rim of his bass drum during a hot chorus. Here, as elsewhere, Armstrong emphasizes the importance of the rhythm section. Armstrong's role as second trumpet meant that he could never "go above" Joe Oliver in range. Trombonist Honore Dutrey had beautiful fill-ins, which he derived from published cello parts. Clarinetist Johnny Dodds played beautiful "variations." Oliver and Armstrong worked out stunningly successful duet breaks that others feebly imitated. A sense of musical dialogue between members of the band is a mark of high quality. Oliver was the most inventive player Armstrong had ever heard. In the vaudevillian atmosphere of the early 1920s, Armstrong did a dance routine (a little more detail is given in "Joe Oliver Is Still King"), but, to his frustration, he did not yet sing.

her name because we always called her Grammaw. She sat down and chatted with us about Old New Orleans—she hadn't been there since Look Out Mountain was an ant hill. Quite natural all the things we talked about was new to her because she left near the time I was born.

Filo was a Creole gal, but she had lived in the Back of Town Section on Gayaso and Cleveland avenue. I knew she and I would hit it off just right because she cherished Papa Joe's friendship therefore she was allright with me. By this time I knew my trip up North would be quite successful—in the first place, no one could get me away from home permanently but Papa Joe. Now with so many New Orleans Boys and Gals I knew I could not get homesick as I had done so many times before when I left New Orleans. . . . .

All of a sudden I had to pull away from Filo and her mother to catch a bit of rest. From a kid in music, I was taught by the old masters that sleep was the essence of good music. A musician cannot play at his best when he is tired and irritable. So I had made it a habit to get as much sleep as I could when ever I could.

When I awakened and just about dressed, Filo came in; she said, "Although you have had a hearty dinner, you must have a sandwich. You got to do a lot of blowing and you need something to hold you up." As good as Filo cooked I did not argue with her. When I went down she gave me a big simmering ham sandwich covered with pineapple and brown sugar. Boy was it good. When I had finished that good old sandwich I started out for opening night at the Gardens.

Opening Night

I kept saying to myself as I was getting dressed, putting on my old "Roast Beef"—P.S. that was what we called an old ragged *Tuxedo*; of course, I had it all pressed up and fixed so good that no one would ever notice it, unless they were real close and noticed the patches here and there. Anyway—I was real sharp, at least I thought I was anyway.

We hit at Nine O'clock that night at the Lincoln Gardens. At eight-thirty on the dot a cab pulled up in front of Filo's house for me. Filo had called the cab because she did not want me to be late. Good Filo was as excited as I was because she wanted things to go on right for my debut, that night with the King.

I ran down stairs and jumped into the cab and before I knew it I was right in front of the Gardens. It's a funny thing about the music game and Show Business, no matter how long a person has been in the profession, their Opening Night always seem to give the feeling that you have little Butterflies moving around in your stomach.

Mrs. Major, the white Lady who owned the Lincoln Gardens, and Bud Red, the colored Manager, were the first two people I ran into, as I walked through the long Lobby. They were both sort of elderly people. The next one I ran into was King Jones, the master of Ceremony. He was a short fellow with a big loud voice. I'll bet you could hear him over a block away, when he yelled "Ladies and Gentlemen." I don't think Jones was a colored fellow. I think he was from some Island. He tried to be everything but colored but that real bad English gave him away.

I finally reached the Bandstand where King Oliver's boys were warming up, Johnny and David Dodds, Honore Dutrey, Lil Hardin, Bill Johnson and the master himself. They were having a smoke before the first set and waiting for me to show up.

The place had begun to fill up with all the finest Musicians from downtown. This was the time I met Louis Panico who was the ace Trumpeter (white) at that time. Isham Jones was the talk of the town in the same band.

We cracked down on the first note and that band sounded so good to me after the first note that I just fell right in like old times—Papa Joe really did blow that horn. The first number went down so well we had to take an encore. That was the moment Joe Oliver and I developed a little system whereby we didn't have to write down the duet breaks—I was so wrapped up in him and lived his music that I could take second to his lead in a split second. That was just how much I lived his music. No one could understand how we did it, but it was easy and we kept it that way the whole evening. I did not actually take a solo until the evening was almost over. I never tried to go over him, because Papa Joe was the man and I felt any glory that should come to me must go to him—I wanted him to have all the praise. To me Joe Oliver blew enough Horn for the both of us. I could just sit and listen to him and play second to his lead. I never dreamed of trying to steal the Show or any of that silly rot.

I particularly enjoyed Lil that night, with that four (4) beats to the bar—for a woman I thought she was really wonderful. She got her training from Joe Oliver, Freddie Keppard, Sugar Johnny, Lawrence Dewey, Tany Johnson, in fact all of the pioneers from New Orleans. She was lucky to come out of Fisk University into the arms of all the real great Jazz musicians. It was startling to find a woman Valedictorian to her class fall in line and play such good Jazz. If she hadn't run into the New Orleans Greats she probably would have married some big politician or maybe play the Classics for her livelihood.

I later found out that Lil was doubling to the Edelweiss Garden at 41 and State Street. I wondered when she was able to get any sleep: of course, Johnny, Baby, Dutrey and Joe Oliver—I knew what to expect of them. Those cats could take it. They used to pull up to a corner in an advertising wagon and play (Tailgate) music. I'd follow them for hours and forget about all that good Creole food, I was scared to go eat because I might miss one of those good notes.

Dutrey was one particular Trombone player from New Orleans who I admired ever since I heard him blow the first note on his horn. He used to play so pretty, with such a beautiful tone, until I could not see how he did it. Yes sir I really wondered about that boy, especially his solos and *fill-ins*—they were so beautiful. Later I found out that he mostly played the Cello parts. The last time I saw Dutrey and heard him play was in New Orleans and that was around 1915—immediately after I saw him he joined the Navy. Dutrey and Bunk Johnson were around the same age when I last saw him in New Orleans, around 25 years old. I hadn't seen him again until I joined Joe Oliver and his Band in Chicago, in 1922. . . .

A particular situation raised its ugly head in the life of Dutrey. While he was in the Navy traveling on a Big Battle Ship he fell asleep in a magazine aboard Ship and contracted an awful case of asthma. When he was discharged from the Navy, instead of him going back to New Orleans, he went to Chicago to live. He joined Joe Oliver a few weeks before I came to Chicago. I listened real close to his horn and I found that he still played beautiful horn, but he suffered something awful with that asthma. Often he would suffer from shortness of breath. When ever he had a real hard solo to play he would go to the back of the bandstand and take out the spray that he always kept in his pocket and spray his nose—and when he finished that spraying so he could get his breath—look out because he would sit down and blow a whole gang of Trombone. How he did it was beyond me.

Dutrey, with his wonderful sense of humor and fine disposition—used to knock me out talking about my childhood days; when I used to follow behind he and Joe Oliver all day in the Street Parades. Johnny Dodds was a real healthy boy and those variations of his were still mellow and perfect. His hobby was watching the Baseball Scores, especially the White Sox team. Johnny and I would buy the Daily News and all he would take out was the Baseball Scores, then he would give the rest to me.

There is so much about that band that I shall mention from time to time, as they come to me because those guys held many interesting moments for me. In my estimation the Band was not too different from previous Bands that I had played in, but I would sit and think, often I would say to myself, this can't be me here playing with all of these masters. To play with such great men was the fulfillment of any child's dream, and I had reached that point in Music. For instance a drummer such as Baby Dodds; to watch him play, especially when he beat on the rim of his Bass in a hot chorus, he sort of shimmied when he beat with his sticks, Oh! Boy that alone was in my estimation the whole worth of the price of admission. I had watched him on the River Boats in St. Louis. When he played on Excursions with Fate Marable, I would find myself watching him so hard that I would loose my place with the music. When he would beat on the rims of his drums behind one of my hot choruses he would make me blow that horn.

When I joined the Joe Oliver Band in Chicago I was happy to find that Baby Dodds had stopped drinking excessively and settled down to music. He had always wanted to settle down but like so many good musicians, they would get that one too many drinks which would throw him off and cause some awful embarrassing moments. Good musicians have to guard against such things in music.

There was Bill Johnson the Bass player—that cat really interested me that first night at the Gardens. He was one of the original Creole Jass band and one of the first who came North and made such a musical hit. You looked at Bill and you would swear he was a white boy. He had all the features, even the voice—yes he really did look like an o'fay boy (southern boy) at that. His sense of humor, Oh! Boy it was unlimited. He had traveled from coast to coast as a member of the Original Creole Band until it disbanded. Most of the boys from the Creole Band went to different places but Bill Johnson and Freddie Keppard made up their own Band. Lil doubled from Joe Oliver to Freddie Keppard's Band after hours.

As opening night progressed, every number Joe Oliver's Band played was a gassuh. Finally they went into a number called "Eccentric"—that is the one where Papa Joe took a lot of breaks. He would take a four bar break, then the Band would play, then he would take four more. At the very last chorus he and Bill Johnson would do a sort of Act musically. While Joe Oliver would be talking like a baby, Bill Johnson would pet the baby in his high voice. The first baby Joe would imitate was supposed to be a white baby. When Joe's horn had cried like the white baby, Bill Johnson would come back with, "Don't Cry Little Baby." The last baby was supposed to be a little colored baby, then they would break it up. Joe would yell, "Baaaah! baaaaaaah!" Then Bill would shout, "Shut up you lil so and sooooooo." Then the whole house would thunder with laughs and applauses. Bill Johnson was really a good bass man.

After the floor show was over and they went into some dance tunes the crowd yelled, "Let the youngster blow"—that meant me. Joe was wonderful. He willingly let me play my rendition of the Blues. Gee I was really in heaven at that particular minute. I was so happy to get the chance to play for Joe and his boys.

Papa Joe was so elated over his new band that he played half hour over time. The boys from downtown stayed right there until the last note was played. When we finally went off, all of the Musicians from downtown came back stage and talked with us while we packed our instruments. They really congratulated Joe on his fine music, and for sending to New Orleans to get me. I was so happy I did not know what to do, because they were right if it wasn't for Joe Oliver I probably never would have left home. I always was afraid to leave home because so many of the boys from home had gone up North and came back in such bad shape. I swore I would never leave home for no one but Joe Oliver, I had just that much confidence in him.

When I got home that night I was so happy to find that Filo fixed up one of those real fine Creole Dutch Lunches—she had Home Brew and everything. That Home Brew is not like any ordinary Brewery Beer, it is so much stronger. They made it from malt, yeast, sugar, some corn and water, then they let it set in a keg until it has become ready to bottle. They put a lot of other ingredients in that stuff but I don't exactly remember. At any rate it was really good with a great kick.

Although Filo had the lunch and everything ready, she was too drunk to serve the food. She boot-legged on the side. She had a lot of friends who ran on the road, from Chicago to all points, and when they came in they all gave Filo a play (bought drinks from her). Instead of her staying up and serving drinks and collecting, the guests had to put her in bed and help themselves. She really couldn't drink at all. When she got two she was out. All of her friends knew her and they never took advantage of her. The next day we sat around and talked. Filo said Jack Johnson, the ex-prize-fighter of the world, lived right up the streets in a big mansion. Later he sold the house.

Night after night the Lincoln Gardens jumped until winter began to set in. After the bad weather set in we had three bad nights a week, and on these nights Mrs. Major would turn off the heat. Johnny Dodds would actually play his horn with gloves. That was the first time I had ever witnessed that sort of thing. I could not much blame him because after each set my mouth piece would seem to have icicles hanging from it. Practically all of the fellows wore their overcoats. That was some winter. The only thing good about it was that we got a chance to do a lot of rehearsing, and that kept us right on the ball.

Mr. Bud Red (manager of the Gardens) and Joe Oliver thought so much of me that they both kidded me all the time. They would say, "Can you imagine this lil so and so coming up here and blowing all of that horn" (meaning me playing the Cornet).

One night I came to work smelling real sweet and Bud Red gave me the devil about it—saying, "Where the so and so did you get that cheap stuff you are wearing?" I did not dare to tell him that one of the roomers gave me that perfume—it came from the Stock Yards in a big bottle. Bud made such an issue of it, and laughed so hard at me, just when I thought I was dressed to kill, I just had to stop wearing it on my clothes to stop all of those cats from ragging me. Before I made up my mind fully to lay off that perfume, it started to smell like lineament. I got up enough nerve to ask the man what it was made of—he told me they made it from fertilizer. That really ended the smelling session.

As our nights progressed at Lincoln Gardens, Lil (who I found later was very fond of me) and I began to have long chats every night. I did not know that all the fellows in the Band were trying to make her. She would carry me around Chicago to visit all the big spots that I mentioned, in order to visit and hear different musicians. She really knew all the places, because she had been in Chicago all the time. At this time she and I became very chummy.

One night we were alone talking over different things and trying to think of some place to go. I told Lil there was something I wanted to ask her to do. Take me to see Ollie Powers, a tenor, swing singer, and Mae Alix. Ollie was a light [skinned] heavy built fellow. He had just come off the Road with Shelton Brooks, a comedian who reminded you of Burt Williams. Ollie was working at the Dreamland with Mae Alix. They were both young at that time, especially that Mae Alix—some vivacious. In all they were great in their field.

Ollie would sing a song, like "What Will I Do," in Fox Trot time. He would sing the first two choruses on the floor, then he would go from table to table. No matter how much noise the people made you could still hear, very clearly, the golden voice of Ollie Powers.

Mae Alix was an attractive, high yellow gal. She had a good voice herself, but she made most of her money in tips. All the big time Pimps, hustlers, and good time Charlies would visit the Dreamland. They would line up a big line of dollars across the floor and Mae would take a long running split and pick up all of those dollars. Sometimes she would have a whole basket of dollars. Those cats would keep her splitting. The dollars would come in so fast sometimes Mae would over look some of the money and the musicians would call her attention with the horn and show her all the money she had missed. I was on the edge to meet Ollie and Mae. So one night we got off early and Lil suggested we go over so I could meet them in person. This was a thrill.

The night was Sunday. We were kinda early and the place wasn't so full, so Lil decided it was a good time for me to meet them. Ollie and Mae came over to our table and sat with us. Lil introduced us, she told them I was the new Cornet man with Joe Oliver's Band and Bla, Bla. (On the Q.T.) I asked Lil if it was O.K. for me to give Ollie a dollar to sing for me, and to give Mae one to do that split for me. Lil smiled and said it was quite all right. Gee, I thought I was somebody, sporting the up. Two dollars, boy, was I something. I could hardly wait to get back to the job to tell the fellows what a big sport I was. When I told Joe Oliver, he looked at me and said ump, ump. As if he wanted to say, "Why you country so and so."

Lil and I had become so chummy by now, we refused to go any place without each other. We went to all the picnics on the South Side. Chicago had some of the best picnics in the summer. We went to many Church picnics but the best one that I recall was St. Thomas. Evidently I had more fun there, because I remember it most of all.

All of the big wigs on the South Side, would get all dressed up and drive out with their chicks dressed to kill, each trying to out do the other. They would be half juiced when they arrived and later on they would get real booted. Those cats really showed off. Sometimes good friends would start a friendly debate and it would end up in a brawl. After they had clowned enough at the picnics they would get ready to leave the grounds and head for the highways in a dead heat. They would race each other so fast and half of them were so drunk they could hardly see. Lil was scared half to death, and to me I thought they were a pack of fools who was not used to anything—since they were up North they just had to show off. The cats back in New Orleans acted differently when they were supposed to be the big wigs. When we got back from the picnics we were happy. Then we could admit we had fun in spite of the danger.

There was something else that Lil and I attended which stand out in my memory. This incident particularly interested me because it was the very first time I had seen an all colored Auto Race. Ump! Now this is going to kill you.

That event was so well advertised, everyone knew about it—the South Side, West Side, and every place colored people lived in the city. You can imagine how long they had the advertisement going continuously. It was to be held at the Harthorne Tracks. Some Colored organization thought up the idea. There had never been an all Colored Race in the city before, and they got together and rented the Tracks and got the contestants together and the race was on. This was sure going to be something. Everyone was so nervous the night before they could hardly wait for the day to come. I was really out of my mind with excitement. I had never before seen a white Auto race to say the least about an All Colored one, so you can imagine how I felt.

That day finally arrived. Lil and I met and went on out to the Tracks early, so we could see everything. As we were en route to the Tracks in a taxi cab we could see the Racers headed for the field. Everyone had their bottle—I mean everybody, even had a little bottle on my hip myself.

Everybody got seated by the time the man dropped the flag. The Race was on for all it was worth. One round then another round, the thousands of spectators cheering like mad, I am sitting here thrilled to the gills. Just as I said, "Gee, Lil this is going to be a swell day," and Lil sanctioned my idea. Before she could finish telling me, she yelled, "Look over there!" I turned around and there was three cars, not one but three cars spinning in the air like a spinning wheel. I thought the people would get excited, but all they said was, Ooh! and turned toward the next cars as though that was a part of the race. They yelled like mad at the next cars. The men went out with stretchers to pick up the men, I went down to see what was going on. When I got there those cats were really stretched out. I don't know how many it was, but it was too many for me so I went back to my seat. When I got back to Lil, I looked down at the rails by the tracks and there was a man standing there waving to someone across the Track. He had evidently forgotten he was at a Race Track, and thought he was on the streets or something. Unconsciously I kept my eye on him. I had no idea why that guy he was waving to was so interesting that he was going across there to talk to him. I have never been able to figure out what that fellow had on his mind. As he walked out he missed the first two cars but the third one got him. He went into the air like a dummy. That really got the people. They became real panicky. Lil and I left long before the Race was over. When we were safely in the cab, I told Lil, "From now on I don't want to see a foot race let alone an Automobile Race."

Three months passed, we were still working at the Gardens, and it was beginning to get cool. My mother May-Ann was getting restless down in New Orleans. She would ask everyone who had been to Chicago and gone back to New Orleans about me. She wanted to know how her boy was getting along. As much as I wrote and sent money she still worried about me. What made it worst, some cat who said he had been to Chicago told her he had seen me and I was in real bad shape. I was not working, broke, sick and hungry. This was too much. She packed her bundle, she was so frantic, and left for Chicago right away. She didn't take time to send me a wire or nothing, she just got the very first train that she could get and started for Chicago.

One night just before the show got started, I looked up and to my surprise there was my mother coming across the stage, bundles, bags and all. She had spied me and no one on earth could stop her. She had seen her boy and that was all it was to it. She ran like mad into my arms to greet me. Everybody turned around to look at us. My dear mother didn't care what the world had to say, all she was interested in was her little sloe-footed boy (that was me). I was speechless.

When my mother reached me, across the Band Stand, I hadn't closed my mouth and it had been opened ever since I spied her. I was so very happy, I didn't know actually what was going on until she said, "How is my boy. How are you doing?" I realized my mother was actually there before me, in Person. Everything was real great. Oh! my such a hugging and kissing. Everybody in the band got around my mother including King Oliver. The first intermission all of us gathered around her. There wasn't anything to do but sit and listen to her talk. May-Ann told us all the news from home after she found out I was O.K. That was when she told us about some cat coming down to New Orleans and telling everybody she had better go to Chicago at once and see about her boy (me of course). May-Ann asked the fellow why her son didn't come home? That cat told my mother, he had asked me the same question. He said, "Louis just held his head down and cried." Dig that cat. I told mama, "Can't you just imagine me turning up this face of mine and crying." That gag put my mother in very good spirit—she laughed out aloud. The rest of the night she had lots of fun meeting the cats in the band . . . . . .

When the Lincoln Gardens show was over, we played a short dance set, then we were off for the rest of the night. I rented a room for the night for my mother, until I could get an apartment for her. While we were on our way home I asked my mother how she liked the big city? She said in a sad voice, "Son I don't think I like it up North with all of these new fangled gadget," (meaning) all the modern things they had in Chicago, which they didn't have in New Orleans. New fangled gadget was May-Ann's pet phrase. It was used to express New Inventions, etc . . . .

Joe Oliver was as glad to see my mother as I was. . . . Oh! she was very proud of her son. . . . She beamed all over every time she looked at me. When the show was over at the Gardens, Papa Joe and I took May-Ann to Thirty-Fifth and State streets, to the Arlington Restaurant and had a real good Southern cooked breakfast . . . .

Speaking of the good old times, we really had one with my mother her first time to Chicago. She was in good spirit by the time we had finished our breakfast and talked about all the happenings around New Orleans after we had left. We nearly talked her to death. Each of us had different people we wanted to know how they were doing and where they had gone. There were so many I wanted to know about, all of my old (white boys) childhood pals, the ones I played cowboy and Indians with in our good old school days . . . . (We were the Indians.)

After we had "scarfed" (eaten), we decided to call it a day and go home. We needed a good night sleep. May-Ann needed to go in too—so we cut out. I was so happy when I got her straightened out. I knew she was tired but she wanted to be sure I was fine. Somehow I wanted her to like Chicago now that she was in town. I hadn't seen her in such a long time—until I just couldn't take my eyes off her. *My My*—This is the very first time I have ever had a 'chance' to really do something real decent for my dear 'mother, *and* 'pal—we were so 'poor, while I was learning music and growing up.

The next morning, while my mother was still sleeping (she was so tired from the long ride on that James Crow train, Jim Crow that is), I thought she should sleep while I went out to look for an apartment. I wanted her to have an apartment—maybe she would like Chicago better. I wanted her to have every comfort. I wanted her to stay up North with me. I decided *that* the very first minute I laid eyes on her.

I finished my breakfast and got dressed. I left orders for no one to disturb my mother—she was to sleep until she woke up. I called up Lil Hardin, she was my very good friend. There wasn't any better piano player than Lil. We became friends, while we played together in Papa Joe Oliver's Band. Lil played at the Gardens with us. She always knew just what to do in most situations. I had explained to her, I wanted to keep my mother with me. When she got up in the same morning she called up a very good friend of hers who was a Real Estate man. She explained to him about the situation and he told her he would have the *very* thing for me. She phoned me and told me the good news. I was very happy, everything was working out alright for me. I met Lil at the appointed place . . . . . and away we went. All of this was to be a surprise for my mother. The only trouble now was to convince her to stay with me at 43rd and St. Lawrence Ave.

When we arrived at the office, the Realtor—he was very kind—took us over to a big apartment building. There was a whole lot of apartments to choose from. Lil and I picked out a three room deal on the fifth floor. We thought this would be just what she would like.

While we looked over the place I was reminded of New Orleans—May-Ann had been so wonderful to me. She and Mama Lucy had done everything they could do for me. Now was my turn to prove how thankful I was for the sacrifices she had made for me.

I would need Lil to help me keep her here. She would get lonesome for her friends back in New Orleans. She would have to make new friends. While Lil and the Realtor talked, I wandered back to the old days. I was going around with an Old gal and I mean an *old* gal, named Nootsy. She was about the ugliest gal in the gang of smart gals around New Orleans at the time. I must have been sixteen or seventeen years old. This ol gal had money all the time and she was stuck on me. I would slip up to her place.

May-Ann never approved of me going around with that gal. She was a *bad* gal too. I didn't have any business over there but I wanted to be in with the cats. I went with this chick for a long time—one night she wanted me to spend the night with her. I wasn't going for that jive. When I started out of the house she stuck me in the back with a *chib* (knife). I *cut* out on the *double*. When I got home May-Ann saw the blood on me and she took me back to the chick's house and grabbed her in the collar and gave her the whipping of her life. Every time she saw the blood on me she gave her another blow. That taught me a lesson. I have never been in any other cutting scrape since. That is when I was directly involved. There she was fighting my battle. She was always in my corner. So there was nothing too good for my mother and sister.

Lil and the Realtor continued to talk—I came out of my trance and joined them. We decided to take the place. Lil and I left the building—this was at 43rd and St. Lawrence Avenue—there was no elevator to be found any place. If you took the apartment, the only way you would get up there was two-footed . . . meaning you had to walk all the way. This situation sort of *had* Lil and I—because May-Ann had such a bad trip to Chicago, and she never had to walk up so far just to go to sleep in New Orleans. I told Lil we really had a problem here because back home we don't have very many buildings that's very much higher than five stories . . . Other than the Mason Blanche building, the Gauchaux building, the Hibernia bank, and several other of the real popular places . . . But not too many of them . . . Of course, those that are built down there are stronger than the rock of Gibraltar . . . Those buildings in New Orleans just have to be built real strong, on account of the damp weather, and lots of water, etc., which will keep a stranger with an awful cold . . . That is, if they don't latch on to the weather right away . . . Of course, in the section where we lived, there were mostly brick houses and good, good lumber houses, built to stay for years . . . We didn't have any tall buildings at all in our neighborhood . . . That's why, I was wondering if my mother would squawk on the issue that Lil and I were about to *lay* on her. . . . . Evidently, since I have not seen my mother in a very long time, I forgot that she was a very congenial woman and appreciate every little favor that I've ever done for her . . . Even, when I was a very small boy selling newspapers, and brought my little change home and gave it to her—it wasn't very much . . . But, she would *make* over-it, the same as I gave her *dollars* . . . Evidently, that's where, I adopted my appreciations from . . .

Yessir—'Lil and I had it all figured out . . . That is,—'Lil, did, anyway . . . We both agreed to wait until we got some furniture in the flat (apartment) and make it look like something before we have mother come in and make herself at home . . . So we ordered the things for every space . . . Lil, being up North for such a long time, from Memphis Tenn., her home town, she was really *up* on things, the *modern* things, and she had such wonderful *taste*, such as how to furnish the apartment, etc . . . Which won my little ol heart right away . . . I, not knowing that Lil had 'eyes' for me, the way she did . . . Meaning, I did not know that she, was getting weak for ol Satchmo, by the minute. . . . Yea . . . Of course, I could see that she liked the way I was blowing my cornet, and singing,—the little singing that I did do while with the King (Joe Oliver). But, as for the great Miss Lillian Hardin, that was her maiden name, or should I use that word—? . . . Anyway, —as for Lil, to have eyes for me, —Ump—I just didn't dig it, that's all . . . But as I was going to say—this particular day, when we had the furniture brought to this apartment, we spreaded all of the furniture around the room, in its places, etc. . . . But when we had fixed the bed,—we both looked at the bed at the same time . . . Realizing that we did not buy the first sheet for the bed . . . So with Lil, on one side of the bed and Me' on the other, our minds, ran (seems-like) the same . . . Wellsir,—we both commenced to thinking, like mad . . . We both thought, Hmmmm,—nobody here but the two of us . . . And it seemed like we both came to a conclusion at the same time . . . That we should, play a little tag, right this minute . . . And we did . . . Yes we did . . . .

You see,—? We figured that we'd' probably never get a fine chance such as this one . . . And Lil, being the master mind of the two, and 'me, with my schooling from the old masters from those old good 'coal cart days, —I did get up never to, not at least, be a wallflower or a simple something, etc., as anxious as I was, to just express my feeling . . . But Lil, she was so beautiful to me at such a precious moment . . . One I'll never forget, as long as I'm colored . . . . . And, before we both knew it, we were making violent, but beautiful love . . . And, from that moment, until the day we were married, we fell in love with each other . . . The day Mary Ann (my mother) came to the apartment and saw the big surprise we had for her, she was so thrilled, until, her eyes commenced to watering, with joy . . . She said, ″Oh, Son, I′ve never had an apartment of my own, in my whole life″. . . Which touched me deeply . . . To realize that I′ve finally done something decent for her . . . We were so poor, all of our lives, until we were very glad to get any place to sleep, most of the years, let alone an apartment with all the trimmings . . . Gosh′ . . . Whatta′ happy moment for Moms, and I, and Lil, also . . . Because she was so glad for the two of us . . . Moms thanked Lil, with a big kiss, and wished that she′d someday be my wife . . . Which she witnessed before she died . . . But we will come to that later. . . .

Around this time we started to talk about Henry (Red) Allen Jr. Red′s father had a very fine Brass Band in Algiers. Red was still going to McDonald 35 in New Orleans. He was taking trumpet in school. He was turning out to be a very fine trumpeter. I was in Chicago at the time but I heard from Red often and he was improving quite well on the horn. I was so very happy because I wanted to see more boys come up and keep the ball rolling, as far as Jazz is concerned. It was quite some time before I heard him play. I was still in Joe Oliver′s Band—the King and I would sit and talk of Red and his father. We said Red had to be good because the old man Allen was good on the cornet himself, and Red had a lot of experience with him. Old man Allen had the best Brass Band in New Orleans. It had to be natural for Red, with all of his experience and study, Jazz had to be instilled in him.

The next we heard from Red, we had had our stay at the Lincoln Gardens. Joe had received a contract from M.C.A. (I think that was the first Booking Agent, who booked Bands). The rest of them booked all of the big time acts, such as Bill (Bojangles) Robinson, Will Mahoney and all of those big time cats. That Will used to dance on a xylophone. He was real good. I happened to catch him later on in London at the Palladium.

[When] Joe Oliver [got the contract from M.C.A.], his Band was Playing at the Lincoln Gardens. (I think his band was the first Colored Band ever booked by that company.) The Band almost broke up when Joe got the contract. Johnny Dodds, didn′t want any part of touring. He had a job offered to him at Kelly′s Stable on the North Side of Chicago. So we lost our clarinet man.

Honore Dutrey, Trombone man, had a nasty case of Asthma—he had contracted it while he was in the Navy. He couldn′t travel because of weather conditions. It was in February at the time and snow was all over the place. Boy that was a real sad day for all of us. We had been together for a long time and to break up almost killed us. Joe had to get some replacements because the show had to go on. Joe hired two men. Buster Bailey came from Memphis when he was a kid. He was playing at the Vendome Theater and doubled to the Sunset. The Sunset was owned by my Boss Mr. Glaser. He still owns the building . . . Buster played Clarinet and Alto Sax.

Rudy Jackson, the second man, played clarinet and Tenor Sax. Both of the new boys played at the Sunset with Cal Dickerson's Band. They both quit to join us for the tour. The rest of the band stayed so we didn't' have too much trouble. By Rudy and Buster playing together at the Sunset and Joe and I taking the Duet, we didn't have too much trouble getting together. There wasn't too much music to remember, so after a few rehearsals we were *kicks* to each other. Listening to Joe and I taking the breaks without the music puzzled all of the musicians. Buster and Rudy soon caught on to us and every thing went smooth. Finally they—Buster and Rudy—decided they would try making some *Duet* Breaks together, the same as Joe Oliver + myself. *Well*, the first time they tried it, we were in Madison Wisc. And we had to laugh because when the break came, Buster + Rudy were in a big argument, saying—"*No man*—you started on the *wrong note*"—etc. Ha Ha—They never did try it again.

There were *lots of* the musicians from Downtown Chicago—hurrying from their Jobs—to *Dig* us every night that we played at the Lincoln Gardens on *31st* Street, near the Cottage Grove Avenue. When Joe Oliver's contract was finished at the Gardens, we sure did hate to leave. In fact—that happens to most musicians. They stay at a place for a long time. And they get so used to the joint, until—it *seems* a *Drag* to leave. But—we finally did. We toured all through Iowa—Pennsylvania—Maryland—Illinois—etc. A very nice tour, I thought. King Oliver's Band was the first, All Colored Band to sign up with the M.C.A. Corporation. I used to do my little Dance with the band, when they hit the road. Although I was a Singer when I joined the King's outfit, and he knew that I could sing. But, he didn't seem to bother. And I did not feel that I should—*force* the issue. Maybe "Pappa Joe"—that's the name I used to call King Oliver—felt the same way that Fletcher Henderson *did* concerning my singing with the Band. Not that they weren't for it. It was just the idea that there never was a *trumpet* player, or, any *instrument* player at that time—way back in the olden days the instrumentalists just weren't singing, that's all. So, I gathered that those two Big shot Boys, Joe + Fletcher, just was afraid to let me sing, thinking maybe, I'd sort of ruin their reputations, with their musical public. They not *knowing* that I had been singing, all of my life. In *Churches, etc.* I had one of the finest All Boys Quartets that ever walked the streets of New Orleans. So you see? Singing was more *into* my Blood, than the trumpet. Anyway, we forgot about the singing—All together. But, as I've said before, Fletcher did manage to let me sing, a vocal chorus to the tune of—"Everybody Loves My Baby," on a Banner Label. And—my goodness—the compliments Fletcher received, when the recording was released. And still Fletcher, or King Oliver, never did *pick up* on my *vocalizings*, which until this day was nothing to write home about. *But.* It *was* Different.

Finally—when I went on tour with the great King Oliver's Jazz Band—he decided to let me do everything *and* anything that I choosed. The Customer's really went for it in a big way. Just before the tour—*big things* really happened. Lillian Hardin + I finally stopped Ducking + Dodging with our *secret* romance and *Got Married. UMP UMP UMP! There now*—the whole town *Gossip* really started. The whole King Oliver Band, was so surprised, until they all were speechless. King Oliver was the first one who spoke up. He said to me—but not direct—can you imagine—? Joe said—"This *Country Son of a Bitch* (meaning me) coming up North making a Chick Fall for him real *Deep*. And *We All*, meaning, every member in my band, has been shooting at her—trying to make some kind of a Headway *with her. Hmmm.*" Then King said, as he let out with a little cute smile on his face, "More power to you *Both Son*. You have my *Blessings* and you *know* I am for *you* and *Lil* one hundred percent. After all—I practically Raised the Two of you. But I *still say* that I—Johnny Dodds—Dutrey—Baby Dodds—Bill Johnson—all of us *Guys*, were all trying to see who would be the first one to *Get* into *Lil—first*. And, of course, Here *you* come with your *Sloe* Foot self."

Then—all of a sudden, King Oliver and the entire Band—they all *yelled* at once—"*Congratulations*—to Mr. + Mrs. Louis *Satchmo* Armstrong." *Ooh Gawd'*. Just think, I said to myself—they are calling me Mister Armstrong. The only time I can remember anyone using *those words* would be my boss man whom I worked for in New Orleans, whenever he would *Jump Salty*, meaning when he would get *angry* at me—which would not last long enough to even mention. I only mentioned it here because I was speaking of an *incident—that's all.*

After the Lincoln Gardens let out—the first night *Lil and I* got *married*—we made the *'Rounds* to all of the After Hour *spots*. And Everywhere we went, everybody *commenced* throwing a lot of *Rice* on us. *My my*—I often wondered—where on earth did they find so much *Rice*. *Why*—every place that we would leave—in front of the door was real white—the same as if there had been a real heavy *snow* on the ground—from so much Rice lying thrown around. *Lillian* and myself, we did not take a Honeymoon, or anything like that. We both thought—it would be a better idea to save all the money we could and try and buy ourselves a nice little *pad* (a home)—kinda look out for a rainy day. It is—an old saying, and it has been around for Generations. Instead of a Honeymoon, we went on tour with King Oliver + his Band. We saved our money together. And, we accumulated quite a bit of *Loot* (money) together. And—sure enough—we really did save enough money to buy a very nice family house, in Chicago of course—at 421 East 44th St. We were both lucky in buying this house. Because the people who had it in front of us certainly did leave it in real fine—good shape. We didn't have to do a thing but *move* in with our furniture. At the time Lil + I got married, she was living with her mother, Dempsey Miller. Of course, 'Dempsey's *nick* name, was ''*Dee*cie. Deecie was a Christian woman and very nice. She treated me swell from the first day we were married, and even after we all moved in our home together. Deecie was from Memphis Tennessee. She raised *Lil*, to be a real smart gal. Lil, was so smart, until, when she attended *Fisk* University—She was Valedictorian of the class. When Deecie + her husband came to Chicago she brought *Lil* with her.

By that time *Lil* had turned out to be a fine piano player. She was *so* good, until all the Jazz Bands on the South Side, were Dickering for her to join their Bands. But she settle for King Oliver's Band, which I personally think she made the right move. Lil was in Joe's Band when I came to Chicago. She was the best. She would give out with that good' ol' New Orleans 4 Beat, which a lot of the Northern piano players couldn't do, to save their lives. *Ol Lil*, would make my ''Boy'' King Oliver, really *Give* out, when she would Commence to *Lay* that good 4 beat under *Papa Joe*. *Yessir*—Between Lil and Baby Dodds, Ol Joe Oliver would create more New Riffs and Ideas, than *any* musician I *know* of. And—for a ''woman'' there are very few *men* piano players, who can Swing a Band as good as *Lil.* And I am not just saying this—because I was married to her. If you'll notice—you'll find a lot of good piano players ruined their beautiful Dixieland Style—fooling around that old "Bop Slop Music. *Lil* had, all of the best jobs *Sewed up* when I first came to Chicago to join King Oliver. She would play with King Oliver at the Lincoln Gardens on 31st Street and Cottage Grove Avenue. From 9 P.M. until 2 A.M. And she would go to work again, on an "After hour Job" further out on the South Side. The name of this After hour Joint was the Edelweiss Gardens. *Yea*—they had a many *Gardens*—in Chicago, when I first went there in the year of 1922.

In the After hour band which *Lil* Armstrong played with after she finished playing with us, each night, was a big fine looking Creole fellow by the name of Freddie Keppard. He played a cornet and how. He had the most perfect lips of any man that I've ever heard, through the years of real *good* music. But to me, Freddie Keppard struck me, as a man who wasn't very serious musically. He still kept a lot of little *traits* in him, the same as the older musicians, in New Orleans from *way* back there in Buddy Bolden's time. The reason why I mention this about Freddie Keppard is because, in the olden days when a Big Man such as Freddie would be playing at a Place, and a "Rookie" (young) musician such as *myself* would show up on the scene, the first thing that Freddie Keppard would say—"Hey Boy—Come up here on the Band Stand and Blow a few numbers for me." Quite naturally—as ambitious as *I* was, I jumped the opportunity to even touch Freddie's horn, let alone *blow* it.

Yes, we young Rookies such as *myself*—would *thrill* at just the idea, of sitting in a big shot's *Chair* such as—Freddie Keppard—Manuel Perez—Joe "King" Oliver—Bunk Johnson, etc.—and lots of the other Cornet players that came from New Orleans. They were real great. Freddie Keppard had a wonderful sense of humor. *Why* the first night that I went out there to the Edelweiss Gardens with Lil, Freddie was sitting in his usual place on the left end of the (little) bandstand, which puts him out in the front where he could be seen and heard real good. And also—get *lots* of kicks—talking and jiving the Customers as they go—*to* and *from* the ladies + gents toilet, which was direct in the rear of the Bandstand. And *Freddie* had a lot of fun greeting his friends, disciples, *etc.* I laughed until I cried when Freddie—just before he started to play a tune—a real cute, pretty little Blonde "*Ofay* (white) Chick walked by the bandstand coming from the ladies rest room. Freddie spoke to her real, *Cute*. ''Oh, *Hello''* he said in a real *high* voice. And the cute little *Chick* smiled and said *HELLO* in a Real heavy voice. And it tickled everybody too much until even Freddie—laughed out loud—and almost fell off the bandstand. *Lill* with her little *high* voice, which sounds just like a kid when she laughs, she started to *laughing*, and ''*brother''* when ''*Lil''* laughs out *loud*, it takes *hell* in *damnation* to stop her.

Out of all of the After hour Joints that were running in Chicago at that time (1922–23), I kinda liked the Edelweiss Gardens the best. Later on—during my stay in Chicago, there was another After hour *Joint*—very pretty—opened up at 35th and State Street, called the Fume (or Fieum or Fiume—one of these) [Fiume—ed.]. The *Fiume* was a Black + Tan place, which means Colored (of course) and they had an *All White*, Dixieland Combo playing there' Nightly. Which was Something (at that time) very rare. Of course, there wasn't, no' particular reason why' that I was a *little bit* surprised to see White Boys, playing music on the South Side of Chicago. It's just that I had never seen such a beautiful picture before. I had just come up from the South, where there weren't anything as near beautiful as that 'happening. *White* musicians, playing all of that good 'Jump' music,—making those Colored people (mostly colored) *Swing like Mad*. The Fiume and the Edelweiss Gardens became a toss *up* with me as to' *which* one of the places that I should *hang* out, in the mornings after I finish work with my *man*—Joe King Oliver.

Sometimes I'd persuade *Papa* Joe (I calls *him*) to make the Rounds with me, after work, which would be—two o'clock in the A.M. It was real ''*Kicks*—listening to music, *Diggin'* his thoughts—comments' *etc*. His Conception of *things*—life—Music, people in general, were really wonderful. It is really too bad that the world did not have a chance to *Dig* the real Joe King Oliver and his greatness. His human interest in things was really something to think about. All Joe Oliver had to do—was to just talk to me, and I'd feel just like I had one of those good 'old music lessons of his. It was a *solid gassuh* the way he would explain things. That night the King and I went out. P.S. I should've said the morning, we went out, because we went to the Edelweiss Gardens first—and finished up at the Fiume. When we left there it was day break, and I was feeling pretty *tipsy*. King Oliver doesn't drink at all. He used to drink just like a fish. That was way back in the olden days when it wasn't *anything* for a musician to turn a pint of whiskey up to his *Lips* and never pull it down until the bottle was Absolutely Empty. That the kind of drinker King Oliver was when he was on the Lush Wagon (whiskey train). And all of a sudden' one New Year's Eve—when he was playing down in the red light district, at Pete Lala's cabaret (in Storyville)—which, are called night clubs—Joe King Oliver made a resolution' that year—I think it was the year of 1917. He said, as he turned a *Pint* of *Whiskey* up to his lips—and said—"*Well this* is my *Last Drink* Fellows" (meaning) the members in the *band*. Of course they all turned and listened to Oliver and looked at him as if he was talking out of his head—or *Somphn*.— But—sure enough—Papa Joe hasn't taken a drink or anything alcoholic *since*. Now—that's what I call, having Will Power—*Personified*. He did a lot of smoking. But *Nixed Out* on the drinking. He said, every time he got *drunk* he would, act a fool—*talk loud*—either get into trouble or hurt himself—which he would deeply regret the following morning. The night he and I went out—he drank, soft drinks,—and I did the lushing (the drinking) you see. I came up during the days which were a little more modern—from what I could gather and saw, when the old time greats were holding sway in New Orleans. Those good ol' musician used to drink day and night—and not one of them would even think of taking a good *Physic*, and clean their stomach out, which would *automatically* straighten their stomachs out for fresh food as well as for fresh liquor.

As I've said, all through this story, that I have always been a great observer. All through life, and—as, we, modern 'Cats' expresses, it,—I *Dug*" "All of the Old timers—their lives—their personal' 'livelihoods' etc. *Hobbies*,—Well—the Hobbies of the musicians of *today* (the ones that's left) are *far* more *modern*. For a youngster' who, (I'd say) had, *practically* made his "own' *way*, *I—Mee*—Louis Armstrong,—I didn't do so bad. I at least learned the "real" *right* from wrong. Which is, in everyone's estimation—good common *sense*. I always knew how far to go with liquor. That is, except for about *two* or *three* times. One is when I was about *Seventeen* years old, when *Three* of my School mates brought me home to *May Ann*" my mother whose name is Mary Ann. "Boy" 'Boy 'oh 'Boy—I was so *drunk*, until I didn't know my ankle from my head. My mother—was very kind through it all. Through my whole life, my mother always had the greatest Confidence in me. She always figured that anything I did I was well aware of the fact as to knowing what I was doing and wanted to do.

Oh—I was *so embarrassed* when I awakened to find out—that I had been *drunk* in front of my mother for the first time. I always managed to do my little ''*Nipping,*'' meaning (drink) with the crowd from the honky tonks, but managed to always ''Straighten up'' before I get home to Mama, whom I lived with practically—all of my life, even after I was married to Daisy Parker (my first wife). Because—at that time, I was' only serious about my horn (trumpet). And—not so much, the women. Therefore—I did not take any foolishness off of them. *Yes Lord.* I'd pack my clothes, Clarence's clothes—and away we would go—'back down to Liberty + Perdido Streets, where *May* Ann' lived. She would always be glad to have us. And the most she would ask us, was—''What's wrong? You + Daisy' ''At it again?''

Joe ''King'' Oliver—had given me' an, old beat up, *Cornet* which he had blown, all out of *tune.* I 'prized *that horn.* And guarded it, with my dear life. As strange as it seemed—I blew on that horn a real long time before I was fortunate enough to get another one. In *those* days—Cornets were far more *cheaper* than they are today. When ever, *'one'* would pay, the price of $65.00 for a *Cornet*, why, er' he' was considered a *big shot* musician' which *handles* ''plenty of money. 'Or 'making a great big salary, 'or' playing *lots* ''N'' *lots* of ''Gigs.''I remember the time when Roy Palmer—Hamp Benson—Kid Ory—Jack Carey (Brother to Mutt Carey)—Vic Gaspard—Morris French—Frankie Duson—Bill Mathews—''*Zoo* Robinson [probably Alvin ''Zue'' Robertson]—George Brashere [probably Norman Brashear]—George Fields [probably George Filhe]—Eddie Atkins—Eddie Vincent [probably Eddie Vinson]—Joe Petit (the *father* of ''*Buddy* Petit—one of our Creole Cornet players)—All of those trombone men and several others, whom I shall mention later on, further down in my story—All of those fellows'—I played music with, when they received their *new* horns, some time or other. And they couldn't have *Beamed* all over, anymore, than if they had *All* received a brand new *Cadillac.* And don't mention the proudness in the *Cornet* players, including me. The first Brand new Cornet that I was fortunate enough to *buy'* with a little bit' *down* 'and, a little bit more money toward the finishing of the *bill* when ever the collectors, can catch up with me. Ha Ha. You 'talking about the *Phrase ''Now 'N' then''* when ever My Collector would Catch up with me. I would tell *them*—''may give ''*y'all*'' something *Then*—but, I'll be *damned*—if I can give' *y'all* anything *Now.*'' P.S. A case of *now* and *then.* ''*Latch?* It was a known thing for cornet players to pawn their instruments when ever there would be a *lull'* in' funerals' parades' dances' etc.

I can remember *twice'* that I actually went to the pawn shop, and picked up some Loot on my *horn*. The first time was, to play *Cotch*, and to be around in the company of those good ol' old time Hustlers and Gamblers. I've already explained, the way they played with 3 cards, and, which, fascinated me—no end. I was working on the excursion boat—the Steamer Sidney—for some real fine white people' the Streckfus family. They were *real Groove* people. And loved music, the way that *I did.* ''Especially'' *that great man'* Captain Joe. He was really on the Ball. He went in for the finest in 'Jazz.' He understood it. And, when ever he was on the *mound'* he'd pull up a chair at our rehearsals' and *watch' look* and listen, very carefully' to every note' which came out of our instruments. *And'* Oh '*Brother* if those notes weren't, right, or those *Chords'* etc.' that's when you'd hear from him, and how. As for *me''* I could not play anything decent when ever I saw Capt. Joe angry. I think I am justified in saying—not only was I sort of' on' edge, when Capt. Joe was on the war path—but, there were *lots* others, of the Crew and Band' who shuttered the same as I. They were *Fate Marable*, Colored boy' whom the *Streckfus* Brothers, picked up on' ever since he was the size of *Sugar Child Robertson.* They '*Reared* ''*Fate.* P.S. I'd—rather' my' 'way of explaining it—They' *Raised'* Fate Marable. They discovered Fate in Paducah, Kentucky. Fate learned to play the ''*Calliope''* very good. Of course, I am not trying to make myself any *too* ''younger than Fate. Although, he is older than I. But—I can easily remember ''Fate playing the *Calliope* on the Steamer Sidney when I was a boy' Selling Newspapers. I used to go out to the foot of Canal Street—out there by the L. + 'N' Station—and Just *sit* there listening to Fate Marable 'Swing those Calliope Keys down to a low gravy. And—not with the slightest intention or knowledge that I would be, featured trumpet in his famous orchestra. It just goes to show you—it's a *small* and beautiful world.

Getting back to Captain Joe Streckfus. Not only was the musicians, waiters and checkroom folks perked up when ever he was around, but there were his devoted Brothers—Mr. Vern—Roy—John,—they also, would really get in there and really *do* the thing Right. There were also a Mr. Lax, whom the Streckfus Boys raised. He was *First Mate.* And, a *Darn Good* one. It was really a great day' in St. Louis, Mo., on the Steamer St. Paul the day' Captain Joe Streckfus married Lola, the young Cashier on the boat. As surprised as everyone were there were a lot of rejoicing—and everyone had a grand time. Even we musicians. They (Capt. Joe + Lola)—sure did have a lot of children. And "Ol" capt., my boy—He wasn't anybody's "Chippy. He was a big, well built' fine man' not too fat. In fact, he wasn't fat at all. His Physique was something to marvel at. And fine—strong frame' would' sorta' make 'one *say "Gee'* I wish that I was as healthy looking as "that man." Later on, we'd, talk about Capt. Joe again. Because, in his later years, *he* and his family made a trip, all the way from St. Louis to New York to hear me play. He loved the way that I played the trumpet. *Yessir"* 'Capt. Joe was a real Jazz fan at heart. Which, to *me*, was *really "Somphn."* When, Joe Oliver came from Chicago down to St. Louis to hear me play the *trumpet*, and spend *four* days of his vacation with me as my personal Guest, he got a big boot out of watching Joe Oliver's expressions and admiration, as he watched me *play*.

And the big baskets of *lunch'* my *landlady* would fix for me, during those' all day excursions—I would not get any of it. I would turn the whole basket over to Joe. And with two Cups of Coffee and a tin bucket full of real Cold Ice Water, he would really go to town. Honest, I used to love to see him eat. Pappa Joe, as I used to call him, as far back as 1917. He would be actually enjoying himself *So* well, as he would Devour my lunch—which was consist of 4' porkchops, a bowl of steamed corn, a bowl of rice, a half dozen slices of bread, well buttered, 2 *Hunk'* Slices of plain pound Cake' (P.S.) I Just *love* plain pound cake. Anyway" Joe Oliver cleaned the whole basket, of food to my *dee'*light. I bought a couple of ham sandwiches for myself, and was *tickled pink*. Ever since the first time I met Joe Oliver, he always play the part of something real precious in my life. He always seemed just a little different from anyone, I had met. And, as a *kid*, I couldn't help but notice the difference in the kindness in Mr. *Joe'* as I once called him. All the rest of the musicians around New Orleans (including "Bunk Johnson') at the time when I was a kid' were full of "you *"know what"* and they never had time. They' just couldn't be *bothered, that's* all. My step father Mr. Gabe, in my estimation, came very close to Joe Oliver, with his kindness to an 'up and coming youngster.— *Gabe"* Oh' I just *love* that name. And—I—being a *Trumpet Player,* and heard all about *Ol* Gabriel so many times, just makes me think that I' know *Gabriel personally." Hmm—silly Boy Satch."*

In the year of 1923, *we* were still in the Lincoln Gardens in Chicago. I mentioned "*We*' meaning' King' Joe' Oliver's Jazz Band. As I've mentioned before' Oliver's *Band' Almost* Broke *Completely* "up" when he accepted a contract from M.C.A. to travel on the road' making a long *tour* of *One* Nighters, which was lots more pay in Salaries, and much shorter hours. But, fellows, in the band' such as Johnny Dodds' Bill Johnson' *etc.'* just wouldn't leave Chicago. That's where Buster Bailey' the great clarinetist + alto saxophonist—and Rudy Jackson—Tenor sax man—came in. They were also in Chicago at the time' playing in Carroll Dickerson's orchestra.

Carroll Dickerson was a violin player, a very good one. And was well known to the public and 'very very popular among the Chicago musicians. At the time, he was playing at the *Sunset Cafe* for "Joe Glaser' whom I later worked for, and *now* 'my present manager. Dickerson's band was the best Cabaret Band, on the South Side of Chicago at that time. Andre Hillare' a very *fine* drummer—was in the band. And—was known' as the *finest* drummer in Chicago at the time. Hillare' was a Creole Boy from New Orleans' my home town. He, was a very delicate sort of fellow' very much fragile. And—as 'we' New Orleanians expresses it, he was very' "Puny." *But*—the only way to put it, so everyone can understand it—he had—T.B. P.S. "Somphn' like that.

Of course the word' "tuberculosis" never did cross my mind very much because my mother had always kept us' Physic minded, from kids. She had my sister Mama Lucy and I to realize—that—just such a thing as a 'slight physic' once' or twice' a week' would throw off many symptoms—germs' etc. 'congregates from out of nowheres' into your stomach. We could not afford a doctor. Nay Nay. Why the fifty cents, or dollar, which was the Doctor's fees, way back there when I was a boy—with *that* money" May Ann could cook a great big pot of Red Beans and rice' which Mama Lucy and I—could really *Annihilate ourselves on*. And the next morning, we would have some beans and rice left' for breakfast before we went to School. By doing that little routine of our Mother's we did not have any sick days at all. Of course, it's a well known fact that a child 'who *came up* during my time' and went *bare* footed practically' all of his young life' the same as I *did'* are' *bound* to pick up a *nail*—splinter' or a piece of glass, the same as I and Mama Lucy did. Quite naturally, we were *young—healthy*—and tough *as ol hell*—so a little thing' such as a *Locked Jaw'* didn't even stay with us very long. Mother and a couple of her friendly neighbors would take an ordinary basket 'each and go out by the railroad tracks' and fill their baskets full' of' Pepper Grass'—they called it. They would bring home this grass, which grows wild. Mother put a whole gang of it—into a big pot—boil it until it get real ''gummy'' then she'd—rub it on the Afflicted *Wound''* and Brother' within two or three hours' we kids' whom were afflicted' would automatically' get up—out of that bed—and out in the streets—playing just like nothing happened.

As the old saying goes'—the Lord—take care of fools.— Just think' of the danger' we kids were in' at all times.— For instance'—after school' we Colored Kids' whom were very friendly with the White Kids that lived in the same neighborhood' their 'parents' were owners (maybe) of the neighborhood' grocery store' or drug store or saloon' or' maybe they just lived in the neighborhood' *period*. Just the same, it did not matter. Kids—will be kids. There would always be a house or *etc.''* being torn down, or rebuilding. And we kids would go into those old broken down lots, where there's so much rubbish, such as old slates, pieces of broken bottles, broken window pains, etc. We 'Kids' Accustomed to seeing the movies concerning *Wars''* we all, decided to play—war—as we saw it. We also decided to appoint—officers of different Rankings' etc., not particularly knowing the real meaning of different appointees'' they made me—Sergeant at Arms. My post was, (dig this) to help when ever a member of my tribe (I mean my regiment) get wounded on the battle field' and I being the Sergeant at Arms. The leader of our Crowd' which was one of the fightingest guys in the world, his name was *One Eye Bud*. He (like Hitler) appointed himself—the General of the Army. And nobody detested it. One Eye Bud—appointed me 'Sergeant at Arms.' And when I asked' ''What does 'that mean?'' He said—when ever a man get wounded' my position is to go out there on the field—take the wounded comrade by the *arm* and lead him off the battle field. Coming off the field one day—a big piece of *Slate'* which' came from one of the old' houses, were in the air in the same direction as my ''Big head'' when all of a sudden, one of my *soldiers* hollered' (real frantically) *''Lookout* ''Dipper'' (my name) *Lookout.''* I gotten *So* excited—I threw my head directly into the direction of that great big piece of Slate and it landed right in the middle of my Head—*wow*. The force from that big piece of slate hit my head *so* hard' until' it penetrated' real deep' down' into my head' which caused me to suffer something terrible. That *Blunt lick*—then *too*, the sharpness of the Slate, immediately shocked my whole body, and—on top of it all—gave me a locked jaw. Mary Ann, my mother'—with tears in her eyes, worked frantically' with her herbs and roots and stuff—all boiled up' along with a glass of Pluto water. She put me to bed—sweated me out real good over night. *Shucks*—the next morning I was on my way to school just like nothing happened. And—with my step' father' working in the kitchen at one of the largest Hotels in the City of New Orleans—he used to bring home a big fat *pan* of those rich white folks' leavings, each night he'd get off from work. Mother would fix *me out* with the very *best* in *Steaks*.

Imagine me,—a young Colored boy—living in a poor neighborhood going to school with a "Filet Mignon" Steak Sandwich. *Hmmm?*—I was the most popular lad in School. You see?—that was the difference between kids such as Hillare, who was also from New Orleans, and we were kids together. But, from different Branches and environments. Hillare's family were—well, I won't say that they were real rich' or' anything like that. But—I'd say—they were real' good *livers*—which means' that they were *well* off." P.S. We' so' amusingly put it, they were *"Nigger rich."* But—wonderful people. Of course, you can see the difference, why youngsters such as myself were much more Healthier than kids such as Hillare, and a' many' other kids whom I *grew up* with. It would take, pages + pages for me to call names of all the unfortunate youngsters who did not get the real chance to rough it out like we kids—the kids whom, I grew up with. Of course, it wasn't no fault of mine, that my parents were poor as *Job's Turkey*, etc. And we kids didn't have everything that we wanted' through life. Like the kids who families were better situated. But—after *Summing* it *all* up, from the lessons' of *'good common sense'* that my Mother, who did not have an *awful* lot of learnings herself, taught my Sister + I—the real Rudiments in life, I feel, right to *this* day—that we both' Sis + I' have gotten the very best of the deal. In life that is. And since I've gotten to be a man," and has been practically' all over the world playing my trumpet, which' no millionaire can boast any more than I can as far as traveling to places where it take lots of money to go.

Hillare and the rest of us kids who turned out to be good musicians, migrated from New Orleans—to Chicago, when times were real good. There were plenty of work, lots of *Dough* flying around, all kinds of beautiful women at your service. A musician in Chicago in the early twenties were treated and respected just like—some kind of a God. And a real 'good one such as Hillare' and as little + cute and' as good looking as "he 'was, why the "women just "Swarmed him" 'constantly. Hillare' being a 'small 'delicate sort of a fellow" and—with' so many *inducements*, etc., which caused him to dissipate, along with his' *late* working hours at the *Sunset* Cafe." The youngster, commenced to going into bad health. And still a trouper 'all the way. Although he commenced to *waning*—looking pale, etc., he still had that *good ol'* pleasant smile for me and the gang when ever we came around." I mostly mentioned the case of Hillare the drummer because—from a kid—I was always a great observer. I Dugged" (I watched) the reactions of "other 'Actors and Musicians, all through our goings 'on' and travels. And I've noticed,—the majority of them—they *scuffled* to the top in music, or their sole ambitions as professional entertainers. But—very few of them—stopped—once to consider that, *health* plays the most important part of it all.

And, in speaking of Hillare, as well as many of the other well off folks who probably had just about the best of everything since their childhood. I was trying to make clear, that where there's health there's *wealth*. My parents did not have a lot of money to display on my sister and I, as children. But, what my mother taught me concerning health' was worth more than any *rich* man' in the whole world. Hillare was one of the finest young men' and musician' that I have ever met. When Buster Bailey (alto sax) and Rudy Jackson (tenor sax) play in Carroll Dickerson's band alongside Hillare at the Sunset Cafe' in the days when Chicago was really jumping, which was the year 1922. I am telling you Folks—That was really Something. My my whatta band. With Bobbie Williams playing 1st trumpet. He had just returned from Service in the United States Army, and only been in Dickerson's a short time. I met Bobby about a week 'after I had joined King Joe Oliver + his band at the Lincoln Gardens, on 31st Street and Cottage Grove Ave. The Sunset Cafe was located at 35th and Calumet Ave. Bobby was a nice looking, Stout—Brownskin man, a little on the heavy side, and rather short. He had a very pleasant smile, and a very good looking personality. Always had a kind word for anyone, whom he should meet. And' from some of the musicians whom I met, on the South Side of Chicago, they all said the same things' about Bobby and his abilities—that' he was the young man' while serving in the Army and playing 1st trumpet in the Band' he wrote the "Bugle Blues," the world famous' "Bugle Blues." He used to feature this tune' nightly at the Sunset, during the Band

Specialty. Of course′ on account of my hours and Bobby′s hours′ I could not hear him as often as I wanted to. And—in fact I did not hear Bobby ′play his trumpet until one Halloween Night, when the Band played an extra engagement at the Eighth Regiment Army, which was located on Giles near 35th′ just around the corner of the Sunset Cafe. In fact—I did not hear Carroll Dickerson′s *Whole* Band′ until this Halloween Dance. They ″tore out″ (started out) with *several Jump Tunes′ then′* here *come* this famous ″Bugle Blues,″ with Bobby′ *Blowing like mad.* I′ve never heard it played so *well* and perfectly *phrased.* Beautiful *tonation*, etc. Afterwards, it became a real treat, to myself′ to hear Bobby′ *play′* when ever I could. Look like, as soon as I was *settling* down to really getting a *good load* of Bobby Williams he taken suddenly Ill—And died.— *Gee′* ″ What a Shock *that* was to the whole South Side (Chicago′s South Side, that is). All Pimps, Prostitutes, Hustlers, Gamblers, Porters, Waiters, Musicians, etc., were All′ brought down, when they were heard the news about, Bobby′s death. Of course, nobody could interfere with the personal part of—as to how Bobby was killed or ′who ′poisoned him. Whom could do *such* a thing to—*such* a *fine* man. They never did′ get the straight of the *Mess*. Somebody would *Accuse* this *Chick* or that *Chick*. Anyway—the whole thing died out, like a *flash.* Bobby Williams was the first Cornet, we′ll say, Trumpet player, that I first *saw* play the trumpet with one hand. Sometimes′ he would play a whole show with just *one* hand. *That* I did not particularly care for. Because the old school where ″I″ came from, the good old timers wouldn′t *dare* to *insult* a good piece of music by holding the horn in one hand to play. All of the hard *music* a musician, runs′ *into*—play one of those hard

6

LETTERS TO ROBERT GOFFIN

(MAY 7 and JULY 19, 1944)

Chapters 6 and 7 are discussed here together. Chapter 7, The "Goffin Notebooks," is a memoir that Armstrong wrote sometime between July 4, 1943, and July 3, 1944. He wrote it for the Belgian Robert Goffin to use in his biography of Armstrong, which would later be published in English as *Horn of Plenty*. Armstrong wrote the letters in chapter 6 to Goffin while in the middle of the project.

Armstrong mentions payments of $500 to Goffin, who was working in war-torn Belgium. Perhaps these payments reflect Armstrong's legendary generosity. But we should at least note the likelihood that Armstrong had a strong interest in seeing the biography come forward. His hopes for this material may be signaled in the letter of May 7, 1944, where the possibility of a film about Armstrong's life is mentioned. In two letters to Leonard Feather from 1941 (one published in this book; both held at the Institute of Jazz Studies, Rutgers University), Armstrong again mentions such a film, which he expects to be directed by Orson Welles. Perhaps Armstrong and his manager hoped that Goffin's biography would form the basis for a biographical movie. Armstrong has done his part by supplying Goffin with lots of colorful anecdotes—as well as cash.

Armstrong didn't mind what Goffin did with this material: "There may be several spots that you may want to straighten out—or change around . . . Whatever you do about it is alright with me." Goffin did indeed treat the material freely, and *Horn of Plenty* belongs, in the balance, to a kind of historical fiction that is no longer fashionable. It cannot be relied upon as a documentation of jazz history. Armstrong's memoir can now take its place. It is bracing to realize that publishing priorities were reversed in 1944.

Tucson Arizona.
May, 7th, 1944,

Greetings My Friend;

No doubt you've wondered why the delay . . . But I just didn't get around to it . . . I've been so busy traveling and making trains, etc . . . How's everything? . . . I do hope that you and the wife are as happy as ever . . . I shall meet my wife out in California in a few days . . . She went on ahead of me from Chicago . . .

Here's fifty dollars more—which makes, Three Hundred . . . I shall finish' up in California . . . Which won't take me long to get the other two hundred . . . I am opening up at the Trianon Ballroom Tuesday night May, 9th,. . . . I have four books of stories to send to you the first chance I can get to a Post Office . . .

There may be several spots that you might want to straighten out—or change around . . . What ever you do about it is alright with me . . . I am only doing as you told me . . . To make it real—and write it just as it happened. . . . And Brother believe me I have a lots for you this time. . . .

Write me a line to this address—2219 Hobart Blvd, Los Angeles California. . . . I am stopping at Mrs. Louise Beaver's Home out there. . . . She certainly is a swell person . . . And incidentally—if ever you should film the story of my life you should see that Mrs Beavers get a good part in the picture . . . She could really play the part of my mother since she looks so much like Mary Ann (my mother) and acts just like her . . .

And as great an actress as Mrs Beavers is—why she and I could get together and really make a big thing in a film together . . . I only mentioned her . . . Sometimes it saves one a lot of worry as to whom to get to play some parts, that's really to be played. . . . So Goffin I shall get to work now . . . And you can look for the rest of my story in a few days. . . .

Courtesy Institute of Jazz Studies, Rutgers University.

So goodnight pal . . . Am dying to lay eyes on you again . . . Am always glad to see you . . . You can tell from the way I explained in my story that you are really my boy . . . So stay happy and write me . . . And God Bless yous . . .

Am Pluto Waterly Yours,
Louis Armstrong

Bremerton Washington.
July, 19th, 1944,

Dear Pal Goffin;

'Man—I've been trying ana trying to get in touch with you . . . I had to write to Leonard Feather—And the gentleman in Chicago (the editor of 'Esquire) Mr Ginsrich . . . He told me that you were somewheres up State in New York . . . I wired you there and still there were no answer . . . I said—'Ump . . . And I wondered and wondered . . . I still haven't heard from Ol Leonard Feather . . . I'll never forgive him for that . . . He could have eased my mind a little—by no more than sending a short Wire, etc . . . I've done ever' so much for him and didn't even charge him one nickel . . . He know I'll tell him so too. . . . 'Oh 'Well—that's not so important anyway . . . So lets forget about him. It's you that I'm interested in. . . . . . .

How are you? . . . How's the wife? . . . Is she feeling fine these days? . . . My wife Lucille sends a big hello to you both. . . . . There's no need of me asking you how did you all enjoy your trip . . . I just know you both enjoyed the State of New York . . . Because—I personally think the State of New York is very very beautiful . . . Here's another hundred dollars toward the five hundred . . . That makes a balance of one hundred dollars more . . . Ain't that right?. . . .

In the Telegram I sent to you at your home on Riverside Drive there were Two Hundred Dollars in it—which would have wounded up the whole amount . . . But the money came back . . . And you know how I am with money . . . The sooner I get my hands on it—the faster I spend it . . . Tee Hee . . . Soooooo—when that money came back—on my way to the bank to put it away until I heard from you—I saw something in a downtown store that caught my eye—and—'Shucks—before I knew it—'WHAM'—the money was gone. . . . Haw haw haw. . . .

So accept this hundred and I'll send the other before a 'Black Cat can 'Lick his *'Bu'hind'*. . . . . haw haw haw. . . . Nightie night my friend . . . And God Bless you and your dear wife . . . You both are the finest people I've

Courtesy Institute of Jazz Studies, Rutgers University.

met in my whole life . . . So stay happy . . . And I do hope to see yous real soon . . . . . . I'm opening up at the Golden Gate Theatre the week of the 26th, of July . . . So I'd be Oh so happy to hear from you. . . . . . . Hear? . . . . . .

Am Pluto Waterly Yours,
Louis Armstrong

7
THE "GOFFIN NOTEBOOKS"

(CA. 1944)

Armstrong organizes the Goffin notebooks by year, covering the period 1918–1931, but within each section he ranges somewhat freely outside of the designated year. His marriage to Lil is placed in a section headed "1923," but the wedding took place February 5, 1924. Armstrong probably made an error when he headed a second section "1923," for the events that follow, including Oliver's tour and Armstrong's departure for Henderson's band in New York, happened in 1924. He has numbered the notebooks 1, 2, 3, and 5. Notebook 3 ends with the year 1926, with Armstrong at the pinnacle of his Chicago years, and notebook 5 begins with the year 1928, with Armstrong and friends scrambling for a job—" 'Things gotten so 'Tough with us until 15¢ (Fifteen cents) looked like $15.00 (Fifteen dollars)"—and in the middle of a story about a car that was not covered earlier. Thus, even though Armstrong mentions "four books of stories" in his letter to Goffin, it seems likely that a fifth notebook (numbered "4"), covering 1926 and 1927, has been lost.

New Orleans (1918)

When ''Daisy (my wife) and I separated—I went home to my Mother ''*May Ann*,''—That's her '*Pet*' *name*'' (''alias''), as I've mentioned before.—Anyway—I moved back home with my mother. And stayed there with her

Courtesy Institute of Jazz Studies, Rutgers University.

the whole time I was working at ″Tom Anderson′s Cabaret—located on ″Rampart (between) Canal + Iberville Streets. That′s one of the most well known places in the History of New Orleans. All of the ″Race Horse ′Men′ used to come every night.— They certainly used to give us ′Lots of ″Tips″ when they′d request a number. Lots of the Big shots from Lu Lu White′s used to come there—And we made lots of ″Tips.— I was in the Band with ′Paul Dominguez (The Leader)—Albert Francis, Drums—his wife ′Edna Francis′ Piano—And I was playing the Cornet. We played all sorts of arrangements from the ′Easiest to the Hardest—And from the Sweetest to the Hottest.— T′was [*recte* T′wasn′t] called—′Jazz Back there in those days. I was also doubling with the *Tuxedo Brass Band*. Was *really something*. Finally ′quit the Band at Tom Anderson′s to go on the Boat—Excursion Boat called the ″Steamer Sydney.″ I Joined Fate Marable′s Band on there. That′s when—during our Intermissions—He would help me out with my ′reading music. And me Being a very Apt young man, I learned a whole lots of reading music Real Quick.— Fate Marable was a good Band Leader—And very Strict on us, when it came to playing that music Right. He is Absolutely responsible for a lot of ″youngsters Successes. Anybody whom ever worked under Fate′s Directions can gladly verify this. And will Admit he′s one of the Grandest and Finest Musicians in the Biz—(meaning) Business.—The first time I left New Orleans I went to St. Louis Mo with Fate′s Band on the Boat and to my Surprise—we were the first Colored Band to play on the ′Streckfus Steamers—including our Boat, the Steamer Sydney—The Steamer St. Paul—And the Steamer ″J.S.″—Those were the Boats in those days—And the people admired it wonderfully.

The most Amusing incidents about the days of the Streckfus was the First we left New Orleans, to meet the Boat in St. Louis at the beginning of the Season (summer season). We left New Orleans ′by ″Train and by me not traveling to any place before, I did not know what do as far as Lunch was concerned. So I went to ″PRATS ′RESTAURANT and Bought myself a Big ″Fish Loaf—I think it was trout. I also Bought myself a Big Bottle of ″Olives′ I had it and the Fish Wrapped up in a Paper Sack. We had to change trains at a little town called GAILSBURG ILL. The Station was Crowded with people Changing Trains for All Directions. Our Train Arrived and by me rushing along to catch the train with David Jones (mellophone player)—I Dropped the ″Fish Sandwich on the ground the *′Olives Dropped′* also and the Olives Bottle Broke and ″Olives were running all over the place. The Fish Sandwich Bag Busted and the Fish fell all over the ground. ''Oh Boy'' was I Embarrassed—I thought sure, David Jones would help me pick up those things—But ''*SHUCKS* He only walked Away Embarrassed also. So the only thing I saw to do—is to Just Walk off And leave the whole thing on the Ground and Catch my Train for St. Louis. David Jones and I '*laugh* about that situation every time we run into each other.

One awful thing happened to me just before I left New Orleans to go to St. Louis. About a week before I left there—I happened to Run into ''Irene—She's the girl whom I was living with—as we express it—It's called Common Law—Man + Wife. That was a long time before Daisy + I were married. So—Irene and I were So glad to see each other. We went and had a Drink together for old time sake. Then of course—After two or three—we were Right in the mood for a very fine Session of Romance. But I was very Careful in asking Irene who was her Sweet Man. I had heard'—She was going with a Real Bad Spade (meaning) Colored Guy named ''*CHEEKY BLACK.*'' Cheeky Means—A person with a lot of nerve, etc. I asked her if she was still going with him—To make sure that nothing will happen since she had invited me up to her house. She tells me—''Oh No, I am no longer going with him.'' I said O.K.—And we went to her house. The minute we undressed and gotten into bed we heard a knock on the door. A real ''Hard Knock at that. She answered (in her little voice) ''Who is that?''—

The Sound came from the door—''It's me—Cheeky Black.'' Aw—Aw—I said to myself—here's where there's going to be Trouble. She answers—''I have Company ''Cheeky''.— In those days, when a girl's Sweet Man or Pimp came to the door and it was locked—And if she'd say she had Company—he immediately would go away. Most of the times the gal is making Money, And he's sure to get some of it. But in this case it was different. Cheeky Black knew that 'Irene has never stopped loving me. After all we did have a lots in common from our younger days together and they were happy ones. She never forgotten how I'd taken Good Care of her—in my little Country Boy Way—When she were suffering so badly with female trouble,'' and King Oliver gave me a chance to make a few extra Dollars by working in his place a few nights—Knowing I couldn't play the Cornet good enough to play in his place but anyway did. And it was through his great influence that they let me work until he came back on the job. So in cases like those makes it rather hard for Irene to just forget about me all together just for "Cheeky Black" and Cheeky Black knew this all the time— in fact he saw us when we went into the house.— So She said once again— "Cheeky—I tell you I have Company." And—I knew the door was locked good—because I locked it myself. But "Shucks just like a Flash of Lightning Cheeky Black Broke the Door Down—Irene Screamed and ran out into the streets justa Screaming—And cheeky Black pulled out his Razor and started cutting at "Irene's Rear." Whether he really cut her—I really can't say.— I was so busy—putting on my clothes trying to get out of there before Cheeky Black came back looking for me.— After all—he's the type that would do a thing like that. Anyway—I finally gotten into my clothes—And Ran as fast as I could to "May Ann" my mother. Mother laughed out loud at me. She said—"*AH—HUH*—you'll know better next time—Never go into a man's house and go to bed with his woman." I said "*Mother* I will never do that again—As long as I am 'Colored.'"— I heard later that Irene' was saved when a "Cop" came along just in time—ooh wee—whata—Close Shave that was.

1922

From the First Day I arrived into Chicago to join my Pal Joe Oliver to play 2nd Trumpet in his Band was—and will always be—Thrilling Memories to me. First Place—I shall never forget how Joe Oliver and his wife Mrs. Stella Oliver, were so nice to me in New Orleans, when I was quite a youngster. And I used to go to their house and run errands for Mr. + Mrs. Oliver. And Joe Oliver would Teach me a lesson or anything I wanted to know concerning the trumpet. I have been always Crazy over Joe Oliver and his playing. So when Joe sent for me to join him in Chicago I was happy because I know I'd feel at home and he'd see after me. I ate my meals at his house. His wife used to fix us Two real Healthy Plates of food. And Ol Man Joe could really Devour some food—Of course I didn't do so Bad myself.

My Romance with Lil Armstrong

In 1922 when I joined Joe—I had already separated from Daisy Armstrong—Down in New Orleans.— From the first night on the Bandstand of Joe's Band at the Lincoln Garden at 31st street near Cottage Grove Ave—

I noticed that all of the Boys in Joe's Band had been very busy trying to make a play for ''Lil whom was the Belle of the Windy City of Chicago at that time. Well—as for me—I was wrapped up in music. I did not pay any attention at first—to the fact that 'Lil was 'Stuck (had a crush) on me instead of those Guys. But *who was I* to think that a Big High-powered 'Chick like 'Lillian Hardin who came to Chicago from Memphis Tenn—the year of 1917—Right out of ''Fisk University—Valedictorian of her Classes—Who Me?—I thought to myself. I just couldn't conceive the Idea—That's all.—

Lill—was already married, to a Singer named Jimmy. They were on the 'Outs when She and I started 'Running together after work. She would take me, to the 'Dreamland Cafe, lots. I liked very much to go there and give May Alix and Ollie Powers, money to Sing for me. I'd give them each a Dollar—Shucks—I thought I really was a *grand Sport*—And be with great 'Lill—That too was a solid sender.— The Boys in the Band Commencing to get rather suspicious of she + I. And for a while they all gave she and I, a lot of ''Ice'' (meaning) they treated us rather cool when we went to work.

But it wasn't one of those Drastic Hates. It was more of a Astonishment than anything else. For instance, one of the Boys in the Band made an ''Assertion—in other words they made a Crack—UMP—''Just think—here we are a Bunch of 'Hip' (hep) musicians—been up North for years—making a 'play for Lil. And here—AH—Real 'Country 'Sommitch' come up here, and take her from right under our noses—'Shucks.''' Lil an I was really in there by that time. She used to tell me her troubles Concerning her Married life—And I would tell her mine. It seemed as though—we felt so sorry for each other we decided out of a Clear Skies to get together for good. Of course we did not really get together until my Mother came to Chicago. Someone went down in New Orleans from Chicago—Put out a False Rumor that they had seen me in Chicago—And I looked 'So Bad—from being 'Hungry—'Raggedy and 'Weak from being 'Sick. And the Guy said—when he asked me—why don't I go back Down Home in New Orleans?—He said—All I did—was to hang my head down and *Cried.* AH—Damn Liar. I haven't ever been in such a terrible position as that—in all my life.

Just the same—it worried my dear Mother almost Crazy. She immediately grabbed a train for Chicago to see about her 'Child—'Mee.'' May'

Ann'' arrived in Chicago and she came directly to the 'Lincoln Gardens—That's where I was playing with Joe. We were sitting on the Bandstand—waiting for the show to get started. ''May 'Ann came in—to the dance floor—looked up and saw me sitting up there besides Joe—Lil—Johnnie Dodds—Baby Dodds—Bill Johnson—Honore Dutrey. 'Shucks—May Ann—gotten so 'Excited.— She came 'Straight across the Dance Floor—Held up the show for over ''Twenty Minute.'' When she came up on the stage or rather—Bandstand—the first words she said were ''My Gawd' (God) 'Son—They told me you were Dying—So I rushed here to see about you. But Thank God—you're really Alive and Healthy. Thank God.''

Everything fine after ''May Ann came up on the Bandstand. First,—Joe Oliver—with his Fresh self—''Cute fresh'' used to always be kidding me that he was my Father.— That went on for a long long time.—Even in New Orleans.— So when May Ann came on the stand I whispered into Joe's ear, ''Well, Papa Joe—Mother's here—shall I tell her what you've been saying?'' ''Oh Gosh you should have seen Papa Joe blush all over the place. And May Ann Thanked him for being so Swell to her Son—UMP—I thought he'd—Just ''Swoon''—or somethin like that.—

Me + Lil
[Book 2]
Lincoln Gardens 1922
Chicago Ill.

It was really ''Cute'' to see the ''Shy'' Expression on Joe Oliver's Face—when I asked him about how he was 'Rubbing' me about he was my 'Step Father' in the presence of my 'Mother May Ann.

Joe Oliver as well as myself—felt that we were very close Relatives. He was always 'Kind and very Encouraging to me—And willing to help a poor 'youngster like me out.— And until the very last day—he drew his last Breath, I stuck right by him. And every one who knew him admired him greatly. He was one of the great pioneers.

The night my mother came to Chicago to see about me—she had decided to return to New Orleans the next day. But 'Lil and I gotten our heads together—And came to a conclusion that mother should stay in Chicago at least a while longer, since she's already there. 'Lil and 'I were close 'Sweethearts by this time and were really *in there''* with each other. So with a little persuasion we induced 'May Ann' to stay. The very next day 'Lil and I went out looking for an apartment for mother, and found a very nice one at 43rd and St. Lawrence Streets. It was a very nice one too. And unbeknown to mother, Lil and I furnished it up very fine with fine furniture. And when we had her to leave her Hotel where she was staying to come to her new apartment—"Gee," She certainly was Surprised. She was so happy until "Tears came 'Rolling down her "Cheeks. Then she said—"Thanks 'Son + my future daughter in Law" (Lillian). Then she said—"Just think—I never thought I would live to see the day that I would be the proud owner of such a fine lovely apartment like this—After living in those dilapidated houses down in New Orleans all of my life. Well Son," she said, "one thing—We were Happy there in New Orleans." Then I said—"Yes Mother—But it's always been my highest ambition to do something real big for you—And make you real happy. Because you Certainly have been a wonderful mother to my Sister *Beatrice'* and me." They call my sister *"Mamma Lou"*—That's her 'Pet Name. She remained in New Orleans when Mother left to come see about me in Chicago. Mama Lou" is the only 'Sister—and I have no Brothers—other than my 'Step Brothers on my Father's Side. I have a adopted Son by the name of 'Clarence. His maiden name is "Clarence Hatfield.' But I adopted him when his Mother (Flora Miles whom's my cousin) died—And there weren't anyone in the family that could take care of him properly. I just could do it myself—I had a little ol Beat up Job—wasn't paying much. But the kid liked me so much and I was crazy about him too. I used to take him every place I went.

We were just attached to each other. Clarence was born August, 8th, 1915. The same year, New Orleans witnessed such a "Terrific 'Storm. Ever since Clarence was a little 'Shaver' (a little baby) in Dresses—He obeyed me and I always felt as if he was my Son,—He's Called me 'Papa all his life—And still do at the age of 29.— And still devoted deeply—He's still the happiest youngster there is today. And Just Jumps with 'Joy when he know that his 'Papa 'Louis (me) is coming to Town. One little unpleasant thing happened to Clarence when he was a little baby. He was playing on the Back Porch one day, in New Orleans, and it was one of those Awful Heavy Rainy Days—And this porch was awfully 'Slippery and 'Wet. And Clarence was out there playing by himself on this porch which were in the back yard—And the 'porch' was one story high from the ground. Thank God 'it was only one story—because Clarence "Fell off of this "Slippery

+ Wet Porch to the Ground, and 'Landed directly on his *'head*—UMP—UMP. The only way we found it out that he fell—he gotten up off of the ground—Came up the back steps Justa 'Crying—We ran to him immediately to see if he was hurt—Rushed him to a Doctor. They had some of the Greatest in the world examine him. All the Doctors said the 'fall Clarence had—set him back 'Four years behind the average normal child—They called it ''Feeble Minded.'' As Clarence Grew older he outgrew it all—And now is doing wonderful. When Clarence was around ''Six years old—I had just married 'Lil.' She and I moved into a fine apartment also just like mother's. I had the folks down in New Orleans whom I left Clarence to live with while I went to Chicago—I had them to put a 'Tag on Clarence—put him on a train and send him to me. It was one swell—Grand Re-union. He's been in Chicago ever since. He stayed with ''Lil and I the whole time we were married. Then when 'Lil' and I Bought a Home on 44th St. in Chicago, Clarence had his special room. Went to school everyday—They transferred him to a School where they teach the Backwards Boys, etc. There he turned to be one of the Best 'Base Ball, 'Basket Ball and 'Foot Ball Players in the whole school. And everybody knows him—And calls him Little 'Louis Armstrong. In fact—that's the only name he knows of now. Since I've taken care of him, all of his life I see no reason why I should expect him to go out and get a Job. He has a tendency to be rather nervous—I am sure it came from that fall—I always see that he is with people whom understand him and know how to treat him and keep him happy. Of course I pay them well. Of course that happens nowadays since I travel quite a bit—And too much traveling and exertion is a little strenuous for Clarence.

When Lil and I had our home together, She, Clarence and myself used to sit in our 'Parlor' Evenings After Supper. And she would Run over some of the finest Classic, etc. on that Brand new Baby Grand Piano I Bought for her. Lil's mother was very 'Fond of me also. She had a 'Stroke in one Arm. I bought her an ol second hand Oliver Typewriter and it was just the thing for her to pass the time away—She had gotten pretty good at typing with one hand. She died shortly after Lil and I separated.

My mother stayed in Chicago almost a year. And she being a Christian Woman—belong to Rev. 'Cozy's Church' on Perdido street across from Fisk School (where 'Mrs. Martin' taken care of the school), she just couldn't stay in Chicago any longer.— She missed her Congregation so dearly.

Then too during the time Mother stayed in Chicago I bought her a lots of fine clothes—All Kinds of Silk ''Lingerie''—otherwords—Women Underwear (underwhere). And she told me—''Son' now that I know you are alright—and I have these 'fine 'Clothes—I just can't stay another minute—I must go back to New Orleans and show these 'Things.'' It was really 'Cute to hear her say these things—but to make her happy to go back I agreed.'' 'Purchased her Ticket to New Orleans—sold her apartment. The night before she left Chicago we made the rounds of all the Night Clubs, + Dances, etc.—I requested it of her, I said—''Mother Darling—now that you are leaving me—How about you and me going out and have a real grand time just by *'ourselves,'* no one else.'' She agreed right away—And the police had to show Both of us where we lived the next morning—Coming from those places. Mother + I laughed over that event a lot of times.

Mother stayed down in New Orleans about *''Two years'*—And she taken Sick—And I had to send for her to come to me in Chicago again. This time—she was really *'sick*. She suffered with the 'Hardening of the ''Arteries''—A Drastic thing to have. I did everything in my power to save ''May Ann'' (my mother)—I gave her the Finest Doctors—And the whole time she was in the Hospital,—it Costs me over $17.00 (Seventeen) Dollars a Day—I didn't care what it Cost—As long as I could save ''Mary Ann.''

That was the year of 1927 when she died. I buried her at the 'Lincoln Cemetery—Just outside of Chicago. I've never cried in my life before—even when ''May Ann' was Dying—and grabbed my hand and said God Bless you my son. And Thank God—I live to see my Son Grow up to be a big successful young man.— Also my daughter.— Thank God they are grown and can look out for themselves. Then she passed away. The undertaker taken her body to the 'Chapel'—And the moment that really ''Touched me was when the Sermon was finished and the Undertaker began to *Cover up her ''Coffin''—UMP.* I let out *plenty* of ''Tears—and I just couldn't stop Crying. And 'May Ann' was laying there looking so natural—Just as though she was just taking a ''nap.''— I never forget what Mother told me before she died. She said ''Son—Carry on, you're a good boy—treats everybody right. And everybody—'White and 'Colored Loves you—you have a good heart.— You can't miss.'' I used to take Clarence with me to visit her when she was sick in the Hospital. It broke his heart when she died. She was so nice to him.

1923

When Lil an I gotten married we made the rounds of the night clubs. And everybody threw rice on us as we were getting in an out of the Cabs. And they all invited us out to their homes etc.

1925

Daisy Armstrong, My First wife, came to Chicago thinking that I was still married to her. Quite naturally she tried to go through the same processions as she did in the old days down in New Orleans. But things had changed—And she could not give me any more trouble. I showed her my Divorce Papers which convinced her immediately. I also told her that I was a changed man since I came to Chicago and married Lil. No more 'Boisterous—'Barrel house 'stuff. Am trying to 'Cultivate Myself. Now we can be the very best of friends—And if there is anything that I can do within my power I will gladly do it. She said—that's fair enough. Because—after all—you and I haven't been together for over Three or Four years. So 'that was 'that.— I ran into Daisy several times after that incident. And she and I would go to a 'Tavern and have a few 'Nips (drinks) together. And she told me that she wouldn't ever stop 'loving me no matter if we are not together. After all—I'm the only man she'll ever love as long as she live.

Daisy gotten into a whole lots of 'Trouble in a 'Tavern one night. It was some ''Guy'' (Colored) Talking about 'me—in other words he was justa ''Panning—me. Daisy happen to be sitting there—she didn't like it—in other words she resented it. So she taken it up. She went over to the 'Guy and told him—''Louis Armstrong is my Ex Husband and I don't like the way you talked about him—After all you don't know him that well.'' The fellow was half 'Drunk—And said Something to Daisy she did not like also. So from one word to another the argument got real 'Hot. And this 'Drunken Guy' pulled out his Big 'Knife. And 'Daisy always carries her ''Razor so when he pulled his 'Knife she pulled out her 'Razor' and they both turned out the Joint—''Cutting on 'one 'another. The 'Ambulance had to come get 'both of them. She's 'O.K. again—It's a few 'Scars left in her face. Her 'hair has turned Grey. When I married Daisy in 1918, I was only 18 years old and Daisy was 21 years old. At this writing I am 43—which makes Daisy's age around 46, or, etc.

1923 [*recte* 1924]

King Oliver still had his Band at the Lincoln Gardens in Chicago Ill. And one day he received an *offer* from a big Booking Office Down Town. I was still playing 2nd cornet in his Band. So the night after we finished the job Joe called a meeting with the Band and told them about the Swell Contract he had just signed. Told them about the Salary, etc. which was very good. But when he told them they had to be traveling—the 'Whole Band 'Backed out Except 'Lil And 'I. Joe had to engage a whole new 'Band to go on the Road. Well that wasn't so Hot. Because those *new* players didn't understand our own way of playing like—'Johnny Dodds—'Baby Dodds—'Bill Johnson + 'Honore Dutrey. But we did the best we could Considering the Situation. I danced—taken a lot of 'solos—you know—help the ol man (Joe) out. After all—I was in there with him with all my heart. Because I loved Joe Oliver—And would do anything in the World to make him Happy.— And he really did appreciate my every efforts.— Our 'Tour was a big Success even though things were like they were. Then too—the *fellows* whom replaced the ones whom didn't go with us were all 'Top Notch musicians—Such as 'Buster Bailey, who now is playing with John Kirby's Orchestra, and 'Rudy Jackson who was the 'Ace 'Tenor Man in those days. Joe Oliver's 'tour lasted until way up into the year of 1924. Then Joe Oliver Broke his Band up—And went into the Plantation Cafe in Chicago, at 35th + Calumet Ave., as a 'Featured Cornetist in 'Dave Peyton's Band—And later formed his own Band right there at that same Club. And he sent down to New Orleans and hired—'Barney Bigard'—'Luis Russell—'Albert Nicholas—'Paul Barbarin—Which made him have another good Band. I guess I would have been in that Band too—But I had already received a telegram from the great 'Fletcher Henderson to join his big Band in New York.—

Now that was another great moment in my life. I arrived in New York on the day 'Fletcher was having "rehearsal—And I was rather nervous when I walked into the place. Shook hand with "Smack"—That's the name I later learned they all called Fletcher Henderson. He was very nice to me. And he could see I was a wee bit 'Frightened etc., his Band being the first Big time Orchestra I had the pleasure of joining. 'Fletcher said to me—"So you're 'Louis Armstrong?"—I said "yassuh." He gave me a 'Cute little Smile of Approval and said—"Your 'part is up on the band stand." I said ''yassuh'' in my little Bashful way—and 'A'way I went up to the stand. Now when I gotten on the stand—to my Chair—I notice that every thing was so quiet, etc.— Just like Musicians—when a new man joins a Band, the other Players doesn't have much to say to the New Man.— It looks like they were all waiting to see what I was going to do—They were figuring on me—And I was doing the same thing by them. The first arrangement they played was ''By the Waters of *Minnetonka.''* I had the 3rd Trumpet part—And was 'Thrilled at playing a part in such an All Star Band as Fletcher Henderson's Band. Finally I *''Cut Loose* one night while we were down at the 'Roseland Ballroom and all of the Band Boys just couldn't play for 'watching me.

In that Band were: Trumpets—Elmer Chambers—Scottie [Howard Scott] + myself. Later it was—Russell Smith—Joe Smith—and myself. Sax—Don Redman—''Buster'' Bailey + Coleman Hawkins. Trombone—Chas Green. Banjo—Chas Dixon. Drums—Kaiser Marshall. Bass Tuba—Ralph Escudero. Fletcher Smack Henderson piano. And Whata *Band.*

[Book 3]
1925

I stayed with Fletcher's Band from the last part of 1924 to almost [the end of] 1925. We played at the Roseland Ballroom for over Six Months, then we went on tour. We were the First Colored Big Band to Hit the Road. We went All through the New England States. We spent our First Summer up in Lawrence Mass—That was our Headquarters, while we played dances to all the Surrounding Towns. Was quite a Thrilling Experience to have most of my days off and we would go 'Swimming' etc. Buster Bailey was exceptionally good at Swimming. He would Swim all the way cross that big 'River in Lawrence Mass. Of course I am not so bad myself at 'Swimming.—In fact it's one of my' famous 'Hobbies, outside of ''Typing.''— I loves that also.

I was still married to 'Lil' in those days. She would visit me from Chicago when ever she could. But owing to the fact she had to work on her 'Job in Chicago, it kept us apart quite a bit. So She finally gotten tired, and made a ''Squawk' to me that I should quit Fletcher's Band and come home to her in Chicago. So I had to choose between—My Wife + Fletcher's Band. After all—I chose'd being with my wife. So I put in my ''notice with

Fletcher. Fletcher was very nice about it. He told me—"Although I hate to see you leave the Band—But after all—I do understand your situation. Well, you can always come back when ever you get ready." That's just what I wanted to hear him say. Although I never went back—I always felt that I'd return to the Band someday.— I had 'Wedged' in there just that much.

All the boys in the Band hated to see me leave—And I hated like hell to leave them too. Just before I left the Band we were in New York—And Fletcher Henderson gave me a Big Farewell 'Party at 'Small's Paradise—135th + 7th Ave. in New York. We all had a wonderful time. We had a Special reserved Table—And the Place was packed + Jammed. And after 'Fletcher made his 'Speech and I made my little 'Speech—most of my 'Speech' was Thanks to Fletcher for the wonders he had done for me—etc. Then the whole Band sat in and played several fine arrangements for the Folks—Another Thrilling moment for me.— After we finished playing we went back to our table and started drinking some more 'liquor.— I gotten so 'Drunk until Buster Bailey and I decided to go home. And just as I went to tell Fletcher Henderson Goodbye as I was leaving New York for Chicago the next morning, I said—"Fletcher 'Thanks for being so kind to me." And—er—wer—er—wer—And before I knew it—I had "Vomit" (*"Puked"*) directly into Fletcher's *"Bosom."* All over his Nice Clean 'Tuxedo Shirt. 'Oh—I'd gotten so sick all of a sudden.— I was afraid Fletcher would get sore at me, but all he said—"Aw—that's allright 'Dip' " (my nick name at that time). Fletcher told Buster Bailey to take me home and put me to 'bed, so Buster did. The next morning—'my 'Headache and all—Boarded the Train for Chicago.

I arrives in Chicago—'Lil—and Clarence was waiting for me. I was glad to see them too. But it had taken quite some time for me to forget Fletcher and his fine Band.— Anyway I remained in Chicago—doing odd jobs, etc. Lill—had the Band at the Old "Dreamland Cabaret at the time. The Dreamland was located at 35th + State Streets. She had a nice little Swing Band—but not like Fletcher's. Somehow—Lil's Trumpet man quit her band—so she gave me the job.

I held the job down a long time. And during the time I was there playing in Lil's Band—I became more popular every night—And was the Talk of Chicago. King Oliver was still at the Plantation Cafe on 35th +

Calumet Ave—Just across the Street from the ''Sunset Cafe'' 'owned' by Mr. Joe Glaser.

1925

I had become so popular at the Dreamland until ''Erskine Tate from the 'Vendome Theater came to Hire me to Join his 'Symphony Orchestra—I like to have ''Fainted.'' Erskine Tate had a 20 piece orchestra playing at a moving picture house called the 'Vendome Theater located at 31st + State Streets in Chicago. In those days they had ''Silent Films'' instead of the Talkies—His Orchestra would Furnish the Music for all the 'Scenes in the Films. And when the picture would Break the Orchestra'd play Overtures etc.' and then they'd, finish up with a Red Hot Number—Then—*'Black out'*—Then the 'Picture would start over again.— And for anyone to play in *'Tate's* Band was Really Really Somebody. So when 'Erskine Tate came for me—After all—you've been wanting to get the experience of playing Classic and Symphony Music, etc.— Well here's your Chance.— I said ''Aw Lil.'' She said ''Boy—if you don't get out of this house and go on down there to Erskine Tate's rehearsal, I'll Skin you Alive.'' I said, Slowly—''Well *'All right*—I'll go.'' I went 'down there and the 'opening night was sensational. I remember the first 'Swing Tune we played—Called ''Spanish Shawl.'' I wasn't in *'Tate's* Orchestra 2 weeks before I was making 'Records with them for the Vocalion Recording Company.— I became quite a 'Figure at the 'Vendome.' Especially with the Gals.

I met 'Alpha During the time I was working there. Alpha was a little cute young girl 19 years old when, she used to come to the Vendome Theater twice a week. They changed pictures there Twice a week. People used to come from all parts of Chicago to hear that Band + see the Pictures. Alpha used to sit in the 'Front Row every time she came.— And She would sit Right where I could get a good look at her. And she had big pretty eyes anyway—I couldn't keep from *''Diggin Her*. There were times when 'Lil would be in the Vendome at the same time as ''Alpha.''— Well—On those nights we couldn't 'Flirt so much.

The whole time I played at the Vendome, Alpha and I began to get ''Thicker + ''Thicker. We would meet—after the show was out. For awhile I did not have but the one job—The Vendome. So quite naturally I had a lot of time to be with 'Alpha. Of course it was '*unbeknowing* to 'Lil.— I tried to keep from wedging into Alpha too Deeply—Knowing I was Still married to Lil—And 'Alpha' was so *young*—and '*Fine* with it. Then too I thought about how 'Lill—had been Running Around with one of the Chicago 'Pimps' while I was at work. So as we colored people used to say—is just as good for the 'Goose as it is for the ''Gander''—meaning—if Lil could enjoy some one Else's Company, I could too.

Ever since I was a little Boy in New Orleans hanging around those ol' Hustlers and 'Pimps down there and they all liked me very well—And they used to tell me—''Never worry over 'No 'One Woman—no matter how pretty or sweet she may Be. Any time she gets down 'wrong, and ain't playing the Part of a Wife—get yourself somebody else, also.— And get another woman much better than the last one at all times.'' Alpha commenced inviting me to her house.—

Alpha was a fine gal. She was a poor girl—not near as Fortunate as 'Lil was when I First met her—Maybe the one reason why Lil + I didn't make a good go of married life together. Alpha was working for some nice *White* people out in 'Hyde Park Chicago' taking care of their little Baby. Mrs. 'Taylor thought a lots of 'Alpha—in fact she practically 'Raised her. I used to go out to her job in the afternoons and Alpha would fix some of the most 'dee'licious meals for me while Mr. + Mrs. Taylor would be Down Town Shopping, etc. Oh it was just wonderful. Alpha + I would 'Straighten up the house just perfect by the time the 'Taylors would return Home.

One night the ''Taylors 'Came home—And Alpha and I was in their parlor having a Grand Time playing Records—Dancing—Opened up one of their Choice Bottles of Whiskey, etc. They were surprised at first. Then Alpha introduced me to them. She said—''Mr. + Mrs. Taylor I want you's to meet my new Boy Friend, his name is Louis Armstrong. He's the Cornet player in Erskine Tate's orchestra down at the Vendome Theater.'' Mr. + Mrs. Taylor—were very nice to me—and seemed to be very happy for Alpha. It seemed as though—All of the rest of Alpha's Boy Friends turned out to be no good ones. So the 'Taylors saw a bright 'future for, 'Alpha' by taking me for her 'Sweetheart. Even if I *was* a married *man*. Alpha had me come to her house in Chicago and meet her mother Mrs. Florence Smith.—

Mrs. Florence Smith—from the first introduction I had to her I could see right then and there that I could like her and I would like to be around her. She was so Friendly—and ′pleasant—And could tell some of the ″Funniest ′Jokes.— Right off the Bat—I fell for Alpha′s Mother and tried to stay as long as I could whenever I was invited to their apartment. I must have been seeking some kind of comfort in life—Lil and I had one of the finest homes in Chicago at the time I was ′Sweethearting′ with Alpha. But still with all of that swell Home, Lil, and I had—There was not happiness there. We were always Fussing and threatening to ′Break up if I ′sat on the ′Bed after it was ′made up. Why—′Lil would almost go into ″Fits″ (Spasms)—etc. And poor Clarence my adopted son with his nervous self—used to almost Jump out of his ′Skin when ′Lil or Lil′s mother would ′Holler at him.— Most of the times it was uncalled for. Lil and her mother had some bad tempers. And it would make my Blood ′Boil when I′d see them Abuse, my Son ′Clarence. When ever they—especially Lil—would ′holler at me I′d tell her ′Just where to go. I′d say—″Aw ′Woman—*′GO ′TA ′HELL.*″

I kept visiting Alpha and her Mother—Down where they lived—in one of the ′Poorest Districts in Chicago. It was at 33rd + Cottage Grove Ave. where they lived—in a very ′Dingy Apartment—with a Wooden Bath Tub. They had a big ol ′Tom Cat name ″*Sit.* And that big ″Sommitch″ used to Jump up on the Window Sill of the room ′where I was sleeping and ′scared the hell out of me. But with all of that ″Dinginess″ etc. I was more happy Down there the nights I would stay there (sleep) with Alpha than I would if I went home. And Mrs. Smith, Alpha′s Mother, would see that I had my correct meals, while Alpha was at work. And after meals—Mrs. Smith used to tell my ″Fortunes—By Cutting a Deck of ′Cards.— She was very good at this sort of thing. I offered to set her up in Business at it—But she didn′t have the time.— I liked Mrs. Smith because she′s the type of woman she has ″*been around*″ and seen everything. The first night I taken Clarence down there to meet Mrs. ′Smith, Mr. ′Woods (Mrs. Smith′s husband) and ′Alpha—′Clarence was so ′glad over it. Just the idea—he could talk ′free without some one ′Hollering at him and ridiculing his ′Affliction, etc. And he didn′t have to put on ″*Airs* with a certain ′Spoon for this and a certain ′fork for that. And as well as Clarence loves to eat and as well as I love to see him eat—He could eat at Mrs. Smith′s house until his little heart′s content. I could see the ′Joy in Clarence′s eyes when he looked around at me and said, as he ′Bit down on a nice Hot ′Biscuit—He said—″Pops″ (that′s what he calls me) he ′said—″this is where I should be living instead of staying out there with Lil.'' Well sir—I was 'Speechless for a moment then all of a sudden I smiled at him and said—''Yes' Clarence—you are right.— And here's where you are going to stay—Right here with Mrs. Smith. Not only that—'you are going to spend the rest of your life with Mrs. Smith.'' I had a sorta feeling within myself that I'd soon get with Alpha anyway. Then Alpha had fallen deeply in love with me by this time anyway—And I was crazy about her from the very first start.— In less than a Month's time—Lil and I had another Fuss (argument)—And I immediately moved Clarence's 'Bags and 'Baggage—All his clothes and mine and we 'Both moved down at 33rd + Cottage Grove Ave. with Mrs. Smith, Mr. Woods and Alpha.— ''Hooray''—

I felt so much more satisfied to know that Clarence was happy there with Mrs. Smith when I was Away. I was still playing at the Vendome Theater.— And real soon I was offered a job to Double from the Vendome Theater which I finished work there at Eleven O' Clock—to the Sunset Cafe—Directly across the street from King Oliver and his Band. Carroll Dickerson had the Band at the 'Sunset'—owned by Joe Glaser (my present manager) and Carroll gave me the Job. Now I was making nice money so I had a good chance to 'Buy Alpha some nice things with my extra money' Lil' didn't know about.— I bought Alpha a very lovely overcoat—the first and the finest she'd ever had before then.— I paid $90.00 for her coat.— It was a fine one for a young gal her age. It was a Heavy Blue Coat—Very Plain—and a nice 'Lamb Collar—but' a' not too big a one. She really did look Smart in it.— And I used to love to take her out on Sundays and we would Drive way out to Blue Island, or, etc.— Bill Bottoms (Joe Louis' Ex-Dietitian) was the owner of a 'Road House out there and 'Alpha—'Me—''Tubby Hall whom was the Drummer in Carroll Dickerson's Band at the time, and his girl, the 'Four of us would drive out in my Bran New 'Ford Car with the 'yellow wire wheels and have 'dinner out there. And 'Alpha would look like a 'Million—She had lovely ''Tastes for Clothes—Even before I was really able to really buy her a lot of fine 'Clothes—'Furs and 'Diamonds galore. She was always a young girl was very 'Neat and 'Clean—And always loved the ''best'—you could tell *'that* when she 'picked me. 'Then, if 'Alpha was going downtown to Buy a Couple of 'dresses and she didn't have enough money to get 'Two good ones—She'd come home with that 'one 'good one. She did not have a whole lots of 'clothes when I met her—but what few she did have was good. And was she 'Innocent' 'my 'my 'my. To believe that Alpha turned out in later years to be a no good 'Bitch'' Why—I am 'Still *''Flabbergasted''* (''*Surprised* as *Ol Hell*).

1926

I finally left the Vendome and Settle down to the 'one Job at the ''Sunset.'' I liked the *set up* there better—With ''Earl Hines'' at the 'Piano—'Tubby Hall on Drums—'Darnell Howard Sax + Clarinet—And Down the line of the good 'ol timers. Mr. Joe Glaser was the Boss of the Place. In fact he was the 'Owner of the whole place.— And Still owns the Building. I always admired Mr. Glaser from the first day I started working for him. He just *impressed* me different than the other Bosses I've worked for. He seemed to understand Colored people so much. And he was wonderful to his whole show and Band—Would give us nice 'presents etc. And' don't you think for once that Mr. Glaser didn't *'Pitch a 'Bitch* when things aren't Jumping Right. I did not know about Managers etc. like they have nowadays. I don't think Mr. Glaser was thinking about it either or else he would have 'Signed me up then.

[Book 5]
1928

'Earl—'Zuttie and 'I—Stayed out of work so long until it was impossible for me to get my 'Car out of the 'Shop, even after it was fixed. 'Things gotten so 'Tough with us until 15¢ (Fifteen cents) looked like $15.00 (Fifteen dollars). But we did not lose our Spirit. And we all kept that good 'ol Clean Shirt 'on everyday, and 'ol 'Earl Hines kept the Big Fresh 'Cigar in his 'mouth 'everyday. Zuttie and 'I both 'admired that. We were still riding in this *'Pneumonia 'Special*—'that's the name we gave this 'Hauling 'Car. You'd be surprised to know how 'happy we were. Lots of the 'youngsters would just 'Rejoice' to get in there with us. One night the 'Three of us 'decided to go over on the 'West Side of 'Chicago and give a 'Dance. After all—we were still *'Hustling* and the 'Three of us would go 'Anywhere as long as we felt that we could make a few *''Dimes* or *'Dollars* too. We still had our 'Expenses to keep up at 'home—And 'money had to come from 'Some place.— So we 'Rented this 'Dance Hall on the 'West side.— It was a very small place—but was enough to make a 'piece of 'money. Only 'one thing'—The Darkies 'were so bad over there. The little joint was doing fine—With 'Earl (piano)—'Zuttie (drums)—'Myself (trumpet)—playing the music. I shall never forget the ''UPRIGHT' piano 'Earl were playing. We had a pretty nice 'Crowd.'— We 'Three had just been saying how 'nice it's going to be after the 'dance. And we'd 'Divide up some 'pretty nice 'money for a change. Where the 'Bandstand was 'situated—it was 'straight back from the door.— The minute you'd come in to the 'door you couldn't help but *see* the 'Bandstand. Comes 'Intermission time—Just as the 'people were deciding what to do during that 'period in walks a 'Drunken *'Darkie*— pulled out a ''45 'Pistol and 'Leveled it, directly at the direction of us on the 'Bandstand. *''Well Sir''*—'UMP.—

The 'Crowd 'Scattered *''Everywhere*—that left the 'Hall rather 'Clean— so this *Drunken* 'Darkie' could get a 'good 'view at us on that little 'Bandstand.— Now when he 'raised his 'pistol again as if he really was going to 'shoot at us.— *''LAWD 'TADAY''*—We were so 'Scared until 'Earl Hines *'tried* to go through his *'UPRIGHT' piano*.— And 'Heaven knows where 'Zuttie + 'I went. But I know we came off of that 'Bandstand 'right away.— Somebody went and found the 'Cops' from somewhere out that way—And they 'chased that Black *''Sommitch''* downstairs, and this 'Drunken 'Guy 'ran under a 'house.— And the 'Cops' Shot all up under that 'house and Filled that 'Guy full of 'Holes.— Of course I was rather sorry to hear about that part of it. But later on, I heard that this ''Spade'' (colored boy)—had some 'trouble over there with some Cops the week before our dance and he 'Killed one of them. And they were on the 'lookout for him 'Anyway. So as we puts it—Death was really 'on Him. Earl—Zuttie—Myself—did pretty good at the 'ol Hustling game. After all—we were the 'Top Notch' players in 'Chicago in those days.—

EARLY—1929.

The Savoy Ballroom, by this time had really gotten under way and was doing all the business in town. They even had a 'Basket Ball Team 'named after the Savoy—And 'whata *'Team*. They were so good until they played some of the 'best *'teams* in the U.S.A. They'd always have a 'Basketball game first—then the dance would start later. After the 'Savoy Ballroom' had been 'Running for quite awhile—they decided to change Bands. The First Two Bands to open the place were 'Clarence Black's Band and

Charles Elgar's Band—They were 'two good Bands.—They would 'Cut' any-Band that came to the 'Savoy' for 'one night—'Especially that Clarence Black's Band. He had 'one 'Tune he used to play—And after he would finished playing it—Couldn't no other Band 'follow behind them—The 'tune was called "I 'Left My 'Sugar Standing in the 'Rain"—"*That's All Brother.*

So when the 'Savoy 'changed one Band they hired 'Carroll Dickerson and 'Carroll had all of us 'ol timers 'rejoin him. Of course "Earl Hines couldn't make it, on account he had just given Jimmy Noone his word to play in his little 'Four piece Combination down at the 'APEX' Night Club on 35th St. So 'Carroll hired "Gene Anderson on piano. Gene was a First Class man—Could Read music perfect. And was also a good "Swing" man. Of course there weren't 'Earl Hines around at all in those days. But just the same—With 'Gene—'Zuttie—Fred Robinson—Homer Hobson—Jimmy Strong—Bert Curry—Crawford Wethington—Peter Briggs—Mancy 'Peck' Carr—Louis Armstrong—and Carroll Dickerson himself—If I have to say it myself—We made up one of the 'Damnedest Bands, there were and taken it into the 'Savoy Ballroom and '*Battled* 'ol 'Clarence Black's Band down to a "*Low Gravy.*"— *After all*—Black's Band didn't have anything but that '*one number*'—called—"I left my Sugar Standing in the Rain." And after he'd finished playing that one tune he was 'finished as far as 'Breaking it up was concerned. And there we were with all of those good 'tunes' we'd just finished 'Recording, etc.— So it all turned out Just fine. Then we became the favorite band of the house also. The Basket Ball Team like us also. We went out on several Dates with them and after the game we'd play the 'Dance. We did this in Several towns outside Chicago—Especially 'Detroit and St. Louis. The Amusing incident that I witnessed at the 'Savoy Ballroom was the night the 'Savoy Team was playing a real big 'League Team. And the manager of the place, decided a week before the big game came off that he let each of the Bands pick out a Team from the Band and play a game of Basket Ball, before the big 'Teams went on"—'Sorta give the 'Customers a good 'laugh. And by the time the big game started everybody would be in good Humor. I 'am 'tellin you 'it was some Fun for all.— 'Clarence's Band was made up with 'young Boys—And our Band was made up of ol 'timers' and Hustlers. Quite naturally we 'dissipated a little more than those 'young 'Cats. Clarence's Boys would go in to the Park, every Morning—Run for 'Miles'—getting all that good Fresh 'Air, etc. And all we were doing was, going out 'every night, "Lushing" (drinking liquor).— Staying up all night long, etc. Well sir—the night of the Dance and the 'Basket Ball game Clarence Black's Boys were all dressed just like real Basket Ball players. Clarence Black himself—a tall lanky fellow—even had on a Knee 'Guards, like the real players. And we had on all kinds of Suits. And I was weighing 230 pounds at the time. So was 'Tubby Hall who was Clarence Black's Drummer at that time.

So we couldn't get a suit to fit us. So Tubby and I had to wear our own Bathing Suits.— Zutty looked good in his suit—so did Crawford—Didn't either one of us knew the 'Rules of the game. The 'Whistle 'Blew, or the 'Gong Sounded and the Game was on.'— The minute we all ran out on the floor, just like the real players—the Crowd went Wild, with applause.— The game started—And those young 'Cats of Clarence Black's nearly Ran us 'Crazy Trying to get a hold of that Ball. Finally I got a hold on the 'Ball and instead of *'Dribbling* the Ball until I could get it near the Basket so I could Throw it in there and make a couple 'points, which we didn't have any—And the Crowd was Laughing so hard and I was so excited, I taken that Ball,—put it under my arm and started 'Running like mad with it. And the 'people 'Laughed and 'Roared "Thunderously." I ran almost to the Basket—taken my position—took a good aim at the Basket—threw it up there—Then I 'missed it (the basket).— Both of our "Teams were so weak from laughing at me.— 'Oh what Fun we had. There wasn't but one 'Basket made in the whole game, and one of Clarence Black's Boys made that one. And the way it happened—when he had gotten a hold of the Ball,—instead of *us* trying to stop him from making the Basket we just stood there watching him (we all out of Breath) to see if he really going to make it.— And when he did make the Basket, we would look at each other in Approval, "'Hmmm' we said—he did make it didn't he?"—And you talking about a Bunch of 'Guys' out of Breath and glad to hear the whistle Blow for time out, 5 minutes.— We were so tired we would just Drop down on the floor, *"lifeless."*— "Zuttie gave me a big laugh when he asked, *"Ham Watson" our* "Captain to please pull him out. He said "Ham'— 'Pops—Can't you pull me out?—*'AH'M'* So 'tired." And *"Ham* said "No 'Zuttie, you are one of my Best players." 'Zuttie said—"Damn 'AH'M' Tired." I said "AH'M' Too." But we had to finish the game out anyway— And look like the time would never come to quit. But it all ended up Swell, with the score 2 to 0 in favor of Clarence Black's Band.

I did not know that Basket Ball taken so much Wind an 'Energy. Why

I'd gotten so out of Breath until I Couldn't Catch my Breath and the little Breathing I 'was doing I wasn't breathing a thing but Hot Air—Tch Tch. I shall never do that again unless I get the proper training.— I was in Bed 'Sick a whole week with ''*Flu* from all of that sudden exposure. Honest I thought I was going to die. Every Bone in my body were ''ACHING.

The life of the Savoy were very interesting.— Business began to get slow, just like any other big Amusement, etc. that opened up in Chicago—go real big for awhile then, ''*KA'BLIP*''—The 'Bottom would 'drop out.— So Mr. Fagan the 'owner would come to us with a *hard luck 'story'* every week. And the way he would *'lay'* this Story on us, we Just couldn't leave him that's all. After all we were all ''Troopers. But look like Mr. Fagan was laying that hard luck story on us a little too often. And payments on our (Lil + I) home was *'way* 'past due. And Zuttie and I would talk it over every 'pay night and we would say to each other—If Fagan comes with no money this week we were sure to quit.

Again the usual thing would happen—no money.— So I was still signed up to the 'Okeh' Record Co.— But Mr. Fern turned my Contract over to Mr. ''Tommy Rockwell whom was Stationed in New York. And at the same time Mr. Fagan was coming up short with our money—Mr. Rockwell sent for me to come to New York immediately to make some 'Records' and also Book me into a show called ''Great Day'' produced by Vincent *Youmans.''* It was a great show. When I received Mr. Rockwell's Telegram in Chicago I showed it to Carroll Dickerson, Zuttie and the rest of the Band Boys. They as well as myself we were so attached to each other until we hated like hell to Break up our Band.— Because it was a good Band.— And we just couldn't see the idea of Breaking it up. And although Mr. Rockwell only sent for Me—I was one Guy who always stuck with a Bunch of fellows, especially if I liked them. Then too we were getting along so nicely in Chicago together—We Rented our own ''Flat'' (apartment)—Gene Anderson's wife run it for us. And when we would get off from work we would go to our 'Flat' and have our own private 'Balls,' etc. No outsiders were allowed unless one of us would invite them there. Muggsy Spanier and a few other Choice Friends would come visit us when ever they Choosed.

Lots of times—Zuttie would cook a big pot of Creole Gumbo. We would ''Eat and 'Drink until our Bellies would poke 'way out.— Then if we felt like—we would have a 'social game of—Poker—Black Jack—or

Shoot a little 'Craps.' Win or 'lose it was all in fun—And we were all good Sports about it.

Mr. Rockwell 'wires me again to come to New York Right Away. Myself and the Band held a private meeting.— I told them—"Well fellows—you all know how well I love you all—And you Boys love me too—What say if we have our Cars fix up and Mr. Rockwell has just sent me enough money—And I can give each man in the Band $20 to eat off of and help Buy Gas, and we'll all go to New York together?"— They all jumped up into the air with Joy, and said that's great.— And it makes us all very happy to know you're not going to leave us, and we'll still be together.— I told them, "When we get to New York and Mr. Rockwell won't have anything for us to do, we'll just 'Take ourselves a job that's all—Because we have a Band good enough to get a Job Any place." So finally we had the 4 cars overhauled—I had gotten my old Hupmobile out of the shop—Carroll Dickerson bought a second hand Marmon Automobile—Gene Anderson had a little 'Essex Car and Fred Robinson had a Bran New light weight Car—I forget the name. Anyway—We left ol Chicago.— All of our Friends were on hand to wish us luck, etc. Just think—had we known it we could have made ourselves a nice piece of money on our way to New York—We were popular all through the 'Towns we passed through—Toledo Ohio—Cleveland—Detroit—Buffalo. We went 40 miles out of our way to see 'Niagara Falls, etc. And everybody were so glad to see us. They all had been hearing our Broadcasts from the 'Savoy' Ballroom in Chicago the whole time we were there. Come to think of it, we would get a lot of Requests from all of those towns. Anyway—we enjoyed our trip and passing through those Towns, because everybody made it real pleasant for us. At last we all 'hit the Town of New York. Zuttie and I were riding in my 'Car, in fact Zuttie did pretty near all of the Driving—I did most of the 'Sleeping.' We had lots of car trouble on our way there. Our Gas line gave us lots of trouble and it kept us stopping to fix the 'Damn thing all the time. And when 'Zuttie arrived in New York the minute we were Crossing '42nd and Broadway—My Radiator Cap Blew off—And Steam was going every place—And were we Embarrassed.— The 'Cops' came over and saw we had a Chicago License on our car, and asked us, "Hey there have you boys any 'Shot Guns in that Car?" We gladly said "No Suh Boss." He smiled and went away. In those days, the gangsters were very popular in Chicago.— So we fixed the car and on our way up in 'Harlem.'—

All the Boys Arrived in New York except 'ol Carroll Dickerson and his Crew. Carroll had an Awful Wreck on his way to New York. Turned his Car over and Completely 'Smashed it up something terrible.— Luckily no one was Killed—Just slightly Hurt.— Carroll left the Car there in the Town. And when the car was fixed two weeks later—Carroll did not have the money and from that day on Carroll hasn't seen his Marmon since.— It was a beautiful big *'Sommitch'* Too. We all finally arrived in Harlem, *'everybody 'Suffering* with the *'Shorts* Meaning—We were all Broke.— So I immediately went down town to Mr. Rockwell's Office—He certainly was glad to see me.— He said "'Louie'—I've just arranged to put you in The 'Great Day Show.'" I said—"Oh fine Mr. Rockwell—But—'er, wer—I brought my Band with me and you'll have to Book us Some place." Mr. Rockwell Hit the Ceiling saying—"Band? I did not send for your Band—I sent for you only." I said, (very calmly) "Just the same Mr. Rockwell, we're here now—I just couldn't leave my Boys 'that's all—I know you can Book us 'Some place. 'Another thing we all need money—so you'll have to let me have about $__Dollars to keep us eating—Room Rent and our Laundry until we go to work. After all, they must hold their heads up, and 'stay 'sharp because they're all Sharp Cats, and can play their 'Asses off."

Finally Mr. Rockwell gave in and gave me all the money I *wanted* and inside of "Two Weeks' we had a job Down in 'Connie's Inn' in Harlem, at 131st + 7th Ave. That Club and the Cotton Club were the Hottest Clubs in Harlem at that time.— And Harlem was really 'Jumping.' All the white people would think it was a real treat to spend a night up in Harlem. After my Band was set at Connie's—I started 'Doubling in 'Connie's Hot Chocolate' show, down town.— Then later on I also had a show of my own at the Lafayette Theater, in Harlem just opposite Connie's Inn—Connie's Inn was downstairs in the basement. My Band really used to 'play the hell out of Connie's Show.— 'Ol Louise Cook—I shall never forget her, and her Dance.— She was so wonderful in her 'Shake dance she would take 5 and 6 Encores. And 'ol 'Zuttie used to 'kill me Beating those Tom Toms for her to Shake that thing. 'Immediately after the show we would go in to a Dance set before we'd take intermission—and the Tune we would play was our Recording of "Indian Cradle Song." We would start 'off the 'Introduction in a slow Fox Trot Tempo—And 'Zuttie would be Beating those 'Tom 'Toms in Such Fine Fashion, without 'wiping the perspiration off of his Face.— That alone, would really 'Send me. And of course we would finish the rest of the Dance Set with some fine dance numbers.— One night, a Sunday, all of the White Musicians from Down on Broadway, came up to Connie's Inn' gave me a big 'party—certainly a Swell Affair.— 'Ben Pollack 'Presented me with a Beautiful gold 'Wrist 'Watch, that was from the Boys from 'Down Town. The inscription on the watch Read as ''follows—

GOOD 'LUCK ALWAYS
TO 'LOUIS ARMSTRONG
FROM
THE MUSICIANS
ON
BROADWAY.

And did we have a Ball.'' My My My.

1929—New York

My Band (Carroll Dickerson's) stayed down in 'Connie's Inn for over 'Six Months.' Then the 'Guys in the Band Commenced to making 'Late Time' etc.— Especially Bert Curry (alto sax)—'Jimmy Strong—'Carroll Dickerson, and several others. Of course it was 'still 'Carroll Dickerson's Band, but the Band had to be 'Billed under my name when it got to New York. Because 'Carroll wasn't known to the 'New Yorkers as I was there from the year of 1924, in Fletcher Henderson's Band. But everything turned out alright at Connie's Inn until the Band Boys Abused the Job. Then 'Connie 'gave us a 'two weeks notice. The Band Broke up the minute we came out of Connie's Inn. Some of the Band Boys went back to Chicago. Carroll, Zuttie and Gene stay in 'New York.— I stayed also. Ally Ross taken a new Band into Connie's Inn and Zutty went back in there with him. Of course Zuttie consulted me before he accepted the job. I told him to take the job. Because I did not have any work in sight for an Orchestra—Then too—Mr. Rockwell my manager had booked me as a single 'act. So 'Carroll and 'Gene went with the ''Mills Blue Rhythm Band.— I did a 'Single Act the Rest of 1929. And the Beginning of 1930, I went to 'California—'me and My 'Trumpet. I was 'Booked into the ''Frank Sebastian's ''Cotton Club. It was located out in 'Culver City California. About 30 Minutes 'Ride (by car) from Los Angeles California, where I lived. Mr. Sebastian had a 'band at the 'Cotton Club, already ''*in tact*. It was 'Elkin's Band. In the 'Band were such fine 'players as Lawrence Brown on Trombone 'and Lionel Hampton on 'Drums.— I discovered the 'greatness of those 'Two youngsters the very first day I went to 'Rehearsal. And 'Lionel was so 'young and 'vivacious (still is) on those 'Drums. And he had taken to 'like me (personally) so well and I felt the 'same way about him. And he was one of the Swinginest Drummers I had ever seen and heard in my life. And he was playing some little 'Bells' which he kept besides his 'Drums. And he was ''Swinging'' the '*hell* out of them too—like I had never heard in my 'life before. 'Right then and 'there I 'predicted that someday 'Lionel would 'go 'places in the 'music world. 'Lionel used to get so 'Enthused over my ''playing ''Trumpet he would get ''*Soakened Wet*.'' And 'Beat a 'whole *gang* of Drums, saying to 'me ''*WA—WA'WON'MO'POPS*.''— Meaning—' ''One More' 'Chorus,'' 'Especially on Tunes like ''Tiger Rag'' and ''Ding Dong Daddy.'' And 'me 'enthused over 'him being 'Enthused—would play, 'Chorus After 'Chorus—I went up to 'Forty 'one night. Well I was much younger in those days myself.

1931—California

After about a year out to the 'Cotton Club 'Broadcasting every night, with everybody in 'California for 'miles and 'miles around catching our 'Programs which were the ''*Last Words*''—I went back to 'Chicago Ill.— 'Played the 'Regal Theater for 'one week.' You couldn't get 'Standing Room the whole week. After the 'Regal 'engagement—I 'Cooled' (*laid off*) for about 'Nine Days,' Having a Little Fun—*etc.*

I was still married to 'Lil 'Armstrong—she was also out in California with me the whole time I was out there. Also the man she 'claimed she had him 'travel with her from New York everywhere she would go to '*Massage* her '*Hips*.— Keeping them from getting too 'large.— 'UMP—She sure must have thought I was a *Damn fool 'Sho Nuff*.' As if I didn't know her 'Hips are sure to '*Ignite*' from the 'Friction.'— Later on, I found out that this 'Guy' and 'Lil had been ''Going together and 'he'd been 'Spending my 'money for years.

So while I was out at the 'Cotton Club out in 'Culver City—'Alpha came out there too. The 'Lord Must have sent her out there to me.— As 'surprised as I were, that she came—I was 'Glad to see her also. 'Alpha said she 'love me so, she happen to be thinking 'strongly 'about me in 'Chicago. And after she had finished doing her 'Show out in 'Cicero Ill., which she was a 'chorus girl, in 'Al Capone's Night Club—'Lucky Millender was the 'Producer. 'Alpha said she was so 'Blue from 'thinking about me, and 'missed me so ''terribly much,'' that she 'Boarded a 'Train for 'California. And before she *knew it*—she wuz in 'California getting off the 'train. Now after she 'arrived in 'California she gotten 'Scared—'lost her 'nerve—and thought that I'd get 'sore with her for 'coming 'way out there. But I was so 'glad to see her again, which I hadn't for 'months and 'months. I just couldn't help but say to her—''Now that you are 'out here you might as well 'stay and I'll find you a 'room''—which I 'did. So after 'Lil and her 'sweet 'Daddy return from 'California in my 'Car, I sent for 'Alpha to come back home in 'Chicago. Alpha's 'mother Mrs. 'Smith was still staying in that old 'Shabby Apartment at '33rd and 'Cottage Grove Avenue. So since I was back with 'Lil,' Alpha went back 'home and lived with her 'Mother.—

1931

After 'Resting a few days, after the 'Regal Theater' engagement, Mr. 'Johnny Collins whom was my 'Manager in California through 'some 'Deal he made with Mr. 'Tommy Rockwell my other 'manager—'*Damn*—Come to think of it—I sure had a 'Manager's 'Fit. Anyway—Mr. 'Collins 'Booked me in a little 'Night Club 'Down Town in 'Chicago called the ''*Show Boat*.'' This place used to be the 'old 'My ''Cellar''—where ''*Wingy* 'Manone once ''held Sway'' and used to '*Rock*' the '*Joint*. I made up a little 'Band and taken it into the ''Show Boat. The members of this Band were—'Charlie Alexander (piano)—'Zilner Randolph (trumpet)—'George James (alto sax)—'Al Washington (tenor)—'Preston Jackson (trombone)—'Tubby Hall (drums)—'Lester Boone (alto sax)—'Johnnie Lindsey (bass)—'Mike McKendricks (banjo) and 'Myself (trumpet). Now there's a Band that really 'deserved a *whole lot* of '*Credit* that they *didn't* get.— They made some of my 'finest recordings with me. I can right now remember some of them as follows—''Sleepy Time Down South''—''When your Lover has Gone''—''Between The Devil And the Deep Blue Sea''—''I Got Rhythm''—''Stardust''—''Wrap your Troubles in Dreams''—''The Lonesome Road''—''Laughing Louie''—''All of Me''—''I Surrender Dear''—''Kickin the Gong

Around"—"World on a String"—"Gotta Right to Sing the Blues"—*'AW 'hell'*—I would be here all night 'Jottin down the names of these fine 'recordings. And the 'Incidents with this particular Band is about the most interesting—At least I think so anyway.

We had a very interesting engagement down at the "Show Boat.— The 'opening night down there—we stayed on the air practically all night.— And all the Big time 'Band Leaders were on hand to say a few words in favor of *Louie* Armstrong—All White Folks call me Louie. 'Carlton Coon of "Coon Saunders Orchestra, were there that night.— He was one of my 'greatest Fans.'— It 'Broke my heart when he 'died. 'Louis Panico' is another 'Fan. 'Oh—'things were going real 'Swell 'there at the "Show Boat. But 'funny thing 'how I did not know that 'Johnny Collins and 'Rockwell were having a "Feud" (fuss) over my 'contract.

'Why—And for 'what'—I've 'never 'found out 'until this day.— All I know is—Whom ever were the 'Gang in 'New York sent 'Gangsters to 'Chicago where I was 'working and tried their *'Damnedest* to *'Frighten* me into 'Quitting the 'Job and Come to New York, to 'Open up back at 'Connie's Inn again.— And I felt that—as 'dirty as 'Connie 'Fired me and my 'Band, I did not want any 'parts of those 'people 'ever again—I am just that way. If you 'Kick my 'Ass' 'Once you can 'bet I won't come back if I can 'help it, so you can 'Kick it Again.— And *"Connie's Inn"* was 'going 'Down, by the 'degrees. And at 'that time I was the 'Rage of the 'Nation (U.S.A). But 'Nay Nay—'Never no 'Connie's Inn.

One night the 'Gangsters started a 'fight in the 'Show Boat in 'Chicago, right in front of where I were 'standing. 'Playing my 'Trumpet,—I usually 'stood playing with my eyes closed—'leaned against a 'post that was made into the 'Band stand was 'built down on the 'Dance floor. I 'mean they were *really* 'fighting 'worst than a Bunch of "Spades" (colored folks). One of the 'Gangsters took a chair and *'hit* a 'woman over the 'head with it—And the 'Chair "Crumbled up all in a lot of little 'pieces. Some of the 'pieces 'hit my 'horn. But 'even *'that could not* make me 'leave the 'Bandstand—you 'know? The 'Captain must go 'down with the 'Ship."— Then too, things like that never 'frightens me. I"ve seen so much of that Bullshit 'during my days of 'playing music. 'Ain't but one *incident* at the 'Show Boat' that *kind of* 'got me.— And it happened one 'night—As we were justa playing and the 'people were all 'Dancing—And having a 'Ball.— Our 'Dressing Room was also located on the 'same side of the 'Band Stand.—

A pretty 'large one 'at that. I usually 'Blows my 'Trumpet with both of my eyes 'Closed. And as I was 'Blowing" I 'felt some one, 'touching me very 'quietly—speaking in a whisper.— It was a big 'Burly looking 'Gangster saying—"'Somebody wants you in the 'Dressing Room." I said "Sure—I'll go as soon as I finish this 'dance set.'" And I didn't pay any attention to it. So after the 'set was over, I 'ran, "Lickity Split" (real fast) to my 'dressing room to see who it was. I 'rushed to the door thinking it was one of the "Cats" (the gang). And 'there *bless My* 'Lamb—who I 'did see was a 'White 'Guy with a *'Beard* on his 'Face—'Thicker than one of those 'Boys from the 'House of 'David.— So he spoke 'first,—"Hello" (kind of 'Sarcastically)—I still ain't 'Hep to the 'Jive.— I said "Hello" (very 'pleasantly). *He said* "Do you know 'who I am?" *I said* "Why'er—*'No*—'No I *don't.*" In fact it really didn't *matter.* As long as he 'talked about *'music* I just 'knew—'he and 'I were going to really 'Run our 'Mouths awhile musically. Then this 'Guy said—"I am 'Frankie Foster." At 'first—I 'still didn't 'pay it any 'Attention—to 'that extent. 'Anyway—*Then* it 'dawned on me what he said—And I 'turned in 'Cold 'Sweats as I 'Back 'Cap'd—'Mugg'd—And took a 'double look'—As I said to him—"What you say your 'name wuz?" By this time he had his Big 'Pistol—Pulling it out—As he said—"My name is 'Frankie Foster." And he said he was sent over to my place (Show Boat) to see that I 'Catch the first train out to 'New York. I 'still try to make it appear that he ain't 'Frightening me.' I said—"New York? 'Why—that's 'News to me. Mr. Collins didn't tell me anything about it." 'Frankie Foster (a bad "sommitch") said, "Oh yes'—'you're going to 'New York to work at 'Connie's Inn. And you're 'leaving 'tomorrow morning." Then He Flashed his Big 'Ol' Pistol and 'Aimed it 'Straight at 'me. With my 'eyes as 'big as 'Saucers' and 'frightened too I said—"*Well* 'Maybe I *'Am* 'going to 'New York." "Ooh 'God." Then 'Frankie Foster said—"O.K. The 'Telephone 'Receiver is 'Down 'waiting for you to come and 'say you'll be there. Now—'you and 'me are going to the 'telephone booth and you'll 'talk." By this time—'Anything he 'ordered of me was 'alright—because it's no trouble at all for a 'Gangster to 'pull the 'Trigger—'especially when they have you 'Cornered and you 'Disobey them." "Soooo" we went to the 'phone (with a gun in my side) and sure enough, someone said hello, a familiar voice too—yes sir—I know that voice if I heard it a Hundred years from now. The first words he said to me was—"When are you gonna open here?" I turned and looked 'direct 'into Frankie Foster's face—and said "Tomorrow AM."

8

"THE SATCHMO STORY"

(EARLY 1959)

Armstrong titles this document "The Satchmo Story, 2nd Edition." This can only mean that he wrote it as a sequel to *Satchmo: My Life in New Orleans*, published in 1954; the forthcoming sequel was announced at the time of publication. Gary Giddins (1988: 16) discusses Joe Glaser's decision to break off *Satchmo: My Life in New Orleans* with Armstrong's arrival in Chicago, as well as the suppression of subsequent material that dealt with marijuana. According to Giddins, Armstrong read parts of the sequel to friends, doubling them up with laughter in reaction to his claims for the medicinal value of marijuana. Giddins thought the book had been lost. But the present document, held at the Louis Armstrong House and Archives at Queens College/CUNY, is surely the beginnings of it. Armstrong says, at one point: "This whole second book might be about nothing but gage"—"gage" being slang for marijuana.

Armstrong says that he was introduced to marijuana by white musicians in Chicago during the mid-1920s. John Hammond (1977: 106) and others identified Mezz Mezzrow as Armstrong's first source. (A 1932 letter from Armstrong to Mezzrow, asking for shipments while on tour, is now held by the Library of Congress; see the Appendix.) Armstrong also mentions his arrest for possession of marijuana, which occurred in Los Angeles during March of 1931. At the Cotton Club in Los Angeles, Armstrong performed with a young Lawrence Brown and an even younger Lionel Hampton. His memory of the latter inspires recollection of a number of drummers with whom he has worked during his career.

Perhaps Armstrong was thinking of combining this document with leftover material from the end of volume 1 (published as "The Armstrong Story" in this book) to form volume 2 of his autobiography. Beyond the obvious obstacle of writing about marijuana, it is not clear why volume 2 never emerged. Certainly, it would have been hard to sustain a narrative with the charm and cohesiveness that made *Satchmo: My Life in New Orleans* so appealing. Volume I was about a single and somewhat exotic place; volume 2 would have to be largely a story of a musician's life on the road. In any event, Armstrong occasionally jumps back to New Orleans in the present document, as he often does in other writings.

The Satchmo Story 2nd Edition

The first time that I smoked Marijuana (or) Gage as they so beautifully calls' it some time, was a couple of years after I had left Fletcher Henderson's Orchestra—playing at the Roseland in New York . . . And returned to Chicago . . . It was actually in Chicago when I first picked up my first stick of gage . . . And I'm telling you, I had myself a Ball . . . That's 'why it really puzzles me to see Marijuana connected with Narcotics—Dope and all that kind of crap . . . It is actually a shame. I was 26 years old then. And it never did impress me as dope. Because my mother and her Church Sisters used to go out by the railroad track and pick baskets full of Pepper Grass, Dandelions, and lots of weeds similar to gage, and they would bring it to their homes, get a big fat slice of salt meat—and make one most 'dee-licious pot of greens anyone would want to smack their lips on. . . . *physics you too.*

So it's against the law to smoke Marijuana . . . The days when I first found out about gage—there weren't any law against it . . . New York weren't 'up on it—when I first went there . . . Of course 'I wasn't 'either at the time . . . I probably wouldn't have paid any attention to it either . . . But to me—I being a great observer in life, I happen to notice the white young musicians coming every night to this swell night club where I was playing—and although they had just finished their jobs, they still looked fresh—neat and very much contented . . . And they would really enjoy my trumpet playing with the highest enthusiasm that any human being could do for another . . . I just came up from the South, I was just thrilled with the closeness and warmth of these great musicians, performers, etc. In fact, it gave

Used by permission of Louis Armstrong House and Archives at Queens College/CUNY.

me such a lift until, the Leader could see the beam all over my face when it was time for us to play a dance tune or play for the show. And we had a real big show . . .

Mind you—I'm still in the dark as to Gage, or who's smoking it and who ain't. That's why, right in these times, I just can't conceive the idea that it's actually narcotic . . . But who am I to tell the law what to do about what's what. These fine musicians (it wasn't necessary to learn their names). Good Jazz Music was always that way . . . So I learned—especially when I came up North—From New Orleans Louisiana . . . A good jazz musician is so glad to see one 'nother until they'll call one 'N' other almost any kind of name (but affectionately) just to get to that good hand shake . . . And they would praise me, which sounded to me like they were swinging a tune . . . Beautiful . . . So it wasn't any problem when I went places with them . . . After all this knowing each other and when they'd 'Light up, why—during the conversation, of whom ever be sitting around the room,—and at the same time—somebody or everybody would be 'blasting like Heavenly,'—out of a clear skies a *stick* of gage would touch the palm of my hand—or the tip of my finger . . . I never was born to be a Square about anything, no matter what it is . . . My Mother always told me, to try anything at least once . . . You either like it or you don't . . . She also said—and you 'don't like it, never ridicule it . . . Which reminds me of a lot of people that I've met through life . . . The first time' picking up, the first thing that they will ask you, "What does it make you do?" . . . I had to tell a chick off when she asked me such a stupid question—I said, "How 'N' the 'hell do 'I know"—I told the Chick—"How 'N' the hell do I know how it's gonna make' you feel or what it's gonna make' you do—all that I know is—it makes me feel 'good as 'gracious". . . . Then everybody would agreeably laugh. . . . That's one thing that I personally found out about Gage, or Marijuana, Narcotic, P.S. Maybe that's why that it is put on the Narcotic list—those two names does sound real bad. Marijuana—Narcotic . . . Sometimes names—just the sounds can cause one, grief of somewhat . . . Such as big stars . . . Just a change in the names sometimes, bring them big successes, fortunes, and stuff like that . . . Maybe someday—some big Authority on things—anything, just as long as he's a big man and has convincing words . . . Then he can probably someday have 'Marijuana name changed to 'Gage—'Muta—'Pot—or some of that *good shit* . . . Maybe it isn't necessary to bother about it these days . . . Because since the days when I was actually

'Wailing—smoking gage, it was plentiful—much easy to get, the Judges weren't so heavy with them years like he gives out these days. Why I'd much rather shoot a nigger in his ass than to be caught with a stick of *shit* . . . The Judge would honestly respect you better . . . . . .

It's Brutal how everybody 'Hawks' on the same thing and the same person for doing something that they're thinking is wrong . . . Meaning—everybody want to point their finger at you with scorn, just because you probably taken your last quarter (that's all that gage costed in those good old heydays) it had just went up from ten cents per stick, when I so fortunately got hip to the tip . . . P.S. Can you imagine anyone buying narcotic for ten cents? . . . Or twenty five cents . . . Hmmm? . . . Somebody's nuts. . . . But when Judge give a man twenty years for the word from a cop who'd probably had it in for the victim (could be you—me—or—anybody) the accused man is charged with just having marijuana in his possession . . . For that he gets twenty years—he's an outcast—nobody want any part of him (especially the one's never smoked it or even tried it to see for themselves . . .) Why Condemn a man for something that you 'think you should . . .

I am different . . . I smoked it a long time . . . And I found out one thing . . . First place it's a thousand times better than whiskey . . . It's an Assistant—a friend a nice cheap drunk if you want to call it that . . . Good (very good) for Asthma—Relaxes your nerves . . . Great for cleanderness . . . Much different than a dope fiend . . . A dope addict, from what I noticed by watching a lot of different 'cats' whom I used to light up with but got so carried away—they felt that they could get a much bigger kick by *jugging* themselves in the ass with a needle—Heroin—Cocaine—etc.—or some other unGodly shit . . . Which would not ever phase a man like myself, who've always had a sane mind from the day he was born . . . As I said before, I've always been a great observer from a baby . . . Mary-Ann—my mother told me when I was very young, She said—"Son—Always keep your bowels open, and nothing can harm you" . . . And she never said truer words than those . . .

This whole second book might be about nothing but gage . . . Of course there'll be a lot of sore heads who'll probably resent this . . . But when you sum it up—a man such as myself who've played nothing but good music for his public all over the world—and all of his fans—and his public feel the same as our respect for each other . . . Never has let them down during the whole forty five years (that I've been blowing my trumpet) . . . Lived the same ways a musician should . . . You know—?— I am my own public myself . . . I never wanted to do anything wrong that I personally would not like . . . I felt at no time when ever I ran across some of that good shit, that I was breaking the law, or some foolish thought similar to it . . . There isn't one person in the whole wide world—white—black—grizzly or gray who ain't breaking the law of some kind, for their kicks—contentment . . . Right? . . . That's why we have the laws . . . So many people still more fortunate than I am these days . . . I lost my contact . . . Traveling all over like a bunch of adagio dancers . . . Good thing I have my wife Lucille with me on all of the trips . . . Shucks, I wouldn't have any fun at all . . . When I was in Sweden a little young, cute little newspaper reporter came up to me while I was autographing one of my little teenage fan's book . . . He said to me—"*Hey Louie Armstrong* how do you like our Swedish Women?" . . . I looked up at him and said "Man—'My wife have the best Smorgasbord in the world" . . . He cut out—very swiftly . . .

I feel that I have a right to say the words that I am saying here . . . I served my time in California in 1930 while playing at the Cotton Club in Culver City California . . . One night Vic Burton, who was really the greatest drummer of all at that time—playing in all of the studios . . . I was blowing like mad at the Frank Sebastian's Cotton Club—upsetting all of the Movie Stars . . . They would pack that great big fine place everynight . . . Mr. Sebastian, a fine looking 'Cat looked sharp in his Vines (clothes) was crazy about Vic . . . And Vic and I were the same way about each other . . . Still are . . . Nope—he's now dead . . . I felt bad over Vic's death . . . Just like a brother . . . But I always remember what my mother said where ever or when ever somebody would die with gas or indigestion . . . And still uses the phrase—"They didn't *shit enough*" . . . . And that's what I said about Vic Burton . . . Now it could have been something else . . . But—it all derives—from negligence of the bowels. . . . I am about to be fifty nine years old . . . This Fourth of July—1959 . . . Born July Fourth 1900 . . . And if I have to say it myself, I am blowing better and twice as strong as I was when I was in my twenties . . . Well I won't mention my sex sessions these days, because I hate to be called a braggadosha. . . . Wow . . . Did that come *outa Mee*. . . .

It's a funny thing how Vic and I got busted . . . It was right in front of the California Cotton Club during my intermission and Vic came over for a few drags—we'd pick a stick alternately . . . Then too—the law wasn't so strict on gage, even out at that time . . . And we—not only Vic, anyone who liked the little buzz that came from it . . . I did not know why we were busted until after the arrest and I was talking to the two Detectives who took me down to the Station from the club . . . Now dig this—that's why I still say, there's no actually written law against gage, but, the person with the evil mind—or thoughts, and with a little money to spend for his own personal evil Spirit—or Method in his Madness (that's for sure)—or I could even say—Jealousy—with a little money, the no good person,—set up a trap, (if it means, anything to them,) or out of a clear sky—from you . . . Because they know that you, don't have a leg to stand on . . . That's what happened to Vic and I . . . You see, I've always been a happy go lucky sort of type of fellow in this way—I never tried in no way to ever be *real real* filthy rich like some people do, and after they do they *die just* the same.—

But Mary-Ann had already 'hipped me to what was happening in this healthful wide beautiful world . . . So, by me doing that (even before I ever heard of gage) I was always the happiest young trumpet player that anyone wanted to ever meet . . . From the first time that I picked up my trumpet, or the one that was out to the Orphanage, I was a popular youngster . . . Success has always been—mine . . . So was never a thought for me to do dirty things to people or think that there was anyone whom ever wanted to do me any harm . . . Hmmm . . . But they did . . . Here's how we were busted (arrested to you)—When I left my home town New Orleans and went to Chicago with Joe Oliver, and the Band disbanded, I went to the Sunset Cafe, playing in Carroll Dickerson's band. We stayed so long at the Sunset until we wedged into a pretty good band . . . Later on—Zutty Singleton (one of the greatest pioneer drummers—Humorist good natured guy—my idol, and a many many things, good, that he is) . . . Joined the band . . . Then it *did* jump. . . .

We felt that we were good and had it . . . So we all (the whole band) members who had some kind of automobile, had it checked up one day and we all just went to New York on our own—and 'took us a job . . . That's how 'good we were. And we proved it . . . Right down into Connie's Inn, on a hundred and thirty first street and seventh avenue . . . We used to rock the joint (I mean the place) every night . . . After six months, the boys, (the Lushies) commenced to *messin* 'up (with a Capitol F) and Mr. Connie who was a very nice man to us said—"I just can't stand it any longer" . . . So the *'Ax Hit Us* . . . After he gave us a notice—I had a friend who ran on the road from New York to California . . . And would always tell me he could get a Pass for me any time I should see fit to go out there . . . And always I would ask him, "What's out there?" . . . Not knowing that I was as popular as I actually was in California . . . With the White People of course—mostly . . . I'll tell you why I said that—Because when I went out there, quite naturally in those days, the minute a colored man gets off of a train anywhere West or South, the first thing that a Red Cap, or a Negro (had to call him *Negro—) because he's in with Mr. Charlie, and he would have my head whipped worst—than a kettle drum . . .

I went to a Hotel on Central Avenue and Forty Second Street called the Dunbar . . . There was a Barber Shop in the front . . . I checked into my room . . . With nothin in particular to look for or forward to either . . . But, I had my right *Loot* (means money). So I'm Straight enough—not to have to *Cop A Beg*—or have to 'blow my horn right away, unless I actually was satisfied and willing . . . I didn't have anyone to depend up on me at that time . . . So, with a few real new Vines, and a nice weight, and young,—blowing my ass off—I felt pretty ready. . . . Thought I'd hit the stroll . . . Stopped in the Barber Shop for a little touch up and ran into a fellow called Soldier Boy,—A record fan, personified . . . Wow. Soldier was all I needed to complete—not only my trip, but my life . . . Of course, you know, he 'latched on to me . . . Taking me around to the Barbers, the *Cats* Laying back being steamed on their faces, etc., . . . Then on his way out of the door there was one more chair with a towel steaming over this gentleman's face, the man whom Soldier Boy said and always said after that particular meeting—"There's a guy whom missed a million dollars, just for being a big shot playing Louis Armstrong, 'Cheap" . . . Soldier Luther Gafford Touched Curtis Mosby on the leg—Curtis Mosby was 'A' drummer—playing downtown in Los Angeles at a Jitney dance. That was—long time ago . . . He made quite a nice little taste (lots of money), which he saved enough to take over the Club Alabam on Central Ave, a very big fine building with a large Night Club into it . . . The Club was jumping every night. The rest of the building he rented out to Doctors—Lawyers—beggar men—chief. Oh hell, Curtis Mosby was *'it"* when I went out to California, in 1930 . . . Soldier Boy, when Curtis pulled the towel from his face,—pretty nice looking chap—brown skin—a little on the plump side . . . I guess that came from raiding the ice box, the way one usually does when they sudden become rich . . . Anyhow—Soldier Boy (Luther Gafford) Said to Curtis—(evidently they knew each other personally—for Soldier to take so much personal interest)—he said—"Curtis I want you to meet Louis Armstrong, the best Cornet Player back East". . . . Then Curtis raised up from his chair real slowly (seemed as though, he did it because he didn't want to ignore Soldier), Raves over my playing . . .

But, by him being some what of a musician himself, he just has to give me the once over anyhow, if no more than for 'doggass-sake . . . When Curtis raised up, he looked straight at Soldier Boy (he hasn't said anything to me—'yet). He said to Soldier—"Oh' Yea, I kinda, have heard of him. —Er 'wa—' Take him into—my dining room and give him a good meal". . . Soldier Boy Jumped sky high and said to Curtis—"Man—'this man don't need no free meal . . . He has his own (Loot) meaning money—he just thought since he's making his first appearance out on the Coast, and you being a man of his Race, he just wanted to give you the first preference to present him . . . He's already a Star. And get all the work anywheres he choose . . . And here you come with that old signifying shit. Not only did you insult him, but you have insulted me . . . And for *that* I'll wait for you outside—so when you finish in here (the barber shop) I'll be waiting for you, and you must apologize to him and me. Not so much me, but I'll demand that you apologize to him . . . And if you 'don't—'you and 'Me—we will 'tie asses together . . . And that's no shit". . . . He apologized . . .

We all said later that Curtis Mosby missed the boat by not hiring me, because the next night Soldier Boy took me out to Frank Sebastian's Cotton Club, which was really jumping (already) out in Culver City California . . . There was a band playing there at the time, was kinda' mixed up . . . The leader was an elderly fellow who, I'm sure, was a fine trumpet man in his heydays . . . His last name was Elkins [Vernon Elkins] . . . He was surrounded by some of the finest musicians that I had witnessed playing music in my whole life . . . From New Orleans to St. Louis—Chicago to New York . . . Through all of those towns where I had already heard some of the greatest men on their instruments, yet, these boys sort of had a little something on the ball (musically) that I had not witnessed . . . Such as endurance—tones, perfect sense of phrasing, and the willingness and the spirit that the Eastern Musicians or the Southern Musicians 'used to have before they got to Broadway and became stinkers, looking for power and egotisms, the desire to do practically anything 'but enjoy their first love—

which is their instrument. . . . These boys in Mr. Elkins band had all of the good qualities and a little more besides . . . Which fascinated me no end . . .

Mr. Elkins was a very smart man . . . He realized that he was aging but fast and the trend of music which I imagine was really a 'pip, in his days were sort of Blaa'zay—in the beginning of the late 'thirties . . . So he would let these youngsters play and run the band the way that they' saw fit . . . And could they swing . . . My God . . . I'll never forget the first time Soldier boy took me out to the Club, when I first heard that band play, I almost jumped out of my skin. . . . The little slick headed drummer (with his hair—gassed to kill) and he kept it slick and shiny . . . A fly would have slipped and broken his neck immediately . . . And that's for sure . . . Konks were the thing in those days . . . I can remember that time when I joined 'Smack Henderson (Fletcher's pet name). I spent the whole day having my hair gassed—so I could make a big hit when I left Chicago to join Fletcher Henderson's Band . . . More about that later . . .

Speaking of Konklines (hair do). As far back as I can remember,—this little cute drummer in Elkins 'band and Arthur Bryson, our once great dancer—were the only two guys whom I admired the way they kept their hair looking so pretty and so shiny all the times . . . Most of the show people and musicians who used to konk their hair, were too lazy to keep it up . . . Because when your hair is konked—in order to do a good job, the barber had to use real lye—mixed up with some kind of stuff looked like putty . . . And if he put this stuff into your hair and if he's a split second late getting to the wash bowl—or if another barber happened to be using the wash basin, 'Man—that lye is *liable* to burn all of your hair out of your head and make a gang of great big fester bump Sores—head sores that is. . . . So you had to be real hipped and *be sharp—feel sharp—and stay sharp* . . . And that's just what this cute little drummer—playing in Elkins band did . . . His smile was infectious (I think—that expresses what I mean.) When this little 'Cat would be drummin smiling while twirling his drum sticks he never missed—he was perfect at it. Smiling with his chops stretching from ear to ear . . . I couldn't stand it . . . I'd just let out a yell and a scream . . . He was too much . . . Folks—that little drummer was Lionel Hampton . . . Whom I think at that time was the greatest that I'd witnessed in my life . . . And that's saying a lots . . .

I have witnessed and played with quite a few masters of the drums . . . Up until that time I was especially carried away with—a few that I'll mention here, otherwise I would not have the room . . . Without insinuations, and with all the greatest respect to all the drummers that I've ever blown my horn with, here's a few that used to gas me through my early years blowing my trumpet and who used to really make Ol' Dipper (that's me—then) get up and blow his ass off . . . From the real early days up to the present time when I first heard Lionel . . . 1915—during the days of the Redlight District (which they now called Storyville) P.S. I imagine they changed it to a much milder name—they thought for the sake of the Teenagers—I guess . . . What is it telling a kid the life of the musicians who played there—and give them a phony name such as Storyville, which has never registered with me, like the magic word—redlight district . . . It sounds more musical to say the real thing . . . To me—doing a thing like that—is just like someone telling a joke and beat around the bush when they get to the punch line . . . Because it's Risqué . . . Ya Dig?

Anyway in 1915 when King Joe Oliver had his Creole band in the district and was playing every night for Pete Lala's Cabaret, on the corner of Conti and Maraise Streets—His drummer was Henry Zeno. . . . A little guy (not too short but with very small waist line) loved to gamble and could gamble, when he was *finished* work at Pete Lala's around four o'clock in the mornings. He would go to a place right down there in one of the neighborhoods, called (25) . . . They used to have some mighty big games there with the Pimps and Hustlers, who gambles nightly and also killing time waiting until their women get through Hustling, and—then they'd take them home—give them some good loving, so whether they'd win lose or draw, they'd have fresh money every night to just piss up if they wish. . . . . Henry Zeno also had a few hustling women on the side. A wife also—but in those days, all the musicians were healthy guys, with lots of energy nature to do whatever he wished. . . . They'd have themselves a ball with a woman—all night, or drinking at the Eagle Saloon where all the greats hungout. And the next you'd see them wailing away in a brass band playing for a *funeral* or the Odd Fellows—or the Labor Day Parades, and 'Blowing. . . . .

Henry Zeno was an all round drummer . . . I'll probably make the same phrase—for quite a few of the fellows whom I speak of so affectionately—(musically) and I probably won't say too much about some of them . . . But one thing that you can bet on—-I won't say anything 'bad about them . . . Because all through my travels in life—I've always lived like the Sister that was in my mother (Mary Ann's) Church. Everybody in that Church just loved their Pastor 'Reverend Cozy to death . . . Hmmm what a coincidence—(Rev. Cozy)—will be talking on Cozy Cole later. . . . Anyway speaking of the certain Sister in Mamma's Church—I noticed one day when Rev. Cozy took a short Vacation and *put in* a substitute ''Preacher—most of the congregation didn't seem to have liked him as well as they did their own Rev. Cozy . . . But, there was 'one Sister sitting in Church, and I noticed that she seemed to be enjoying him just about the same as she did Rev. Cozy. . . . So when Church was out and all of the brothers and sisters were coming out—they all made a bee line over to where she was sitting and why did she enjoy the 'Sub Pastor as well as she does our own Pastor? . . . So—she said to them—''When ever our Rev. Cozy is Preaching, I can look right straight *through him* and see Jesus—and when the 'Sub Preacher was Preaching sure—I realized that he wasn't as good as our own Pastor—-So just looked 'over him and saw Jesus just the same''. . . . That's the only way I've wanted to be—just like that sister. . . .

When Henry Zeno would pull the handkerchief from under his snare drum when playing a funeral and they'd taken the body to the Cemetery. And, the preacher have said his last words. He would actually thrill me when he'd make a long clean roll on his snare (which is real clear now) and when the musicians would come from different places while the sermon's going on, and Henry Zeno would start the march. For a while then he'd get his cue from the Cornet player—the leader to start em up, and old Black Benny would hit that base drum three times to be exact—Boom Boom Boom—Oh didn't he Ram-bled didn't he Ram-bled—he Rambled til, the Butcher cut him down. . . . The parade in on its 'way then taking the members back to the hall. . . . Zeno used to kinda' tilt his head to one side while drumming in a street parade . . . Good man . . . When Henry Zeno died, the whole city turned out for his funeral . . . That's how popular he was . . . In fact the biggest two funerals that I had ever seen in New Orleans when I was a kid were two members of the district . . . One was Henry Zeno the drummer and the other Clerk Wade the sharpest Pimp that New Orleans ever had . . . He was a real dark brown skin young man—who kept his hair cut real close (Konk wasn't known in those days). Clerk wore the very best of clothes and he also had diamonds in his garters for his socks . . . The next funeral which came pretty close to those fellows—was a young kid who lived in my neighborhood by the name of Arthur

Brown . . . He was a plain looking light brown skin boy—about 15 years old when a little simple boy killed him accidentally playing with his father's pistol . . . The pistol went off and killed Arthur Brown with the first bullet . . . That kid upset the whole city, boy all of those pretty young girls from everywhere crying at his funeral . . . I played his funeral in Joe Oliver's brass band . . . His Cornet player whom were working in the day time, couldn't get off . . . 'T'was so sad until tears even came to my eyes . . . After all he was one of my childhood playmates. . . .

My next favorite drummer in the olden days was Henry Martin . . . A sort of a sophisticated young man, whose mother was a widow and was left with a large family of goodlooking children . . . She was made a caretaker of the Fisk School, the school that I went to when I was a little boy . . . In fact, the only school that I went to in the City . . . Most of my schooling was done in the Waif's Home for boys . . . (boy's jail) . . . The Martin family were all musically inclined . . . All except one Son . . . There were four boys and three girls . . . The oldest brother left home real early in the years . . . Went to East St. Louis, Ill. with his Violin, and we didn't hear from him very much after he left . . . Most of the family stayed on the school premise with their wonderful Mrs. Martin—who was such a grand person . . . And loved by everybody in the neighborhood and afar . . . There were Alice Martin—I was home when she got married to one of my childhood playmates by the name of John Cootay . . . He could easily pass for a white boy . . . But he couldn't be bothered . . . So he had one of the best jobs in town working a big sportsman club, waiting on the white rich gamblers with drinks, new decks of cards and things, of that sort . . . So he was already a good liver (as we used the phrase) when someone's 'Negro rich . . . Alice and John were living together when I left New Orleans in 1922 . . . I don't think they ever had any children . . . There was Orlenia, another sister who got carried away with show business and fell in love with an Actor (a beat up one at that) who never did get to the big time in show 'Biz'—why he never did get to any kind of time at all . . . Because he could not act in the first place . . . But Orlenia thought that he was heaven on earth . . . She got so carried away with this Ham Hamlet, until she ran off and got married without even letting Mrs. Martin know about it. . . . And boy' did that guy lead her to destructions . . . He had her up North—hustling and doing everything to make a dollar, so he could spend the money on a lot of trifling broads around Chicago, who were laughing at him—calling him a hick from Louisiana, etc . . . . . . With all the things—he did to our Orlenia, we were just as glad to get her back home . . . It was a hard thing for her to get over the sudden shock . . . Something that she never dreamed—would happen to her . . . Especially when she'd reminisce over the proposals she used to get when we were kids together . . . Then there was the one sister by the name of Wilhelmenia . . . Now there was the gal . . . Everybody would try to woo her . . . But she was the only one whom Mrs. Martin depended on. And Wilhelmenia used to clean all of those school rooms everyday . . . And Believe me there were loads of them . . . From the first grade to the six . . . All those rooms were just like a drop in the bucket to Wilhelmenia . . . Every time I saw her she would probably be looking over the schoolhouse's picket Fence, saying hello or maybe a conversation to a few passer-byers, etc . . . And I was in love with her until I was afraid to dare say it to her . . . I was real young at the time and she would say the nicest things to me . . . Such as encouragement on my horn and she would always tell me, "Dipper (for Dippermouth) don't you never stop practicing your cornet . . . Because you are going to be real good someday" . . .

Of course Wilhelmenia was much older than I was . . . She was 20 years old then and a perfect Virgin . . . Never been kissed . . . (Well, I don't know whether she'd been kissed or not) . . . I didn't try to find out . . . All that I know is—I wasn't fixing to insult her . . . At that time—I probably wouldn't have known what to say to a nice girl like her anyway . . . But, I sure was in love with her . . . I was just a News boy selling the daily papers . . . And the little money that I made selling papers and shooting craps on the corner with the other News boys, I had to take that money and support 'my sister Mamma Lucy . . . Beatrice is her real name . . . And she's two years younger than I . . . And May'Ann my mother and my real Father Willy Armstrong were separated, and nothing much was happenin with the few Step Fathers that she had calling around every now and then . . . Most Step Fathers in those days never had nothing anyway . . . They weren't the type that could go down in (25) and gamble . . . Because they never could get their hands on that much . . . They'd bring a few nickels, now and then . . .

So you see—it was a useless thing to even think of trying to marry a girl as nice as Wilhelmenia . . . And a Virgin too . . . Huh . . . My luck always ran with the girls that came to the dances where I was playing . . . Lawn Parties or some kind of social function . . . They were goodlooking girls also . . . But there were great differences in them from Wilhelmenia . . . When as young as I was I could feel it . . . Most of them were already master minded . . . And had already—layed and been schooled by the elderly (cheap) Pimps—Gamblers, etc. Which made them sort of feel that they were a little more superior to a young musician like me . . . As young as I was, I didn't know then about the little traits—and what to say or do—to sweep a gal off her feet . . . Ya Dig? . . . So when it came to me and my young comrades, it would be more of a toleration and an admiration for the Blues that I played than anything else . . . Which was—alright with me . . . Because it was the cornet and the musicians that I wanted to be around mostly anyway . . . And if I never had a sex session with a girl—it really didn't make any difference with me . . .

It all comes 'back to me now . . . I noticed that the most affection I received when I was a young musician were from the elderly women . . . Way above my age . . . They seemed to take the time—to tell me the real things, that I must always do, or say, in order to keep the Ideal woman, that's on my mind . . . And until this day—I'm still ever so grateful to all of them . . . I was such a small boy at 17 years old until the Whores, used to come into the Honky Tonk where I was playing every night—with Boogus on the piano—and Gobee on the drums . . . Three Pieces . . . And they used to come around four o'clock in the mornings, especially Sunday Mornings after a big night's take in their stockings (which was genuine silk even in those days) and they have me blow them blues' for them . . . And they would almost fight as to whose lap that I was to sit in while having a drink with them . . . I didn't' drink anything but a cold bottle of beer, which only cost, *a nickel* . . . Yea, those were my people my crowd and everything, and still are . . . Real people who never did tell me anything that wasn't right . . . I wound up getting married . . . And my first was the prettiest and the 'bad'est 'whore in Gretna Louisiana . . .

The joint was right up the river from New Orleans . . . We would go over on the Louisiana Avenue Ferry every Saturday night and play all night for a dollar and a half . . . Which was pretty good money in those days . . . Daisy Parker was the Chick and the Apple of everybody's eyes . . . Especially those who worked in those Oil Foundries over there, and were paid off every Saturday night . . . Daisy kept on flitting across the floor in front of the bandstand where I was blowing the blues, and giving me the wink with the stuff in her eyes. . . . Hmmm. . . . As soon as I could get off the bandstand I went up to her and said—"Lookheah' Babe's—Suppose you wrap it up for the night? And—spend the rest of the night with me upstairs? . . . I'm buying 'all the rest of your time, etc" . . . That sounded great to Daisy. . . . More about it later . . .

Back to the drummers . . . Henry Martin as I told you before, wasn't to me as flashy as Henry Zeno. Red Head Happy—Little Mack—Facia—Zutty Singleton—Tubby Hall (they called him Baby Hall)—Minor Hall also a drummer (who now plays with Kid Ory) Baby Dodds—Cantrell [Louis Cottrell Sr.]—Walter Brundy (the best reader of them all) he played John Robichaux's Orchestra, the best Orchestra in town because they could read music fluently on sight . . . Yea, they could read even a fly speck if it got on to their music sheet . . . Tee Hee . . . Brundy swung nicely but he couldn't get down there and really get like Ole Paul Barbarin—Black Benny and those young 'Cats who came up in my era . . . Barbarin is still a swing modern drummer. And has always had a good band . . . Right til this day in N.O. Barbarin was the drummer who played on my recording of "When the Saints go Marching" which was the very first recordings of the "Saints" . . . Ahem . . .

There was a white drummer in New Orleans when I was coming up around there by the name of Paul Detroit, was real great . . . He played at the Orpheum Theater Wailing for those big time R.K.O. Acts which came from up North to appear there . . . Such as Sophie Tucker—Lew Dockstader, and many others . . . Of course we had to sit in the Buzzard Roof to dig em . . . As determined as I was to hear every 'Livin' (A)sperin'—I didn't mind the climb at all . . . Young too . . .

I said all of this to show you just how much—I appreciated this young boy—called Lionel Hampton. . . . I had never seen anyone that was so vivacious as Hampt . . . I sat in with him for two nights at the Cotton Club, and when we did open up for the public—we were so wedged in together until the public thought that we had been together for six months . . . . . .

I thought when Fletcher Henderson formed his band in 1924 at the Roseland Ballroom (which was at 51st and Broadway at the time) . . . Gee, I thought when he sent for me to leave Chicago and join his first big Orchestra, I really did think that was something . . . Which, come to think of it, it was. . . . It was the first big band that was ever heard of on these United Shores and about the biggest thing that Fletcher had done up until that time . . . In that band were also some of the all time greats—such as—

Kaiser Marshall on the drums . . . He was a real sharp 'Cat indeed . . . I'd never seen or heard of anything that was anywheres near the ever sharp Kaiser Marshall . . . Oh' he'd sit up there behind those drums, and whip those hand cymbals to death . . . Then there was Charlie Green on the trombone who could hit a Bell Tone so solid and distinct . . . Things that just wasn't being played in New Orleans or anywheres . . . Charlie Green had some of the strongest 'Chops (lips) of all the trombone players in New York at the time . . . And was the *best*est for a long long time . . . Of course Mr. Jackson Teagarden came up to Harlem one night he had just arrived from Texas . . . The first thing Jack said to me—"Where's all of these trombone players around here—I want to cut them" . . . He did . . .

Ralph Escudero, Fletcher's Bass Tuba Player. But (very) good. And what a sense of humor he 'had . . . You see' I'm just a new man in the band. And I'm diggin' all of these big wigs of music as I went along—night after night in N.Y.C. I thought that Escudero was one of the finest tuba players I had heard in years . . . Charlie Dixon was a good guitar man . . . Later he turned arranger . . . Scottie [Howard Scott]—Elmer Chambers who were in the trumpet section with me were also men whom I'll always have respect for . . . And there was the sax section which were Don Redman—Coleman Hawkins and Buster Bailey . . . Smack (Fletcher) played the piano . . . I really appreciated that band . . . And felt that I was getting some place in music . . . . . .

9
"JAZZ ON A HIGH NOTE"
(1951)

For this article, *Esquire* asked Armstrong to comment on some recordings from the middle years of the 1920s—mainly the legendary Hot Five and Hot Seven recordings that made him one of the central figures in jazz history. Along with some colorful stories, Armstrong reports on what the initial experiences with recording were like for him and his colleagues, who did not form a working band but were assembled for this studio work. Armstrong and Lil Hardin Armstrong collaborated on the back steps of her apartment, composing songs specifically for the recording sessions. If, near the end of a session, the studio asked for an additional song that the musicians did not have, they simply made one up on the spot, happy to accept a flat fee and assign royalties to the company. "Mike fright" was a problem, and a mistake in handling a sheet of lyrics produced one of the first recorded examples of a scat vocal.

Armstrong says that "Cornet Chop Suey" could be performed "as a trumpet solo, or with a symphony orchestra." Here we get a glimpse of the complicated context surrounding the three-minute recordings that survive on disc. William Russell (1939: 134) reports that "Cornet Chop Suey" was arranged for twenty-one orchestras in a concert promoting Okeh records in 1926. "Trumpet solo" probably refers most directly to the Hot Five format. But the piece may well have been performed with Armstrong fronting Erskine Tate's orchestra, which, according to William Kenney (1993: 49) "plugged Clarence and Spencer William's 'Royal Garden Blues' at the 1500–seat Vendome Theater by performing an arranged version in which each section of the orchestra, hidden in different parts of the theater, began 'Royal Garden Blues' when cued by the 'old familiar minstrel roll off,' and played it while marching toward the pit." This performance was reported in the *Chicago Defender* on February 20, 1926, the very month that Armstrong recorded "Cornet Chop Suey." With its collective improvisation and many breaks, "Cornet Chop Suey" is, as Armstrong implies, not far from the New Orleanian street music that he had been performing only a few years earlier. It reminds him especially of the good-natured "carving contests" between cornet players in New Orleans. Indeed, its bravura made it a dazzling display piece; crafting it, Armstrong must have realized how well suited the virtuosity of the cutting contests was to the kind of theatrical display that was featured in the Vendome Theater. It is the kind of piece that made Armstrong's reputation in Chicago. Recently, a copyright application for "Cornet Chop Suey" has been discovered, confirming the ambitions of Lil and Louis, sitting on their back steps sketching out what they hoped would be the next pop hit.

''POTATO HEAD BLUES.'' Louis Armstrong and his Hot Seven. Kid Ory, trombone—Johnny Dodds, clarinet—Johnny St. Cyr, banjo—Baby Dodds, drums—Pete Briggs, tuba—Lil Hardin, piano—Louis Armstrong, trumpet . . . This particular recording really ''gassed me'' because of the perfect phrasing that was done by Johnny and Ory . . . I could look direct into the Pelican Dance Hall, at Gravier and Rampart Streets in New Orleans, during the days of the First World War . . . That was in the years of 1918–1919 . . . And their bandstand was built in the left-hand corner of the hall . . . And the stand was up over everybody's head . . . in order to say hello to any member of the band, you had to look up . . . And all of that good music was pouring out of those instruments—making you want to just dance and listen and wishing they'd never stop . . . ''Potato Head Blues'' was a tune they really did swing out with . . . My man, Joe Oliver, bless heart . . . Papa Joe (I used to call him) he really used to blow the kind of cornet I used to just love to hear . . . His playing still lingers in my mind . . . There never was a creator of cornet any greater than Joe Oliver . . . I've never heard anyone to come up to him as yet . . . And he's been dead since 1938 . . . ''Potato Head Blues'' . . . Hmm . . . Every note that I blew in this recording, I thought of Papa Joe . . . ''Yass Lawd'' . . .

''TWELFTH STREET RAG.'' Louis Armstrong's Hot Seven. Although I haven't heard this recording for quite awhile . . . at one time, I had about pretty near every recording that I've ever made . . . That was when I was

Used by permission of The Louis Armstrong Educational Foundation.

married to Lil, and was living with her in Chicago, on 44th Street . . . I was also playing at the Sunset Cafe . . . for my manager (of this day) Mr. Joe Glaser . . . I had just left Fletcher Henderson's Band in New York, to come home to Lil, in Chicago . . . So—since I had to come home—I stayed home . . . and went to work at the Sunset Cafe . . . Fletcher, his boys and I were such wonderful friends, until, when they had an engagement at the Congress Hotel, downtown Chicago, I invited the whole band out to our home for a big party I and Lil gave for them . . . Now, here's where the reason why I haven't heard "Twelfth Street Rag" comes in. The night of the party, all the boys had their choice chicks and friends with them . . . I played all of my record collections and *somebody*—when they got ready to say good night—had several of my choice recordings inside their "bosom!" Soooooo . . . That's why I have not heard my "Twelfth Street Rag" for ages . . . Ha Ha Ha . . . But I'll take the risk and say—"Twelfth Street Rag" is a "Livin Aspirin" . . .

"CHICAGO BREAKDOWN." Louis Armstrong's Band. "Chicago Breakdown" . . . Featuring Earl Hines . . . This recording features mostly Earl Hines . . . Of course, everybody knows that Earl was really in his prime in those days . . . Before he organized that great big band of his . . . And he taking so much time, or should I have said "wasting so much time," just directing the band . . . Of course, Earl being a born, good musician, overcomed it right away . . . In the early days, Earl didn't do anything but play the hell out of that piano . . . He still attain the name of "Fatha," in my estimation . . . Earl is now playing with my All Stars Band . . . Along with Jack Teagarden, Barney Bigard, Cozy Cole, Arvell Shaw and myself. And I'm "tellin yoo" Earl is back to his ol' self again. PS. Ol' self—not *old* self. Ha Ha. And in all, I think that everyone will enjoy the recording of the "Chicago Breakdown" . . . I know, I did—before they *stole* it the night of Fletcher Henderson's party, given by me—at my home in Chicago . . . "Chicago Breakdown" . . . The correct name . . . Huh???

"MUSKRAT RAMBLE." Louis Armstrong's Hot Five. "Muskrat Ramble" was recorded in Chicago . . . In the good old days when Joe Oliver was blowing his cornet like mad—at the Plantation—at 35th and Calumet . . . That's when I was playing just across the street—at the Sunset Cafe . . . The Sunset was owned by my manager, Joe Glaser . . . Of course, I was just a member of the Carroll Dickerson's Orchestra at the time . . . And Mr. Glaser hadn't started managing anyone—then . . . Along about that time—

Kid Ory, John A. St. Cyr came to Chicago . . . And the minute I heard that they were in town—I jumped sky-high . . . You see? I had just signed a contract to record for the Okeh Recording Company . . . And they told me to hire anyone for my recording band that I desired . . . Boy O Boy . . . The minute Mr. Fern (the President of the Okeh Company) gave me the go sign—I hit the phone and called the Musician's Union, and asked permission to hire Kid Ory, Johnny St. Cyr and Johnny Dodds (who was already in Chicago, playing at Kelly's Stable) . . . Of course—Lil Hardin joined up with me for my recording dates . . . She was working with King Oliver (Joe Oliver) every night—at the Royal Garden . . .

After our first date—the band impressed the bigwigs of the Okeh Co. so well that they signed us up right away . . . Then we began to really get into the groove, the New Orleans groove . . . That's when we started making records every day . . . It was a good thing for us . . . Because when we went down to the Okeh Recording Company for the first time, we were all Mike Fright. We did not realize just how much we were frightened—until the day we recorded the "Gut Bucket Blues". . . Tunes such as "Muskrat Ramble"—and other instrumental tunes—which were being recorded through the old Horn System—as unaccustomed as we were, we finally got used to it . . . But the day came for the recording of "Gut Bucket Blues". . .
Ump . . .

"GUT BUCKET BLUES." Speaking of what happened the day of the "Gut Bucket" recording—the joke was actually on Johnny Dodds . . . He seemed to be a little more frightened than the rest of us . . . Because—if you'll notice in this particular record where each member of the band had a few words to say during one solo . . . I said, "Oh, play that thing or blow it Kid Ory,"—while he played his solo on his trombone . . . So—quite naturally, when I played my solo, Johnny Dodds was supposed to say, "Oh (play-it) Papa Dipp" (that was my Nick (Alias) name down in New Orleans before we all went to Chicago) . . . And don't you know that Johnny Dodds could not open his mouth to say one word—when it was his time to say, "Play it Papa Dipp". . . Ha Ha Ha . . . We ruined several Masters . . . And finally had to give those lines to someone else . . . But we sure did have a lot of fun making that recording . . . Incidentally, "Gut Bucket Blues" was the first recording made by my Hot Five . . .

"STRUTTIN WITH SOME BARBECUE." Louis Armstrong's Hot Five. "Struttin with Some Barbecue". . . This tune was derived and thought of during the days when Zutty Singleton and I were playing at the Savoy Ballroom on the South Side of Chicago . . . And, after the dance was over every night, Zutty and I would drive out to 48th and State Street . . . There was an old man there who made some of the most delicious barbecue that anyone would love to smack their chops on (their lips). One order never was enough for Zutty and I . . . Some nights that man's barbecue was so good, until I almost hurt myself, from eating so much . . . One night, while Zutty and I were manipulating those "Chime Bones" (barbecue), a thought came into my head . . . I said to Zutty—"Say Zoot, as I sit here eating these fine-tasting ribs, it dawned on me that I should write a tune and call it, "Struttin with Some Barbecue" . . . Zutty said, "Dush, that's a real good idea" . . . So then and there, "Struttin with Some Barbecue" was born . . .

That same night at this rib joint, a funny incident happened . . . I had been carrying a hundred-dollar bill in my pocket for a long, long time . . . I used to have a nice Creole roll in those days . . . A Creole roll, as we called it in New Orleans, consists of a small bunch of money wrapped around an empty thread spool . . . Quite naturally it will look like a big roll of money . . . And the girls would fall for that jive . . . So on this night Zutty and I were eating these fine ribs, when I thought about my pocket . . . Which I only had this hundred-dollar bill wrapped around this spool, that I used to show off with . . . I said, to Zoot—"My Gawd, Zoot—don't you know? We have eaten all of this food and I only have this hundred-dollar bill—and that's all . . ." Then I asked Zoot, "are you stickin?" (meaning) "Have you any money on you at the moment?????" and Zutty said—"No man" . . . Then we both agreed to just hand the hundred-dollar bill to "Dad" (the barbecue man) and if he hasn't that much change, he probably tell you—bring it back later when we get paid off tomorrow . . . So I handed Dad the hundred-dollar bill, with Zutty and I looking out of the corners of our eyes at Dad . . . Watching his every move . . . Huh . . . Dad took my hundred-dollar bill, went back behind his old raggedy counter, opened an old greasy cigar box, and gave me my change back from my hundred-dollar bill so fast, our heads commenced to swimmin' round and round . . . Haw Haw Haw . . .

"HEEBIE JEEBIES." Louis Armstrong's Hot Five. "Heebie Jeebies" was another recording, was another incident that I shall not ever forget . . . This time the laugh was on me . . . When everybody heard about this record was made they all got a big laugh out of it . . . They also said that this particular recording was the beginning of Scat Singing . . . Because the day we recorded ″Heebie Jeebies,″ I dropped the paper with the lyrics—right in the middle of the tune . . . And I did not want to stop and spoil the record which was moving along so wonderfully . . . So when I dropped the paper, I immediately turned back into the horn and started to Scatting . . . Just as nothing had happened . . . When I finished the record I just knew the recording people would throw it out . . . And to my surprise they all came running out of the controlling booth and said—″Leave That In″ . . .

My, my . . . I gave a big sigh of relief . . . And sure enough—they did publish ″Heebie Jeebies″ the same way it was mistakenly recorded . . . Kid Ory—John A. St. Cyr—Johnny Dodds—Lil Hardin—and myself on this recording . . . Boyd Atkins who used to play the violin in my band at the Sunset Cafe wrote the tune . . . He must have made a nice little ″taste″ (meaning) the tune made a quite a bit of ″loot″ (meaning) they sold lots of records and made lots of ″dough″ (meaning) ″money″ . . . On this record the players were—Kid Ory, trombone—Lil Hardin, piano—John A. St. Cyr—Johnny Dodds, clarinet—oh yes—St. Cyr, banjo . . . Louis Armstrong, trumpet . . .

″YES I'M IN THE BARREL.″ Louis Armstrong's Hot Five. Like a lot of the old tunes we recorded—I wrote most of them myself . . . It's a funny thing how I used to sit on the back steps of Lil's home and write five and six songs a day . . . Just lead sheets . . . And Lil would put the other parts to them . . . cornet, clarinet, trombone, etc. . . . Then I would sell them to the recording companies outright . . . Mostly the Okeh . . . In this recording were Kid Ory, Johnny Dodds, Lil Hardin, John A. St. Cyr, Louis Armstrong (me) trumpet . . . P.S. cornet rather . . . The title came from an old ″saying″ from the good old days in New Orleans, La., my home town . . . Whenever one of those Gambling guys would get busted in a gambling game—such as shooting dice, playing poker, or, etc.—they would pawn their best clothes, to pay off their gambling debts . . . Quite naturally they would have to go back to their old raggedy clothes until they get lucky and get the good ones out of pawn again. So, that's why, we used the expression ″Yes I'm in the Barrel″ . . . Yes . . . I too—were in the barrel lots of times . . .

″CORNET CHOP SUEY.″ Louis Armstrong's Hot Five. Written by Satchmo Louis Armstrong . . . On the steps (back steps) of his second wife Lillian Hardin Armstrong . . . ″Cornet Chop Suey″ turned out to be a very

1 Louis Armstrong + the Jewish Family in New Orleans La.
The year of 1907

Written by Louis Armstrong – Ill in his Bed at the Beth Isreal Hospital
March 31, 1969
New York City N.Y.

A Real life story and Experiences At the age of Seven years old With the KORNOFSKY FAMILY The year of 1907.

All Scenes happened in New Orleans La. Where Armstrong was Born. The Year 1900.

The Neighborhood was Consisted of Negroes, Jewish People And lots of Chinees. But The Jewish People in those early days were having problems of their own. Along with Hard Times; from the other white nationalities who felt that they were better than the Jewish Race. And they took advantage of every Chance that they had to prove it.

Page 1 of "Louis Armstrong + the Jewish Family in New Orleans, La., the Year of 1907" (Louis Armstrong House and Archives at Queens College/CUNY).

Tucson Arizona.
May,7th,1944,

Greetings My Friend;

Nodoubt you've wondered why the delay...But I just didn't get around to it...I've been so busy traveling and making trians,etc... How's everything?...I do hope that you and the wife are as happy as ever...I shall meet my wife out in California in a few days...She went on ahead of me from Chicago...

Here's fifty dollars more-which makes,Thee Hundred... I shall finish up in California...Which won't take me long to get the other two hundred...I am opening up at the Trianon Ballroom Tuesday night May,9th,....I have four books of story,to send to you the first chance I can get to a Post Office...

There may be several spots that you might want to straighten out-or change around...What ever you do about it is alright with me...I am only doing as you told me...To make it real-and write it just as it happened....And Brother believe me I have a lots for you this time....

Write me a line to this address-2219 Hobart Blvd, Los Angeles California....I am stopping at Mrs Louise Beaver's Home out there....She certainly's a swell person...And incidently-if ever you should film the story of my life you should see that Mrs Beavers get a good part in the picture...She could really play the part of my mother since she looks so much like Mary Ann(my mother)and acts just like her...

And as great an actress Mrs Beavers is-why she and I could get together and really make a big thing in a film together.. I only mentioned her...Sometimes it saves one a lot of worry as to whom to get to play some parts,thats,really to played....So Goffin I shall get to work now...And you can look for the rest of my story in a few days....

So goodnight pal...Am dying to lay eyes on you again...Am always glad to see you...You can tell from the way I explained in my story that you are really my boy...So stay happy and write me... And God Bless yous...

Am Pluto Waterly Yours,

Louis Armstrong.

Letter to Robert Goffin, May 7, 1944 (Institute of Jazz Studies, Rutgers University).

Right: Page 1, book 1 of the "Goffin Notebooks" (Institute of Jazz Studies, Rutgers University).

New Orleans – 1918

When "Daisy (MY WIFE) And I Seperated – I went home to my Mother "Mayann". – That's her 'Pet' name." "ALIAS" As I've Mentioned before – Anyway – I moved back home with my mother. And stayed there with her the whole time I was working At "Tom Anderson's Caberet – Located on "Rampart (BETWEEN) Canal + Iberville Streets. That's one of the most well Known places in the History of New Orleans. All of th "Race Horse Men" used to Come

1 Lincoln Garden - 1922
Chicago Ill

It was really "Cute" to see the "Shy" Expression on Joe Oliver's Face - when I asked him about how he was 'Ribbing' me about he was my 'Step Father' in the Presents of my 'Mother

Mary Ann -
MAY ANN

Joe Oliver as well as myself felt that we were very Close Relatives - He was Always 'kind' And very Encourgaing to me - And ENCOURAGING Willing to help a poor 'youngster like me out. - And until the very last day - he drew his DIED last Breath, I stuck right LAST Beside him - And everyone who

With May Ann and Mama Lucy, 1922 (Louis Armstrong House and Archives at Queens College/CUNY).

Armstrong with "Papa" Joe Oliver, Chicago, ca. 1923 (Louis Armstrong House and Archives at Queens College/CUNY).

Left: Page 1, book 2 of the "Goffin Notebooks" (Institute of Jazz Studies, Rutgers University).

Fletcher Henderson's Orchestra, 1924 (Louis Armstrong House and Archives at Queens College/CUNY).

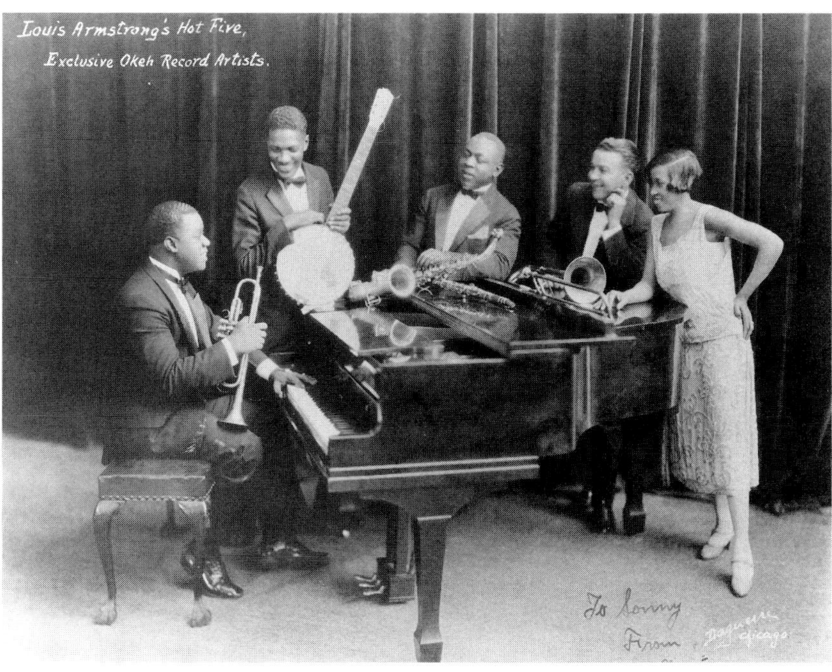

The Hot Five, 1926 (Louis Armstrong House and Archives at Queens College/CUNY).

"Of course I am not so bad myself at "Swimming.— In fact it's one of my' famous 'Hobbies, outside of "Typing."— I loves that also." (Louis Armstrong House and Archives at Queens College/CUNY).

Chicago, 1933 (Louis Armstrong House and Archives at Queens College/CUNY).

Bill "Bojangles" Robinson (Institute of Jazz Studies, Rutgers University).

Endorsing Selmer trumpets (Institute of Jazz Studies, Rutgers University).

Fronting the Luis Russell Orchestra, 1936 (Institute of Jazz Studies, Rutgers University).

With Joe Glaser, signing a contract for Fleischmann's Yeast Hour, 1937 (Louis Armstrong House and Archives at Queens College/CUNY).

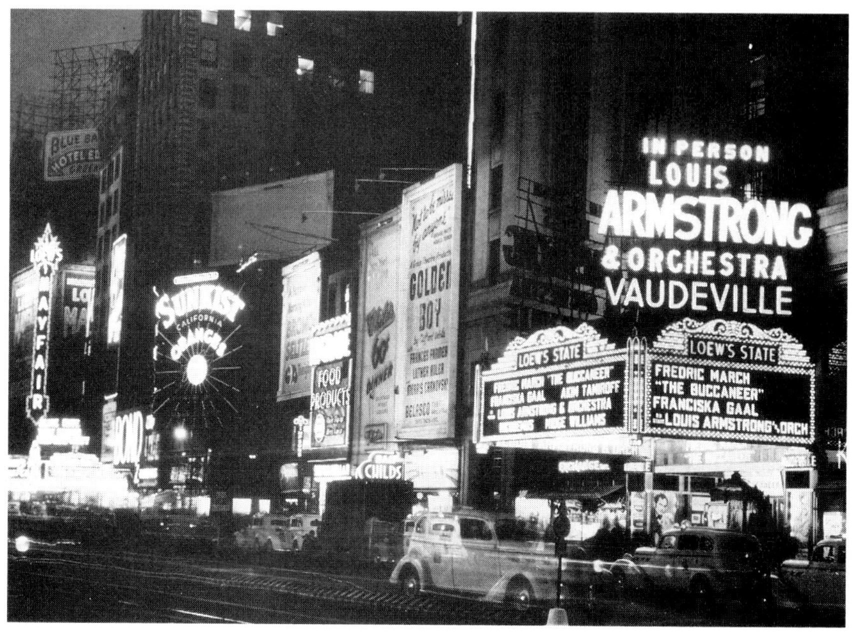

Times Square, New York, 1938 (Louis Armstrong House and Archives at Queens College/CUNY).

A quiet place backstage (Louis Armstrong House and Archives at Queens College/CUNY).

Louis and Lucille, newlyweds, 1942 or 1943 (Louis Armstrong House and Archives at Queens College/CUNY).

On the set for a soundie, 1941 (Institute of Jazz Studies, Rutgers University).

Performing "When It's Sleepy Time Down South" in a 1942 soundie (Institute of Jazz Studies, Rutgers University).

The All Stars, late 1940s (Louis Armstrong House and Archives at Queens College/CUNY).

Rehearsing with the All Stars (Institute of Jazz Studies, Rutgers University).

King of the Zulus, Mardi Gras 1949 (Louis Armstrong House and Archives at Queens College/CUNY).

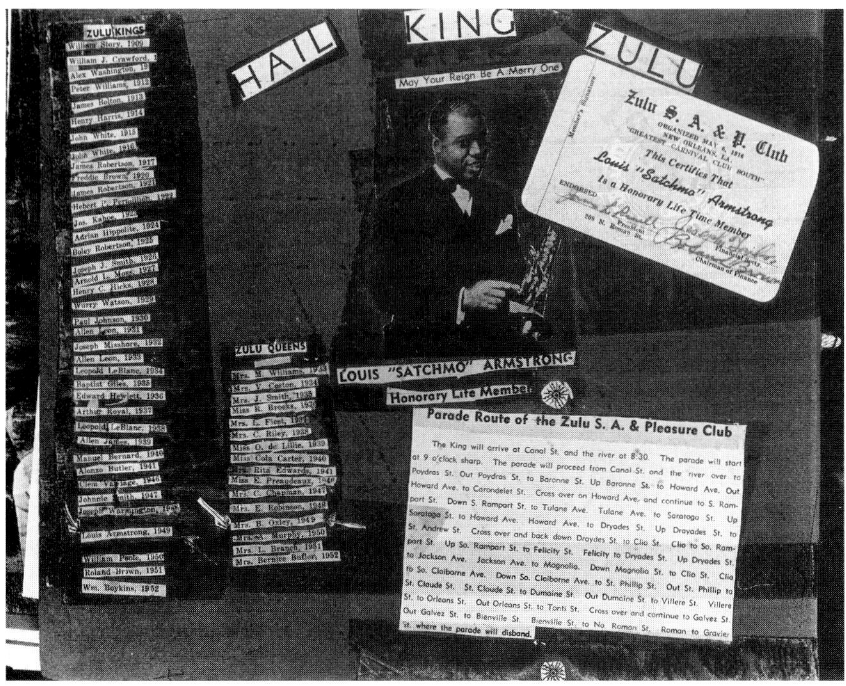

Collage decoration was another hobby (Louis Armstrong House and Archives at Queens College/CUNY).

Honored at Leopoldville, Congo (now Kinshasa, Zaire), 1960 (Louis Armstrong House and Archives at Queens College/CUNY).

Warming up (Institute of Jazz Studies, Rutgers University).

Airport greeting, England 1968 (Louis Armstrong House and Archives at Queens College/CUNY).

The house in Corona, New York (Louis Armstrong House and Archives at Queens College/CUNY).

Neighborhood music in Corona (Louis Armstrong House and Archives at Queens College/CUNY).

popular tune—especially among the musicians & actors and music lovers ... Kid Ory—Lil Hardin—Johnny Dodds—Johnny St. Cyr and myself played on the recording date also ... Those variations in this recording remind me of the days when we played the tail gate (advertisings) in New Orleans ... We kids, including Henry Rena—Buddy Petit—Joe Johnson and myself, we all were very fast on our cornets ... And had some of the fastest fingers anyone could ever imagine a cornet player could have ... And to us—we did not pay any attention to the idea that we were fingering our horns so terribly fast ... And all of those boys had good tones ... And when I say tone, I'm speaking of tones that blend with the tone that a trumpet man should have when playing a swing tune—And you'll hear a lot of them blowing like mad ... But they never lost essence and the mellow fragrance of the tune. "Cornet Chop Suey" could be played as a trumpet solo, or with a symphony orchestra.

"SKID-DAT-DE-DAT" Louis Armstrong's Hot Five. It seemed as though ever since I made that mistake in "Heebie Jeebies," by dropping the paper with the lyrics on them, and I kept on Scatting—and the recording company kept the record and released it just the same—and it made such a tremendous hit—a lot of tunes were written right after that, with a lot of 'scat' choruses in them ... Such as "Skid-Dat-De-Dat" ... Of course I do not want to be quoted on this Jive. But, everybody who hear the recordings of "Heebie Jeebies" and "Skid-Dat-De-Dat," they all seem to think that Be Bop Singing and Riffing derived from "Jeebies" and "Skid-Dat." Hmmmmmm ... Think So? ... Anyway, it doesn't make any difference one way or the other ... It's all Jive ... No matter where it came from ... And it all seem to have a friendly attitude ... I, myself, just love to hear those guys swing their Chops—Scatting. To me, Scat Singing is just like playing an instrument ... That is, when they sing with the right chords, and beautiful changes ... Of course, I'm not responsible for catcalls, and all of that kind of stuff. Wow ...

"ORY'S CREOLE TROMBONE." "Ory's Creole Trombone" is one tune that always did fascinate me ... I remember when I was a kid in short pants (years ago in New Orleans, when Kid Ory and his band used to play every Sunday night at the St. Katherine's Hall), I used to sell newspapers and save up enough money to pay my admission, which wasn't much ... And I would just listen to them play this particular tune ... Mutt Carey was playing cornet in the band at the time ... Johnny Dodds, who was really in his prime, played clarinet—Kid Ory, trombone—Henry Martin played the drums—Bob Lyons played the bass—Lorenzo Staulz played the guitar—Emile Bigard (Barney's Uncle) played the violin and led the band . . . And when those guys would play the tune "Ory's Creole Trombone," everybody would dance . . . They had a rhythm on this tune wherein, after several choruses, they would get 'way down, real soft, real soft, and Kid Ory would make those slide tones on his trombone, and the more choruses they played, the softer they would get . . . And they would get so soft until you could hear the feet of the dancers, "justa shufflin" . . . My, my, they sure used to knock me out on "Ory's Creole Trombone" . . . And it's also a very fine recording . . .

"THE LAST TIME." Of course, some recordings such as "The Last Time," I haven't heard very much since the recording . . . So all I can say about this tune—it was well recorded by some of the most Jazz Genius there is . . . And their names will linger in the music world for the next generations to come. I admire every one of them. Whether I made records with them or not . . . Men such as Kid Ory, Mutt Carey, Bud Scott, Minor Hall, Joe Oliver, Bunk Johnson, Eddie (Montooly) Garland, Johnny Dodds, Jimmie Noone, and many many others of the good old New Orleans Era, their names shall never die . . . Those boys are the ones who actually started this stuff about getting together and really play good music together . . . Later years they called them Jam Sessions . . . In those days that I'm speaking of, we would just meet on a job, no music whatsoever and blow . . . The same as if we'd worked together for over six months . . .

"THAT'S WHEN I'LL COME BACK TO YOU." Louis Armstrong's Hot Seven. Vocal chorus by Lil and L. Armstrong. It certainly was real kicks making this record . . . especially with Lil Hardin . . . who later became Mrs. Satchmo Louis Armstrong . . . This is our first time singing together . . . It amused the recording company so well until they started looking around for new material for Lil and I . . . Honest . . . Lil also knocked me out with that cute little voice of hers . . . And to me, she always could "Swing Sing" (an expression of mine) with feeling . . . If I'm not mistaken I think that Lil wrote this tune . . . She was very much versatiled when she and I were married, between us we wrote some pretty good songs together . . . "That's When I'll Come Back to You" was written as a comedy number . . . You'll notice in the recording that Lil sings these words—"You Can Beat me, Kick me, Blacken my eye, but please don't quit me" . . .

Which knocked everybody out . . . Then, my line is, "When the rain turn to snow and it's fifty below-er—that's when I'll come back to you" . . . Blaa Blaa Blaa . . . All in all, the tune brings a little laughter . . .

"WEARY BLUES." Louis Armstrong's Hot Seven . . . "Weary Blues" was derived from the good old days of tail gates in my home town, New Orleans, La. . . . There were a lot of bands advertising on Sundays for some kind of affair . . . And pretty near every band will play the "Weary Blues." The recording we made for the Okeh people reminded me so much of New Orleans, until I was looking direct into New Orleans when we were recording it . . . The trombone player on this recording date is named John Thomas . . . He is now a big embalmer in the Windy City of Chicago . . . And the bass tuba player, Peter Briggs (a little flat-nose fellow) but a darn swell guy . . . And one of the finest musicians and has one of the finest big hearts of any man . . . And recordings such as this particular tune, every time I play it, I find something else to write and tell the world about . . .

"BASIN STREET BLUES." Louis Armstrong & His Savoy Ballroom Five—featuring Earl Hines. This is another recording date that was a real "Gassuh" . . . with Earl Hines, piano—Mancy Cara, banjo guitar—Jimmy Strong, clarinet—Fred Robinson, trombone—Louis Armstrong, cornet . . . "Basin Street Blues" was also a tune written from the good old days of Storyville . . . In fact, there's a street named Basin Street in New Orleans . . . Lulu White, the Octoroon Chick, had a very famous house on that street in those days, called "Mahogany Hall" . . . Jelly Roll Morton, the great jazz man at the piano, played for Lulu . . . In the days when money was flowing like wine, down there . . . Basin Street is what travelers call a "landmark" nowadays . . .

"GOT NO BLUES." Louis Armstrong's Hot Five. Louis Armstrong, trumpet—Kid Ory, trombone—Johnny Dodds, clarinet—John A. St. Cyr, banjo guitar—Lil Hardin, piano . . . Was one of those quickies that was made up right there in the studio . . . You know?—some of the best records were issued from some of those incidents . . . Say f'rinstance—records such as "Gut Bucket Blues," the record that we had so much fun making—why, it was made up right there in the Okeh studio . . . And lots of times, when we would finish up with the tunes that we had set for that particular date, the recording manager would ask if we had any other tune we could make up right away . . . Quite naturally we would say yes . . . Then to thinking about those extra bucks that would be involved—Hmmm, we'd find ourselves automatically going into a tune that sounded good to the "man" (the recorder) and he would say—O.K.—that's very very good . . . Let's make it . . . They used to either buy the tune outright, or ask us if we cared to collect the royalties . . . P.S. Of course you don't have to make any guesses as to our decisions . . . Aye? . . . Sure . . . Our slogan was, A bird in hand gathers no moss. "Got No Blues" got a nice little "Taste" for us . . . We split the royalties [*recte* flat fee] . . . Of course, it wasn't enough to make one "Hump Back" from carrying it . . . But, as we New Orleans musicians used to express it—it did beat a blank (meaning) the money came in handy . . . And it was more than we had . . . Yea man . . .

"I'M NOT ROUGH." Louis Armstrong's Hot Five. Now, here's a recording that I always have a great thrill and get a great boot out of playing as well as I did when we recorded it . . . "I'm Not Rough" . . . Lord to Day . . . I can see King Joe Oliver, right this minute, blowing his cornet, and playing this tune in the advertising wagons on Sundays . . . And—I—just a kid following him all over town . . . Just to hear that horn . . . He was with Kid Ory's band at the time . . . And they played an arrangement to "I'm Not Rough" which we tried to remember the idea when we recorded it . . . But I'd give my right arm right to this day, to hear the master-papa Joe Oliver toot this tune . . . So what little creations we did in the recording of "I'm Not Rough"—just remember that I was looking right into the Chops of my idol—the great King Joe Oliver . . . Folks—Joe Oliver was a creator . . . Most of your modern Riffs you might hear in these late-day arrangements came from Papa Joe (my man) . . . And since I am searching like mad for all of my records, so I can record on my tape recorder—you can bet I am in a mad search for "I'm Not Rough" . . . Yarsuh . . .

"HOTTER THAN THAT." Louis Armstrong's Hot Five. "Hotter Than That" was another one of those recordings that I wrote on the back steps of Lil Armstrong's home . . . The minute Mr. Fern, who was headman of Okeh, heard it, he got Lonnie Johnson to sit in with us and play his guitar on this date. Yes—that's Lonnie playing so wonderfully . . . I have always wanted to make a record with Lonnie . . . In fact, just to play with him. I can remember as far back as 1915, when Lonnie and his brother, Rooster, played a whole lot of violin . . . So you can see my delight in blowin' with that fine boy and a wonderful musician, Lonnie was also signed up to the Okeh . . . In fact, he was a member, way longer before I was.

III. "Book Anywhere–Anytime":

Life on the Road during the 1940s and 1950s

"Book Anywhere–Anytime. Just let me know what's happening–in time. I'm sure–you "Dig me" Huh?"

10

EARLY YEARS WITH LUCILLE

(CA. 1970)

This untitled document begins in mid-paragraph and ends in mid-sentence. Armstrong describes his courtship with Lucille, beginning in 1938, their marriage in 1942, and their purchase of a house in Corona, New York. A good supplement to this document is an article from *Ebony* (Armstrong 1954b) titled "Why I Like Dark Women," which includes reflections on Lucille's success as a dancer at the Cotton Club: "When I first saw her the glow of her deep-brown skin got me deep down. When we first met, she was dancing in the line at the old Cotton Club and was the darkest girl in the line. Dark, that is, by prevailing standards of Negro beauty. Lucille was the first girl to crack the high yellow color standard used to pick girls for the famous Cotton Club chorus line. I think she was a distinguished pioneer. I suppose I'm partial to brown and dark-skinned women, anyhow. None of my four wives was a light-colored woman."

And if you want to know *what* kind of Eyes' that I am talking about—I am talking about *Bedroom Eyes*. ''You're Just' the *Gal* for me. Now I know' you're going to tell me that, you might be a little too young for me' since there is a difference in our ages.'' ''I am only 26 years old'' she said—And *you* (meaning me) are around 40 or 41 *somewhere* around there. And I'm wondering if it would turn out O.K. Being married to a man with so much Experiences behind him (3-ex-wives). After all I'm just a little small Chorus

Girl, Lucky to come in contact with a Bunch of Lovely Well Hipped People.''

That's when I stopped her from Talking by slowly reaching for her *Cute* little *Beautifully Manicured hand'* And said to her, ''Can you Cook' Red Beans and Rice?'' Which Amused her very much. Then it dawned on her that I was very serious. *She*—being a *Northern* girl and *Me* a *Southern* boy from N.O. She could see why I asked her *that* question. So She said: ''I've never cooked that kind of food before. But—Just give me a little time and I think that I can fix it for you.'' That's All that I wanted to hear, and right away I said' ''How about Inviting me out to your house for dinner tomorrow night?'' She said, ''Wait a minute, give me time to get it together, or my wits together, or *Sompthing*. We'll say a Couple of days from now?'' Gladly I Accepted. Two days later I was at her house on time with Bells on. Also my best Suit. I met her Mother Mrs. Maude Wilson. Then later I met, Jackie, Janet and Sonny. They all impressed me right away as the kind of Relatives that I could be at ease being around for the rest of my life. The Red Beans + Rice that Lucille Cooked for me was just what the Doctor ordered. Very much delicious and I Ate Just like a *dog*. I said forgive me after I had finished eating. I Just had to make *some* kind of excuse. She accepted it very cheerful. Because I am sure that Lucille has never witnessed any *one* Human Being eating *So* much. Especially at one *Sitting*. I had her to save the rest of the Beans that was left over. Then I'd come another time and finish them. We commenced getting closer ''n'' closer as time went by.

And when I went out on the Road with Luis Russell's Band' and when we played in Chicago—I had to appear in Court, to get my Divorce from my 3rd Wife, *Alpha*. It was ''10 'o'Clock in the Morning' And I had been out Balling all night stumbling over Chairs from drinking (meaning) having one *drink* after another. No sleep and Juiced (Drunk) personified quite naturally. 'By the time I got to the Court house at ''10 'o'Clock in the *A.M.* I was very *hoarse* + could only be heard above a whisper, just happy to get the trial over with' one way or other. Just so I could go to my Hotel' Room and get some sleep and a well needed Rest. Good thing that we had a night off.

Just before our trial started—I happened to slowly scan' (look around) the court to see if I could see anyone I knew outside of Daisy [*recte* Alpha]. And *there Bless* my *Lord* I looked straight into those beautiful eyes of

Lucille (Brown Sugar) Wilson. *Wow*—I lit right up. And Sharpened up for the Questions that the Judge were going to ask me′ concerning Daisy [*recte* Alpha] and I′ divorce. Lucille had surprised me by taking the weekend off to come to Chicago to *Dig*′ my *Trial* and be with me. Just then the Judge turned to me and commenced ′Asking me a few Questions. I was so hoarse + my *voice* sounded ′*So* Bad until the Judge immediately looked straight at me + said—″*Look here* young *man* have you Caught a Cold?″ I Said—″*No* Judge it′s Just this ′*Saw Mill* voice that All of my Fans said that I have.″ The Judge Gave a little *Chuckle* (of laughter) and *immediately* said—″Divorce Granted.″ Lucille came over to me, and we went home′ to my Hotel. Played the *Gig* in Chicago.

St. Louis was next. My vocalist′ Velma Middleton who came from St. Louis were with our Band at the time. On our way to St. Louis by Train′ I mentioned to Velma (privately) that I had planned to marry Lucille real soon. And I won′t let her get out of my Sight′ by returning back to New York, before she have our marriage *License* in her hands. And *Velma* Bless her′ right away she said—″Since We′re here in my home town′ why don′t you and Lucille get married at *my* house. I want you to meet My Mother—Brother and My Son Manny anyway. My Mother belong to a Large Church in St. Louis and her Pastor, a *fine man* is loved by the whole congregation of the Church. We can engage him to marry you and Brown Sugar and our Band Boys could all be Invited *Guests*,″ Which sounded very good to me, Even when I told Lucille what Velm had said.

So we all agreed and set Oct. 12th, as the Wedding Date. All Set. Then a Day before the Wedding there was a real situation which raised its ugly head. Lucille is Catholic and I am a Baptist. We went to several priests and they all turned us down, and would not O.K. our Marriage License. So the time was getting near′ And Lucille + Myself were getting desperate and so distraught until it wasn′t even funny. But we would not give up. Then all of a Sudden it Dawned on Lucille + Me—after all we both are deeply in Love, which Priests or *no* Human could understand or care less. So we decided to Forsake all others, and go on with the Wedding. Lucille had already sent for her mother to come from New York to Witness the Ceremonies and happenings, etc. She was all Smiles and seemed so satisfied over everything as far as Lucille + I were concerned. So that was it. I bought a beautiful *orchid* and pinned it on Lucille. That was the (1st) orchid I′d ever bought in my Life. Whether it was Lucille′s 1st, or not, I don′t know. I only went by how nice "n" pretty *mine* looked on her. We made a very good looking couple with me (at that time) was down to my *Fighting* weight (Very Slim). And I had on a *Sharp' Hard* Hitting *"Grey"* (suit) as we *cats* expresses it. Luis Russell + his Boys' All looked *'nice* and had a real good time. All the Liquor "n" everything that they 'wanted.

The next night we played at the Tune Town Ballroom, the place where Bix Beiderbecke—and Frankie Trumbauer' used to *Blow'* a lot of times during the old days when it was *running* and Really Jumping, A Real Popular Place. Bix played cornet. Frankie play the C" Melody' Saxophone. And what a team that those *fellers* made. I played there several times myself through those years. I met a lot of Teenagers of those days. I even played there with my 1st, All Star Band *including*—Jack Teagarden on Trombone—Barney Bigard on Clarinet—Early Hines on Piano—Arvell Shaw on Bass—Cozy Cole on Drum—Velma Middleton Vocalist—Myself on Trumpet. And I mean we really had a Band if you ask me. The last time we the All Stars appeared at the Tune Town Ballroom Big Sid Catlett played the Drums. He died soon after that. We sure hate to lose him. Now there was a man on the Drums" All that I'd have to do is to turn around to *See Big Sid* Sitting behind those Drums *doing just* any old *thing miscellaneously* and Brush off a cymbal, etc., and it would Hang me (make me feel good). That man really had a Soul' On those *Drums*. He's gone' but not, forgotten. Nay Nay.

Speaking of Lucille and *I's* Wedding. After we finished our engagement at the Tune Town, we left St. Louis to go on the Road, for six months of one night stands. So I sent Lucille and her mother back to N.Y. and to wait until I return from my long trip. I had no fear. "Learned to know Lucille like I did' I felt that She had the same thoughts as *I* did. And it *worked* out Just *fine*. The *Rev.* who married Lucille + *I—Hmm"* his *wife* who was also at our *wedding'* surprised us when *two* weeks *later*, 'since our *wedding*, she *Sued* her *husband Ol Rev"* for a *Divorce. Well Sir'* she *caught 'Reverend'* in a *peculiar position* with one of the *young Church Sisters* who sings in his Church *Choir*. That certainly did struck us all funny. But I did not have any fear of something like that ever happening to Lucille and I—We had too much sincere Love + Devotion. In other words, never Divorce' each other. *Our* home must be our *castle* where we could *pleasantly* lock our *Bedroom Door* at *Infantory* time (sex). A *Clean Well Damped Wash* Rag Just before getting in bed, so if Anything—"Anything 'should come into *both minds"* it *Won't* be any *Problem* at all' as to *where* to *begin.*

So we *wrapped* it *up* in our *minds.* That has been over *Thirty Years* ago. And we're *still* married' and still at it. "Yess "*Lord.* (*It's all sex.*) We never *worry* or *interfere* with other *people's* Love *problems.* Because it's *no* good. You'll probably *lose* their *Friendship*, any way. Can you *imagine* these *Kids* of my neighborhood at my home listening and grinning as I was telling them about *Aunt Lucille's* and my *Beautiful* life together! They would have stayed *longer.* But their *mothers* commenced *calling* us on the *phone sayin* for us to send the *kids* home just a few doors away. Because it's time for their *supper.* Lucille called me at the same time to our dining room to have *my* supper also. I was a little *scarfish* (hongry) from Riding on our Bus *all night* and *half* of the *day.* So the Dressing Room Chat that I had with *Ceelie* (Lucille)—another *one* of my *Pet* Names that I *layed* on *Ol* Lucille during our *Sexy* years. The more we *wedged* in together which's' gotten *better each* time' I *commenced* to calling *Ol Lucille Moms. My Moms.* She's So Attentive, And she *reminds* me and *does* a lot of *things* just like my mother, *May Ann.* And since she *passed* in 1927' it seems as if *Lucille* has close *features* just like *May Ann*—Some of Lucille's ways and little *gestures* are just like my mother. Unconsciously it happen. Lucille—not knowing anything about it until I told her about it. And then she *did* feel proud.

Everybody in Harlem were glad to see us again—but *married* this time. Then I came to a *conclusion* that I must *set* Lucille down. Not just to be a *Housewife* or anything like that. I figured if we want the Comfortable Happiness that I seek with that girl, She must stay home. And Keep our *Citadel* (I *call's* it) with that *wall* to *wall* Bed' *Fresh* "n" *Ready* to *go* at *all* times. Like we first met' and Checking in a lot of Hotels with those *Twin* Beds, *my my* how Lucille + I suffered every time that we did the Vonce (sex) you know? We had to *tie* those *beds* by *their bed posts*, in order to have a little happiness while we're *Wailin"* (sex) *Ya Dig*? And *now—Old Wall* to *Wally"* (wall bed) is *just* what we'd' been *looking* for all *through* the years. The house where we live in Corona' Lucille bought it while I was traveling on the Road. The money that I could afford to send to her' After paying expenses at home' she would save as much as She could.' And when she saved enough for a Down Payment on a house' she came out here in Corona' And was very lucky to run into the *same* White family whom *their*

Children were *raised* with *Lucille* when she + her family lived in Corona in her young School days.

These White people were *moving* out—going to *Another Neighborhood.'* And when they found out that Lucille come *All* the way from Harlem out in Corona looking to buy a *house*, why' they were *so* glad to know that she liked *their* house and she told them that she would *buy* it—*Hmmm.* They *almost gave* her the *house* for *nothing*. And they didn't know anything about me. The house *was* (+ *still* is) so *high* powered' and *distinctive* looking' until' the night I came home off of the road—*Caught* a *Cab* Downtown' after we *unloaded* our Bus. I gave the *Cab* Driver the address and told him to *drive* me to this *address*. Corona is a *good half* hour *drive* from New York' by *'Car.* 30 minutes (maybe) by *Subway*. And *''Me'* I've never' *been* to this *house* before, why I could not tell him *anything* as far as' the directions' (etc.) how to *get* there. So the *Cab* Driver finally *found* the *house*. And when he looked around to the back of the Cab and said to me, ''O.K. this is the place.'' *One* look at that big *fine* house, and *right* away I said to the *driver ''Aw man quit Kidding'* and *take* me to the address that I'm looking for.'' It was in the *wee* hours in the *morning* and I was *real beat* for my *youth. Tired* as old *hell*. Lucille and the family were *all* in *bed* sound asleep. *Not* knowing *when* or *what* time that *Our Bus* would get into the City of New York. Anyway, I get up enough courage to get out of the Cab, and Ring the Bell. And sure enough the door opened and who stood in the doorway with a real thin silk Night Gown—*hair* in *Curlers*. To *me* she looked *just* like my *favorite flower'* a Red Rose. The *more'* Lucille *showed* me *around* the *house* the *more thrilled* I *got. Yea you hear?— I got''* (tee hee). Right then and I felt very grand over it all. A little *higher* on the *horse* (as we expresses it). I've always appreciated the ordinary good things. I noticed Lucille being the same way. Of course she and I have *our* little

11

LETTER TO LEONARD FEATHER

(SEPTEMBER 18, 1941)

Leonard Feather was one of many writers with whom Armstrong established mutually beneficial relationships. In this letter, Armstrong asks Feather to relay a request for some written arrangements of recent recordings he has made, since he has experienced the common twentieth-century phenomenon of audiences demanding to hear in person what they have grown accustomed to through recordings. Though other jazz musicians resented such demands, Armstrong happily obliged.

Feather has apparently asked Armstrong to reflect on the most important events in jazz during the past twenty-five years. Near the end of his life, Armstrong would respond to this question with a review of the golden days from his New Orleanian youth ("*Scanning the History of Jazz*"). But in 1941 his mind moves first to 1937, when he hosted radio broadcasts sponsored by Fleischmann's Yeast—one of many occasions upon which Armstrong broke the color barrier. (In a different setting, his wife Lucille broke the color barrier one year later; see the introduction to Chapter 10.) The radio hosting was an important step along Armstrong's path of participating in nationally organized sectors of the entertainment industry. Indeed, Armstrong's next thought about the most important events in jazz during the previous twenty-five years is of his participation in movies.

Atlanta Ga.
September, 18th, 1941,

Dear Feather;

'Man—I didn't know that you were waiting to hear from me again . . . And as much as I like to write—Why man—I would have been on you just like 'White is On Rice . . ha . . ha . . . Gee 'Gate I am really sorry if I kept you late . . . You know?—by taking so long to write . . . I'll try to speed up with my answerings from now on . . . Well How's everything else going with you these fine days? Are you still knocking yourself out in the dear old 'Apple? . . N.Y . . .

We're getting ready to play a swell dance here tonight for the colored folks and the white folks are invited as spectators and I'm tellin you Leonard you never seen such wonderful gatherings in all your life as they do'' all down in these parts . . . Honest they get along down here at these dances just like one 'beeg family . . . It would be 'kicks some times if you could 'Dig some of this jive so's you can realize just what I am talking about . . . And do these 'Cats Jitterbug . . . 'Whooooo' Weeeee . . . ha . . . ha . . . Alpha Kills me when she sits on the bandstand some night and watch them . . . She said she watches them for so long and concentrating on 'them too—she said she gets the 'swimmin in the head . . . ha . . . ha . . . So you can tell by that—that they really 'Jumps for Joy . . . No Foolin . . .

Oh yes—when you go to the office (Mr. Glaser's office) please tell him that all of the records that myself and band make should be arranged and given to me . . . Because these people hear those tunes on these Venders . . . And quite naturally when they come to my dances they request these tunes . . . Now tell Pops he don't have to have those spectacular (Ump) arrangements, etc . . . Just have them taken off the very same way we recorded them . . . George Washington (my trombone man) is very good for this sort of work . . . He did some work for me some time ago . . . I know for sure that he can take a tune off of the records—Note for Note . . . Now don't forget to tell Father Glaser about this because it's very important—I think

Courtesy Institute of Jazz Studies, Rutgers University.

. . . Of course I'm going to write Mr. Glaser and tell him about it also . . . But since I'm already writing to you I thought it a good idea to stipulate . . . 'Dig?. . . . .

That was real swell news when you told me that you are going out in Hollywood to help me out with my picture . . . Gee—that's swell Leonard . . . I don't know of anything that could 'Send me any better than that . . . To show you how glad I was to hear of it—I wrote to Mr. Elliott Paul the producer of this Flicker that I'm to make . . . And man—I sent you sky high . . . Honest I did . . . I told him—if there's anyone that knows about my life it's Leonard Feather . . . I also told him about the days when we all were in England . . . I also told him how to get in touch with you through Mr. Glaser in case he lose your address . . . Nice?. . . . .

Alpha and all of the boys said hello to you and the rest of the company . . . They all seemed as glad as I did to know that you will be there in good ole Hollywood . . .

I 'Dug'd that write up in the *Down Beat* about the Trumpet players and thought it was pretty nice . . .

Oh yes—what about this celebration—and the anniversary, etc. . ? . . . When is this supposed to happen? . . . As far as the most important events in Jazz during my 25 years—well the first one was when Pops booked me for my first commercial program over the—N.B.C.—for Flieshman's Yeast—(I guess that's the way you spell his name ha . . . ha.) [correct spelling is "Fleischmann"—ed.]. . . .

Then too—those pictures—"Pennies From Heaven"—"Artists 'N' Models"—"Everyday is a Holiday"—and that fine "Going Places". . . Jeepers Creepersly Speaking . . .

As far as the people that I've met during those 25 years—the important ones . . . Well—if I'd start to mentioning them—it would make a book as tall as you are . . . ha . . . ha . . . But I've actually met some swell 'Cats in my runnin up and down these highways and by ways . . .

And you talking about 'My—how times have changed . . . 'Man—you said a mouthful . . . I remember the times when there were so much work in New York until I was holding down Three Jobs . . . One was down town playing with Connie's Hot Chocolate Musical Comedy . . . I was the Hot Trumpet man in the Pit at that time playing under the direction of the then famous Leroy Smith . . . Oh Boy—Whata Show . . .

In this particular show I used to feature the Theme Song of the show called—"Ain't Misbehavin' " . . . I played this solo during the Entree act of the show . . . In other words—I played this tune between the First and Second Act . . . And take it from 'me 'Gate—it was really in there. . . .

Now that was one job . . . The other two were—after I'd finish the show down in the Hudson Theater—I'd rush immediately up town and do a Show at the Lafayette Theater—up in Harlem . . . Then from there I'd wind up down stairs at the Connie's Inn Cabaret. . . . . That's what one might call 'slinging a whole lots of 'Chops into one Trumpet . . . 'Huh? . . . . .

I wished I had time to just call about—oh well a whole gang of my recordings that I personally think were kinda good . . . AHEM . . . ha . . . ha . . . Now if anybody disagree with me—just tell them to forget it . . . After all—I'm talking to myself and I don't want any answer . . . ha . . . ha . . . Personally I like—"Memories of You"—"West End Blues"—"Ol' Man Mose"—"Swing That Music"—"Confessin' "—"Lazy River"—and—Oh Gawd—To tell the truth they're all—ALL REET with me . . . Every Old "Crow thinks her children are White as Snow . . . ha . . . ha . . . Well—that's the way I feel about my own records . . . All of my records 'Knocks' me out . . . After all—I am the public too . . . I criticizes myself too . . . When I find it necessary . . . Some people criticizes just to be saying something that's unbecoming—or—something like that . . . tee hee . . .

I went down to my home town New Orleans—of course you know . . . And as usual I had a swell time . . . In fact I had a much better time this time than before . . . Well for one thing—we had a day off which gave me some time to get around a 'Dig some of the folks whom I hadn't seen for—oh—years and years . . . And that good Gumbo they serve down there . . . *'M M—mmmmmm* . . . Makes' my big mouth run water just to think about it right now and I am almost a thousand miles away from—Deah Ol New Orleans . . .

I saw quite a few of the old timers (meaning the musicians) . . . And they certainly were glad to see me . . . They came to my dance that night—which was really something unusual for those fellows like 'Picou—'Manuel Manetta—'Maurice Durand—'Recou—and many more of the good good good boys from the old school . . . It's a grand feeling I'm tellin you . . . To have the health to still live and run into the boys whom you used to 'Swing with over Twenty Years ago . . . Why—if you ask me—'That is really Something. . . . .

I also saw the famous and fine man of the trumpet of over thirty years ago . . . And that man is none other than 'Bunk Johnson . . . I saw him in New Iberia when we played there . . . Leonard—he's over Sixty Years of age and he looks like anybody's 'Chippy . . . Marvelous—Huh? . . . Suppose you and I could keep breathing that long—you'd be a happy 'Cat—Eh?. . . . But between me and you 'Gate—I think I'm gonna 'Dig it—no foolin . . . After all—a man ain't no older than he feels . . . And most of that lies in his mind . . . And God knows—I keeps a young mind . . . I have to—to enjoy my trumpet the way I do . . . That's why I say—my trumpet even sounds good to me most of the times . . . tee hee . . .

Bunk was telling me that he had heard from Sidney Bechet in New York . . . And he was expectin to join Bechet real soon to make some recordings of the good old days . . . Now if this happens—it ought to be real good . . . Bunk was tellin me that he still remembers those good ol good ones that was written by Scott Joplin . . . You know?—"Grace 'N' Beauty"—"African Pas"—"Maple Leaf Rag"—etc . . . Aw—I used to play 'em 'all . . .

Well Leonard Ol Boy—I hate like hell to stop this letter to you . . . But on account of it's getting ready time (as we expresses it) . . . And I have to go to work . . . So until I hear from you or 'Dig You out 'thar' in Sunny California—I shall endeavor to do the Cutout . . . ha . . . ha . . . So take em slow and give my regards to Mr. Glaser and all of the folks of the office . . . And also the Hot Fans—Jitterbugs and the folks who loves' real music . . . Good luck always.

Am Red beans and Ricely Yours,
Louis Armstrong

12

LETTER TO BETTY JANE HOLDER

(FEBRUARY 9, 1952)

In this letter Armstrong writes about his infamous experience as King of the Zulus in 1949. During Mardi Gras festivities, he rode the float sponsored by the Zulu Aid and Pleasure Club, dressed outrageously in black-faced makeup and a parody of tribal garb. James Collier (1983: 311) suggests that the publicity generated from this incident served as a turning point in Armstrong's career. On the one hand, he became a genuine media "star." On the other hand, he was criticized for promoting vestiges of minstrelsy which, no matter how firmly grounded in New Orleanian tradition, seemed to outsiders like an embarrassing retreat from racial progress. As Dizzy Gillespie put it, "Louis is the plantation character that so many of us . . . younger men . . . resent" (*Down Beat*, July 1, 1949: 13).

Armstrong explains that he cherished the honor of King of the Zulus, since he grew up admiring the Zulu Aid and Pleasure Club. As the day approaches, he visits with old friends, who call him by childhood nicknames and emphasize the special nature of the coming event. Yet his description of how the makeup was applied reveals unease. He puts himself in a passive role: "No sooner that I had fallen asleep, when I felt something crawling all around my chops* (my mouth)—etc . . . It was a member of the Zulu Club, whom the President had sent to my hotel to—'make me up . . . You' know? Put all of the white stuff around my lips,—eyes, in fact, everywhere he could *swerve a brush*."

But immediately Armstrong recalls the same makeup having been put on his stepfather, twenty years earlier, and it is this sense of tradition as much as anything that made the event so special. Elsewhere, Armstrong recalls the importance of "masking" for his mother and his father during similar celebrations (see the Appendix). The practice of masking would seem to provide a useful reference for this event and for Armstrong's conception of entertainment, generally. One might relate masking to the shifting images that are associated with Armstrong—facial images that shift from moment to moment in a performance and public images that shift through the dramatically different phases of his career.

Riverside Hotel
Reno Nevada,

February, 9th, 1952

Mary had a little bear
The bear was mighty fine
Everywhere- 'Mary, went,
You'd, see her bear behind.

Dear Miss (Mrs.) Betty Jane Holder''

Received your fine' letter . . . And was really glad to get it . . . It came as a surprise . . . But 'Man, 'Whatta 'surprise.'' Especially when it comes, to telling, how thrilled I was, being the 'King of the Zulus on Mardi Gras Day . . . Several years ago, I witnessed those very fine moments . . . Moments, that I—as a lil, ol, kid, selling newspaper up and down Baronne Street—St. Charles Street—Canal Street, in fact, all of those busy streets where I used to love to hop on those fast street cars, selling ana hollering—''Paper-paper—read the New Orleans Item—paper paper''. . . And sometimes, the street car would not slow down, and the first time I went to jump off of one of them, I wasn't 'Hipped- to trotting a little bit when jumping off, something going as fast as they—and—' My 'Gawd'—I couldn't sit down for a 'whole week . . . ha ha . . .

The Zulus' Social Aid and Pleasure Club, was originated in the neighborhood that I was 'Reared I should say—Raised—? . . . I don't like the word 'reared. . . . . All of the members of the Zulus are people, for generations,—most of them—brought up right there around, Perdido *and* Liberty—Franklin Streets . . . So finally, I grew into manhood—ahem—and the life

Courtesy Hogan Jazz Archive, Tulane University.

long ambition, never did cease . . . I have traveled all over the world . . . And no place that I've ever been, could remove the thought, that was in my head,—that, someday, I will be the King of the Zulus,—my life long ambition . . . And there, bless my 'Lamb, I won it in the year of 1949 . . . Wow . . . 'Whatta wonderful feeling I had . . .

The night before the Mardi Gras parade we my band (the -All Stars-) played for a dance in New Iberia Louisiana . . . That was the last time we all saw the great trumpet man—Bunk Johnson . . . Bunk came to the dance (as he always does) when ever he saw the name—Lou—is—Armstrong in the lights, or the 'marquee—or, just a plain old sign. Bunk knew, he was as welcome as the flowers in May. . . . He used to sit in with us, every time he came . . . Sort of, made him feel good, and we too . . . I shall never forget the look, of happiness in Bunk's face, when I told him, that I was going to be the King of the Zulus' parade, the next day . . . He gave me a great big smile, and said—"Go—'On 'Dipper" . . . That's the 'nick name, the early settlers, of the Zulus' neighborhood, gave me when I was just a shaver (a small boy) Dippermouth . . . That's the name. . . . .

Bunk said, he wouldn't miss the Mardi Gras for the world . . . And he didn't either. . . . We finished playing the New Iberia, around two o'clock in the morning . . . And by the time we had a bite to eat (which every band does after a hard night of swinging)—by then, it was three A.M. . . . Then we tore out for New Orleans, by bus . . . Our chartered bus . . . We reached home (at the hotel where we were staying—the wife Lucille and I) it was six o'clock a.m.—so I thought I'd stretch the old frame—my body, for an hour or so. . . . No sooner that I had fallen asleep, when I felt something crawling all around my chops* (my mouth)—etc . . . It was a member of the Zulu Club, whom the President had sent to my hotel to—'make me up . . . You' know? Put all of the white stuff around my lips,—eyes, in fact, everywhere he could *swerve a brush*. . . . .

As much as I was not accustomed to this sort of, creepy feeling, I did remember my step father—having the same stuff, put on his face, some 20 years before I was the King. . . . So, after I realized, what was happening, I stretched out and went fast asleep, while he still swung the brush . . . What amused me the most about the whole thing at my hotel that morning, was when Earl Father Hines—who was playing the piano with my All Stars at the time, he and his wife Janie, came into my room looking for me to take a picture with his camera . . . And when Lucille pointed toward me, with all of this jive on my face, Earl's eyes got as big as saucers, saying "WHAT THA HELL IS THAT—?". . . . . He said it so loud, he awakened me . . .

It was time for me to get up and get dressed for the grand parade, and to meet the Barge, which Mr. Janckie—the great gravel man—loaned us each year we had our parade . . . Lucille, had a cute little secretary working for her at the time . . . Her name was Selma Heralda . . . And Selma lived next door from us, in Corona Long Island, where we have our home . . . Everybody were trying to help me, get into my Costume, etc, which was really a gem. The very best and finest material . . . Everything went down and fit perfect except for the hat . . . And for that reason,—all day long, I had trouble trying to keep that hat on my head . . . Wondering to myself—Hmm—there must be 'some way, to keep this, so 'N' so, hat on my big head. . . . Anyway—we had a real time, all over the city, throwing coconuts to the people, and saying hello, and waving to the old friends, etc. . . .

Just think—twenty thousand coconuts, which each member on my float threw to the crowd . . . I happened to look up on a porch where a young man was justa yelling to me, "Come on Satchmo" (meaning me) "throw one of those fine coconuts up here". . . And I taken a real good aim, and threw one at him, with all of my might . . . The guy waited until the coconut reached him and the coconut hit the tip of his finger, and fell down on a bran new Cadillac. . . . . . . 'Geeeee. . . . I just turned my head to the direction in front of me, just as nothin happened. . . . Wow . . . Close shave,—huh? . . . I shall never forget the incident, when our float reached Dumain and Claiborne Streets, and as high as I was sitting, I see straight down Claiborne street, for miles, seemingly, and the whole street were blocked with people waiting for the parade to come down their way . . . But instead—the float, turned the other direction . . . And—all of those people made one grand charge at once, toward the float. . . .

The real surprise of the day, was—when the float that I was on turned the corner, my eyes looked direct in to Hugues Panassié's . . . He's the President of the Hot Club de France . . . Paris France . . . His secretary Miss Madeleine Gautier was standing—eagerly waving with him. . . .

Panassié and Madeleine followed us, until we reached Orleans and Roman St. and it was getting rather late in the evening . . . Around six-thirty in the afternoon . . . And, with all of those people riding on top of my float with me, I'm sure, those four mules, when they looked around, in our direction as if to say, "Hey there—What goes—?". . . Just then, my float commenced to crumbling down to pieces. . . . . Ha ha ha . . . The extra people were my vocalist, Velma Middleton, who weighs, a good two hundred and fifty pounds—Big Sid Catlett, who was the drummer of the All Stars, that year—*Stuff* Crouch, a friend of mine who came all the way from Los Angeles California just to witness me doing my stuff on top of that float . . . And several others, along with six Zulu Members who were supposed to be up there in the first place . . . Now you can see, the load we had on those mules . . . And I, once being a teamster for the C.A. Andrews-Coal-Company, from Ferret and Perdido Streets,—making—fifteen cents per load—but I did—O.K. 'Anyway—I could easily understand those mules . . . Because, I used to—all but talk to 'mine (my mule) every morning, five o'clock, when I went to hitch him up to the coal cart I was driving. . . .

When I was a youngster, hanging around the corner of Liberty and Perdido—all of the all time great teamsters, took great interest in me . . . Taught me the ropes, as to how to load up my cart, without all but breaking my back in two . . . And they're the ones—especially my step father-'Gabe—he'd say to me, "Son, always have a kind word for your mule in the mornings when you'd go into his stall to hitch him up . . . Because, a mule is a very sensitive and stubborn animal . . . You'd might go into his stall one morning, and find him in one of those old nasty feeling—just like a human being, and he's liable to kick your brains out . . . Savvy??. . . . So, I never forgot that piece of advice . . . In fact, anything 'Gabe, and Joe Oliver had to tell me, I was always, ready to listen . . . They wouldn't tell me anything that wasn't right . . . That's why, I give Joe Oliver all the credit in the world, when it comes, to telling who went out of their way to show me things' on my trumpet. . . .

When that float broke down, Mardi Gras day, I was so glad to see Panassié (whom) I hadn't seen for quite some time . . . Since the last time I was in Paris France, playing concerts at the Salle Pleyel Concert Hall . . . A hall similar to the Carnegie Hall in New York . . . Panassié and secretary *stayed* with me the whole time their *visit* in this country permitted them . . . When we left New Orleans, we made a tour, all through Mississippi, and all the other points, down there in *Galilee* (south).— By them being from Europe, they did not pay any attention to, what's happening . . . Such as, white people going to colored dances, etc . . . You know, they did not know, because everywhere we played, he and his secretary would sit right up on the bandstand where they could hear that horn . . . Which was what they came all the way from France to hear . . . And the Law, who saw them sitting up there, did not say one word to them . . . And, Oh, was I happy . . . My My . . . The day before I mounted the float for the Zulus' Parade, I had a very fine afternoon with our great (sharp) Mayor DeLesseps . . . Oh, we had a ball at City Hall . . . His office was packed and jammed with the press—his friends and my friends, and I'm telling you Janie, ol, deah, we really did pitch a boogie woogie . . . The Mayor and I killed 'em, when he said to me, ''*Satch*'' P.S. that's a abbreviation, to Satchmo . . . The English People gave the short name Satchmo—because they thought I had more mouth. . . . . . . Getting back to our boy' (the Mayor of New Orleans)—when he said—''Satchmo I read in *Time* (Time magazine) where—you said—all you wanted, was to be the King of the Zulus and you were ready to die—??'' . . . I said, ''Yes Mayor, I do remember saying those words—but it ain't no use of the Lord taking me *literally*''. . . . . And the house came down with laughter . . . P.S. Did'ja' get the 'Laughter—?. . . .

I would like to say a whole lots more to you Jane . . . But, since this is my first letter to you, I won't wear my welcome out . . . That's one thing about me, when I start to writing, especially, to someone whom I really 'want to write to, huh,—'girl,—I can write until times get better . . . Of course, I remember you saying in your letter, that I should send in about six hundred words, etc . . . Of course I did not count them . . . And since I am here in Reno (not getting a divorce)—just doing a show, here at the Riverside Hotel, with my band,—I have to write between shows . . . And you can imagine, trying to write, and shaking hands with your fans at the same time. . . . But I managed to get in there, just the same. . . .

So, you can tell everybody, that Ol' Satchmo, has 'Octopus hands . . . I have my tape recorder right here by my right side, which I have, pretty near all of my recordings, on reels . . . So, when I listen to my records, I can get food for thoughts, since I'm writing my life's story . . . But I wouldn't miss a fine opportunity, to write you and let you know how thrilled I was to be the King of the Zulus . . . And I'd gladly *livit* (live it) over again, if I had the chance . . . In fact I'm looking forward to another year of it before I die . . . Hmmm??? . . . Who said something about dying . . . Tee hee.

So Janie, thanks very much taking your precious time out to drop me a line and let me in on the know as to what's happening there in my home town . . . As far as this New Orleans Item deal . . . I'd—just love to be able to get my hands on one of the articles, you said, would appear in the Item . . . Maybe, you will be kind enough to grant me this little favor,—Hmmm?. . . . Thanks in advance Jane . . . And I am so very happy to have had the opportunity to jot down a few 'gappings' for you . . . And most of all—I am very glad to meet you . . . You give a big hello to the Mayor, and all the rest of my Jazz Fans down there in my home town . . . And,—as the little boy who sat on a block of ice, said,—My Tale Is Told. . . . Yea . . . Goodnight and God Bless 'Ya'. . . .

Am Red beans and ricely yours,
Louis Armstrong

13
LETTER TO JOE GLASER
(AUGUST 2, 1955)

This letter reveals a side of Louis Armstrong that does not neatly conform to his public image. Writing to his manager, Joe Glaser, from the Moulin Rouge hotel in Las Vegas, Armstrong wants to "get my seriousness over with" before his wife Lucille arrives on a late-night flight. The seriousness involves a series of financial commitments that Armstrong wants Glaser to assume while Armstrong tours overseas. Armstrong liked to have his manager take care of all business arrangements, leaving him free to concentrate on performing. He was happy to give up control as long as he received regular and generous stipends. He knew that he could make more money under different contractual arrangements, yet he also knew how to assert his will upon occasion, as this letter reveals.

Armstrong needs Glaser to take care of payments to a "sweetheart and secretary," to a mistress (the name has been deleted from this edition) who, he thinks, has borne him a child, to in-laws, and to a friend. Anticipating Glaser's resistance, Armstrong spells out, as clearly as he can without being offensively blunt, that a trade is taking place: If Glaser wants him to go abroad on tour, then these payments must be made. Referring to previous conversations that must have involved similar situations, Armstrong throws Glaser's words back at him—"give me a little chance to Govern Myself Accordingly (your expression)." And he uses humor to lighten the situation: "I—Just, Love, Your, Checks, in, My POCKETS—''OH'' They look so *pretty*, until, I hate like hell to cash them. Honest to God, I usually keep them as long as I possibly Can. But Suddenly, some Situation raise its ''UGLY HEAD.'' And ''bye 'bye Joe Glaser's' signature."

Armstrong recalls advice given him by Black Benny during his youth: "always have a *White Man* (who like you) and can + will put his Hand on your shoulder and say—*''This is ''My'' 'Nigger''* and, Can't Nobody Harm' Ya." The anecdote allows Armstrong to say as directly as he can that he has chosen Glaser, not the other way around. No matter to what extent Armstrong may agree to give up business control as a means of coping with a racist society, he will control ultimately the hiring and firing of his manager. As if to compensate for his assertiveness, Armstrong calls Glaser his "Boss Man" and signs off as "Your Boy"; nevertheless, his demands are in place.

Moulin Rouge
Las Vegas, Nevada

Aug. 2nd 1955

Dear Mr. Glaser''

Am sorry that I have to write this letter with a pen, but, on arriving at the air port in Las Vegas yesterday, My typewriter fell from on top of all, that luggage that was on the truck, And the ''Jolt''Sprung' everything. Tch, Tch, isn't it A Drag? And I wanted so badly to swing a lot of *Type Writing*, ''Gappings'' on ya'' Of course, they're fixing it up for me. So, I Guess, that's all that matters. I like to say that I hope, *Moms our dear Mother* (Mrs. Glaser) is feeling better. She is, Such A Wonderful Person. We (Lucille + I) love her very much. And you too. I know you are quite surprised to get a letter from 'ol Satchmo—since you haven't heard from him in a long time. I like to write you Daddy, but, you keep my 'ol ass 'So Busy' until I only have time to *'Shhhit Shhave* and *'Shower''* Ha. Ha. But I Just love it. When, one keep busy' they usually forget about, old age. Which Seems very logical to me.

But what I am really writing you for' Lucille (my darling) is arriving here at 1148—P.M. Las Vegas time. So I thought I'd get my seriousness over with you before she gets here. First—I want to make myself very Clear.'' You know deep down in your heart, that I love my wife Lucille + She love's Me. Or else we wouldn't been together this long. Especially' doing the Crazy things that I usually do for *Kicks*. That's why I love her, because she's smart. The Average woman would have ''Quit' my 'ol ass—long long ago. The Woman understands me and there's no, ifs' and ans'

From the collections of the Music Division, Library of Congress. Courtesy of the Music Division, Library of Congress.

about it. That's when I explained to her, the reason why "Sweets." And, when we first saw each other up in Montreal Canada we had no intentions about Sex. But—after we had been together sitting in my room, talking about everything in General—Some how, 'it *dawned on us* that we both hadn't had Any *Ass* in ages. With Lucille riding Around in her big and beautiful Cadillac, and would only travel if persuaded by "you, period. Which was, O.K. I still enjoyed Blowing my horn every night Cunt or No Cunt. Sweet's him, Slim, havin been dead for several years—going into Seclusion, until we both met, after the Show in *Montreal.* I'll never forget it. As much as she tried to talk me out of it—I just *Kept On* laying those hot Kisses up on her fine "Chops." When two people are in a room by themselves, Kissing will lead to fucking every time. P.S. Of course Sweets + I didn't *Swing* but once in Montreal. Sort of "Warm""Up." Once in Toronto—Minneapolis, etc.—But where we really *Whaled* and that Cute little baby Girl was made—was in Las Vegas—during the time when we were appearing at the *Sands Hotel*—And Robert Merrill and I did that *fine* finale together. Every night' we *Whaled.* I mean, I really *Grined* in that Cunt. I Could feel it Just as good when I *Struck Oil*—And planted that cute little Baby. Oh Mr. Glaser You + Dr. Schiff have got to see that baby. You see—? I don't live to do Anything wrong. It's so much easier, and more wonderful to do things Right. 'I like to see people happy. They've" made me happy All through these beautiful years. And still are. All the Money in the world, Couldn't make me any happier than I am right now—this minute. Why? Because I've Just Came from the bathroom taking A Good "Sh—t" And, what's any better than A Good Sh—t—?—*Hm*?

A Man Just don't have to be with a woman all the time to feel good. But, it's so grand + Glorious to be with a woman, so why fight it, As Billy Kyle expresses it. That's why I have several Chicks that I enjoy *whaling with* the same as I do with Lucille. And She's, Always had the Choicest *Ass* of them All. But regardless of the *Genuineness* of *Asses*—I was taught when I was a "teenager' hanging around Gamblers, Pimps, People of All Walks of life, they all loved the way I played My *Horn"* and they did everything within power for me, an, "innocent kid at that time, Even to the whores, they didn't do, or, tell me anything wasn't right. When the older *Cats*, such as *Black Benny* whom was loved by everybody in My Neighborhood—these are the same words Black Benny said to me, when I was getting ready to go up North (Chicago), He said *"Dipper"—Abbreviation* for

Dipper Mouth which was my cute little pet name at the time. He said to me, "You're, going out into this wide wide world. Always remember, no matter how many times you get Married.— Always have another woman for a Sweetheart on the outside. Because, *Mad* Day might Come, or she could be the type of woman whose Ego, After realizing that you *Care* deeply' may—for no reason at all, try giving you a hard time. And with no other Chick whom you're Just as fond of—on the out side—two Chances to one you might do Something "*Rash*' which is a *Mild Word*." I find—the advice—Benny gave me—turned out, to be very logical. Because I can look back through all of my marriages, with the Comfort of my "*horn*" (trumpet). I" told All, those Bitches' when ever they'd start showing they '*Asses*: "You Can go to *Hell*." Because, I have my horn to keep me warm. Something else Black Benny said to me, came true—He said (to me) "*Dipper*, As long as you live, no matter where you may be—always have a *White Man* (who like you) and can + will put his Hand on your shoulder and say—"*This is "My" Nigger*" and, Can't Nobody Harm' Ya." By, Sweets having that baby for me, gave Lucille one of the best *ass* whippings in her life. As nice + sweet + as wonderful as she is she still has a sense of "*Aires*' that I've never particularly cared for—Being raised around people who were, just plain human beings, and love (at least) respect for each other. Not from the Attitude that you're just a Musician a low trumpet player, Smokes, Reefers, etc. That, I am more than you type, which is all *Bullsh—t*. Which Goes to show, that I Can tolerate Anything, as long as it doesn't interfere with my trumpet.

See ol Man—I am saying these Words to say this—I heard by the Grape Vine (band rumors) that you are getting ready to send us down to *Australia* then direct to Europe—After we leave Los Angeles the finish of our engagement at the *Crescendo*. Which would be Just fine. I am in the best of shape—I am fit as a fiddle—ready for love. P.S. You Can tell by Sweet's baby—Tee Hee. But Seriously Mr. Glaser there's one thing that's going to be a big *drag*—And that is these 'Personal bills of mine. Which runs up to $1100.00 per month. I don't care how soon we leave—where' we're going. Just if you'll, Personally, Pay these Bills while I am over seas, It's alright with me. And for Godsake stop telling Lucille when ever you give me, extra Money. I give her a good healthy Allowance, (which you also, set—) thanks. I also, give her extra Money. What ever' you + Lucille get together, concerning our home has no "bearing" on this Nine hundred (etc) dollars that I have been paying out my small allowance after Lucille + the Hotels, Pugh [Doc Pugh, Armstrong's valet], Laundry, Cleaners, get theirs. I manages to gladly pay.

Now here are the *Bills* as follows. I want you to see that *Sweets* + Baby' get *one hundred per week* [''fifty'' was added to ''one hundred,'' then crossed out—ed.]—or you can send her, a month's gappings, now + pay her monthly. Either way daddy, I want her to get this money the whole time, I am abroad. Now—the next Monthly Bill is my Sweetheart + Secretary Miss, Velma Ford my sharp Chick whom you met while she was helping with my Satchmo story. She's very good at taking Dictation, etc. I gave her a real beautiful ''Fleetwood Cadillac'' for a Christmas Present. Oh, She look' so sharp in that Car Pops. I Paid $2200.00, down and the ''Man (one of my fans—car salesman'') was nice enough to set my Payments as low as he could. He brought the installments down to, one hundred—sixty one dollars and some odd cents. The Payments on the Car is to be Paid on the 12th of every Month until Paid. I usually send Miss Ford a check for $200.00 (two hundred), instead of the amount of $161.00, etc. The extra Change helps her with her Monthly Bills, around her (Beat up) Beauty shop. Tee Hee. Of course, Daddy, you being a strictly business man, it must be *impossible* to realize *whatta* thrill I get seeing that fine young Chick, sit her big fine brown ass into that fine Cadillac—*whow*.

These next two Bills won't be so high. But Just the same, they've 'got to be Paid. If I could send this money back from Europe, I wouldn't bother you at all my dear Boss Man. Of course, you already know about the Car, which is a Chrysler, New Yorker, that I bought for my dear and *Bosom* Pal, Stuff Crouch. Fine boy, that *Stuff*. Would give you his shirt off of his back. His Car's almost paid for. Just a few payments more. Of course, you can check with all of these people. I'll give you their Address's—. Julius—Stuff—Crouch. Send to him, $150.00 per month. Now last but not least—There's another Bran New Chrysler New Yorker, I've Just bought for my Brother + Sister in law Mr. + Mrs. Charlie Phipps. The Monthly Payment on his Car runs around $150.00, the same as Stuff's. I will Give you the correct address on Charlie's bank. Then you can mail it there yourself.

Well, I guess that's about it. Other than send me some Cash money out here, so I can weather these big Bills while Lucille + I are out here. And which will furnish me with a little smile to take Down in ''Australia, then to good 'ol' Europe, the Countries that I dearly love. So, Pops, do these, "essential things for me, and I will be prepared to stay Away from America, as long as you can find bookings for me. All you have to do is to *Sorta* give me a little chance to Govern Myself Accordingly (your expression). So that's why I am Asking you for some Cash Money. I want to Govern myself Accordingly. "YA DIG?" Of course—if you should change your mind, concerning the European as to Cancel them—etc—Just forget about the whole thing. Forget I mentioned it. But, when ever you send me to Europe, these personal of mine I've Just mentioned still stands + still has to be taken care of by one of us. Just the same—trip or no trip I could use a little help out here.

Dig these addresses.
1. the 1st of the month—$400.00 per month
[. . .] (Mother of Satchmo's baby)
2200 Madison Ave.
Apt. 10—F
New York

2. 12th of month—$200.00 per month
Miss Velma Ford (Fleetwood Cadillac sedan)
266 Second St.
Richmond Calif.

3. 25th of month
Julius "Stuff" Crouch (Chrysler New Yorker)
Address—122 West—53rd, St.
Los Angeles, Calif.

4. 1st of the month
Charlie Phipps
Later—for address.
New York.
Chrysler—New Yorker

Louis, Satchmo, Armstrong
Address above—
A rented beautiful Cadillac car.

Well, ′ol ′man, I don′t think, I′ve left not one thing unturned. ″Nay Nay.″ The ″Joint will really ′Jump—when that frantic, ″Hampton,″ open here at the Moulin Rouge where Lucille + I stay. Everybody seem to be looking forward. ″Oh Yes.″ On our World Wide tour, if we should go to *Israel*, see that we *play* there for *nothing* also. If a broken ass *″Sommitch″* like Lionel Hampton can afford it, so can I. I′m very serious. Of course, it′s Cheap *Notoriety* but, Anything ″Goes′ with an, Ass hole, like, him. Don′t fail to write me immediately. Let me Know ′your plans. If we should go to Europe direct from Australia, why, we′ll have Lucille at the finishing of our engagement here in *Vegas*—spend the week packing our overseas clothes, while I play the week in San Francisco Calif. And—Meet me in Los Angeles the week that we play the Crescendo. ″Right? Then we Can ″Cutout″ for a world tour if necessary. All I ask of you—is Answer right away which will give ′ol′ Satchmo lots of time to get himself Straight. Then You Can Keep us in Europe, til the Dodgers win a World Series. Regards to the Staff. Look into your drawers real good. There might be some old A—S—C—A—P—or, *etc.* checks, all, old forgotten and stuff. I—Just, Love, Your, Checks, in, My POCKETS—″OH″ They look so *pretty*, until, I hate like hell to cash them. Honest to God, I usually keep them as long as I possibly Can. But Suddenly, some Situation raise its ″UGLY HEAD.″ And ″bye ′bye Joe Glaser′s′ signature. ″HM . . . It has been such a real Pleasure writing to you, Boss. Hope, I didn′t bore you. Just wanted to let you know. As long as I am Slated to blow this Trumpet don′t spare the Horses. I love the instrument. *Then too*—the *loot* looks good in my pocket. P.S. so I can gladly, put it—in—the—Harry Bank. *UMP*. It′s, near the time for me to go and meet Lucille. So I′ll Close—Now that I have made myself very Clear. Book Anywhere—Anytime. Just let me know what′s happening—in time. I′m sure—you ″Dig me″ Huh?

From Your Boy
Goodnight + *Love*,

Louis Armstrong

14
"LOMBARDO GROOVES LOUIS!"
(1949)

As *Metronome*'s introductory paragraph for this story explains, Armstrong was given a "blindfold test" by Leonard Feather, in which he was asked to identify and comment on six unnamed recordings. A similar article was published one month later. Predictably, for 1949, the test was set up to give Armstrong an opportunity to voice contempt for Bebop. The following month Armstrong critiqued Dizzy Gillespie, Miles Davis, and Lennie Tristano, quipping: "this is all right according to the current trend, but not for no jazz fan." Armstrong's management vigorously promoted the Bebop–Armstrong controversy as a media event (see Appendix).

More interesting than Armstrong's scorn, perhaps, is his praise. His admiration for blues and Swing needs no explanation, for these are the two styles in which he excelled from early on. But the high praise of "eight stars" for Guy Lombardo may be surprising. Armstrong often expressed his admiration for "sweet music" generally and for Lombardo particularly. He says a little more about Lombardo in an interview published in *Down Beat* (Armstrong 1948): "It's always the same thing in all languages. You make a pretty tune and you play it well and you don't have to worry about nothing. If you swing it, that's fine, and if you don't, well look at Lombardo and Sinatra and they're still not going hungry. We'll be around when the others will be forgotten." According to James Collier (1983: 219), Armstrong's admiration for Lombardo was shared by other African American musicians during the 1920s; furthermore, the admiration was mutual, to the degree that Lombardo invited Armstrong and Zutty Singleton to perform with him in 1928.

The following is an introduction to Armstrong's comments, by Leonard Feather: "Louis was sitting out on the stoop of his neat, cozy home in Corona, Long Island, playing with a happy group of neighborhood children. He had a few days off, one of his rare chances to relax and forget music for a while. It seemed almost shameful to drag him through the ordeal of a blindfold test, especially since he's one of those good-natured people who hate to stick their necks out. However, before long Louis got warmed up to his subject and talked freely and forcefully; in fact, he gave me enough material to divide this piece into two installments. And here, as near to verbatim as possible, is what he had to say."

The Records*

1. Piano sounds like Count Basie . . . that trumpet has some of Roy's phrases . . . now this one, could this be Frank Galbraith? . . . It's a darn good record, ain't a thing wrong with it. Sounds like at least two trumpets; if there's three, a couple of 'em sound pretty much alike. Well, being a jazz fan, I'd give that at least a trey.

2. Ah, the blues! . . . the blues will last forever. You can hear from the first note that this has *soul.* The bopsters will probably think it's old fashioned. That clarinet is trying to tell a story—you can *follow* him. You can give that four stars right off. You can dance to it! In bebop, they don't know which way they're going to turn.

3. Now you take this trombone solo . . . Jack Teagarden will take a solo like that, and it'll be so much prettier, it'll say something, and it'll be just as hot. This thing looks like everybody is trying to kill themselves. That kind of music is liable to start a fight! That's Woody, isn't it? I guess musicians would dig this more than the untrained ear . . . I liked Norvo, he has that essence that I appreciate. Two stars.

4. For a moment it sounded like Johnny Dodds; for a moment it

From *Metronome*, September 1949.

*Leonard Feather: "These are the records which Louis Armstrong heard during his blindfold test. He was given no information whatever about them either before or during the hearing of the records. 1. Little Jazz Trumpet Ensemble. "Fiesta in Brass" (Keynote). Roy Eldridge, Joe Thomas, Emmett Berry, trumpets; Johnny Guarnieri, piano. 2. Bunk Johnson. "Franklin Street Blues" (Victor). Johnson, trumpet; George Lewis, clarinet. 3. Woody Herman. "Keeper of the Flame" (Capitol). Bill Harris, trombone; Terry Gibbs, vibes. 4. Art Hodes. "Way Down Yonder in New Orleans" (Blue Note). Hodes, piano; Wild Bill Davison, cornet; Sidney Bechet, clarinet; Fred Moore, drums. 5. Benny Goodman. "Sometimes I'm Happy" (Victor). Arr. Fletcher Henderson. Bunny Berigan, trumpet; Goodman, clarinet. Rec. 1935. 6. Guy Lombardo. "Always" (Decca)."

sounded like Ed Hall. That trumpet wouldn't be Dominique, would it? Wingy? This thing gets a good mood . . . Sounds like Baby Dodds on drums. Piano didn't impress me . . . they're touching them pianos up a little different nowadays. Trumpet's all right; but he didn't make them phrases Bunk made—he didn't hurt himself. Give it three stars.

5. This has a nice, easy swing . . . that's swing music, hot music, whatever you want to call it. It's done up with 'tonation, everything . . . like a basketball team, everybody passing the ball just right. The trumpet phrases a lot like Bunny Berigan. I believe it is Bunny. *(Sax chorus)* Mmmm, that's pretty, this reminds me of when we used to play them good old dance numbers. Real good musicianship here. Sounds like Benny Goodman on clarinet. Four, man!

6. Give this son of a gun *eight* stars! Lombardo! These people are keeping music alive—helping to fight them damn beboppers. You know, you got to have somebody to keep that music sounding good. Music doesn't mean a thing unless it *sounds* good. You know, this is the band that inspired me to make "Among My Souvenirs." They inspired me to make "Sweethearts on Parade." They're my inspirators!

IV. "Music Has No Age":

Late Years in Corona, New York

"Just want to say that music has no age. Most of your great composers–musicians–are elderly people, way up there in age–they will live forever. There's no such thing as on the way out. As long as you are still doing something interesting and good. You are in business as long as you are breathing. Yeah."

15

LETTER TO L/CPL. VILLEC

(1967)

This letter was written to a Marine stationed in Vietnam, who must have written to Armstrong and expressed his fondness for jazz. Armstrong responded with one of his most direct testimonies about the power of music. The references to religious music are similar to those made by other jazz musicians, though rarely by Armstrong. To conclude the letter Armstrong quotes the inspirational "You'll Never Walk Alone" from *Carousel* by Rodgers and Hammerstein, revealing the broad range of his musical tastes.

34–56–107 St.
Corona New York'
U.S.A

Dear L/Cpl, Villec''

I'd like to 'step in here for a 'Minute or 'so' to ''tell you how much—I 'feel to know that 'you are a 'Jazz *fan*, and 'Dig' 'that 'Jive—the 'same as '*we* 'do, ''yeah.'' ''*Man*—I carry an 'Album, 'loaded with '*Records*—'Long playing 'that is. And when I am '*Shaving* or 'Sitting on the 'Throne with '*Swiss Kriss*' in me—*That* Music 'sure 'brings out those 'Riffs 'Right Along with 'Swiss Kriss, which I 'take 'every night or when I *go* to bed. '*Yeah.* I

Courtesy of The John C. Browning Collection.

give myself a 'Concert with those 'records. 'Music is 'life it'self. What would this 'world be without 'good music? No matter 'what kind it is.

It 'all came from the Old 'Sanctified 'Churches. I can remember—'*way* back in the 'old days in 'New Orleans, La—'My home town. And I was a little Boy around 'ten years old. My Mother used to take me to 'Church with her, and the Reverend ('Preacher that is') used to '*lead* off one' of those 'good *ol* good '*Hymns*. And before you realized it—the 'whole 'Congregation would be ''*Wailing*—'Singing like 'mad and 'sound *so* 'beautiful. 'I 'being a little boy that would ''Dig'' 'Everything and 'everybody, I'd have myself a 'Ball in 'Church, *especially* when those 'Sisters 'would get 'So 'Carried away while ''Rev'' (the preacher) would be 'right in the 'Middle of his 'Sermon. '*Man* those 'Church 'Sisters would '*begin* 'Shouting 'So—until their 'petticoats would '*fall* off. Of course 'one of the 'Deacons would 'rush over to her and 'grab her—'hold her in his 'Arms (a sorta 'free 'feel) and 'fan her until 'she'd '*Come* 'to.

Then there were those ''Baptisms—that's when someone wants to be *converted* by Joining the 'Church and get '*religion*. So they have to be '*Baptized*. 'Dig this—I remember 'one Sunday the 'Church had a 'great big *Guy* they had to 'Baptize. So these 'Deacons all 'Standing in this 'River—in 'Water up to their *waist* in their 'white 'Robes. They had 'Baptized 'several 'women and a few 'Men—'saved their 'Souls. When in 'Walks' a '*Great* 'big' 'burly '*Sinner*' who came down the line. So—'these 'Deacons whom were 'very 'strong 'themselves, they grabbed 'hold of this '*Cat* and said to him as they 'ducked him down into the water, as they let him up they asked him—''*Brother* 'do you 'Believe?'' The Guy didn't say 'anything—Just looked at them. So they 'Ducked him down into that 'River again, 'only they 'held him down there a 'few minutes 'Longer. So when the 'Deacons looked in the guy's *eye* and said to him—''Do you 'Believe?'' This Guy finally 'answered—he said ''*Yes*—I Believe you '*Son of Bitches trying* to '*drown me*.''

P.S. I guess you think I'm 'Nuts. 'Nay 'Nay.' I only 'mentioned these incidents because it all was 'built around 'Music. In fact, it's 'All Music. ''You 'Dig? The 'Same as we did in my 'Home Town 'New Orleans'—those 'Funeral Marches etc. ''Why '*Gate*'' '*Villec*, we 'played those 'Marches with 'feeling from our 'hearts. 'All the way to the Cemetery—'Brass Band of course. The 'Snare drummer would put a 'handkerchief under the 'snares of his 'drum to 'deaden the 'Sound while 'playing on the way to the Cemetery—''Flee as a Bird.'' But as 'soon as the 'preacher 'say ''Ashes to 'Ashes—'Dust to 'Dust''—the ''*Snare Drummer* Commence 'pulling the handkerchief from his 'drum, and make a 'long roll' to 'assemble everybody, including the members of the 'dead man's 'Lodge—or 'Club. 'Then we'd 'return 'back to the 'headquarters 'playing ''Didn't he 'Ramble'' or ''When the Saints Go Marching In.'' *You 'See? 'Still Music.''*

I said 'All of that to Keep 'Music in your 'heart the 'same as 'you're 'doing. And '*Daddy*—you '*Can't* 'go 'wrong. 'Myself and my 'All Stars' are 'Playing here at the 'Harrods 'Club (Reno) for 'Three weeks. My 'wife 'Lucille has 'joined me here. The 'rest will do her *lots* of *good.* She was 'operated on for a 'Tumor, about the 'Middle of 'July. She's *improving* 'very 'Rapidly. Her 'Doctor who 'operated on her at the 'Beth 'Israel Hospital' in New York told her—'She could go to 'Reno and 'spend some time if 'you (Lucille) + your 'husband (*Satchmo*) 'promised to 'behave 'yourselves and 'don't try to 'do the ''*Vonce*'' (''meaning '*Sex*). I 'Said—''Doc I 'Promise—But I'll 'Just 'touch it 'lightly every 'morning—to see if *it's* 'still 'there.'' 'Ha 'Ha. 'Life's 'sweet. 'Just the 'thought that 'Lucille is 'through with her 'little 'Hindrance—and ''soon ''be *well* and 'happy—'be 'her '*lil 'ol 'cute 'self* 'again—'Just ''knock's' *me out.*

'Well 'Bre'r 'Villec,' I guess I'll '*put* it 'down, and get some '*shut* eye.'' *It's* the '*Wee* 'hours in the 'Morning. *I've 'Just* 'finished 'Work. I am *too 'tired* to '*raise* an '*eye 'lid. Tee hee.* So I'll leave this little message with you. ''*Here goes'*

When you 'Walk—through a 'Storm—
Put your '*Head—up 'high*—
And 'Don't be Afraid of the 'Dark—
At the 'End of a 'Storm—
Is a 'Gol-den 'Sky—
And a Sweet *Silver* 'Song—
Of a 'Lark—
'Walk—'on—through the 'Wind—
'Walk—'on—through the 'Rain—
Though your '*Dreams* be ''Tossed and 'Blown—
'Walk—'on—'Walk—'on—
With 'Hope in your heart
And 'You'll '*Nev-er* 'Walk '*A-'lone*—

You'll *'Nev-er 'Walk A-lone*—
(one more time)
'Walk—'on—'Walk 'on—with 'Hope in your 'heart—And 'you'll
Nev-er 'Walk *'A-lone*—'You'll *'Nev-er 'Walk—'A————lone*. ''Savvy?

Give my regards to the fellows that's in your company. And the other fellows too. And now I'll do you 'Just like the 'Farmer did the 'Potato—I'll 'Plant you 'Now and 'Dig you 'later. I'll 'Close now. It's a *real* 'Pleasure 'Writing—'You.

''Swiss Krissly''

Satchmo
Louis Armstrong

16

"SCANNING THE HISTORY OF JAZZ"

(1960)

Asked by *The Jazz Review* in 1960 to "scan" the history of jazz, Armstrong reflects first on the golden age of his youth. He then comments on more recent and less desirable music—"modern slop." Not to end sourly, he offers a story (a simpler, less personal version is told in "The Satchmo Story") that explains by analogy his appreciation of a great deal of music, even when it is less than first-rate. Just as the sister in church appreciated the inferior preacher, since she could "look *over* his *shoulder* and see *Jesus just the same*," so Armstrong discovers the superior qualities of a great musician like Joe Oliver shining through music played by inferior musicians—as long as they "display their *willingness* to play as *best* they could." It is a powerful analogy that sheds light on Armstrong's musical and spiritual values.

The word 'Jazz,' as far as I can see or can remember, was [not used—ed.] when I was a little boy, five years old. The year of 1905. In those days it was called *"Rag Time Music."* And when ever there was a *dance* or a *Lawn Party* the Band, consisted of Six Men, would stand in front of the place on the Side Walk and play a half hour of good rag time music. And *us* kids would stand or dance on the other side of the street until they went inside. That was the only way that we young kids could get the chance to hear those great musicians such as Buddy Bolden—Joe Oliver (cornet—my idol), Bunk Johnson (cornet), Freddie Keppard (cornet), Henry Allen Sr. (cornet + his brass band), Old Man *Moret* (and his Excelsior brass band—cornet wonder and leader at "60"), Frankie Duson (trombone), Kid Ory (trom), And a whole lot of the other players who will for ever live in my mind as the greatest musicians that I have ever heard since I was big enough to realize what was happening. Even to the Brass Bands down in my home town New Orleans, to witness them playing a funeral march, will make something inside of you just 'tinkle. Even to a 6–8–march, they always expressed themselves, and their very souls in the music. Joe Oliver (cornet—my idol) and Manuel Perez (cornet), had a Brass Band by the name of the Onward Brass Band. And—'My 'My, how they could play in the street parades & funerals. [. . .]

Of course there were many other greats even before my time, and my days of the wonderful music that every musician were playing in New Orleans. But to me Joe *King* Oliver was the greatest of them all. He certainly didn't get his right place in the mentionings in Jazz history as he so rightfully deserved. He was a Creator, with unlimited Ideas, and had a heart as big as a whale when it came to helping the underdog in music, such as me. I was just a kid, Joe saw I had possibilities and he'd go out of his way to help me or any other ambitious kid who were interested in their instrument as I was. When he played his cornet, there were always happiness. And a certain closeness that he gave out whenever he played and whatever he played. Take "Dipper Mouth Stomp," for instance, no one living today could express themselves while playing that tune like Joe Oliver did. [. . .]

Of course there have been many styles in music since those days and in my younger days, such as Bop—Music of tomorrow—"progressive," "cool," etc. But not anyone of them styles have *im*pressed me as *Oliver*. And the *good ol* musician played in those days what I am talking about. The *tail gate* those *street parades*, *funerals*, *lawn parties*, Balls, they're called *Dances* nowadays. We didn't resort to different styles, etc., we just played good *ragtime music*, *sweet* when necessary. All these different new styles of this day doesn't do anything for the up + coming youngsters and they leaves not *any*thing for the kids to derive on, like the old timers did for us. Ever since this new stuff has been in port, I myself has been for ever so long—trying to figure out what the *modern* musicians trying to *prove*. And the only solution that I came to is, the majority of them are inferior musicians. Where there would be a real *solid note* to be *hit right* on the *nose*, they would make a *thousand* notes, rather than attempt that *one*. *Screeching* at a *high note* and *praying* to God that they'd *hit* it. The results is a very few musicians are working nowadays. The public itself gotten so tired of hearing so much *modern slop* until they refused to continue paying those big checks. And now if you'll notice it, only the *fittest* are *surviving*. No matter *where—who* I play with, I never forget my *first love*—real good music. That's why I am at home, when I am playing *any* kind of music. Most of the fantastic players of today can't even *read music*. They never did want to. All they want to do is *scream*. And if they don't watch out, *I'm gonna scream*, right along with the *public*.

Always remember—Louis Armstrong never bother about what the other fellow is playing, etc. A musician's a musician with me. Yea—I am just like the *Sister* in our Church in N.O., my home town. One Sunday our pastor whom we all loved happened to take a Sunday off and sent in another preacher who wasn't near as good. The whole congregation "frowned on him"—except one Sister. She seemed to enjoy the other pastor the same as she did *our* pastor. This aroused the Congregation's curiosity *so much*—until when Church service was over they all rushed over to this *one Sister* and asked her *why* did she enjoy the substitute preacher the *same* as our regular one? She said, "Well, when *our pastor preach*, I can look right through him and see *Jesus*. And when I hear a preacher who's *not* as good as ours—I just look *over* his *shoulder* and *see Jesus just the same*." That applies to me all through my life in music ever since I left New Orleans. I've been just like that Sister in our Church. I have played with quite a few musicians who weren't so good. But as long as they could hold their instruments *correct*, and display their *willingness* to play as *best* they could, I would look over their shoulders and see *Joe Oliver* and several other great masters from my home town. So I shall now close and be just like the little boy who sat on a *block* of *ice*—*My Tale is Told*. Tell all the Fans and *All* musicians, I love *Em Madly*.

Swiss Krissly Yours
Louis Armstrong Satchmo

17
"OUR NEIGHBORHOOD"
(CA. 1970)

During the last years of his life, Armstrong loved to write at his house in Corona, New York. Phoebe Jacobs (quoted in Balliett 1994: 75), a friend who visited him often, observed how important his hobby was to him: "His real therapy was writing. He'd say to me, 'You lick the envelopes and the stamps, I'll do the writing.'" In this document, Armstrong describes domestic life with Lucille, his neighbors, their favorite Chinese restaurant, and their dogs, Trumpet and Trinket. His warm feelings for the Corona community are clearly stated, even while he acknowledges the difficulty of finishing his Chinese dinner.

Our Neighborhood

When my wife Lucille + I moved into this neighborhood there were mostly white people. A few Colored *families*. Just think—through the (29) years that we've been living in this house' we have seen just about (3) generations come up on this particular block—107 Street between 34th + 37th Ave. Lots of them have grown up—Married' had Children. Their Children + they still come and visit—Aunt Lucille + Uncle Louis. And when there's *Death* in our block Lucille Always Bake a Turkey—Ham, *etc.*, put it in a big basket and take it over to the house—so the people who come and sit up with the Deceased will have Sandwiches, coffee, etc. Recently (8)

Used by permission of Louis Armstrong House and Archives at Queens College/CUNY.

people has *died* since Louis Armstrong came out of the Hospital. Even the new neighbors get to know us. And we Respect each other greatly. When (Pops) was sick and just out of the Hospital—nobody bothered him and kept very quiet so that he wouldn't be disturbed. Now that he has recuperated—feel good—*blowing* his horn every evening before supper with his Doctor's permission' the whole neighborhood rejoice at hearing his horn everyday. And when (Pops) miss blowing his horn, a couple of days, the neighbors, will call on the phone saying "Is (Pops) OK?—We haven't heard his horn for a few days. Is there anything wrong?" Then Lucille will tell them, "No *Pops* is alright. He's just been busy doing other things' such as Interviews in his *Den* for his Fans—all over the world, which pleases them very much. That's why *Lucille* + *Pops* feel that we should [not—ed.] move. We don't think that we could be more relaxed and have better neighbors any place else. So we stay put. After all—we have a very lovely home. The house may not be the nicest looking front. But when one visit the Interior of the Armstrong's home' they' see a whole lot of comfort, happiness + the nicest things. Such as *that Wall to Wall Bed*—a Bath Room with Mirrors *Everywhere'* Since we are *Disciples* to Laxatives. A *Garage* with a magic up + down Gate to it. And of course our Birthmark *Car'* a Cadillac' (Yea). The Kids in our Block just thrill when they see our garage gate up, and our fine Cadillac *ooze* on out. They just rejoice and say, "Hi—Louis + Lucille—your car is so beautiful coming out of that raise up *gate*," which knocks' me out.

There's a Chinese Restaurant in Corona where Lucille + I have our Chinese Food when we're in the mood. While sitting there in the Restaurant waiting for our food to be served. And by the time our food is being served—the kids of the neighborhood might pass by and look through the window and see *Satchmo* and round up *all* the kids in the neighborhood, tell them that Satchmo + Lucille is sitting in the Restaurant, and the whole neighborhood of kids come and as soon as the waiter—bring our food, all of these kids make a bee line in the Restaurant to my table for Autographs. *Soo*—I *Still* haven't eaten my food' for Autographing for the kids. The funny thing about it *all*—they all must have *their* names, on their autographs. So by the time I finished' *hmm* my food were very cold. So I ate my Fortune Cookies. One read—"Social pleasure and a *most* fortunate future." The other Fortune Cookie said—"Your romance will be a long and lasting one." So we left the Dragon Seed and when we went home Lucille fixed me a beeg Dagwood *Sandwich*. At home where we live in Corona is *so lively*. We have *two* dogs. They are *Schnauzers*, Male + Female. And they are two very *fine* watch dogs. They not only Bark when the door bell rings, but anybody who Comes' up our steps' they Bark their *(A)spirin* off. The Male Dog who is the older one' his name is "*Trumpet*. The Female, the baby' her name is *Trinket*. I gave *Trumpet* to Lucille and Mr. Joe Glaser gave us *Trinket*. And when the two of them start Barking together—Oh Boy what a *Duet*.

18

OPEN LETTER TO FANS

(JUNE 1, 1970)

Armstrong wrote this document during his recovery from heart and kidney ailments. He begins by telling how he tried to convert the hospital staff to Swiss Kriss, a laxative that he praises often in this book. Laxatives were important to him from early childhood, when his mother used local herbs as a kind of folk medicine. Armstrong explains in "The Satchmo Story" that he regards marijuana as an herbal medicine very much akin to herbal laxatives. Perhaps it is not too much to say that he regarded laxatives as cleansers for the body, marijuana as a cleanser for the mind. Thus, access to his chosen laxative is a primary concern as he begins to restore his health. Armstrong acknowledges the help of friends, associates, and the beautiful nurses. The vitality of his own "beautiful imagination" was certainly important for restoring health; to this one might add his sense of humor. He also reports here on the pleasure of telling stories to neighborhood children about his early courtship with Lucille while both were working at the Cotton Club with Bill Bojangles Robinson.

Well Folks, here I am—at Home at last. I've just gotten out of the Beth Israel Hospital after being there *Twice* for *Fatigue—Rundown* Body, *Exhaustion*—and a *Kidney* Ailment which *effected* my *Heart* and *Liver*. My Doctor, Gary Zucker (a *Great* Man and Jazz Fan of mine), he worked hard over me and took me out of my *Crisis*. He took me out of *INTENSIVE CARE*

TWICE (2 times) which is *something* very seldom heard of' with *any* Human Being. While I was in intensive care and was coming back to normal and life again, and I talk to Dr. Zucker whenever he *visited* me, he and I would have some heart talks. Knowin that he was also one of my Dear Fans, I felt at ease talking to him. The first thing that I said to Dr. Zucker was—"*Doc* God Bless you and I love you. Now there's one more thing that I'd be very happy' if you'd O.K. it. And that is "*Swiss Kriss.*" Because *Doc* the kind of Laxatives that they've been Giving me hasn't *worked* me at all. It has been (Four Days) now' and I haven't been to the "*John*" (the toilet). And my mother Mary Ann (May Ann—for short) She always told me + my sister (Mama Lucy) *Beatrice* (real name)—at the same time she would be giving us a Physic (a laxative) some *Herbs* "which she picked up by the Railroad Tracks in N.O., bring those leaves home—ground + Grind them down to almost a powder—And would give me a large tablespoonful on my Tongue—And a *tablespoonful* to Mama Lucy' and a *heaping* tablespoonful for herself. Then she would run three Large Glasses of Water from the Water Faucet or hydrant—and she pass a glassful to *us*—And one for herself—and Down the *Hatch* we went, to Bed. The next morning when we awakened' "*OOH*" We had such a *ball* trying to be the *1st* one to get to the *toilet—pull that lever*, and get that good eye opener. From real Young' Mama Lucy + I heard May Ann say—You may never get Rich, but no Drastic "Ailments' that'll *take* you off this earth—Just like *that*—you won't.'" So after explaining all of this to Dr. Zucker, and asked him to O.K. the *Herbs*, *Herbal Laxative*—etc. etc.—which happens to be *Swiss Kriss*. And I've been *taking* for many many years. He automatically picked up the Telephone and called my wife Lucille Armstrong and told her—She may bring all of the Swiss Kriss' he needs 'to Louis Armstrong's room, because he prefers *it* instead of the Laxatives that they serve here in the Hospital. And Lucille—Who was the discoverer of Swiss Kriss by Reading Dr. Gaylord Hauser's, Health Book—"All About Herbal Laxatives and Etc."—it was a pleasure to Lucille to bring our Laxative which helped me to Recuperate—Beautifully.

After a few days, taking Swiss Kriss and in a Beautiful private toilet and *Wailin* on time Hitting it on the *nose*' everybody commenced to noticing the Rapid Improvement in me—my skin—my weight gaining and everything—appetite—much better. So the patients as well as the Nurses became inquisitive about *Swiss Kriss*. Since Lucille *brought* to me quite a bit (sample packages), I had enough to give everybody who wished to try it. And the *Head Nurse* at the Beth Israel Hospital, who was very strict to the (*Chart*) she carried around, *consulted* me concerning Swiss Kriss' and was about to hit that telephone (in my room) and talk to Dr. Zucker when I told her, as she put the phone back on the hook. I said to her, "Honey, Dr. Zuck has given me permission' for Swiss Kriss' everybody in this Hospital is taking it and having beautiful results—Jumping over Hurdles at Laxating times—And they're *All* Happy—Good "feeling. Now *Nurse* if you were smart—*tomorrow* when you have your day off." I handed her a small box of Swiss Kriss' saying—"Take a large *tablespoonful'* just before you hop in bed. Put it on your tongue—Rinse Down with a large glass of water—*two* glasses is better. The more Liquids' the better. A little nip afterwards if you desire. As long as it's anything wet." O.K. The Head Nurse did as I told her, that she must try Swiss Kriss, her *personal* self' And then there won't be anybody that could change her mind about it or turn her ever against it. And just as I figured she would—she came to her own conclusions. The next night when she came on Duty—the *first stop* that she made' was *my private* room. She came in looking at me *Straight* into my eyes—pointing her finger at me at the same time—saying—"*Satchmo'* You are a *Naughty Boy*." And smiling' beautifully' looking as pretty and fresh as she could be. That *Swiss Kriss* is just wonderful. I feel *cleaned* and great. Coming from her' I was very happy. She was just about one of my Toughest Customers I do believe.

Dr. Zucker + me would *Chat* everyday as he saw such a good improvement in me. Every time he came—he would talk about Releasing me (sending me home). My *two* nurses, whom I had gotten to know commenced to showing that they'll surely miss me when I left. And I'd began to feel that way about them.

My Day Nurse was a good looking' *cute* white Jewish Girl by the name of [left blank—ed.] and my night nurse a real fine beautiful (big fine gams) Brown Skinned Gal from Jamaica, W.I. They both were well "Hipp'd" and on the Ball. I loved the *words* that they would say to me, of *encouragement*. The both followed my career + life in music. What I *stood* for, in *music*, and the Situations that I had to go through in life—54 years of *one night* here, and there, *all over* the world. So, I could see on their *faces* that they were very glad to comfort me and nurse me back to health. God Bless Em. My night nurse's name—Mavis Andrews. Of course, I must give thanks to the extra nurses.

Finally going home time came around. First thought of happiness came into my mind' was my Dear, and very much devoted wife Lucille (Brown Sugar) Armstrong. Brown Sugar was her stage name or Show Biz name. Every one loved her. I thought to myself now Lucille can catch up on some well needed rest, from visiting me at the Hospital when I was sick, she religiously came to visit me *every* day. And *stayed* with me until the Curfew *rang* and she'd have to cut out. For her' I was *thrilled.* Of course Ernest Debman whom has been with us for many many years and Bernice Dixon who also has been with us for many many years. They *held* the *Castle* (I call's our house) down while my Dear Lucille visited me. Even our *two* Dogs (German schnauzers) love Bernice and Ernie. One Dog is named *Trumpet*—He's the He—And the younger dog is named *Trinket.* They're Both Schnauzers. We had Trumpet for a long time. And Mr. Joe Glaser brought *Trinket* to me from California, just before he died. Ernie—Bernice—Lucille—Myself—we just love those dogs. They're like Human Beings.

Yes—a big thanks to the Extra Nurses who looked after me—the times that my Regular Nurses weren't with me or during their time off (they'd visit during their *Recess'* or etc.). Also they came from other wards serving other patients, etc.—they would congregate in my room to *chat* with me while I was resting. And those girls used to let their hair down and would talk More *Trash.'' WOW—Whatta* sense of Humor *they had.* By us all being of age and broad minded and having been *around* somewhat they didn't *Spare* no Horses—I'm sure they *Dugged* the Expressions on my *Face.* As they *spoke* about Sex. But a man such as me—at 70 years old—and *sick* as old hell they had no fear. As for me, they kept my cheeks Rosy Red. *The Cute Things.* Then too—All of those beautiful young nurses felt that they could relax talking anything around me (in my presence) anytime. As for me, at 70 years old—I *still* had my thoughts and a beautiful imagination which I'll always have. It also comes out in my music. *Think So?*

My Manager Mr. Joe Glaser visited me every day. Dr. Alexander Schiff our company Doctor, who travels *all* over the world with me and my *All Stars'* Band. They would spend *lots* of time, with me' talking about *everything* in General. I enjoyed their Company very very much. Ira Mangel' our road manager would visit me quite often. And would tell me of lots of interesting things such as what's *Happening'* on the outside which would knock me out. Of course as I've said before—*''Moms''* that's what I call's my Dear Wife Lucille—She was there 'everyday looking pretty and Fresh, as ever. ''Oh'' I love that woman. We both have our *ups* and downs, in our early stages in life, and so marvelous how Lucille who is (14) *years* younger than I am, how we could get together, and make such a beautiful marriage so far for over (30) years. And still happy. We've both seen (3) Generations grow up in our Block where we bought our home in Corona. *White + Black*, And those kids' when they grew up and got *married*—their children—Still comes around to our house and visit their Uncle Louis and Aunt Lucille. That's how close 'they feel toward us. During my (54) years traveling on the Road playing one night stands, and when I would return home, all of those kids in my Block would be standing there' right in front of my door' waiting to help me unload my Luggage and take it into the house. And you talking about Something real cute—that was some scene, I'm ''tellin'' you. While Lucille would be in the kitchen fixing a little something such as Ice Cream + Cake' etc.—the kids would all be on the floor in front of the *Television* watching' a Play' (a Shoot Em Up movie) or *Something* and my *Tiredness* would *hit* me. And I'd automatically Doze off to Sleep. So I would quietly *lay back* and go to sleep on the floor. By the time Lucille would bring in the Ice Cream to us we would all be sound *asleep—yissir* we would be spreaded out on the floor which would remind you of the *massacre* in Chicago.

Those kids' would wake up' and while we were eating our Ice Cream + Cake' I would relate some of my past, of Lucille + I. How we met and etc. I told *em* about the time' when Lucille + I met. It was at the Cotton Club Downtown New York. We both were on the bill with our Idol Bill Robinson (Nickname) Bojangles. She + I still think that Bill Robinson is the greatest showman that we've ever had in our Race. And to us, that takes in everybody' in the Negro Race. He was the sharpest Negro Man on stage that I *personally* ever seen in my life. Since the first time that I ever layed eyes on Bojangles at the Erlanger Theater in Chicago in ''1922. I had just came up from New Orleans, my hometown. And I was playing 2nd, *trumpet* at Lincoln Gardens with King Oliver (another great man in my life long memory book)—Bill Johnson (our bass) who had been on the R.K.O. *Circuit* for many years, which was the best. I had Bill Johnson take me to see a matinee show one day so I could see this man whom I had *heard* and *read* about in my early days—in N.O. And Bojangles came up to every expectation + opinion that I had of him before I saw him in person. I am sitting in my seat in the theater′ very anxious to see this man. And sure enough′ the great one appeared. As he came out of the *wing* on stage′ the first thing that hit him was the *Flashlight. Sharp—Lord* know″ *that man′* was *so Sharp* he was *Bleeding″* (our expression when we mention someone that′s well dressed). Anyway he had on a sharp light tan Gabardine summer suit, Brown Derby and the usual expensive thick soul shoes in which he taps in.

It was a long time before Bojangles could open his mouth. That′s how popular he was and well liked by all who understood his greatness as a dancer and a showman. He waited after the Thunderous Applause had finished—And looked up into the booth and said to the man who controlled the lights—Bill said to him ″*Give* me a *light my color.*″ And *all* the lights *all* over the house ″*went out.*″ And *me* sitting there when *this* happened′ with the whole audience just Roaring with Laughter′ When I realized it—I was Laughing so Loud′ until Bill Johnson whom I was with ′was on a verge of taking me out of there. I hadn′t heard anything like that before or witnessed it either. Then Bojangles went into his act. His every move was a beautiful picture. I am sitting in my seat in thrilled ecstasy′ and delight, even in a trance. He imitated a *Trombone* with his walking cane to his mouth, blowing out of the side of his mouth making the buzzing sound of a trombone, which I enjoyed. He told a lot of Funny jokes, which everybody enjoyed immensely. Then he went into his dance and finished by skating off of the stage with a silent sound and tempo. *Wow* what an artist. I was sold on him ever since.

After that show′ I did not see Bill, for many years. I became very popular making records—playing in a Symphony Orchestra, for Silent pictures with an Overture′ right after the picture had finished. This was in 1925 at the Vendome Theater in Chicago. Prof. Erskine Tate was the Director. I had left King Oliver and was on my own. I even toured Europe before running into Bill Robinson again. That was after I had toured all over Europe and went back to Chicago and signed up with Mr. Joe Glaser, whom I worked for in the early days at the Sunset Cafe, to be my manager. I joined Carroll Dickerson′s band at the Sunset through Mr. Glaser. That′s the band I recorded ″When Your Smiling″ with. Mr. Glaser formed a big band for me, and took us out on the road′ to a very successful tour through all the South, etc. We finished that tour—back to Chicago and *Disbanded*. A week later, Mr. Glaser and I went to New York. He settled down with a Booking Office. He signed me up with *Luis Russell* who had a *great band*. I directed his band and played my personal solos whenever it was my time to *Blow*—(trumpet that is). In Russell's band there were several boys (musicians) from my home town, N.O. So you can imagine how well I felt at home with them. Luis Russell was from N.O. also. Although his native home was Panama. But he came to N.O. from there as a real young kid, so there's where he and his family settled down until he came into manhood and *cut out* for New York. He also signed up with Mr. Glaser, who immediately put us together, and put us with the Bill Robinson's Revue. We played quite a few theater dates with Bill before we went into the well known Cotton Club. That's where I met Lucille. She was a sharp, cute chorus girl, very popular with everybody in the show, including the musicians. Red Allen Jr. from Algiers La. was one of the trumpeters in the band. So was J.C. Higginbotham' the best *trombonist* of them *all* at that time. Luis Russell played that good New Orleans piano' very *Lusty* and Swingy. Being from N.O. he had to be good along with all the competitions' that were around' in those days. Nothing but Hellions, meaning the Best of the piano players, such as *Fats* Waller—*Willie* (the Lion) Smith—James P. Johnson, etc. *All* greats.

I was very proud "n" happy to have played in that band every night. And when I told these kids in Corona at my house while we were sitting in front of my television watching one of those Bad *Cats* (Cow Boys) shoot up the whole town and he never stopped for once to reload—we all got a *Boot—Pickin* up on that *Jive*" (the situation). That's when I told them that I started *courting* Aunt Lucille (as they called her) when we were both appearing in Bill Bojangle Robinson's great Revue at the Cotton Club, downtown N.Y. 'Oh' their little eyes lit up like Diamonds' with glee—very Hip'd kids. In fact it dawned on me—it seemed to me that Lucille was the ideal girl for me. In fact our lives' were practically the same. Good Common Sense—great observers (not for any particular reason)' but were not particular about phony people, etc.—what we *didn't* have we *did* without. I came up the same way as Lucille did, somewhat anyway. For instance, regardless what the *other* fellow had or *how* much he had *more* than me, *So what*, it was his, and it didn't Faze me one bit. I always had the thought of the advice that *Mary Ann* my Mother gave to Mama Lucy and I when we were both' little *Shavers* (children that is). She said "Never worry about what the *other* feller has *got. Try "n" get something your self.*" Lucille had the same *slant* on life—the same as me. I paid strict attention to her' when she was working in the chorus at the Cotton Club. Beside the Salary that she were making at the club, which weren't too much (nothing like the *girls* made that were *working* for *Ziegfield* and his *Follies*), with her salary she had to help take care of her family, which consisted of her mother, her two Brothers, Jackie + Sonny, and a Sister Janet, who was once in *show* business before Lucille. But it seemed as though show Bizz'ness just wasn't her Bag. So she put it down, and did just what the Two Brothers did—*lay* on Lucille, *beg* for *support.* To do this—And for extra money' Lucille had to sell cookies to the members of the cast, which taken in everybody, including Bill Robinson and me. Every night before the first show, Lucille would be a very *busy* young Girl trying to get dressed—And put her make up on for her first show, and get rid of the cookies' which she would bring down from Harlem' made by some private family who lived up in Harlem. The cookies were very *Tasty* + *Dee'* licious. We all enjoy eating them very much. They weren't too very expensive *either.*

One night when Lucille came into my dressing room to deliver my Box of Cookies, I asked her, (I said) "Honey? *How* many Boxes do you bring down here every night?" And when she told me—I said to her, "When you come down here with your Bundle of Cookies, from *now on*—Just bring them all in here (meaning my dressing room). I'll take *all* of them." She did, which took a big load off of her mind. The night that she brought in the cookies, I put them aside and when we'd' finish work at the club, *me* and my good man Friday' Bob Smiley would take them up town in Harlem and the next day we'd take them over to the school and divide them up amongst the School Kids. They loved them. I did too.

One night when Lucille came into my Dressing Room to deliver her Cookies, I just couldn't hold back the deep feeling and the warmth that I had *Accumulated* for her ever since I first layed eyes on her in the front line of the Cotton Club floor. And about all things—Swinging in that Front Line every night—Looking *beautiful'er "n" beautiful'er* every night. Then too—She's doing her dance every night direct in front of me standing there directing the Band and *Blowing* my Solos on my trumpet whenever it was time for me to *Blow "n" Wail.* All of those Beautiful Notes along with Lucille's perfect dancing. Me—diggin those cute *lil* buns of her's.

Hmm'' That's when I automatically *said ''Look Brown Sugar,''* the name that we *Show Folks* ''n'' *musicians* gave her during her *early'* or her first days right out of the dancing school into *show* Biz'ness (Business). I always thought that it was a *cute* name. I said to Lucille, ''You must have at least an *Inkling* ''Huh?'' Lucille raised her big fine eyes (at me) as if to say 'My 'My where did he dig *that* word. Of course' she didn't *say it—but* I could *tell* by the *tone* of her eyes' that she was wondering *like hell.* Pretty smart *Chick* to be so young. And around us old timers too. She's *too much.* And to *me'* she's everything. I said Lucille, I might as well tell you Right Now—I have *Eyes* for you. And has been having them for a *long* time. And if any of these *cats* in the show Shooting at you—I want to be in the Running. Lucille looked at me and just laughed. But before we Both knew it—we were taking in the Shows (movies) between our shows. Riding uptown in Harlem every night after our last show. That's when I had that big long Rust Colored Packard Car that Mr. Glaser had *bought* for me. And *Boy* was it Sharp. It was the *Hottest* car in town. And the *Talk* of the Town. *Bob* Smiley—my *Right* hand man, a tall good looking six foot, brownskin *Cat*—used to drive this fine long Packard while Lucille + I would sit in the *Backseat* and—'she looking just like a *Lil Ol Doll* and *me*—Sharp as a wedding (you know what) and *happier* than (2) peas in a *pot* (pod to you)—we would stop by the Bar where all of the Show Folks (colored) would congregate after we all had finished our last show, and go there to sort of Signify, etc.

We'd arrive there around eleven-thirty or twelve at night—and around Four O'Clock in the Morning' Everybody's Juiced (Stoned) drunk and Hungry. Everybody's standing at the bar Drinking like *Mad.* And all of a sudden everybody gets Hungry and want something to *eat.* Right behind this same bar in this same room' there's an old Italian Fellow cooking Italian Foods, good meatballs—and spaghetti—wafting all across our noses. A little room in the back of the Joint with tables. Everybody'll 'load up their plates and just Devour that food. And on top of all of that liquor, some of the Drunks would get *''Two''* orders of Spaghetti. And go home and *fall out*—into the bed and sleep all day until time to go to work. Many a performer lost their cute little figures and acquired big bellies from that situation of eating and going right straight to bed' which was bad.

Even Lucille had began to lose her *cute lil* figure from that situation. And I did too. But by me being *Physic Minded* from what my mother

Mayan taught me when I was young—no matter how much I drank + ate—when I went home′ I would take a Big Physic before I even took my clothes off before I went to bed. And the very next morning all hell would break loose in the Toilet before I′d take my shower. And when I got to know Lucille a *lil* better′ I *Instilled* it in her. And by that—she kept her *lil ol* waist line. All of life I have taken *some* kind of a physic every night before going to bed. *Anything*—as long as it makes you *trot* and cleans me out. I use the word *physic*—which I was taught to say from my childhood days. Finally I learned to say *laxative*. *All* the same. Maybe more expensive than the word physic. They both make you do the same thing.

19
"GOOD-BYE TO ALL OF YOU"
(1969)

For its December 1969 issue, *Esquire* asked twenty-five elderly celebrities to give some advice to younger generations, since "our years tend to be around threescore and ten"—that is, since the celebrities may soon be dead. The celebrities responded with lots of advice. But Armstrong was one of the few to respond with comments about aging. These comments include his opinion that "music has no age," and they provide a fitting conclusion to this volume.

My belief and satisfaction is that, as long as a person breathes, they still have a chance to exercise the talents they were born with. I speak of something which I know about and have been doing all of my life, and that's Music. And now that I am an elderly man I still feel the same about music and its creations. And at the age of "sixty-nine" I really don't feel that I am on my way out at all. Of course a person may do a little less—but the foundation will always be there.

I feel that I did my interesting work as I have gotten up into the older age bracket. I enjoyed being in the band with Joe King Oliver when I was seventeen years old in New Orleans, and when he went to Chicago I joined him again. I was twenty-two years old then. Every word that he told me concerning my music stayed with me all through my career. And

Used by permission of The Louis Armstrong Educational Foundation.

Joe Oliver was way up there in age. I did not at any time think about his age. It was what he was saying that counted. To me, he was the greatest on the cornet which we all played in those days. I was thirty-two years old when I first went to England. Returned the following years and toured all of the provinces of England—we also toured the French countries—the Scandinavian countries—came back to America—toured—traveled the U.S.A. and made movies. In 1947 I organized my All Stars Band—with Jack Teagarden (trombone), Barney Bigard (clarinet), Big Sid Catlett (drums), Dick Carey (piano), Arvell Shaw (bass) and Satchmo (trumpet—leader). Another tour of all America, 1953. We made our first trip to Germany. We were the first attraction there, after the war. I was fifty-three years old. We toured all over Italy. We went everywheres in Africa. 1958—in Italy, I became ill. Not for long, probably a week. 1960's we toured overseas again. This time we went to all of the countries. We returned to the States and played Las Vegas—Reno—Lake Tahoe—in California we made more movies. Went to England—1967. Back home in 1969 still doing the things that I love, playing music and singing. Still pleasing my audiences—appreciative fans. On my sixty-ninth birthday, all of the kids in Corona where I live came in front of my home and wished me a Happy Birthday, which thrilled ol Satch. Saying carry on until you're a hundred years old. I have seen three generations come up in the block where I live. Many kids grew up, married, and brought their children to visit my wife Lucille and I. And those kids grew up—Satchmo fans. Just want to say that music has no age. Most of your great composers—musicians—are elderly people, way up there in age—they will live forever. There's no such thing as on the way out. As long as you are still doing something interesting and good. You are in business as long as you are breathing. "Yeah."

APPENDIX

1: "Louis Armstrong + the Jewish Family in New Orleans, La., the Year of 1907."

Armstrong's handwritten manuscript is seventy-seven pages, numbered consecutively; it is held at the Louis Armstrong House and Archives at Queens College/CUNY. The title is Armstrong's. He dates the beginning March 31, 1969; midway through the manuscript he writes "This is the year of 1970." A hand that is not Armstrong's has glossed the document, here and there (I thank Michael Cogswell for drawing my attention to this detail); these glosses have been deleted from this edition.

A photograph of the Karnofsky family from 1917 is published in Miller (1994: 19). In a letter to Leonard Feather (October 1, 1941, held at the Institute of Jazz Studies, Rutgers University), Armstrong adds the following information regarding the Karnofsky family:

> When we returned to 'New Orleans to play the dance uptown at the Rhythm Club every 'Cat from my old neighborhood were up there . . . And the place was packed and jammed . . . My old boss of years ago Mr. Morris Karnofsky and his wife were also there and enjoyed themselves and our music to the highest . . . He and I talked about the good ol days when I was just a kid working on his 'Coal Wagon with him selling 'Coal to the 'sporting class of people down in the 'Red Light District which were running full bloom at that time . . . It was somewheres around the year of 1915 and early 16 . . . I was so small until I had to put on long pants when ever Mr. Karnofsky would go down in the Dis-

> trict to sell his 'stone coal (as we called it then) 'Five Cents a Water Bucket . . . Oh I really thought I was somebody down there amongst those 'Pimps—'Gamblers, etc.

As I have suggested in the introduction to this chapter, some of the details do not match up with earlier accounts given by Armstrong. It seems to me that (contrary to several assertions in essays published in Miller 1994) the very early date of Armstrong's first employment with Karnofsky, 1907, should not be automatically taken as an approximate date for events described in the document. In the letter to Feather just quoted, Armstrong gives 1915 for his employment with Karnofsky, and in *Satchmo: My Life in New Orleans* (p. 94), Karnofsky is introduced at around this same time in the chronological flow. Perhaps Armstrong picked rags and junk with the Karnofsky family as early as 1907, working for them with coal beginning around 1915. But in *Satchmo: My Life in New Orleans* (p. 109), Armstrong's experience picking rags takes place after his visit to the Colored Waifs' Home for Boys, and it is associated not with the Karnofsky family but with one "Lorenzo," who played tunes on "an old tin horn." Lorenzo inspired Armstrong: "The things he said about music held me spellbound, and he blew that old, beat-up tin horn with such warmth that I felt as though I was sitting with a good cornet player." A report from Jelly Roll Morton (Lomax 1950: 61) suggests that tin horn advertisements were common practice: "Even the rags-bottles-and-bones men would advertise their trade by playing the blues on the wooden mouthpieces of Christmas horns—yes sir, play more lowdown, dirty blues on those Kress horns than the rest of the country ever thought of." Unquestionably, street music was vitally important for Armstrong's musical development. His early prowess playing blues is confirmed by many accounts (see Appendix material for Chapter 2).

Other details in the present document—which, it should be remembered, was written during recovery from a life-threatening illness, barely two years before Armstrong died—also raise suspicion about accuracy. Armstrong says that he learned "Home Sweet Home" after the Karnofsky family helped him purchase his first cornet, but in his two published autobiographies, this song is taught to him on the cornet by Mr. Davis in the Colored Waifs' Home, 1913, before which Armstrong "had never tried to play cornet" (1936: 17; 1954a: 39 and 46; see also Jones and Chilton 1971: 52 and 208). The earlier recollections, from 1936 and 1954, are surely more reliable. I would offer the following view on these discrepancies: It is possible that Armstrong had some early experience with the Karnofsky family in 1907. But it seems more likely that many of the events recounted in this document happened later, after he returned from the Colored Waifs' Home and probably in 1915–1916. It is possible that memory lapses yielded additional inaccuracies, as well.

Armstrong describes Bill Bojangles Robinson as "the greatest comedian + dancer in my race." Gary Giddins (1988: 34) transcribed this passage as "comedian + danger in my race," and he analyzed the word "danger" as revealing an important aspect of Armstrong's own persona. The transcription problem is caused by the fact that Armstrong has written over the "c," blurring it and making it look like a "g." Nevertheless, it seems unlikely that he has written "danger"—unlikely in terms of both physical representation and context—while "dancer" makes perfect sense. (Giddins also misread the connections of phrases in this passage, which is a gloss that does not fall neatly in sequence on the page.) In "Open Letter to Fans," which must have been written around the same time, Armstrong says about Robinson: "That's how popular he was and well liked by all who understood his greatness as a dancer and a showman." Giddins discusses the passage in question while constructing an argument that Armstrong cultivated an image of erotic daring in his film work and music. In any event, I think that it is unlikely that Armstrong ever cultivated an image that he considered dangerous.

Armstrong's most extensive statement on his New Orleanian youth is, of course, *Satchmo: My Life in New Orleans*; see also his 1947 article for *True* magazine. Other chapters in this volume dealing with this period are "The Armstrong Story," The "Goffin Notebooks," "The Satchmo Story," "Jazz on a High Note," and "Scanning the History of Jazz." One biographical detail to keep in mind when reading Armstrong is his birth date, which he thought was July 4, 1900, but which has now been placed at August 4, 1901 (Giddins 1988: 47–53).

Armstrong mentions the controversy that followed his comments on the "*big* Integration *Riot* in Little Rock." He was quoted in the *New York Times* (Sept. 19, 1957) as abandoning plans for a State Department–sponsored trip to the Soviet Union because "the way they are treating my people in the South, the Government can go to hell." Armstrong said that President Eisenhower had "no guts," that he was "two-faced," and that "It's getting so bad a colored man hasn't got any country." A follow-up story by the *Pittsburgh Courier* (Sept. 28, 1957) quoted Armstrong as saying, "I wouldn't take back a thing I've said. I've had a beautiful life over 40 years in music, but I feel the downtrodden situation the same as any other Negro. My parents and family suffered through all of that old South . . . My people . . . are not looking for anything . . . we just want a square shake. But when I see on television and read about a crowd spitting on and cursing at a little colored girl . . . I think I have a right to get sore and say something about it." From Davenport, Iowa, Armstrong sent a telegram to Eisenhower on September 24 (my thanks go to Mr. Dwight Strandberg at the Dwight D. Eisenhower Library at Abilene, Kansas, for locating the telegram and sending me a copy):

> THE PRESIDENT
> THE WHITE HOUSE
> MR PRESIDENT. DADDY IF AND WHEN YOU DECIDE TO TAKE THOSE LITTLE NEGRO CHILDREN PERSONALLY INTO CENTRAL HIGH SCHOOL ALONG WITH YOUR MARVELOUS TROOPS PLEASE TAKE ME ALONG "O GOD IT WOULD BE SUCH A GREAT PLEASURE I ASSURE YOU. MY REGARDS TO BROTHER BROWNWELL AND MAY GOD BLESS YOU PRESIDENT" YOU HAVE A GOOD HEART.
>
> YOU CAN CONTACT ME THROUGH MY PERSONNEL MANAGER MR JOE GLASER 745 FIFTH AVENUE NEW YORK. AM SWISS KRISSLY YOURS LOUIS SATCHMO ARMSTRONG.

The criticism of Lil Hardin Armstrong in the present document is discussed in the Appendix material for "Jazz on a High Note." The spelling of two proper names is in question: Armstrong gives "Crawford Worthington" and "Bernerdine Curry," while Jones and Chilton (1971: 103) give these names as "Crawford Wethington" and "Bert Curry." Armstrong writes about violence among "second liners"; this observation is supported by John Casimer (quoted in Mitchell 1995: 154), who remembered how second liners during this period would hit each other with "bricks and sticks and everything . . . Sometimes used knives, cut you and shoot you too; take an old broom handle, beat you all up." As Armstrong suggests, drummers like Black Benny were relied upon to deal with such violence; Danny Barker describes this phenomenon in more detail in his own memoirs (Barker 1986: 62).

Armstrong's claim that there were a lot of pianists better than Jelly Roll

Morton is supported by Pops Foster (1971: 93–98), who adds the observation that it was not simply the color of Morton's skin but also his flair for entertainment that won him good jobs. Armstrong's statement that Morton denied any "Cullud" heritage is supported by Lomax (1950: 103): "Never once . . . did [Morton] refer to his Negro status." Armstrong's uncharacteristic negativity about both Morton and Freddie Keppard must have something to do with Morton's comment (Lomax 1950: 154) that "Armstrong has never been in [Keppard's] class." Johnny St. Cyr described Keppard as "the most popular trumpet player with the mulatto race . . . when you come darker than Keppard, you didn't score with the mulattos at all" (Lomax 1950: 102). Armstrong reviewed Lomax's book for the *New York Times* (Armstrong 1950a) and he owned a copy of the Library of Congress recordings which formed the basis for the book. As for Armstrong's remarks about Freddie Keppard's clowning and my suggestion that he is, at the same time that he criticizes Keppard, defending his own style of entertainment, consider this from a letter to John Chilton and Max Jones (1971: 220): "Critics in England say I was a clown, but a clown, that's hard. If you can make people chuckle a little; it's happiness to me to see people happy, and most of the people who criticize don't know one note from another." Albert Murray observes, "For the most part, Armstrong's comic mask, which as often as not was as much a matter of vocal inflection as mugging, was a convention for countering sentimentality" (Murray, 1976: 191).

Armstrong says his father "was a *Freak* for being the *Grand Marshal* for the *Odd* Fellows Lodge parade." From Sidney Bechet (1960: 65) comes this description of the performance expected from a Grand Marshal: "And those clubs, maybe the Lions Club or the Odd Fellows . . . they'd have this Grand Marshal who was the leader of the club. He'd have the longest sash. He'd have a sash that would go right down to his shoe tops and it would have gold bangles on it. And on his shoulder, he'd have an emblem, maybe a gold lion. That was his badge. But most of all, the way you could tell the Marshal, it was from how he walked. The Marshal, he'd be a man that really could strut. It was really a question of that: the best strutter in the club, he'd be the Grand Marshal. He'd be a man who could prance when he walked, a man that could really fool and surprise you. He'd keep time to the music, but all along he'd keep a strutting and moving so you'd never know what he was going to be doing next. Naturally, the music, it makes you strut, but it's *him* too, the way he's strutting, it gets you. It's what you want from a parade: you want to *see* it as well as hear it. And all those fancy steps he'd have—

oh, that was really something!—ways he'd have of turning around himself. People, they got a whole lot of pleasure out of just watching him, hearing the music and seeing him strut . . ."

2: *"Joe Oliver Is Still King"*

This is an abridged version of an article Armstrong wrote for *The Record Changer* (July–Aug. 1950, p. 10).

The supposition that Armstrong learned ragtime—which is how New Orleanians during this period described uptempo "jazz"—from Oliver is supported by the fact that by 1914, the year he says he started learning from Oliver, he had already attained noticeable mastery in playing blues. This is reported by several observers, including Pops Foster (1971: 50): "About 1914 I was playing with Ory's band doing advertising for an affair the Turtles were putting on at National Park . . . So then we needed a trumpet player very bad. After we went a few blocks, I saw Louis Armstrong standing on a corner watching, and said, 'Hey, there's little Louis over there!' We got him in the wagon and he went on to play the advertising with us, and then we carried him out to the park to play. The only thing Louis could play then was blues, so we played them all day long. Louis played them good too. As far as I know, that was the first time Louis played with a big-time band. Before that Louis just played with kid bands."

In his battle with Bebop, Armstrong would sometimes say that Bebop musicians played merely "routines" or "figurations" similar to what he used to play before Joe Oliver taught him to value beautiful melody. For example, he told Dan Morgenstern (Morgenstern 1994: 97) that Oliver taught him to "always play the lead. I used to run all over the horn, playing those figurations—something like what they call bop now. But King Oliver taught me to play the lead."

Armstrong's comments on Oliver's inventiveness are supported by Fess Williams (Wright 1987: 335): "I remember another night at the Royal Gardens when a bunch of white musicians were at the ring-side table and offered Joe a dollar for each break he played that was different from the last. They thought he wasn't any kind of a creative musician. Joe broke them that night; took all their money, and was still playing breaks afterwards!"

In a 1938 issue of *Jazz Hot*, Armstrong wrote this obituary of Oliver:

King Oliver, the great trumpet player of the Good' ol' Days of Yore—has just passed away . . .

King Oliver died way down south in Savannah Georgia . . . We had his body shipped from down there in Savannah to New York . . . All the musicians in New York were present to get the last look at the man that gave all of us our starts . . . I sure do hate to see King Oliver leave this Earth . . .

He was a wonderful man indeed . . . I can remember way back in New Orleans, Louisiana . . . When I was just a boy . . . I used to go to the grocery for Mrs. Stella Oliver (his wife) and when I'd return with Mrs. Oliver's grocery King Oliver would give to me a music lesson free as his thanks . . . I would much rather the lesson than to get the cash monies . . .

Of course, we all know that Death is one thing that we cannot do anything about: all we can do is thank the Lord, that He has stuck by us and has watched over us . . .

3: "Bunk Didn't Teach Me"

This document is abridged from an article in *The Record Changer* (July–Aug. 1950, p. 30). The heading of the article reads "Bunk Didn't Teach Me, as Told by Louis Armstrong." Published here is material that appears in quotations marks in the original article, signaling Armstrong's words, which may have been spoken during an interview, though it is just as likely that Armstrong wrote them.

For more on Armstrong's denial of a teacher–student relationship with Johnson, see Jones and Chilton (1971: 51). This denial is supported and extended by Pops Foster (1971: 47):

> Bunk played a beautiful horn and nobody else around New Orleans played the same style Bunk did. He played the most beautiful tones. After a while Bunk got to drinking so bad they fired him and then he went with Frankie Dusen's band . . . Bunk would show up to play so drunk he'd be draggin' his coat across the floor and couldn't find the bandstand . . . He'd drink til he passed out and then sleep it off on a pool table, get up, and start drinking again . . . He got to drinking so bad that even the

> Eagle Band fired him about 1910 and no one else would hire him. He left town with a minstrel show and I didn't see him again until 1937 when I was playing with Louis Armstrong's band in New Iberia, Louisiana. Bunk claimed he got Louis his first job, but Bunk wasn't even around New Orleans when Johnny Dodds and Peter Bocage got Louis the job with Fate Marable on the boats. Until that, Louis just had one night gigs with different bands.

Foster (p. 77) places trumpeters in two different stylistic groups, the hot trumpeters like Oliver, Ned, Bolden, Penerton, Petit, Keppard, and Armstrong, and the sweet trumpeters like Johnson, Celestin, Metoyer, and Perez.

Barney Bigard (1986: 88) supports Armstrong's denial, as well:

> Bunk, well, he was pathetic to begin with . . . He went around telling people that he taught Louis Armstrong, and Louis, bless his soul, he was so good about the whole thing that he wouldn't let you know any different. But he knew Bunk didn't teach him anything. I mean Bunk never could play like Louis in his life or like Buddy Petit, and Petit was Louis' big influence.

In a letter to William Russell of October 3, 1939 (now held by the Historic New Orleans Collection), Armstrong describes his efforts to help Johnson:

> Say′ ′Gate′—concerning the Trumpet for my boy Bunk—I haven′t forgotten it at all . . . I just hadn′t had the time to go over to Rudy Muck′s place, and ′Intercede . . . ′Ump -′′Diddat Come Outa Mee? . . . Ha . . Ha . . . That′s a $5.00 ′Word isn′t it? . . . . . . Anyway I usually go to my boy Rudy Muck′s because my Credit′s good over there . . Savvy? . . . I′ll have Muck send Bunk a Trumpet Right Away. . . .

4: Letter to Isidore Barbarin

A photograph of the typed, one-page letter, dated September 1, 1922, is held by the Hogan Jazz Archive, Tulane University. A facsimile of the letter is given in the liner notes (authored by Lawrence Gushee) to "King Oliver's Jazz Band 1923," The Smithsonian Collection R001, CBS records, New York, 1975. An edited version has been published in Giddins (1988: 74). Apparently, there was an active exchange of letters between musicians who stayed in New Orleans and their colleagues who had moved to Chicago. Armstrong reports (1936: 35) that, before he left New Orleans, " 'King' Oliver would write to me quite often from Chicago."

Danny Barker (1986: 27) provides a good portrait of Isidore Barbarin, his grandfather, including this comment about his musical taste:

> Isidore referred to musicians who played jazz music in the many six-piece jazz bands about the city as "routine" musicians. It was a slur. To him, "routine" meant playing by ear, with no music, in the now "classic" jazz pattern: melody, then variations on a theme . . . I heard Isidore once say of [Buddy] Bolden, "Sure, I heard him. I knew him. He was famous with the ratty people." I soon learned what ratty people, ratty joints and dives meant: it meant good-time people, earthy people, who frequent anywhere there's a good time . . . So, ratty music is bluesy, folksy music that moves you and exhilarates you, makes you dance.

Armstrong was very much a product of the musical culture Barbarin disdained. Relations between uptown, darker-skinned musicians and downtown musicians who took pride in their Creole ancestry still await systematic investigation. Armstrong comments on such relations in stray remarks, here and there. In *Satchmo: My Life in New Orleans* (1954a: 142), he describes a tense and revealing encounter between a reading band, lead by John Robichaux, and the (mostly) nonreading band he played with, lead by Kid Ory; the encounter must have happened in 1919 or so, about three years before Armstrong was brought into Celestin's Tuxedo Brass Band, where he probably played with Isidore Barbarin. In a letter to Leonard Feather of October 1, 1941 (held at the Institute of Jazz Studies, Rutgers University), Armstrong told this story:

> Gee—they came runnin from every direction when they heard that 'Louiee Armstrong's Bus was parked at 'Dumaine and 'Claiborn Avenues . . . Two popular streets . . . I remember way back in the days when the Odd Fellows and the Labor day Parades used to pass that corner—I was quite a youngster then—but I still can remember that I had to do a lot of 'runnin—'second lining behind those parades just to hear—'Joe King Oliver or 'Bunk Johnson or Manuel Perez—blow those trumpets . . .

> Those ′Creoles were certainly bad in those days . . . The downtown boys would not let the uptown boys pass ′Dumaine and ′Claiborne without putting up a ′fight or getting ′sapped up . . .

Armstrong's two main mentors during his teenage years were Black Benny and Joe Oliver. The darkness of Black Benny's skin is signaled by his nickname, that of Joe Oliver's by Jelly Roll Morton's taunting nickname for him, "Blondie." Clyde Bernhardt (quoted in Wright 1987: 339) recalled Oliver saying, "There are three kinds of blacks; a *black*, a *lamb* black, and a *damn* black. I'm black and I only seen two other people in the world blacker'n me." According to Baby Dodds (1992: 13), "The [uptown and downtown] musicians mixed only if you were good enough." What is suggested by Armstrong's experiences, then, is that he was initially mentored by darker-skinned musicians; then, as his abilities blossomed in his late teens, he made his way into "downtown" musical circles.

Paul Barbarin died forty-seven years after this letter was written while performing in a parade with the revived Onward Brass Band. The occasion adds another dimension to our understanding of social interactions in New Orleans, for Barbarin's band was breaking the color barrier in this parade, as the first African American band to participate in what had been an exclusively white event. A poignant account of Barbarin's death is given in Buerkle and Barker (1973: 181).

5: "The Armstrong Story"

Partly typed and partly handwritten, this document is forty-eight pages, numbered consecutively; it is held at the Louis Armstrong House and Archives at Queens College/CUNY. The title is Armstrong's. The document is a continuation of *Satchmo: My Life in New Orleans*, Armstrong's published autobiography from 1954, with some slight overlap between the end of that book and the beginning of the present document. Photocopies of the last two pages of this document are on file at the Library of Congress, and on the back of them is stamped "Mail desk, N.Y. Aug. 18 2:52 PM 1954." Most likely, the entire document was written in 1954. Armstrong certainly conceived it as part of volume 1 of his autobiography. The decision to delete most of the present material from *Satchmo: My Life in New Orleans* and to end volume 1 with

Armstrong's first performance in Chicago was probably made by Glaser, as Giddins has reported (1988: 16).

To describe the relationships between this document and copies of it held by the Institute of Jazz Studies, Rutgers University, and the Library of Congress, it will be useful to divide the present document into three parts. The first page of the present document is numbered 121; a different typewriter is used beginning with page 128. So, for this discussion I will call pages 121–127 "section A." Armstrong changes to handwriting in the middle of page 131, yielding a "section B" that goes from page 128 to the middle of 131. And from the middle of page 131 he continues with handwriting through page 168, ending in mid-sentence to form, for the purpose of this discussion, "section C."

Section A overlaps with a complete thermofax copy of the typescript that was used to make *Satchmo: My Life in New Orleans*; this copy is now held by the Institute of Jazz Studies. Apparently, Armstrong held onto the original typescript and sent a copy to the publisher (or probably to Glaser, who forwarded it to the publisher); this copy made its way eventually to the Institute of Jazz Studies, while all that survives of the original is published as the present document. No known copy of section B survives. And, as mentioned already, the Library of Congress holds photocopies of the final two pages of section C. On the back of the second of these two photocopied pages held by the Library of Congress, Armstrong's handwriting appears—in the original, not a photocopy: "Dear Mr. Glaser, these are the two pages, you told me to send them back to you when I finished with them. Regards, Louis Armstrong." Thus, it would appear that Armstrong held onto the original and sent Glaser copies for submission to the publisher. Unquestionably, Armstrong conceived all of the present document as belonging to volume 1 of his autobiography. If sections B and C were written after publication, then Armstrong would more likely have signaled in his prose that he was making a fresh start on a sequel—which is exactly what he does in Chapter 9 of this book.

Doubts have been raised (see, for example, the discussion in Kenney 1991: 47ff. and Morgenstern 1986: viii) about whether Armstrong himself executed the typescript that was used to make *Satchmo: My Life in New Orleans*. Some details about the present document may be relevant to this debate. In a 1955 letter to Joe Glaser (Chapter 14 of this book), Armstrong refers to "my

Sweetheart + Secretary Miss, Velma Ford my sharp Chick whom you met while she was helping with my Satchmo story. She's very good at taking Dictation, etc." It is possible that Armstrong dictated rather than typed section A of the present document. Section A differs from other typescripts that are surely by Armstrong as follows: It has rare use of ellipses (only two instances); rare use of dashes; rare use of irregular capitalization; no irregular apostrophes or quotation marks; frequent use of commas, especially to separate clauses; consistent use of closed quotations to signal dialogue; no spacing after commas and periods. On the other hand, it is similar to other typescripts that are surely by Armstrong as follows: parentheses are wrapped around the number "4"; one—but only one, and that is not typical—case of unclosed parenthesis; some use of irregular capitalization (e.g., "New Orleans Greats"). If one finds these idiosyncrasies sufficiently indicative of Armstrong's typing, then perhaps the lack of more idiosyncrasies can be explained by the possibility that Armstrong has simply been more conventional than usual in typing this document, since he has the publisher in mind.

Section B, written on a different typewriter, contains more ellipses, more dashes, and more idiosyncrasies that mark it as unquestionably Armstrong's typing (e.g., "Yessir—'Lil" or "You see,—?"). The contrast with section A would seem to reinforce the idea that Armstrong did not type section A. This does not mean, of course, that its authenticity is in question. I do not doubt that these are Armstrong's words. But I also think it possible that he dictated them, rather than typed them. Alternatively, it could be that the explanation for the new typewriter and looser style in Section B is a lapse in time. (Recommending this possibility is the reintroduction of Lil Hardin and Honore Dutrey. The same point could be made about section C, where stories are again retold.) Thorough study of the complete thermofax copy held at the Institute of Jazz Studies would certainly shed more light on this problem.

The authenticity of Armstrong's other published autobiography, *Swing That Music*, has been challenged, and a brief comment is warranted here. *Swing That Music* was more heavily edited than was *Satchmo: My Life in New Orleans*, and Kenney (1991) properly identifies different "voices" in the text. *Swing That Music* includes few distinguishing marks of Armstrong's orthographic style, but this is not surprising given the heavy editorial reworking. It does include at least the distinctive use of quotation marks around proper names ("Fate" Marable). The misspelling of Sidney Bechet's last name as Bachet, a misspelling that is found in some of Armstrong's other writings, must surely derive from the manuscript or typescript that he supplied as a basis for the book. Other features are part of Armstrong's style, though they may not be distinctive enough to shore up the argument—occasional underlining for emphasis (transformed into italics for the printed version), use of parentheses, and long dashes. Surely it is inappropriate to dismiss this book as "ghost written," though the editorial treatment of Armstrong's prose makes it difficult to regard the document as directly representing Armstrong's words. I find it likely that the relationship between the published text and Armstrong's original text was somewhat close, that Armstrong was edited and embellished and altered, but that we can read a great deal of him in this book. In any event, *Swing That Music* is not a fictionalized embellishment of Armstrong's words, in the manner of Goffin's *Horn of Plenty*.

Armstrong credits Oliver's tutoring of Lil Hardin in "good′ ol′ New Orleans 4 Beat, which a lot of the Northern piano players couldn′t do to save their lives." Paul Barbarin's comments (Russell 1994: 58) about the early history of this style reinforce Oliver's important role in developing it: "You see, drummers like MacMurray or Jean Vigne. Them fellows they never played no four beats. All those drummers then played two beats. Never played four. The first time I ever heard four beats played was King Oliver and Ory and them playing at Economy Hall. They was playing the blues . . . See, playing this kind of music, this dixieland music, a lot of people are going to dance. See, the older people they don't know where to start. They go out but they can't get started. Too many beats. But see, with this kind of music that we play, they know where to come in and put their foot. The two beats is good for dancing. A good beat."

Armstrong's wedding to Lil Hardin was reported in the *Chicago Defender* (the article is reprinted in Wright 1987: 38). Armstrong believed that Lil Hardin had been valedictorian at Fisk University, and this claim has been repeated often. The claim is unlikely, however; it has been asserted recently that Hardin attended Fisk for no more than one year (Bergreen 1997: 181–82). The story of Armstrong and Nootsy is told in detail in *Satchmo: My Life in New Orleans* (p. 86). Nootsy is unnamed in that source, but the information that Armstrong—who must have been around age fourteen—was working as her pimp is provided.

Armstrong mentions Joe Oliver's distinguished performance of "Eccentric." On this, Preston Jackson commented (Shapiro and Hentoff 1955: 42): "One of the best numbers I ever heard Joe play was 'Eccentric.' He took all the breaks, imitating a rooster and a baby. He was a riot in those days, his band from 1915 to '16 to 1918 being the best in New Orleans. The LaRocca boys of the Dixieland Jazz Band used to hang around and got a lot of ideas from his gang."

Armstrong's moral point (delivered in his story about Hillare the drummer), that youthful poverty yields advantages that are unavailable to those who grow up with privilege, finds an interesting parallel in this discussion of Sidney Bechet by Barney Bigard (1986: 70): "If you're poor you can realize more of something than if you are rich. By just being rich you don't have to bother about things so much. A lot of life just doesn't ever come your way. But if you're born poor, you feel it. That all comes out in your music. So many of the guys that suffered because of the racial situation and the economic situation in New Orleans, for instance, they can't even read music, but they play with that feeling. That's all they have to offer. . . . The old white teachers wouldn't teach Negroes. I was lucky and had a first-rate teacher, but a lot of those guys didn't. You take guys like Benny Goodman, Artie Shaw and Woody Herman. They all play with feeling but they were taught right. Even from the start. It's easy to see how they made it, but now I'll tell you about one of the greatest instrumentalists that I ever heard in my life. This guy didn't have any knowledge about reading music but he became one of the most famous players in jazz. That's Sidney Bechet."

6 and 7: Letters to Robert Goffin (May 7 and July 19, 1944), The "Goffin Notebooks"

The two letters (both typed) and the notebooks (handwritten) are held by the Institute of Jazz Studies, Rutgers University, which purchased them from Goffin's estate. On the cover of each of the four notebooks is the heading "Military Writing Portfolio," decorated with a military emblem, bald eagle, soldiers, and stars and stripes.

Armstrong's personal acquaintance with Goffin began as early as 1932, when Goffin published his *Aux Frontières du Jazz* and dedicated the book to Armstrong. According to Jones and Chilton (1971: 135), when Armstrong was given a copy of the book, "he was so moved by the dedication to 'Louis Armstrong, the true King of Jazz,' that he promptly kissed it." More than usual (though one finds this also in letters to other white journalists, such as Leonard Feather), Armstrong translates "jive talk" for the Belgian Goffin; for example: "spade (that's colored folk)," and "a lot of 'Ice' (meaning) they treated us rather cool."

For *Esquire*, Armstrong wrote another account of the 1920s, also organized by year. It was published in 1947 as "Chicago, Chicago, That Toddlin' Town: How King and Ol' Satch Dug It in the Twenties."

The story that concludes the Goffin notebooks, in which Armstrong is held at gunpoint and instructed to return to New York, highlights the managerial problems that he experienced during the early 1930s. As he says in the Goffin notebooks, "Come to think of it—I sure had a 'Manager's 'Fit." His managerial troubles—and, it seems, the threats from organized crime—ended when he hired Joe Glaser, and this is surely one reason among several that he became so devoted to Glaser. During much of the early 1930s he avoided New York and Chicago, presumably to stay clear of gangster threats.

Armstrong freely praises musicians throughout his writings. But with respect to Coleman Hawkins, the great tenor saxophonist and one of the true giants in jazz history, it is all he can do simply to record his name, as just another member of Fletcher Henderson's dance band in 1924. Armstrong and Hawkins were not fond of each other. A low point in their relationship came in 1934, when Armstrong refused to show up for a scheduled performance with Hawkins (Jones and Chilton 1971: 152). This was not the only clash of egos that Armstrong experienced during his long career; there were also tensions, at times, with Sidney Bechet, Earl Hines, and Benny Goodman.

Armstrong hints at chilly relations within Henderson's band. Rex Stewart (1991: 92–96) paints a fuller picture, with emphasis on problems caused by Charlie Green. Armstrong was a little more explicit about his dissatisfaction in a letter published by Jones and Chilton (1971: 211):

> Fletcher only let me play 3rd cornet in his band. The whole time I was in his band he'd only give me 16 bars to get-off with, but he'd let me hit those high notes that the big prima-donnas, first-chair men, couldn't hit. I stayed and tolerated those fellow-musicians cutting up on the bandstand instead of playing their music. The fellows had such big heads if they missed a note so what? Hmmm. When I talked to Lil on the 'phone and told her what was happening she immediately said 'come on home' . . . As far as Fletcher was concerned he wouldn't even listen to me sing nothing. All the singing that I did before I joined Fletcher Henderson went down the drain . . . [Lil] had a damned good band. To me, it was

> better than Fletcher's, other than all those big arrangements that Don Redman was making, I wasn't moved very much with them, too much airs, etc. Fletcher was so carried away with that society shit and his education he slipped by a small-timer and a young musician—me—who wanted to do everything for him musically. I personally didn't think Fletcher cared too much for me anyway.

Earl Hines (quoted in Dance 1977: 58) adds to this picture:

> Louis went to New York soon after we opened at the Grand Terrace, and I never forgot the postcard he sent me when he got there. It read like this: "Man, everybody up here is trying to cut one another. It's got so bad that when we were at a party one night a guy with a bass horn on his shoulder came and knocked on the door. 'Anybody here I can cut?' he asked."

In several documents published in this book, Armstrong stresses the importance to him of Erskine Tate's "Symphony Orchestra" at the Vendome Theater. In a letter to Jones and Chilton (1971: 212), he adds: "I learned a lot playing under the direction of Erskine Tate, we played all kinds of music. I really did sharpen up on my reading there. We played the scores for the silent movies, and a big overture when the curtain would rise at the end of the film. I got a solo on stage, and my big thing was *Cavalleria Rusticana*. That always started with me, sometimes I used to warm-up with snatches from it." His success with Tate is described by Milt Hinton (see Lax 1974) and also by Lionel Hampton (1989: 26): "I'll never forget the first time Louis Armstrong played with the Erskine Tate band. My uncle Richard bought tickets to the Vendome for the entire family. We were in the front row of the first balcony, and we could see the entire audience go crazy after his first, fifteen-minute solo."

Here and elsewhere, Armstrong mentions his fondness for his cousin Clarence, who died in New York City on August 27, 1998.

8: "The Satchmo Story"

This typed document is eleven pages, numbered consecutively; it is held by the Louis Armstrong House and Archives at Queens College/CUNY. In the body of the text, Armstrong gives an approximate date for the document when he says "I am about to be fifty nine years old . . . This Fourth of July—1959." The title is Armstrong's. A short version of the story of Mrs. Martin and her "three beautiful daughters with light skins of the Creole type: Orleania, Alice and Wilhelmina," is told in *Satchmo: My Life in New Orleans* (p. 30).

Lionel Hampton (Hampton 1989: 37) described how he came to play the vibraphone while recording with Armstrong in California, October 16, 1930:

> We were recording for Okeh, and the recording studio was also the NBC studio and sitting in the corner was a set of vibes. Louis said, "What's that instrument over there?" And I said, "Oh, that's a new instrument that they're bringing into percussion, into the drum department. They call it a vibraharp, some call it a vibraphone." At that time they were only playing a few notes on it—*bing, bong, bang*—like the tones you hear for N-B-C . . . Louis noticed the vibraharp again. So he said, "Can you play it?" I was a young kid, full of confidence, and I said, "Sure." So I looked at it, and it had the same keyboard as the xylophone had. He said, "Pull it out in the middle of the floor and play something on it." . . . Everybody's standing around waiting to record, and I played one of his solos, note for note, that I had taken off one of his records. . . . He said, "Come on, we going to put this on a record. You can play on this record." Eubie Blake had sent Louis a copy of his song, "Memories of You," and I played the introduction on it . . . That's the first time jazz had ever been played on vibes.

The story of the arrest on marijuana charges is told more fully by Armstrong in Jones and Chilton (1971: 113). Armstrong contrasts the severity of punishment for marijuana possession to casualness in the United States about racial violence: "Because since the days when I was actually 'Wailing—smoking gage, it was plentiful—much easy to get, the Judges weren't so heavy with them years like he gives out these days. Why I'd much rather shoot a nigger in his ass than to be caught with a stick of *shit* . . . The Judge would honestly respect you better . . . . . . " On file in the Library of Congress is a questionnaire about narcotic use by jazz musicians—one Paul K. Dougherty was seeking Armstrong's help in compiling a "sort of 'Kinsey Report' of Jazz"—complete with Armstrong's handwritten, indignant responses, such as:

"The Music that comes of a Man's' Horn' is good enough for me—his personal habit—I don't care." Also on file in the Library of Congress is a letter Armstrong wrote from Europe to Mezz Mezzrow, dated September 18, 1932. Though marijuana is not explicitly mentioned, it is clear from statements like the following that this is what Armstrong is requesting from Mezzrow: "see to your 'Boy being 'well 'fixed, because I wouldn't want to 'Run 'Short, because it, might 'Bring me 'Down. *'No might* in it, it *'would.* Ha Ha." According to Ralph Gleason, "Mezz sold his grass by the shoebox coast to coast, mail order, as well as standing on 125th Street underneath the tree of life, dealing with all who came by" (Gleason, 1975: 56).

9: "Jazz on a High Note"

Armstrong wrote this article for *Esquire* (Dec. 1951, p. 185). His criticism of Lil Hardin in "Louis Armstrong + the Jewish Family in New Orleans, La., the Year of 1907" should be balanced against praise for Lil in this document and elsewhere. One source of bitterness was a dispute about authorship of songs from the 1920s. From Armstrong's description in this article of their collaborations, it is easy to see how the matter could have become confused.

Armstrong describes cutting contests between himself and trumpeters in New Orleans in Jones and Chilton (1971: 11). Danny Barker (1986: 129–133) describes a spectacular cutting contest in Chicago between Reuben Reeves and Armstrong. Barney Bigard (1986: 30) describes a victory over Johnny Dunn. A recently discovered lead sheet for "Cornet Chop Suey" is reproduced in Miller (1994: 105; see the discussion by Dan Morgenstern on p. 101). According to David Chevan, Armstrong filed copyright applications for more than eighty compositions (cited by Barrett 1992: 239).

Armstrong suggests several times in this article that certain pieces inspired him to visualize New Orleans: "The recording we made [of "Weary Blues"] for the Okeh people reminded me so much of New Orleans, until I was looking direct into New Orleans when we were recording it." "So what little creations we did in the recording of "I'm Not Rough"—just remember that I was looking right into the Chops of my idol—the great King Joe Oliver." "This particular recording ["Potato Head Blues"] really "gassed me" because of the perfect phrasing that was done by Johnny and Ory . . . I could look direct into the Pelican Dance Hall, at Gravier and Rampart Streets in New Orleans, during the days of the First World War." The imagery calls to mind a story from "*Scanning* the History of Jazz" in which Armstrong says that he is able to look over the shoulders of an inferior musician and see his mentor Joe Oliver, just as a worshipper is able to see Jesus through the preaching of an inferior pastor.

It is generally acknowledged today that Armstrong's scat vocal on "Heebie Jeebies" was not the very "beginning of Scat Singing," though its influence was considerable.

William Kenney (1991: 124) describes "Okeh Race Record Artist's Night" in February 1926:

> The Consolidated Talking Machine Company's promotional cooperation with South Side musicians and music entrepreneurs climaxed in 1926 with two star-studded programs staged at the Chicago Coliseum. The first, called "Okeh Race Record Artist's Night," took place on Feb. 27, 1926, co-sponsored by the South Side Elks Lodge. It was prepared for by an intensive publicity campaign in the sixteen Okeh record retail outlets on the South Side. At the Coliseum, guitar sensation Lonnie Johnson, in company with Louis Armstrong's Hot Five, made records on stage "to demonstrate how it's done." These recordings were played back to an awed crowd immediately afterward. Clarence Williams, Bennie Moten, King Oliver, and Richard M. Jones further entertained the crowd, leading orchestras which accompanied several heavily promoted vocalists. The program was broadcast over the Chicago *Tribune's* radio station WGN, and ex-Mayor Thompson took the occasion to make a speech.

10: Early Years with Lucille

This untitled, handwritten document is thirty-five pages, numbered consecutively beginning with page 20 and ending with page 54; it is held at the Louis Armstrong House and Archives at Queens College/CUNY. Since the document begins in mid-paragraph on page 20 and ends in mid-sentence on page 54 (which is filled), we may assume that the first nineteen pages have been lost and that there was a continuation that has also been lost. Armstrong implies a date for this document ca. 1970 when he writes: "So we *wrapped* it *up* in our *minds*. That has been over *Thirty Years* ago."

The house in Corona, New York purchased by the Armstrongs is now open to the public, under the auspices of the Louis Armstrong House and Archives at Queens College/CUNY.

11: Letter to Leonard Feather

The three-page, typed letter, dated September 18, 1941, is held by the Institute of Jazz Studies, Rutgers University, which holds a series of letters from Armstrong to Feather. Armstrong writes about an integrated dance with the comment that "Honest they get along down here at these dances just like one 'beeg family." It is impossible to tell if this is a sarcastic remark, which the irregular spelling of "big" would seem to be suggest. In an article from 1961 (1961: 84), Armstrong wrote about an integrated event in Miami: ". . . I'd like to recall one of my most inspiring moments. It was in 1948. I was playing a concert date in a Miami auditorium. I walked on stage and there I saw something I thought I'd never see. I saw thousands of people, colored and white on the main floor. Not segregated in one row of whites and another row of Negroes. Just all together—naturally. I thought I was in the wrong state. When you see things like that you know you're going forward." Armstrong thought that his music could work against bigotry (1961: 86): "These same society people may go around the corner and lynch a Negro. But while they're listening to our music, they don't think about trouble. What's more they're watching Negro and white musicians play side by side. And we bring contentment and pleasure. I always say, 'Look at the nice taste we leave. It's bound to mean something. That's what music is for.' "

Armstrong mentions three pieces composed by Scott Joplin in this letter, but only one, "Maple Leaf Rag," was actually by Joplin. "Grace and Beauty" was composed by James Scott, "African Pas" by Maurice Kirwin (identification thanks to Charles Kinzer).

12: Letter to Betty Jane Holder

The four-page, typed letter, dated February 9, 1952, is held at the Hogan Jazz Archive, Tulane University. It appears that this letter was solicited by Betty Jane Holder for use in an article about Armstrong, just as Leonard Feather and others solicited material from him. Gillespie's quoted criticism should be understood in the context of public tensions between Armstrong and Bebop during the 1940s; later, Gillespie and Armstrong became good friends.

Armstrong speaks about his early experience with the Zulu club in *Satchmo: My Life in New Orleans* (p. 126 ff). He describes a parade in 1918 at which an infamous white policeman was parodied by the Zulus; the parody was poignant for Armstrong, since he had been unjustly imprisoned by this very policeman, coming out of prison on the day of the parade. He also writes of the Zulus in a letter to Leonard Feather of June 29, 1953 (Institute of Jazz Studies, Rutgers University), that is worth quoting at length:

> I can remember the mardigras as far back as five years old . . . I remember the first time I saw my mother and father, mask . . . You talking about a sharp masquerader, or masqueradress' I'll never forget how sharp my mother was . . . In those days the women would go the limit to look good on mardigras day . . . They would buy the very best in silk—satins and laces . . . The best silk stockings that were made in those days . . . They wore masks the image of a face . . . And they would carry a—small switch—in their hands . . . That's what they use to let you know that they know you, then they'll give you a little peep from under their masks, and, from then on, or, maybe not, they'll take you into a saloon and buy you a drink, well,—some drinks. . . . . [. . .]
>
> I sure was proud of my mother, in her short, silk mardigras outfit . . . With her lil, ol,—big leg self her silk stockings running all up to her——you'd be surprised—how beautiful those women used to look . . . And still do . . . The Zulus Club was the first colored carnival club to get together in New Orleans . . . The Club has been—for generations consist of the fellows in my neighborhood . . . The members were—coal cart drivers, bar tenders—waiters, Hustlers, etc., people of all walks of life . . . Nobody had very much . . . But they loved each other . . . And put their best foot forward as to making a real fine thing of the Zulu Aid and Social Club . . . It's been my life long ambition to become King of the Zulus, someday . . . And the Lord certainly did answer my prayer (Prayers) . . . Just think . . . New Orleans has been having the Mardigras for generations . . . Even—before I was born . . . I watched a many white Kings Launch in the Mississippi River . . . At the foot of Canal Street . . . He'd get off of his big fine boat looking like a million (which most of

> them have) . . . The King would then get up on his float which was waiting for him to come from somewhere up the river . . . Then the parade was on". . . . . [. . .]
>
> On Mardigras day, everybody do a little masking of some what . . . Even when I was a kid, I'd black my face, pick up on some old raggidy clothes, and burlesque somebody . . . [. . .]
>
> My father was a guy who masked every year . . . He used to mask in a big white monkey suit . . . The trouble with a guy who'll pass you in a monkey suit, he's liable to hit you in the 'chops with their tails . . . Because their tails have marbles in them . . . A lick in the 'chops with those 'tails would make them swell up, just like, 'two beef hearts. . . . .

In "Louis Armstrong + the Jewish Family in New Orleans, La., the Year of 1907," Armstrong drops this brief but provocative reference to what may have been a "white face" contest (for "flower" read "flour"?): "Some nights we' see a moving picture at the Iroquois Theater—10 cents each for May Ann + Tom, 5 cents for Mama Lucy + me. (I won an amateur contest—dip face in flower.)" In any event, it seems clear that masking was a cultural practice that Armstrong was brought into at a young age.

The Zulu tradition in New Orleans and Armstrong's participation in 1949 is discussed by Tassin (1984) and by Mitchell (1995). Tassin (1984: 47) describes Armstrong's costume: "a red feathered crown, a red velvet tunic trimmed with gold sequins, black tights and gold-colored shoes. Over the tights, he wore a yellow cellophane grass skirt. Satchmo was later quoted as saying that his costume that year was what inspired Liberace's wardrobe." The outrageous Zulu rituals parodied the institution of "Rex," the white Mardi Gras king. Writes Mitchell (p. 151): "Zulu did everything that Rex did. If Rex traveled by water, coming up the Mississippi with an escort from the U.S. Navy, Zulu came down the New Basin Canal on a tugboat. If Rex held a scepter, Zulu held a ham bone. If Rex had the city police marching before him, Zulu had the Zulu police . . . All that Zulu did caricatured Rex; a black lord of misrule upsetting the reign of the white lord, a mocker of a mocker." To understand this importance of Rex is to appreciate the full richness of a stage joke made by Armstrong while performing for an audience that included the King of England in 1932. As Armstrong told the story in an interview (1955: 56):

ARMSTRONG: . . . the biggest laugh about me and the King was when I was playin' that tune for him in 1932, "I'll Be Glad When You're Dead, You Rascal You." I hollered, "This one's for you, 'Rex'—that's what I called him, 'Rex.' "

INTERVIEWER: Was he a cat?

ARMSTRONG: He's got to be or I wouldn' called him "Rex." You see, when you're a cat you appreciate your name, your nickname like that.

Probably no one in the hall but Armstrong—the future King of the Zulus—appreciated the full implications of the King of England being nicknamed "Rex."

Shortly after it was given to Armstrong, the honor of King of the Zulus was enjoyed by Sidney Bechet (probably in 1951). Bechet (1960: 197) described his gratitude:

> . . . it is the ambition of every big guy in New Orleans to be the King of the Zulus. So Louis Armstrong, he happened to be the King a year or two before, and it was in *Time* magazine and everywhere. So M. Badel, he asked me, "Would you like to be king for a day?" So I accepted it. I phoned my fiancée up and we accepted it. And it was one of the biggest things that's ever been seen since Aly Khan's marriage. We went right around the town, and there were bands on carts going around just like I remember from way back when I used to be in the second line. It was really something, and I am certainly grateful to all these people and to all those musicianers who made it into a day I won't ever forget.

13: Letter to Joe Glaser

The sixteen-page, handwritten letter, dated August 2, 1955, is held by the Library of Congress, Washington, D.C., which purchased a series of letters written by Armstrong to Glaser. The stationery is headed "Moulin Rouge, Las Vegas, Nevada."

The advice given to Armstrong—that he "always have a *White Man* (who like you) and can + will put his Hand on your shoulder and say—*''This is ''My'' Nigger''* and, Can't Nobody Harm' Ya"—is credited not to Black Benny in this document. However, in a letter (dating probably from 1970) to Max Jones (Jones and Chilton 1971: 10), it is attributed to a bouncer named Slippers. Slippers is also named as the advisor in Meryman (1966: 27), where Armstrong also reports that "Years later I told that to Joe Glaser, my ofay manager, and he said, 'You're nuts.'" Armstrong expressed similar thoughts to Larry L. King (quoted by Balliett 1994: 72) in a 1967 interview: "If you didn't have a white captain to back you in the old days—to put his hand on your shoulder—you was just a damn sad nigger . . . If a Negro had the proper white man to reach the law and say, 'What the hell you mean locking up MY nigger?' then—quite naturally—the law would walk him free. Get in that jail *without* your white boss, and yonder comes the chain gang!"

Armstrong places his promiscuity in two broad contexts. First is the local culture of his youth, when he was a teenager "hanging around Gamblers, Pimps, People of All Walks of life." Black Benny gave him the advice to "Always have another woman for a Sweetheart on the outside." The other context is musician's culture, as it is lived on the road. Armstrong quotes his pianist, Billy Kyle: "it's so grand + glorious to be with a woman, so why fight it." Rex Stewart (1991: 139) spoke frankly about the promiscuous lifestyle of musicians on the road: ". . . usually there would be some amorous encounters. The ladies seemed to think musicians were romantic figures, almost like a movie star, and they wanted to know us . . . To be factual, all of the fellows had little black books crammed with addresses and telephone numbers of fillies from coast to coast." Lucille Armstrong maintained practical attitude: "Let's say the eye sees what it wants to see . . . There are all sorts of women in the entertainment field. They throw their arms around Louis. I have partial vision on purpose . . . I call Louis when I am going to join him while he is on tour" (quoted in Jones and Chilton 1971: 168).

On the reference to Velma Ford taking dictation for "my Satchmo story," see the Appendix entry for "The Armstrong Story." In any event, it is clear from the present document that Velma Ford was a secretary who did more than type.

Armstrong writes: "I mean, I really *Grined* in that Cunt." "Grined" should be understood in the context of African American vernacular "grind," meaning "to copulate" (Dillard 1977: 23–25).

Armstrong's devotion to Joe Glaser must have been due initially to the fact of Glaser solving his " 'Manager's 'Fit," described in "The Goffin Notebooks." In the long run, it was certainly fostered by Glaser's ability to keep Armstrong's career going through the harsh vicissitudes of fashion that have marked the music business in the United States throughout this century. Armstrong must have often reflected on the pathetic decline of his mentor, Joe Oliver, whom he encountered near the end in Savannah, Georgia, during the Depression (see Armstrong 1966: 47ff.). The general problem was articulated in the following way by an African American jazz musician from New Orleans (quoted but not named in Buerkle and Barker 1973: 99): "Scott Joplin and many other composers and musicians faded into the shadows—unsung but fighting and grasping at the fickle American music lovers—who will desert the current music (whatever it is) for the new thing. It's an American pattern. . . ."

Barney Bigard, who played with Armstrong for ten years during the 1940s and 1950s, had this to say about Armstrong's relationship with Glaser (Bigard 1986): "As far as Louis and Joe Glaser went, they really did get along just fine. When Louis said in an interview that Joe was the greatest man he had ever met, he probably meant it. They really were plain old-fashioned friends. Louis wasn't just saying that for business reasons" (p. 115). "Joe hired and fired everybody. Whatever he did it was alright with Louis. If he fired someone Louis wouldn't say anything, even if he liked the guy real well. It wasn't on account of that he was frightened of Joe, or that Joe was a white guy handling him. It was just that Louis long ago figured that he did best out of the world if he didn't get involved with the business side. He didn't want to tread on anyone's toes or hurt anyone's feelings, so he just made no comments on anything that happened" (p. 116). "[Glaser] was a hell of a business man. I don't think anyone else could have taken Louis as far as he did" (p. 117).

14: "Lombardo Grooves Louis!"

This article was written by Leonard Feather for *Metronome* (Sept. 1949, p. 18). A companion article titled "Pops Pops Top on Sloppy Bob" appeared one month later. Leonard Feather (1972: 31) describes putting these blindfold tests together at Armstrong's home in Corona.

Jones and Chilton (1971: 111) report further on Armstrong's admiration of Lombardo in the 1920s: " 'Now you dig that "Sweethearts,' " [Armstrong] pointed out. 'It reminds you of Lombardo . . . When we were at the Savoy in Chicago in 1928, every Saturday night we'd catch the Owl Club, with Guy Lombardo, and as long as he played we'd sit right there . . . We didn't go nowhere until after Lombardo signed off. That went on for months.' Lombardo advertised 'the sweetest music this side of heaven' and Louis said that was what he played. He added that he often sat in with the Lombardo band in Chicago during the '20s. 'And that was before the first mixed session was ever put on record, so what does that make me?' he asked."

William Kenney (1991: 114) reports an additional detail regarding Armstrong's relations with white musicians during the 1920s: "One night, Armstrong, who had never heard [Wild Bill Davison] play, invited him to sit in. Wild Bill played one or two passages which Armstrong himself might have played, and the black jazzman burst into laughter. Davison was never sure whether he was laughing with him or at him. Wild Bill later invited Armstrong to a party at his North Side apartment, where, it turned out, he was the only black. Armstrong refused to leave the kitchen. Davison and his friends therefore moved into the kitchen, too."

The October installment of Armstrong's blindfold test included this provocative remark, in response to Babs Gonzales's "Prelude to a Nightmare": "They're all trying to take everybody to Africa, that's what they're doing . . . advertising Africa! I've got a book I can show you where they prove that all this bebop is nothing but African and Zulus' talk. Put this one right along with the rest of the boppers. I won't rate it."

The bop rivalry was promoted by Armstrong's management. A publicity manual (held at the Institute of Jazz Studies, Rutgers University) distributed by his manager includes the following:

ARMSTRONG ON BEBOP

The national jazz controversy, which began in *Time* magazine will be centered in ———— when Louis Armstrong arrives for his ———— (Date Here) concert at ———— (Name of Hall Here).

The cause of New Orleans 'Ragtime' versus 'Progressive Jazz,' long a heated subject among musicians, has been extended to include all phases of our national culture. It has assumed implications political, psychological and international.

Armstrong focused the debate and brought it prominence, with his statement that ". . . them rebop boys, they're great technicians. Mistakes—that's all rebop is. Man, you gotta be a technician to know when you make them . . . New York and 52nd street—that's what messed up Jazz. Them cats play too much—a whole lot of notes, weird notes . . . most of the so-called modern music I heard in 1918. That stuff means nothing. You've got to carry the melody." [. . .]

New York and San Francisco papers, quick to sense the political implications of the word "progressive" have editorialized that the music of New Orleans, the old style, was the music of the reactionary elements of our culture, who were attempting to preserve the status quo and restrict the ideas of the younger elements. [. . .]

Rebop, bebop, or "Progressive" music, derives its title from the sounds made by the instrumentalists. The high note is the re or be, and the low note is the bop. The notes are generally weird and fast and the result is frantic. Like Chopin or Liszt's lesser efforts, there is the tendency to play too many notes in an attempt to impress the audience.

The next round will be held at (Name of Hall) on (Date) when Louis will answer the bebop followers with the best of America's jazz. Featured also will be Jack Teagarden, Barney Bigard, Cozy Cole and Earl Hines.

Bebop fans are invited to attend.

Sidney Bechet (1960: 192) describes contests around 1949, set up by Rudi Blesh:

> there was to be a bop band and a jazz band to show themselves . . . the bop musicianers came on and played, and the people didn't even move, they didn't move a hand for them. There was nothing for the bop musicianers; Bop was dead. And then we came on and we hadn't even finished the first number before we had them going. They really moved. They were demanding it, they wanted more. . . . Louis Armstrong, he'd been to one of these contests at Bop City before then and he'd been there for weeks. He'd really broken it up. He'd topped all receipts they'd ever had. They told him he could stay just as long as he wanted.

15: Letter to L/Cpl. Villec

This ten-page, handwritten letter is not dated; the envelope is postmarked 1967. The letter is held in the John C. Browning Collection, Durham, North Carolina. The envelope is addressed to L/Cpl. William H. Villec/Sub Unit #2—Headquarters BN/'A' Co. 4th Plt. 3rd engr. BN/3rd Marine Div. (fwd)/F.P.O. San Francisco, Calif 96602 (Air mail Special Delivery 2279387).

Armstrong also mentions his experiences singing in church in *Satchmo: My Life in New Orleans* (1954a: 11). In "Early Years with Lucille," he states that he is a Baptist. When asked in an interview (Armstrong 1955: 59), "Are you a religious man?" his response was "Yeah. I'm a Baptist and a good friend of the Pope's and I always wear a Jewish star a friend gave me for luck." In the present document, he implies that he attended the Sanctified Church when young. Pops Foster (1971: 20) describes musical practice in a New Orleanian Holiness Church in the first decade of this century: "The Holiness church was the only one that didn't consider music sinful. Their music was something. They'd clap their hands and bang a tambourine and sing. Sometimes they had a piano player, and he'd really play a whole lot of jazz. You should've heard it."

On the broad range of Armstrong's musical tastes, well in place from his teenage years onward, see Barrett (1992).

16: "Scanning the History of Jazz"

Armstrong wrote this article for *The Jazz Review*, July 1960, p. 7; it was later reprinted in *Esquire*, December 1971, p. 184. In the *Esquire* article, the first three pages are facsimile of Armstrong's handwriting; *The Jazz Review* gives handwritten facsimile for the last page, as well. Armstrong writes the title on page 1. Portions of the article have been deleted in the present edition, due to overlap with other documents.

By error of omission, Armstrong does not say, in the first sentence of this article, precisely whether the term "jazz" was or was not used during his childhood in New Orleans. Tellingly, this same hesitation is found in "Louis Armstrong + the Jewish Family in New Orleans, La., the Year of 1907" and again in The "Goffin Notebooks." Nevertheless, it seems quite clear that Armstrong means to say, here and in the other documents, that the word "jazz" was *not* used when he was young. As he explains in the third sentence of the present document: "In those days it was called *Rag Time Music*." Other New Orleanians from this period—Sidney Bechet and Pops Foster, for example—concurred. In an interview (Armstrong 1955: 60), Armstrong responded to the question What is jazz? by saying, "I wouldn't say I know what jazz is, because I don't look at it from that angle. I look at it from music—we never did worry about what it was in New Orleans, we just always tried to play good. And the public named it. It was ragtime, Dixieland, gut-bucket, jazz, swing—and it ain't nothin' but the same music." And in an article published by *Metronome* (Armstrong 1945), Armstrong answered a query from Leonard Feather as follows: "Dear Leonard: Your question is— Are Women Capable of appreciating good Jazz . . . You see—you had me stung for a moment—because we Cats use the word good Jazz for something else—too (tee hee) but now I Dig what you mean . . ." Armstrong's opinion was that yes, women could appreciate good jazz.

17: "Our Neighborhood"

This handwritten document is six pages, numbered consecutively; it is held at the Louis Armstrong House and Archives at Queens College/CUNY. Armstrong mentions returning from the hospital, which would place the document in 1969 or 1970. The title is Armstrong's. Armstrong's fondness for Chinese food, which appears to have held strong in his late years, began in his youth, as explained in "Louis Armstrong and the Jewish Family in New Orleans, La., the Year of 1907": "But for a change and something different—My Mother + my *Step* Father used to take *me* + *Mama* Lucy (my sister) down in China Town + have a Chinese meal for a change. A kind of *special* occasion. And the *Bill* in those days were real cheap. And we felt as though we were having something Big. We would also order Fried Rice and *Liver Gravy* with our Red Beans. And *ooh, God*—you would *lick* your *fingers'* it would taste *so* good."

18: Open Letter to Fans

This handwritten, untitled document is dated at the top of page 1 both March 15, 1970, and June 1, 1970. It is twenty-two pages, numbered consecutively, and it is held by the Louis Armstrong House and Archives at Queens College/CUNY; the archivist has supplied the title. It was written while Armstrong was recovering from illness at Beth Israel Hospital.

Armstrong's conviction that laxatives promote good health began as a child. In *Satchmo: My Life in New Orleans* (p. 16) he describes his reunion with his mother at age five (having been raised by his grandmother until this age). The reunion was caused by her need for help during an illness. In her first lesson to him about health, she made him promise to "take a physic at least once a week as long as you live." Armstrong highlighted Swiss Kriss in a

Christmas card that included a photograph of him sitting on the toilet (reproduced in Giddins 1988: 189).

19: "Good-bye to All of You"

Armstrong wrote this for *Esquire*, December 1969, p. 158. In addition to Armstrong, elderly celebrities who responded to *Esquire*'s invitation included Rube Goldberg, Maurice Chevalier, Norman Rockwell, Lotte Lehmann, Buckminster Fuller, and Leopold Stokowski.

BIBLIOGRAPHY OF WRITINGS BY LOUIS ARMSTRONG

This bibliography includes all published writings that I have been able to consult, along with unpublished writings and interviews cited in the present book.

Armstrong, Louis. 1922. Letter to Isidore Barbarin, Sept. 1. Hogan Jazz Archive, Tulane University. Published in Chapter 4 of this book.

———. 1932. Letter to Mezz Mezzrow, Sept. 18. Library of Congress, Washington, D.C.

———. 1936. *Swing that Music*. New York: Longmans.

———. 1937. Letter to Captain Joseph Jones, Nov. 3. Published in "Louis Armstrong's Letter to His 'Daddy.' " *The Second Line* 26 (July 1976): 12.

———. 1938a. "Les Hite et son Orchestre." *Jazz Hot*, Dec.–Jan., p. 7.

———. 1938b. "King Oliver Is Dead." *Jazz Hot*, April–May, p. 9.

———. 1939. Letter to William Russell, Oct. 3. Historic New Orleans Collection, New Orleans, Louisiana.

———. 1940a. "Special Jive." *Harlem Tattler*, July 2, p. 7.

———. 1940b. "Special Jive." *Harlem Tattler*, July 19, p. 7.

———. 1941a. "60–Year-Old 'Bunk' Johnson, Louis' Tutor, Sits in the Band." *Down Beat*, Aug. 15, p. 11.

———. 1941b. "Berigan Can't Do No Wrong." *Down Beat*, Sept. 1, p. 7.

———. 1941c. Letter to Leonard Feather, Sept. 18. Institute of Jazz Studies, Rutgers University. Published in Chapter 11 of this book.

———. 1941d. Letter to Leonard Feather, Oct. 1. Institute of Jazz Studies, Rutgers University.

———. 1944a. Letter to Leonard Feather, Feb. 9. Published in "Louis and Letters." *Metronome*, April 1945, p. 48.

Armstrong, Louis. 1944b. Letter to Leonard Feather, April 2. Published as "Louis and Letters." *Metronome*, April 1945, p. 48.

———. 1944c. Letter to Robert Goffin, May 7. Institute of Jazz Studies, Rutgers University. Published in Chapter 6 of this book.

———. 1944d. Letter to Robert Goffin, July 19. Institute of Jazz Studies, Rutgers University. Published in Chapter 6 of this book.

———. 1944e. The "Goffin Notebooks." Institute of Jazz Studies, Rutgers University. Published in Chapter 7 of this book.

———. 1946a. Letter to Leonard Feather, December 5. Institute of Jazz Studies, Rutgers University.

———. 1946b. "Chicago, Chicago, That Toddlin' Town: How King and Ol' Satch Dug It in the Twenties." *Esquire's 1947 Jazz Book*, pp. 40–3.

———. 1947a. "Storyville—Where the Blues Were Born," *True*, Nov., p. 32.

———. 1948. " 'Bop Will Kill Business Unless It Kills Itself First'—Louis Armstrong." Interview published in *Down Beat*, April 7, p. 2.

———. 1949a. "Lombardo Grooves Louis!" With Leonard Feather, for *Metronome*, September, p. 18. Published in Chapter 14 of this book.

———. 1949b. "Pops Pops Top on Sloppy Bop." With Leonard Feather for *Metronome*, October, p. 18.

———. 1949?. Radio Interview. In a publicity booklet titled "Publicity Manual on Louis Armstrong, 'Satchmo,' Associated Booking Corp." Institute of Jazz Studies, Rutgers University.

———. 1950a. Review of *Mr. Jelly Roll: The Fortunes of Jelly Roll Morton, New Orleans Creole and Inventor of Jazz* by Alan Lomax. *New York Times*, June 18, p. 3.

———. 1950b. "Europe—With Kicks." *Holiday*, June, p. 3.

———. 1950c. "Ulceratedly Yours." *Down Beat*, July 14, p. 1.

———. 1950d. "Care of the Lip," *The Record Changer*, July–Aug., p. 30.

———. 1950e. "Joe Oliver is Still King." *The Record Changer*, July–Aug., p. 10. Published in Chapter 2 of this book.

———. 1950f. "Bunk Didn't Teach Me." *The Record Changer*, July–Aug., p. 30. Published in Chapter 3 of this book.

———. 1951a. "They'll Never Come Back—the Good Old Days." Interview published in *Melody Maker*, Sept. 15, p. 3.

———. 1951b. "Jazz on a High Note." *Esquire*, Dec., p. 185. Published in Chapter 9 of this book.

———. 1952a. Letter to Betty Jane Holder, Feb. 9. Hogan Jazz Archive, Tulane University. Published in Chapter 12 of this book.

———. 1952b. "There Were Three Encores to that Spaghetti!" *Melody Maker*, July 5, p. 9.

———. 1952c. "My Kicks in Europe." *Melody Maker*, July 12, p. 9.

Armstrong, Louis. 1952d. "That Italian Boy Could Sing Jazz Like We Did!" *Melody Maker*, July 19, p. 9.

———. 1952e. "Red Beans and Rice: One of the Only Birthmarks I Can Remember." *Melody Maker*, July 26, p. 9.

———. 1952f. "That Roman Jazz Took Me Back to the Riverboats!" *Melody Maker*, Aug. 2, p. 9.

———. 1952g. "Them Glasses Cost a Load of Loaf." *Melody Maker*, Aug. 2, p. 9.

———. 1952h. "Bop—That's Ju-Jitsu Music." *Melody Maker*, Aug. 16, p. 9.

———. 1952i. "My Kicks in Europe (continued)." *Melody Maker*, Aug. 23, p. 9.

———. 1952j. "My Kicks in Europe (concluding)." *Melody Maker*, Aug. 30, p. 9.

———. 1953a. "A Toast to Mezzrow and Joe Oliver," *Melody Maker*, January 10, p. 3.

———. 1953b. Letter to Leonard Feather of June 29. Institute of Jazz Studies, Rutgers University.

———. 1954a. "Why I Like Dark Women." *Ebony*, Aug., p. 61.

———. 1954b. "It's Tough to Top a Million." *Our World*, Aug., p. 22.

———. 1954c. "Satchmo—My Life in New Orleans." *Saga*, Nov., p. 18.

———. 1954d. *Satchmo: My Life in New Orleans*. New York: Prentice Hall.

———. 1954e. "The Armstrong Story." Louis Armstrong House and Archives at Queens College/CUNY. Published in Chapter 5 of this book.

———. 1955a. Letter to Joe Glaser, Aug. 2. Library of Congress, Washington, D.C. Published in Chapter 13 of this book.

———. 1955b. "They Cross Iron Curtain to Hear American Jazz." Interview published in *U.S. News and World Report*, Dec. 2, p. 54.

———. 1956. Interview with Sinclair Traill and Gerald Lascelles published in *Just Jazz*. London: Peter Davies.

———. 1959. "The Satchmo Story." Louis Armstrong House and Archives at Queens College/CUNY. Published in Chapter 8 of this book.

———. 1960. "Scanning the History of Jazz." *The Jazz Review*, July, p. 7; reprinted in *Esquire*, Dec. 1971, p. 184. Published in Chapter 16 of this book.

———. 1961. "Daddy, How the Country Has Changed!" Interview published in *Ebony*, May, p. 81.

———. 1966. *Louis Armstrong, A Self Portrait: The Interview by Richard Meryman*. New York: Eakins Press.

———. 1967. Letter to L/Cpl. Villec. John C. Browning Collection, Durham, North Carolina. Published in Chapter 15 of this book.

———. 1968? "New Orleans." Published in Gary Giddins, *Satchmo*. New York, 1988, p. 212.

———. 1969a. "Good-bye to All of You." *Esquire*, Dec., p. 158. Published in Chapter 19 of this book.

———. 1969b. "Louis Armstrong + the Jewish Family in New Orleans, La., the

Year of 1907." Louis Armstrong House and Archives at Queens College/CUNY. Published in Chapter 1 of this book.

Armstrong, Louis. 1970. Open Letter to Fans, June 1. Louis Armstrong House and Archives at Queens College/CUNY. Published in Chapter 18 of this book.

———. 1970?a. "Early Years with Lucille." Louis Armstrong House and Archives at Queens College/CUNY. Published in Chapter 10 of this book.

———. 1970?b. "Our Neighborhood." Louis Armstrong House and Archives at Queens College/CUNY. Published in Chapter 17 of this book.

———. 1970?c. Letter to Max Chilton. Published in *Louis: The Louis Armstrong Story 1900–1971*. Frogmore: Mayflower, 1971.

WORKS CITED

Baker, Nicholson. 1994. "The History of Punctuation." In *The Size of Thoughts: Essays and Other Lumber*. New York: Random House.

Balliett, Whitney. 1994. "King Louis." In *The New Yorker*, Aug. 8, p. 70.

Barker, Danny. 1986. *A Life in Jazz*. New York: Oxford Univ. Press.

Barrett, Joshua. 1992. "Louis Armstrong and Opera." *The Musical Quarterly* 76: 216.

Bechet, Sidney. 1960. *Treat It Gentle*. London: Cassell.

Bergreen, Laurence. 1997. *Louis Armstrong: An Extravagant Life*. New York: Broadway Books.

Bigard, Barney. 1986. *With Louis and the Duke: The Autobiography of a Jazz Clarinetist*. Ed. Barry Martyn. New York: Oxford Univ. Press.

Brothers, Thomas. 1997. "Ideology and Aurality in the Vernacular Traditions of African-American Music." *Black Music Research Journal* 17 (1997): 169–209.

Buerkle, Jack, and Danny Barker. 1973. *Bourbon Street Black; the New Orleans Black Jazzman*. New York: Oxford Univ. Press.

Collier, James Lincoln. 1983. *Louis Armstrong: An American Genius*. New York: Oxford Univ. Press.

Dance, Stanley. 1977. *The World of Earl Hines*. New York: Scribner.

Dillard, J. L. 1977. *Lexicon of Black English*. New York: Seabury.

Dodds, Baby. 1992. *The Baby Dodds Story*. As told to Larry Gara. Rev. ed. Baton Rouge: Louisiana State Univ. Press.

Early, Gerald. 1989. " 'And I Will Sing of Joy and Pain for You': Louis Armstrong and the Great Jazz Traditions." In *Tuxedo Junction: Essays on American Culture*. New York: Ecco.

Feather, Leonard. 1972. *From Satchmo to Miles*. New York: Stein and Day.

Foster, Pops. 1971. *Pops Foster: The Autobiography of a New Orleans Jazzman*. As told to Tom Stoddard. Berkeley: Univ. of California Press.

Giddins, Gary. 1988. *Satchmo*. New York: Doubleday.

Gleason, Ralph. 1975. *Celebrating the Duke*. Boston: Little, Brown.

Goffin, Robert. 1947. *Horn of Plenty: The Story of Louis Armstrong*. Trans. James Bezou. New York: Allen, Towne and Heath.

Hammond, John. 1977. *John Hammond on Record: An Autobiography*. With Irving Townsend. New York: Ridge Press.

Hampton, Lionel. 1993. *Hamp: An Autobiography*. With James Haskins. New York: Amistad.

hooks, bell. 1989. *Talking Back: Thinking Feminist, Thinking Black*. Boston: South End Press.

Jones, Max, and John Chilton. 1971. *Louis: The Louis Armstrong Story. 1900–1971*. Boston: Little, Brown.

Kenney, William H., III. 1991. "Negotiating the Color Line: Louis Armstrong's Autobiographies." In *Jazz in Mind*, ed. Reginald T. Buckner and Steven Weiland. Detroit: Wayne State Univ. Press.

———. 1993. *Chicago Jazz: A Cultural History. 1904–1930*. New York: Oxford Univ. Press.

Lax, John. 1974. "Chicago's Black Jazz Musicians in the Twenties: Portrait of an Era." *Journal of Jazz Studies* 1: 107–27.

Lomax, Alan. 1950. *Mr. Jelly Roll: The Fortunes of Jelly Roll Morton, New Orleans Creole and Inventor of Jazz*. New York: Grove Press Books.

Major, Clarence. 1994. *Juba to Jive: A Dictionary of African-American Slang*. New York: Viking.

Miller, Marc, ed. 1994. *Louis Armstrong: A Cultural Legacy*. Seattle: Univ. of Washington Press.

Mitchell, Reid. 1995. *All on a Mardi Gras Day: Episodes in the History of New Orleans Carnival*. Cambridge: Harvard Univ. Press.

Morgenstern, Dan. 1986. "Introduction to the Da Capo Edition." In *Satchmo: My Life in New Orleans*, by Louis Armstrong. Rpt. New York: Da Capo.

———. 1994. "Louis Armstrong and the Development and Diffusion of Jazz." In Miller, ed., *Louis Armstrong: A Cultural Legacy*. Seattle: Univ. of Washington Press.

Murray, Albert. 1976. *Stomping the Blues*. New York: Random House.

Russell, Bill. 1939. "Louis Armstrong." In *Jazzmen*, ed. F. Ramsey, Jr., and C. E. Smith. New York: Harcourt.

———. 1994. *New Orleans Style*. Compiled and edited by Barry Martyn and Mike Hazeldine. New Orleans: Jazzology Press.

Shapiro, Nat, and Nat Hentoff, eds. 1955. *Hear Me Talkin' To Ya: The Story of Jazz by the Men Who Made It*. New York: Rinehart.

Stewart, Rex. 1991. *Boy Meets Horn.* Ed. Claire Gordon. Ann Arbor: Univ. of Michigan Press.

Tassin, Myron, and Gaspar "Buddy" Stall. 1984. *Mardi Gras and Bacchus: Something Old, Something New*. Gretna: Pelican Publishing.

Wright, Laurie. 1987. *King Oliver*, Essex: Storyville.

ANNOTATED INDEX OF PROPER NAMES, PLACES, SONGS, AND SHOWS

COMPILED BY CHARLES KINZER

Reference Sources

Armstrong, Louis. 1936. *Swing That Music.* London: Longmans, Green. Reprint. New York: DaCapo, 1993.

Armstrong, Louis. 1954. *Satchmo: My Life in New Orleans.* New York: Prentice-Hall. Reprint. New York: DaCapo, 1986.

Kenney, William Howland. 1993. *Chicago Jazz: A Cultural History, 1904–1930.* New York: Oxford University Press.

Kernfeld, Barry, editor. 1988. *The New Grove Dictionary of Jazz* in 2 vols. London: Macmillan.

Rose, Al, and Edmond Souchon. 1984. *New Orleans Jazz: A Family Album.* 3d rev. ed. Baton Rouge: Louisiana State University Press.

Abbreviations

as - alto saxophone
bjo - banjo
c - cornet
cl - clarinet
dr - drums
gtr - guitar
ldr - leader
pn - piano
s - saxophone
sb - string bass
tbn - trombone
ts - tenor saxophone
tu - tuba
tpt - trumpet
vln - violin
vcl - vocalist

Entry Format

Name [or title], page # in this volume. Brief description. Further references.

Africa, 190.

"African Pas," 149. Piano rag composed by Maurice Kirwan, 1902.

"Ain't Misbehavin'," 148. Song composed by Andy Razaf and Thomas "Fats" Waller, 1929. Armstrong 1936, 91.

Alexander, Charlie, 108. 1904–c. 1970; pn; active in Chicago 1920s, house pianist at Bert Kelly's Stables before joining Armstrong in 1931, settled in California after 1932. Kenney 1993; Kernfeld 1988; Armstrong 1936, 95.

Algiers, LA, 27, 62, 185. Small city opposite New Orleans on the Mississippi River. Armstrong 1954, 145; Armstrong 1936, 37.

Alix, May, xix, 54, 55, 86. Born 1904; vcl; worked with Jimmie Noone in Chicago c. 1922, recorded with Armstrong in 1926, retired from music in the 1940s. Kernfeld 1988.

"All of Me," 108. Song by Seymour Simons and Gerald Marks, 1931. Recorded by LA and His Orchestra, January 1932.

Allen, Henry Sr., 62, 74. 1877–1952; c; leader of Allen Brass Band in New Orleans, father of Henry "Red" Allen. Kernfeld 1988; Rose and Souchon 1984; Armstrong 1954, 84.

Allen, Henry "Red," 62, 185. 1908–67; tpt; active in New Orleans in the 1920s and later with Joe Oliver, Luis Russell, Fletcher Henderson, and Armstrong; popular leader in New York, 1950s-60s. Kernfeld 1988; Rose and Souchon 1984; Armstrong 1954, 134.

"Among My Souvenirs," 166. Song by Edgar Leslie and Horatio Nicholls, 1927. Recorded by LA and His Orchestra, April 1942.

Anderson, Gene, 101, 103–4, 106. Piano; active in Chicago, 1926. Armstrong 1936, 87.

Anderson, Tom. *See* Tom Anderson's New Cabaret.

Andrews Coal Company, 154. C.A. Andrews Coal Co., New Orleans. Armstrong 1954, 59.

Andrews, Mavis, 182. Nurse at Beth Israel Hospital, 1970.

Apex Club, 101. Nightclub in Chicago 1926–28, located on East 35th Street. Kernfeld 1988.

Arlington Restaurant, Chicago, 58.

Armstrong, Alpha Smith, xix, 95–99, 107–8 140–41, 146–47. Born c. 1907; third wife of LA, married 1938–42. Smith worked at the Vendome Theater in Chicago and met Armstrong there in 1925.

Armstrong, Beatrice "Mama Lucy," 6–9, 12–13, 18–22, 22–23, 29–30, 59, 72, 74, 88, 123, 180, 185–86. Born c. 1902; sister of LA. Armstrong 1954, 11; Armstrong 1936, 2.

Armstrong, Clarence Hatfield, 69, 88–90, 94, 97–98. 1915–98; adoptive son of LA, natural son of Armstrong's cousin, Flora Miles. Armstrong 1954, 81; Armstrong 1936, 88.

Armstrong, Daisy Parker, xviii, 69, 82, 84–85, 91, 124–25. Born c. 1897; first wife of LA; married 1918-c. 1922, New Orleans. Armstrong 1954, 147; Armstrong 1936, 36.

Armstrong, Lillian Hardin, xvii-xviii, xx, 26, 47–48, 50, 52, 54–57, 59–62, 64–67, 82, 85–89, 91–98, 103, 107–8, 127–30, 132–36. 1898–1971; pn; second wife of LA, married 1924–38. Born Memphis, TN, Hardin moved to Chicago in 1917 and met LA there in 1922. In addition to performing with Joe Oliver and LA, she worked with Freddie Keppard (1928), Johnny Dodds (1928–29), and Henry "Red" Allen (late 1930s). Kenney 1993; Kernfeld 1988; Armstrong 1954, 237; Armstrong 1936, 70. And previous husband Jimmy, 86. And her mother, 65, 89, 97.

Armstrong, Lucille Wilson, 11, 35, 80, 115, 139–45, 152–53, 157–61, 163, 171, 176–80, 183–84, 185–88, 190. Born c. 1914, fourth wife of LA, married 1942. Wilson worked as a chorus girl at the Cotton Club and met LA there in 1939.

Armstrong, May Ann [Mary Ann], xvii-xviii, 6–10, 12–13, 16, 18–20, 22–23, 29–30, 57–62, 68–69, 72–75, 78, 82, 84, 86–90, 112–16, 121, 123, 143, 150, 170, 180, 185–88. Died 1927, mother of LA. Armstrong 1954, 7; Armstrong 1936, 2. And unnamed stepfather, 6, 123, 150 (Armstrong 1954, 26; Armstrong 1936, 2). And stepfather Gabe, 71, 154 (Armstrong 1954, 26). And stepfather Tom 22–23, 30, 74.

Armstrong, Willie, 7–8, 20, 123. Died 1933; natural father of LA. Armstrong 1954, 7; Armstrong 1936, 3. And stepmother Gertrude, 8 (Armstrong 54, 55).

ASCAP, 163. American Society of Composers, Authors, and Publishers. Performing rights organization, founded 1914 in New York City. ASCAP licenses music to radio, television, nightclubs, and other music users.

Artists and Models, 147. 1937 musical motion picture, starring Jack Benny and Ida Lupino and featuring Martha Raye, Andre Kostelanetz, and LA and His Orchestra.

Atkins, Boyd, 132. 1900–c. 1960; vl; performed with LA on the SS *Sidney* and later became active in Chicago; composer of "Heebie Jeebies." Rose and Souchon 1984; Armstrong 1954, 186.

Atkins, Eddie, 29, 69. 1887–1926; tu, baritone horn; active in New Orleans with Joe Oliver, Onward and Tuxedo brass bands; traveled with Manuel Perez's band to Chicago in 1916 and settled there. Rose and Souchon 1984; Armstrong 1954, 99; Armstrong 1936, 14.

Atlanta, GA, 146–47.

Australia, 160–61, 163.

Bailey, Buster, 63, 72, 75, 92–94, 126. 1902–67; cl; performed in Chicago in the early 1920s with Joe Oliver, in New York after 1924 with Fletcher Henderson. He spent 1965–67 with Louis Armstrong's All Stars. Bailey was known as a fluent jazz soloist. Kenney 1993; Kernfeld 1988.

Baker, Nicholson xxiii. Literary scholar, author.

Barbarin, Isidore, viii, 42–43. 1872–1960; alto horn; performed with Onward Brass Band, New Orleans, 1910s. Kernfeld 1988; Rose and Souchon 1984.

Barbarin, Paul, 30, 42–43, 92, 125. 1899–1969; d; son of Isidore, active in New Orleans in the early 1920s, joined Joe Oliver in Chicago in 1924 and Luis Russell in NY in 1928, eventually recorded with LA. Barbarin returned to New Orleans after WWII. Kernfeld 1988; Rose and Souchon 1984.

Barker, Danny, xxi. 1909–94; gtr, bjo, vcl; nephew of Paul Barbarin, he performed in New Orleans in the late 1920s before moving north and spending time in the bands of Lucky Millinder, Benny Carter, and Cab Calloway. Returned to New Orleans in the 1960s and remained active there. Kernfeld 1988; Rose and Souchon 1984.

Basie, William "Count," 165. 1904–84; pno, ldr; prominent bandleader of the swing era and beyond. The Count Basie Orchestra recorded numerous hits in rhythmic Kansas City style of the late 1930s, including "One O'Clock Jump" and "Lester Leaps In." Kernfeld 1988.

"Basin Street Blues," 135. Song composed by Spencer Williams, 1928; introduced and recorded by LA and His Orchestra, June 1928.

Beavers, Louise, 78. Actress, acquaintance of LA.

Bechet, Sidney, 149. 1897–1959; cl/soprano saxophone; widely influential jazz soloist. Bechet performed in New Orleans until about 1916. After touring in the South and Midwest he spent much of the 1920s in Europe, but recorded with LA 1924–25. He worked principally in Harlem in the 1930s-40s and settled in France, 1951. He recorded prolifically. Rose and Souchon 1984; Kenney 1993; Kernfeld 1988; Armstrong 1954, 134; Armstrong 1936, 14.

Beiderbecke, Leon "Bix," 142. 1903–31; c; one of the first influential white soloists of jazz. Born in Iowa, active in Chicago and later New York, Beiderbecke performed with Frank Trumbauer, Jean Goldkette, Paul Whiteman, and others; his recordings exhibit a distinctive tone and colorful approach to harmony. Kernfeld 1988; Armstrong 1954, 209; Armstrong 1936, 107.

Benson, Hamp [Hamilton], 69. Born c. 1885; tbn; active in Storyville in the 1910s with Andrew Kimball, Tom Brown. Rose and Souchon 1984; Armstrong 1954, 100.

Bergreen, Laurence, 3. Author, biographer of LA.

Berigan, Bunny, 166. 1908–42; tpt/ldr; performed in New York in the 1930s with

Berigan, Bunny *(continued)* Benny Goodman and Tommy Dorsey before organizing own band in 1937. Kernfeld 1988.

Beth Israel Hospital, New York City, 5–6, 11, 171, 179, 180–82.

"Between the Devil and the Deep Blue Sea," 108. Song composed by Ted Koehler and Harold Arlen, 1931. Recorded by LA, January 1932.

Bigard, Barney, 31, 92, 129, 142, 190. 1906–80; cl; respected jazz soloist. Studied with Lorenzo (Jr.) and Louis Tio and performed in Storyville before leaving New Orleans in 1924. After three years in Chicago with Joe Oliver, Bigard joined the Duke Ellington Orchestra in New York for a stint of fourteen years. Spent much of his later career with LA All Stars. Kernfeld 1988; Rose and Souchon 1984; Armstrong 1954, 125.

Bigard, Emile, 134. C. 1890–1935; vln; performed in New Orleans with Joe Oliver, Kid Ory, Magnolia Orchestra, and Maple Leaf Orchestra before retiring from music in 1924. Kernfeld 1988; Rose and Souchon 1984; Armstrong 1954, 216.

Black, Benny. *See* Williams, Black Benny.

Black, Clarence, 100–102. Bandleader in Chicago, 1926. Kenney 1993.

Bolden, Charles "Buddy," 38, 66, 173. 1877–1931; c, ldr; seminal figure of early jazz. Bolden led a band in the dance halls and barrooms of the black tenderloin district of New Orleans near the turn of the century. In 1907 mental deterioration and subsequent institutionalization ended his career. He was known for a powerful tone and ability to ornament melodies in a personal manner. Kernfeld 1988; Rose and Souchon 1984; Armstrong 1954, 23; Armstrong 1936, 12.

Bolton, Red Head Happy, 125. Died 1928; New Orleans hustler, drummer; performed with Joe Oliver in the 1910s and with John Robichaux's society orchestra in the 1920s. Rose and Souchon 1984; Armstrong 1954, 34.

Boogus, 124. New Orleans barroom pianist, c. 1917. Armstrong 1954, 101.

Boone, Lester, 108. Born 1904; as; performed with LA in Chicago, 1931; also worked with Charles Elgar, Earl Hines. Kernfeld 1988; Armstrong 1936, 95.

Bottoms, Bill, 98. Nightclub owner in Chicago, 1920s. Kenney 1993.

Brashear, George, 69. Trombone; performed with LA aboard the SS *Capitol*, 1920. Rose and Souchon 1984; Armstrong 1954, 100.

Briggs, Peter, 101, 128, 135. Born 1904; tu; performed with Carroll Dickerson in Chicago, 1926, and recorded with LA's Hot 7, 1927. Kernfeld 1988; Armstrong 1936, 87.

Brooks, Shelton, 54. Stage comedian, active in Chicago, 1920s. Armstrong 1936, 70.

Brown, Arthur, 121–22. Armstrong 1954, 89.

Brown, Lawrence, 107, 111. Born 1907; tbn, performed with Vernon Elkins, 1929, recorded with LA and His Orchestra 1930, soloist with Duke Ellington from 1932 to 1951. Kernfeld 1988.

Brundy, Walter, 125. Drums; performed with John Robichaux Orchestra, New Orleans, c. 1917. Rose and Souchon 1984.

Bryson, Arthur, 119. Dancer, Los Angeles, c. 1930.

Buffalo, NY, 104. Armstrong 1936, 88.

"Bugle Blues,"75. Jazz instrumental composed by Bobby Williams, c. 1920.

Burton, Vic, 115–16. Drums; active in California, c. 1930.

"By the Waters of Minnetonka," 93. Song with words by J. M. Cavanass and music by Thurlow Lieurance, 1914.

California, 78, 106–8, 115–19, 190. Armstrong 1936, 95.

Capone, Al, 108. 1899–1947; famous gangster, dominated organized crime in Chicago from 1925 to 1931, owner of several nightclubs in Chicago area.

Cara, Mancy. *See* Carr, Mancy "Peck."

Carey [Cary], Dick, 190. 1916–94; pno, brass instruments; performed on piano with

LA's All Stars, 1947–48; later with Jimmy Dorsey, Eddie Condon. Kernfeld 1988.

Carey, Jack, 69. C. 1885–c. 1935; tbn; active in New Orleans with the Crescent Orchestra, associated with the genesis of the tailgate trombone style and the song "Tiger Rag." Rose and Souchon 1984; Armstrong 1954, 92.

Carey, Mutt [Thomas "Papa Mutt"], 28, 69, 133–34. 1891–1948; c, tpt, ldr; brother of Jack, active in New Orleans 1910s, performed with Kid Ory in Los Angeles in the early 1920s, led bands in California after 1925. Rose and Souchon 1984; Kernfeld 1988; Armstrong 1954, 92.

Carnegie Hall, 154–55. Concert hall in New York City.

Carr, Mancy "Peck," 101, 135. Born c. 1900; bjo, gtr; performed with Carroll Dickerson band in Chicago in the mid-to-late 1920s, recorded with LA in 1928 and 1929. Kernfeld 1988; Armstrong 1936, 87.

Catlet, Big Sid, 142, 154, 190. 1910–51; dr; influential stylist of swing era; performed with Benny Carter and Fletcher Henderson in the 1930s, became featured drummer for LA's big band from 1938 to 1942, also with LA All Stars, 1947–49. Kenney 1993; Kernfeld 1988.

Celestin, Oscar "Papa," 42–43. 1884–1954; c, tpt, ldr; active in New Orleans from 1906, co-leader with trombonist William "Bébé" Ridgley of the Original Tuxedo Orchestra from 1917–25. Celestin enjoyed great popularity as a fixture of the New Orleans music scene in the last decade of his life. Kernfeld 1988; Rose and Souchon 1984; Armstrong 1954, 92.

Chambers, Elmer "Muffle Jaws," 93, 126. 1897-c. 1952; tpt; soloist with Fletcher Henderson, 1923–25. Kernfeld 1988.

Cheeky Black, 84–85. New Orleans hustler, c. 1918. Armstrong 1954, 101.

Chicago, IL, 25–26, 28–29, 33, 39, 42–43, 47–67, 72, 74–76, 87, 85–104, 107–10, 112, 116, 125, 127–35, 140–41, 183–84, 189. Kenney 1993; Armstrong 1954; Armstrong 1936; Kernfeld 1988.

"Chicago Breakdown," 129. Song recorded by LA and His Stompers, May 1927. LA's first recording as leader of a big band.

Chicago Defender, 127.

Chicago White Sox, 51.

Cicero, IL, 107.

Cleveland, OH, 104.

Club Alabam, 117. Nightclub in Los Angeles, 1920s-40s, located on Central Avenue.

Cohen, Oscar, 23. Associate of Joe Glaser; president of Associated Booking Corporation, 1960s.

Cole, Cozy, 129, 142. 1906–81; dr; recorded with Jelly Roll Morton in 1930 and performed with various bands in the 1930s, came to prominence with Cab Calloway's orchestra, 1938–42. Toured and recorded with LA as regular member of the All Stars, 1949–53. Kernfeld 1988.

Collier, James Lincoln, 150, 164. Author, biographer of LA.

Collins, Johnny, 108–9. LA's manager in Los Angeles and on tour of England, 1931–32.

Colored Waifs' Home, New Orleans, 12, 122. Armstrong 1954, 35; Armstrong 1936, 6.

"Confessin'" ["I'm Confessin'"], 148. Song with words by A. J. Neilburg and music by Doc Dougherty and Ellis Reynolds; first recorded by LA, August 1930.

Congress Hotel, Chicago, 129. Kenney 1993.

Connie's Inn, 105–6, 109, 116, 148. Nightclub in New York City operated by Connie and George Immerman. Located at 131st Street and 7th Avenue. Kernfeld 1988; Armstrong 1936, 89.

Cook, Louise, 105. Dancer in New York City, 1929.

Coon, Carleton, 109. 1894–1932; dr, ldr; co-leader with Joe Sanders of the Coon-Sanders orchestra, resident at the Blackhawk club, Chicago, from 1926 through the 1930s. Kernfeld 1998.

Cootay, John, 122. Childhood friend of LA.

"Cornet Chop Suey," 127, 132–33. Jazz instrumental composed and recorded by LA in 1926.

Corona, NY, 139, 143–44, 153, 164, 169, 176–78, 183, 185, 190. Queens, New York, home of Louis and Lucille Armstrong from 1943.

Cotton Club, 105, 139, 179, 183, 185–86. Nightclub in Harlem, opened in 1922 at 644 Lenox Avenue. Moved to 200 West 48th Street in 1936, closed in 1940. Kernfeld 1988, Armstrong 1936, 89. *See also* Frank Sebastian's Cotton Club.

Cottrell, Louis Sr., 31, 125. 1878–1927; dr; active in New Orleans with Onward Brass Band, 1910s, and Armand Piron's New Orleans Orchestra, 1920s. Performed in Chicago with Manuel Perez, 1916–18. Credited with introducing the press roll into jazz drumming. Rose and Souchon 1984; Kernfeld 1988.

Cozy, Reverend, 89, 121, 170. Pastor of a Baptist church on Perdido Street in New Orleans, 1910s-20s. Armstrong 1954, 31.

Crescendo Club, 160, 163. Nightclub in Los Angeles, 1950s. Kernfeld 1988.

Crouch, Julius "Stuff," 154, 161–62. Friend of LA, 1950s.

Culver City, CA, 106–7, 115, 118.

Curry, Bert, 101, 106. Alto sax; member of Carroll Dickerson's orchestra, Chicago, 1926. Armstrong 1936, 87.

Dad, 131. Barbecue cook in Chicago, 1920s, inspiration for the title of "Struttin' With Some Barbecue."

Davis, Miles, 164. 1926–91; tpt, ldr; prominent soloist and one of the most innovative leaders in jazz from the late 1940s through the 1960s. Performed in New York with Charlie Parker from 1945 to 1948, led groups from 1948 on. Influential in the development of cool jazz, modal jazz, bop-based free jazz, and jazz-rock fusion. Kernfeld 1988.

Debman, Ernest, 182. Domestic employee of LA, 1960s.

DeLesseps, Mayor, 155. DeLesseps S. Morrison, Mayor of New Orleans from 1946 to 1961.

Detroit [Dedroit], Paul, 125. 1894–1963; dr; active in New Orleans and on tour with bands led by his brother Johnny. Rose and Souchon 1984.

Detroit, MI, 101, 104. Armstrong 1936, 88.

Dewey [Duhé], Lawrence, 50. 1887–1959; cl; active in the 1910s in Storyville, New Orleans, with Kid Ory; moved to Chicago and led band at Deluxe Cafe, 1917–18. Rose and Souchon 1984; Armstrong 1954, 220.

Dickerson, Carroll, xix, 26, 63, 72, 75, 98, 101, 103–6, 116, 129, 184. 1895–1957; vln, ldr; led groups in Chicago from 1920 into the 1940s. LA was in two of his bands, in 1927 and in 1927–28. In 1929 LA took Dickerson's group (with Dickerson as conductor) to New York; there, back under Dickerson's name and minus Armstrong, the band worked at Connie's Inn for a year. After touring briefly with King Oliver, Dickerson returned to successful pursuits in Chicago. Kenney 1993; Kernfeld 1988; Armstrong 1936, 84.

"Didn't He Ramble" ["Oh, Didn't He Ramble"], 120, 171. Song composed by W. C. Handy, 1902, and recorded by LA and the All Stars as part of the medley "New Orleans Function," April 1950.

"Ding Dong Daddy" ["I'm a Ding Dong Daddy from Dumas"], 107. Song composed by Phil Baxter, 1928; recorded by LA with His Sebastian New Cotton Club Orchestra, July 1930.

"Dippermouth Stomp," 174. Jazz instrumental composed by LA and recorded by LA with King Oliver's Creole Jazz Band, April 1923.

Disneyland, 28, 35. Amusement park opened in 1955 in Anaheim, CA; developed by the studios of Walt Disney (1901–66), prominent movie producer and pioneer of animated films.

Dixon, Bernice, 182. Domestic employee of LA, 1960s.

Dixon, Charles, 93, 126. 1898–1940; bjo; member of Fletcher Henderson's orchestra in New York, 1924–28. Kernfeld 1988.

"Do You Know What It Means to Miss New Orleans," 34. Song with words by Eddie de Lange and music by Louis Alter, 1946; recorded by LA and His All Stars, October 1946.

Dockstader, Lew, 125. 1856–1924; blackface minstrel and vaudeville entertainer, 1870s-1920s.

Dodds, David. *See* Dodds, Warren.

Dodds, Johnny, 48, 50–51, 54, 62, 64, 72, 87, 92, 128, 130, 132–35, 165. 1892–1940; cl; influential jazz soloist, member of LA's Hot Five and Hot Seven. Dodds performed in New Orleans with Kid Ory and King Oliver from 1912 to 1919, then joined Oliver in Chicago. He recorded with Oliver's Creole Jazz Band in 1923 and led a band at Kelly's Stables from 1924 to 1930. Rose and Souchon 1984; Kenney 1993; Kernfeld 1988; Armstrong 1954, 237; Armstrong 1936, 69.

Dodds, Warren "Baby," xii, 48, 50, 52, 64–65, 87, 92, 125, 127, 130, 166. 1898–1959; dr; leading jazz drummer of the New Orleans style, member of LA's Hot Seven; brother of Johnny Dodds. Baby Dodds worked in New Orleans with Bunk Johnson and Papa Celestin before joining King Oliver's band in San Francisco in 1922. He recorded with Oliver's Creole Jazz Band in 1923 and later worked with his brother, Sidney Bechet, and others, usually in traditional New Orleans small group format. Rose and Souchon 1984; Kenney 1993; Kernfeld 1988; Armstrong 1954, 186, Armstrong 1936, 69.

Dominguez, Paul [Jr.], 83. C. 1887–c. 1970; vln, gtr, ldr; led band at Anderson's Cabaret in New Orleans, 1922, which included LA. Rose and Souchon 1984; Armstrong 1954, 215.

Dominique, Natty, 165. 1896–1982; tpt; born in New Orleans and migrated to Chicago in 1913; in the 1920s he performed with Jelly Roll Morton, Carroll Dickerson, Jimmie Noone, and LA. An ensemble musician and section leader, his few recorded solos show influences from King Oliver. Rose and Souchon 1984, Kenny 1993, Kernfeld 1988.

Down Beat, 147, 150, 164. Leading American periodical devoted to jazz, first issued in 1934. Kernfeld 1988.

Dreamland Cabaret, 54–55, 86, 94, 95. Nightclub in Chicago, opened as Dreamland Ballroom in 1912; located at 35th and State streets. Renamed Dreamland Cafe in 1924 and closed in 1928 for violation of prohibition laws. LA first appeared there in 1924 with Ollie Powers and his Harmony Syncopaters. Kenney 1993; Kernfeld 1988; Armstrong 1936, 70.

Dreamland Cafe. *See* Dreamland Cabaret.

Dukes of Dixieland, 35. 1950 to present; dixieland touring and recording band from New Orleans, led by trumpeter Frank Assunto and featuring several members of his family. Rose and Souchon 1984.

Dunbar Hotel, Los Angeles, 117.

Durand, Maurice, 148. 1893–1961; tpt, ldr; performed with the Onward and Tuxedo brass bands in New Orleans in the 1920s, also led dance bands. Rose and Souchon 1984; Armstrong 1954, 180.

Duson, Frank, 69, 174. 1881–1936; valve tbn, ldr; performed in New Orleans in the early 1900s with Buddy Bolden and succeeded Bolden as leader after 1907. Rose and Souchon 1984; Armstrong 1954, 23.

Dutrey, Honoré, 26, 48, 50–51, 62, 64, 87, 92. 1894–1935; tbn; performed in New Orleans in the 1910s with the Excelsior Brass Band and John Robichaux's orchestra. After military service settled in Chicago and joined Joe Oliver's band. Subsequently worked

Dutrey, Honoré *(continued)* with LA, Carroll Dickerson, and Johnny Dodds. Rose and Souchon 1984; Kenney 1993; Kernfeld 1988; Armstrong 1954, 92; Armstrong 1936, 69.

Dutrey, Sam [Sr.], 26. C. 1888–1941; cl; brother of Honoré, performed in New Orleans with the Silver Leaf Brass Band and with Fate Marable's orchestra aboard SS *Capitol*, 1920. Rose and Souchon 1984; Kernfeld 1988; Armstrong 1954, 92.

Eagle Saloon, 120. Nightclub in New Orleans, 1910s, located at 401 South Rampart Street; it gave its name to Frankie Duson's Eagle Band. Rose and Souchon 1984; Kernfeld 1988.

Ebony magazine, 139.

"Eccentric," 47, 52–53. Song performed by Joe Oliver's band at the Lincoln Gardens, Chicago. Oliver imitated baby noises on his cornet and engaged vocalist Bill Johnson in a comic dialogue. Armstrong 1954, 239.

Edelweiss Gardens, 50, 66–67. Nightclub in Chicago, 1920s, located at 41st and State Streets. Kenney 1993; Armstrong 1954, 239.

Eighth Regiment Army Band, 76. Prominent military wind band made up of black musicians in Chicago in the late 1910s and 1920s.

Eisenhower, Dwight D., 9. 1890–1969; distinguished military general and President of the United States from 1953 to 1961.

Eldridge, Roy, 165. 1911–89; tpt, ldr; leading jazz trumpeter of the swing era. Influenced by LA, Eldridge worked briefly with Fletcher Henderson's orchestra before leading his own small group in 1936. Performed with white leaders Gene Krupa and Artie Shaw in the early 1940s and recorded a well-known solo on Krupa's hit, "Rockin' Chair." He was associated closely with Norman Granz's Jazz At the Philharmonic concerts after 1948. Kernfeld 1988.

Elgar, Charles, 101. 1885–1973; vln, ldr; performed in New Orleans on violin and clarinet from c. 1897 to 1903, when he moved to Chicago. In the 1910s he helped New Orleans musicians find work in Chicago, and by the 1920s he was one of the city's most successful orchestra leaders. His groups played in a conservative style geared toward society dances. Rose and Souchon 1984; Kenney 1993; Kernfeld 1988.

Elkins, Vernon, 107, 118–19. Tpt, ldr; led the resident orchestra at Frank Sebastian's New Cotton Club until May 1930, when Sebastian hired LA to take over the onstage leadership. LA recorded with this group in July, 1930.

Ellington, Edward Kennedy "Duke," x, 30. 1899–1974; pn, ldr, composer; leading figure of the swing era and beyond. During his tenure as leader of the house orchestra at the Cotton Club in Harlem (1927–31), Ellington began to share with LA a leading position in the world of jazz. He gained worldwide fame with the 1930 recording of "Mood Indigo," and among his other contributions to the standard repertory of jazz were such hits as "Satin Doll," "It Don't Mean A Thing If It Ain't Got That Swing," and "In a Sentimental Mood." The longevity of Ellington's career and the extent of his influence stand parallel to those of LA. Kernfeld 1988; Armstrong 1954, 202; Armstrong 1936, 81.

England, 190.

Erlanger Theater, 183. Venue in Chicago, 1922.

Escudero, Ralph, 93, 126. 1898–1970; tu, sb; performed with Fletcher Henderson, 1921–26. Kernfeld 1988.

Esquire, ix, 80, 127, 189.

Europe, 160–63, 184.

Every Day's a Holiday, 147. 1937 motion picture starring Mae West and Edmund Lowe, and featuring LA.

"Everybody Loves My Baby," 64. Song composed by Jack Palmer and Spencer Williams, 1924. LA sang this song with Fletcher Henderson's orchestra, and recorded it, his first vocal recording, in November 1924.

Excelsior Brass Band, 31, 42, 174. New Orleans brass band from 1879 to 1931. One of the earliest and most versatile of New Orleans brass bands, it consisted primarily of Creole musicians and performed both scored music and head arrangements of marches, dance music, dirges, and hymns. Rose and Souchon 1984; Kernfeld 1988; Armstrong 1954, 180.

Facia, 125. Drums; active in New Orleans c. 1917.

Fagan, Mr. [I. Jay Faggen], 103. Owner of the Savoy Ballroom, Chicago, 1926. Kenney 1993.

Feather, Leonard, ix, xx, 77, 80, 145–49, 164. 1914–94; prominent British writer, critic, composer; author of numerous books on jazz and regular columnist for the *Los Angeles Times*; contributor of articles to *Down Beat*, *Esquire*, *Metronome*, and *Playboy*. Kernfeld 1988.

Fern, Mr. [E.A. Fearn], 103, 130, 136. Co-president of the OKeh Recording Company in Chicago, 1920s. Kenney 1993.

Fields [Filhe], George, 69. 1872–1954; tbn; performed with the Onward Brass Band in New Orleans, early 1900s, moved to Chicago in 1913 and worked with Joe Oliver, Lawrence Duhé, and Dave Peyton into the 1920s. Filhe helped other New Orleans musicians find work in Chicago. Rose and Souchon 1984.

Filo, 47–49, 53. Friend of Joe Oliver and LA in Chicago, 1922. Armstrong 1954, 234.

Fisk School, New Orleans, 89, 122.

Fisk University, Nashville, TN, 65, 86.

Fiume Club [Cafe], xix, 67. Nightclub in Chicago, located on State Street north of 35th Street, opened in 1919. Kernfeld 1988.

"Flee as a Bird" ["Flee as a Bird to Your Mountain"], 171. Sacred song composed by Mary Dana Shindler, c. 1857. Used as a standard dirge by New Orlean brass bands, and recorded by LA and the All Stars as part of the medley "New Orleans Function," April 1950.

Fleischmann's Yeast, 145, 147.

Ford, Velma, 161–62. Secretary of LA, 1955.

Foster, Frankie, 110. New York gangster, c. 1931.

Fountain, Pete, 34. Born 1930; cl, ldr; prominenet Dixieland soloist; based in New Orleans but gained national television exposure on *The Lawrence Welk Show* (1957–59) and *The Tonight Show* (1960s-1980s).

France, 190.

Francis, Albert, 83. 1894–c. 1983; dr; performed with LA at Tom Anderson's restaurant in 1920; his career in New Orleans culminated in the 1960s with appearances at Preservation Hall. Rose and Souchon 1984; Armstrong 1954, 216

Francis, Edna Mitchell, 83. Piano, vcl; wife of Albert; performed with LA at Tom Anderson's restaurant in 1920 and later entertained as piano-playing balladeer in New Orleans cabarets. Rose and Souchon 1984; Armstrong 1954, 183.

Frank Sebastian's New Cotton Club, 106–7, 111, 115, 118, 125. Nightclub in Culver City (Los Angeles), CA; opened in the 1920s, it featured dancing and floor shows. LA performed with the house orchestra in July 1930 and again for three months in 1932. Kernfeld 1988; Armstrong 1936, 95.

French, Morris [Maurice], 69. Born c. 1890; tbn; performed in New Orleans with trumpeter Henry "Kid" Rena in the early 1920s. Rose and Souchon 1984; Armstrong 1954, 97.

French Opera House, New Orleans, 22. Opera theater in New Orleans, open from the mid-1800s until 1919, when it was destroyed by a fire.

Funky Butt Hall, 14. Dance hall in New Orleans, located at 1319 Perdido Street. Properly known as the Union Son's Hall, it was generally referred to as Funky Butt Hall

Funky Butt Hall *(continued)*
from the 1890s, when Buddy Bolden played there. In the 1920s the building came to be used as a Baptist church. Rose and Souchon 1984; Kernfeld 1988; Armstrong 1954, 22.

Gafford, Luther "Soldier Boy," 117–19. Friend of LA in California, 1930.
Gailsburg [Galesburg], IL, 83. Armstrong 1954, 189.
Galbraith, Frank "Smoothie," 164. Trumpet; performed and recorded with LA and His Orchestra in 1941.
Garland, Ed "Montudie," 29, 134. 1885–1980; sb; performed in New Orleans with various bands, including that of Kid Ory, in the 1900s-10s; moved to Chicago in 1914 and worked Lawrence Duhé and then Joe Oliver. Went to Los Angeles with Oliver in 1921 and remained there. After a stint with Earl Hines in 1955–56, Garland freelanced, playing regularly into the 1970s. Rose and Souchon 1984; Kernfeld 1988.
Gaspard, Vic, 69. 1875–1957; tb; performed in New Orleans with the Onward Brass Band until 1910, and with various dance orchestras including that of John Robichaux, until about 1930. Rose and Souchon 1984.
Gautier, Madeleine, 153–54. French writer; associate of Hugues Panassié and president of the Hot Club de France from 1975–1983.
Gennett Records, 39. Record Company and label based in Richmond, IN, and active from 1917 to 1930. Its catalog was absorbed by Decca in the mid-1930s. Gennett issued some of the most important jazz recordings of the early 1920s, including those of the New Orleans Rhythm Kings, Joe Oliver's Creole Band, and Jelly Roll Morton. Kernfeld 1988; Armstrong 1936, 79.
Germany, 190.
Giddins, Gary, xxv, 3, 111. Jazz critic, author.
Ginsrich, Mr., 80. Editor of *Esquire* magazine.
Gillespie, "Dizzy" [John Birks Gillespie], 150, 164. 1917–93; tpt, ldr, composer; a principal developer of bebop and one of the most influential trumpet soloists in the history of jazz. Gillespie joined Cab Calloway's band in New York in 1939. He soon began to participate in after-hours jam sessions with Charlie Parker, Thelonious Monk, and other young musicians, helping establish the new, more complex style of jazz that came to be called bebop. A decade at the forefront of the movement made him one of the acknowledged leaders of jazz. Kernfeld 1988.
Glaser, Joe, viii, ix, xvi, 3, 6, 63, 72, 95, 98–99, 111, 129, 146–47, 149, 157–63, 178, 182, 184–86. Died 1969; promoter, manager of the Sunset Cafe, Chicago, mid-1920s; personal manager for LA from 1935 to 1969; founder and President of Associated Booking Corporation. Kenney 1993; Armstrong 1954, 140; Armstrong 1936, 85. And Mrs. Glaser, 158.
Gobee, 124. Drums; active in New Orleans, c. 1917.
Goffin, Robert, viii, ix, xxii, 77–82. Belgian writer and jazz critic, author of *Horn of Plenty* (1947), a biography of LA. Armstrong 1936, 103.
Going Places, 147. 1938 motion picture starring Dick Powell, Anita Louise, and Ronald Reagan, and featuring LA, who sang "Jeepers Creepers."
Golden Gate Theater, 80. Venue in San Francisco, CA.
Goodman, Benny, 166. 1906–86; cl, ldr, leading figure of the swing era; Goodman moved from Chicago to New York in 1928 and came to prominence in the mid-1930s as a bandleader and virtuosic clarinet soloist. Especially sympathetic to the plight of black musicians, he crossed racial boundaries to record with Teddy Wilson and Lionel Hampton before WWII. Goodman enjoyed immense popularity until his death. A 1953 tour with LA, however, proved unsuccessful due to severe differences in business style and a clash of per-

sonalities. Kenney 1993; Kernfeld 1988; Armstrong 1936, 33.

"Got No Blues," 135–36. Jazz instrumental composed and recorded by LA's Hot Five, December 1927.

"Gotta Right to Sing the Blues" ["I Gotta Right to Sing the Blues"], 109. Song with words by Ted Koehler and music by Harold Arlen, 1932. Recorded by LA and His Orchestra, January 1933. Armstrong 1936, 96.

"Grace and Beauty," 149. Piano rag composed by James Scott, 1910.

Great Day, 103, 105. Stage show, Cosmopolitan Theater, New York, 1929; music by Vincent Youmans.

Green, Charles "Long Boy," 93, 126. C. 1900–36; tbn; performed with Fletcher Henderson, 1924–26; also with LA in 1927, and later with Benny Carter and Chick Webb. Kernfeld 1988.

Gretna, LA, 124. Small city opposite New Orleans on the Mississippi River.

"Gut Bucket Blues," 130. Song composed by LA and recorded by LA's Hot Five, November 1925.

Hall, Edmond, 165. 1901–67; cl; performed with various bands in New Orleans before moving north in 1928. Notable work includes recordings with Eddie Condon and stints with Teddy Hill's sextet (1941–44) and LA's All Stars (1955–58). Rose and Souchon 1984, Kernfeld 1988.

Hall, Fred "Tubby," 98–99, 102, 108. 1895–1946; dr; brother of Minor; performed in New Orleans with the Eagle Band and Silver Leaf Orchestra in the 1910s, then moved to Chicago and joined Lawrence Duhé's band in 1918. In the 1920s Hall worked with Joe Oliver and Carroll Dickerson. He recorded with LA in 1927 and again in 1931–32. Rose and Souchon 1984; Kernfeld 1988; Armstrong 1936, 95.

Hall, Minor "Ram," 125, 134. 1897–1959; dr; brother of Tubby Hall; moved from New Orleans to Chicago in 1918 and worked with Joe Oliver, Jimmie Noone, and others until 1927 when he relocated in Los Angeles. Performed often with other New Orleans musicians and recorded with LA in 1946. Rose and Souchon 1984; Kernfeld 1988.

Hammond, John, 111. Author, jazz critic, record producer. Kernfeld 1988.

Hampton, Lionel, 107, 111, 119–20, 125, 163. Born 1908; dr, vibraphone, ldr; prominent figure of the swing era. After early work in Chicago, Hampton established himself as a swing drummer in Culver City, CA, with Vernon Elkins' band, and he recorded with LA when the latter assumed leadership of that group (1930). In the 1930s Hampton achieved widespread popularity performing with Les Hite and Benny Goodman on vibraphone, and he formed his own big band in 1940. Hampton's hit recordings include "Flying Home" and "Midnight Sun." Kenney 1993; Kernfeld 1988.

Hardin, Lil. *See* Armstrong, Lil Hardin.

Harlem, New York City, 104–5, 126, 143–44, 148, 186–87. Armstrong 1936, 80.

Harrod's Club, 171. Nightclub in Reno, NV.

Harthorne Racing Tracks, Chicago, 56.

Hauser, Gaylord, 35, 180. Author.

Hawkins, Coleman, 93, 126. 1904–69; ts, ldr; prominent jazz soloist of the swing era and beyond. After starting out in Kansas City, Hawkins achieved widespread fame as a jazz improviser in the orchestra of Fletcher Henderson, with whom he worked from 1924 to 1934. He worked in Europe in the mid-1930s but returned to the United States to lead a big band (1939–40) and numerous small groups during the 1940s and 1950s. He recorded prolifically (with LA as a member of Henderson's orchestra), and his 1939 recording of "Body and Soul" established him as one of the most influential jazz saxophonists of any period. Kernfeld 1988.

"Heebie Jeebies," 131–33. Song composed by Boyd Atkins, 1925. Recorded by LA and His Hot Five, November 1925; considered the first scat vocal recording in jazz. Armstrong 1936, 85.

Henderson, Fletcher, xviii, 63–64, 82, 93–94, 106, 112, 118, 125–26, 129. 1897–1952; pno, ldr; Henderson led the most important of the pioneer big bands. After moving from Atlanta to New York in 1920, Henderson became a bandleader through working for Pace-Handy Music and the Black Swan recording company. In 1924 his group began a ten-year stand as the house orchestra for the Roseland Ballroom, where it performed for upscale white clientele. Henderson immediately brought LA into the orchestra as a featured jazz soloist, and LA stayed with the group until the fall of 1925. Henderson led bands until 1939, when he joined Benny Goodman as a staff arranger. A severe stroke in 1950 forced his retirement. Kernfeld 1988; Armstrong 1936, 26.

Heralda, Selma, 153. Secretary for Lucille Armstrong, 1949.

Herman, Woody, 165. 1913–87; ldr, as, cl, vcl; prominent leader of big bands from 1936 until his death. Herman became famous in the mid-1940s with the success of his bebop-influenced band, known as Herman's Herd. His Second Herd (1947–49) included the distinctive "Four Brothers" saxophone section. All of Herman's groups were known for a driving sound and superb musicianship. Kernfeld 1988.

Higginbotham, J. C., 185. 1906–73; tbn; a widely respected soloist in the swing style, Higginbotham joined Luis Russell's orchestra in New York in 1928 and later worked with Fletcher Henderson, Chick Webb, and Benny Carter. He recorded with LA in 1929 and in the late 1930s when LA fronted Luis Russell's band. Kernfeld 1988.

"High Society," 38. Song by Walter Melrose and Porter Steele, 1901. Recorded by LA and His Orchestra, January 1933. Armstrong 1936, 96.

Hillaire [Hilaire], Andrew, 72, 74–75. C. 1900–c. 1936; dr; performed with Jelly Roll Morton and Carroll Dickerson in Chicago in the 1920s. Rose and Souchon 1984; Kernfeld 1988.

Hines, Earl "Fatha," 99–101, 129, 135, 142, 152–53. 1903–83; pno; ldr; influential jazz pianist and important musical partner of LA. Hines moved from Pittsburgh to Chicago in 1923 and found work with Sammy Stewart, Erskine Tate, and Carroll Dickerson. He became musical director for Dickerson's orchestra in 1927 when LA was its nominal leader, but the following year moved on to perform with Jimmie Noone at the Apex Club. In 1929 he reunited with Armstrong to record the striking duet "Weather Bird." In the 1930s Hines achieved fame as a leader through radio broadcasts of his band from Chicago. He continued to lead bands until 1948, when he joined LA's All Stars for three years. Hines remained active as a leader and freelance soloist until the 1980s. Kenney 1993; Armstrong 1936, 84; Kernfeld 1988. And his wife, Janie, 152.

Hirt, Al, 34. 1922–99; tpt; performed with the big bands of Tommy and Jimmy Dorsey in the 1940s, before returning to New Orleans as a dixieland soloist. Hirt gained a national following in the late 1950s as leader of a group which included Pete Fountain. Rose and Souchon 1984; Kernfeld 1988.

Hobson, Homer, 101. Trumpet; member of Carroll Dickerson's orchestra, Chicago, 1926. Armstrong 1936, 87.

Hodes, Art, 165n. 1904–93; pno, ldr; a member of the Wolverines in 1926, Hodes worked in Chicago through the 1930s, making his first recordings with Wingy Manone in 1928. He later performed in New York with Mezz Mezzrow and led his own band. As a writer and radio/television broadcaster he promoted early jazz into the 1980s. Kenney 1993; Kernfeld 1988.

Holder, Betty Jane, 150–51, 155–56. Acquaintance of LA in New Orleans, 1950.

Hollywood, CA, 147. Armstrong 1936, 95.

"Home, Sweet Home," 1, 12. Song with traditional melody and words by John Howard Payne, 1823.

hooks, bell, xi, xii. Literary scholar.

Hot Chocolate, 105, 147. Musical stage show, Hudson Theater, New York, 1929; music by Thomas "Fats" Waller, book and lyrics by Andy Razaf. Armstrong 1936, 91.

Hot Club de France, 153. French organization of jazz enthusiasts founded by Hugues Panassié in 1932, and dedicated to the promotion of early jazz and swing. LA was honorary president from 1936 to 1971. Armstrong 1936, 103; Kernfeld 1988.

Hot Five, 127, 129–33, 135–36. Recording group led by LA in Chicago, 1925–27. The original members were LA, c; Kid Ory, tbn; Johnny Dodds, cl; Johnny St. Cyr, bjo; and Lil Hardin Armstrong, pn. Lonnie Johnson (gtr) joined the group for one session. Influential recordings include "Struttin' With Some Barbecue," and "Cornet Chop Suey." Kernfeld 1988; Armstrong 1936, 85.

Hot Seven, 127–28, 134–35. Recording group led by LA in Chicago, 1927. Personnel comprised that of the Hot Five with the addition of Pete Briggs (tu) and Warren "Baby" Dodds (dr). Lonnie Johnson (gtr) was occasionally added as an eighth member. Recordings include "S.O.L. Blues" and "Potato Head Blues." Kernfeld 1988.

"Hotter Than That," 136. Jazz instrumental composed by Lil Hardin Armstrong. Recorded by LA and His Hot Five, December 1927. Contains a scat vocal solo by LA.

Howard, Darnell, 99. C. 1900–1966; vln, cl, saxophone; Howard performed with Carroll Dickerson, Charles Elgar, and Joe Oliver in Chicago in the mid-1920s. He came to prominence as a clarinet soloist with Earl Hines's orchestra from 1931 to 1937. Later work included a long stint with Hines in the 1950s. Kenney 1993; Kernfeld 1988.

Hudson Theater, New York City, 148. Armstrong 1936, 91.

"I Got Rhythm," 108. Song with words by Ira Gershwin and music by George Gershwin, 1930. Recorded by LA and His Orchestra, November 1931.

"I Left My Sugar Standing in the Rain," 100–101. Song by Irving Kahal and Sammy Fain, 1926.

"I Surrender Dear," 108. Song with words by Gordon Clifford and music by Harry Barris, 1931. Recorded by LA and His Orchestra, April 1931.

"I'm Not Rough," 136. Song composed by LA and recorded with the Hot Five, December 1927.

"Indian Cradle Song," 105. Song recorded by LA and His Orchestra, April 1930.

Institute of Jazz Studies, Rutgers, the State University of New Jersey, x, xx, 47–48.

Irene, 84–85. Common law wife of LA, c. 1917. Armstrong 1954, 101.

Iroquois Theater, New Orleans, 30.

Israel, 163.

Italy, 190.

"I've Got the World on a String," 109. Song with words by Ted Koehler and music by Harold Arlen, 1932. Recorded by LA and His Orchestra, January, 1933.

Jackson, Eddie, 27. C. 1867–1938; tu, sb; performed in New Orleans with the Onward Brass Band in the early 1910s, and with the Tuxedo Brass Band and Orchestra in the 1920s. Rose and Souchon 1984; Armstrong 1954, 90.

Jackson, Preston, 108. 1902–83; tbn; performed in Chicago in the 1920s with Erskine Tate and Carroll Dickerson. Toured and recorded with LA in 1931. His later career included work with Lil Armstrong

Jackson, Preston *(continued)* and the Preservation Hall jazz band. Rose and Souchon 1984; Kernfeld 1988; Armstrong 1936, 95.

Jackson, Rudy, 63, 72, 75, 92. 1901–c. 1968; ts; performed with Carroll Dickerson and Joe Oliver in Chicago in the mid-1920s and later toured with Noble Sissle's orchestra. Kernfeld 1988.

Jacobs, Phoebe, 17. Friend of LA, 1960s.

James, George, 108. Born 1906; as, ldr; performed with Jimmie Noone in Chicago in the late 1920s, toured and recorded with LA in 1931. He later worked with Fats Waller and as a leader in New York. Kernfeld 1988; Armstrong 1936, 95.

Jankie, Mr., 153. New Orleans businessman.

Jazz Review, The, ix, 173. American periodical devoted to jazz, in publication from 1958 to 1961.

Jeepers Creepers, 147. 1939 comic motion picture, starring Thurston Hall, Roy Rogers, and the Weaver Brothers.

Johnson, Bill, 47, 50, 52–53, 64, 72, 87, 92, 183–84. C. 1872–1972; sb, tu; performed in New Orleans in the early 1900s, toured with the Original Creole Orchestra in the 1910s, joined Joe Oliver for a year at the Lincoln Gardens in Chicago in 1922. Johnson remained active in Chicago through the 1940s, eventually retiring to Texas. He recorded with Johnny Dodds in 1928. Rose and Souchon 1984; Kenney 1993; Kernfeld 1988; Armstrong 1954, 99; Armstrong 1936, 69.

Johnson, Bunk [Willie Geary "Bunk" Johnson], 37–38, 40–41, 50, 66, 71, 134, 149, 152, 166, 174. 1889–1949; c, tpt, ldr; prominent trumpeter of the early jazz style. Johnson performed in New Orleans with the Eagle Band from 1910 to 1914, then toured regionally until retiring from music in the 1930s. His career was revived in 1939 through the efforts of scholars Bill Russell and Fred Ramsey, who were led to him partly through the recommendation of LA. Johnson began recording in 1942 and led bands until his death. Although he helped lead the 1940s revival of interest in the New Orleans style, Johnson's actual involvement with the development of jazz at the turn of the century was exaggerated, both by himself and by enthusiasts. Rose and Souchon 1984; Kernfeld 1988; Armstrong 1954, 23.

Johnson, James P., 185. 1894–1955; pn, composer; one of the foremost stride pianists of the 1920s. Johnson's career began in the dance halls of Harlem in the 1910s and culminated with performances of his orchestral compositions in such venues as Carnegie Hall in the late 1920s. As a jazz pianist he influenced Fats Waller, Duke Ellington, and Art Tatum, among many others. Kernfeld 1988.

Johnson, Jack, 53. 1878–1946; prizefighter acknowledged as the first black heavyweight champion after he defeated Jim Jeffries in 1910. Armstrong 1954, 36.

Johnson, Joe, 133. C. 1890–c. 1928; c; performed in New Orleans with the Eagle Band. Rose and Souchon 1984, Armstrong 1954, 25.

Johnson, Lonnie, 136. 1889–1970; gtr, vcl; guitarist who recorded with LA as an additional member of the Hot Five and Hot Seven. Johnson's career began in New Orleans in the 1910s. After performing on riverboats in the early 1920s he settled in Chicago. He recorded prolifically as a blues vocalist. Rose and Souchon 1984; Kenney 1993; Kernfeld 1988.

Johnson, Rooster, 136. Violin; brother of Lonnie Johnson.

Johnson, Tany, 50. Armstrong 1954, 239.

Jones, David, 83–84. C. 1888–1956; ts, mellophone; member of Fate Marable's orchestra aboard the SS *Sidney;* he later worked with Joe Oliver and co-led the Jones-Collins Astoria Hot Eight. Rose and Souchon 1984; Kernfeld 1988; Armstrong 1954, 182; Armstrong 1936, 47.

Jones, Isham, 50. 1894–1956; pn, ldr; popular white orchestra leader in Chicago in the mid-1920s, recorded and toured extensively through the 1930s. Kenney 1993; Kernfeld 1988; Armstrong 1954, 237.

Jones, King, 49. Armstrong 1954, 237.

Joplin, Scott, 149. 1868–1917; pno; preeminent composer of ragtime. Active as an itinerant pianist in the Midwest in the 1890s, Joplin began to publish compositions for piano at the turn of the century. His more than 40 piano rags, including "Maple Leaf Rag" and "The Entertainer," achieved national success and helped establish the syncopated dance music called ragtime as the prevailing popular style.

J.S., SS, 83. Streckfus Line riverboat, 1910s–20s. Rose and Souchon 1984.

Karnofsky family, 3, 4, 5, 7, 11–12, 14–19, 23, 30. Family in New Orleans which befriended and employed a young LA.

Karnofsky, Alex, 11–13, 16–17, 19.

Karnofsky, David, 7, 23, 30.

Karnofsky, Morris, 13–15, 17, 21. Armstrong 1954, 94.

Kelly's Stable [Bert Kelly's Stables], 62, 130. Nightclub in Chicago, 1920s, located at 431 North Rush Street. Kernfeld 1988.

Kenney, William, xiii, xiv, 47, 127.

Keppard, Freddie, 4, 25–26, 50, 52, 66–67, 174. 1890–1933; c, ldr; prominent cornetist of early jazz. Keppard led the Olympia Orchestra and performed with other groups in New Orleans from 1906 until about 1914, when he migrated to Los Angeles with the Original Creole Orchestra. Settled in Chicago and maintained successful career in the 1920s. He recorded with the Jazz Cardinals in 1926. Rose and Souchon 1984; Kenney 1993; Kernfeld 1988; Armstrong 1954, 52; Armstrong 1936, 14.

"Kickin' the Gong Around," 108. Song with words by Ted Koehler and music by Harold Arlen, 1931. Recorded by LA and His Orchestra, January 1932.

Kimball, Andrew, 31. C. 1880–c. 1929; c, ldr; performed in New Orleans with John Robichaux, the Onward Brass Band, and others in the 1910s and 1920s. Rose and Souchon 1984.

Kimball, Henry, 26. 1878–1931, sb, ldr, performed in New Orleans with John Robichaux and Manuel Perez, toured with Jelly Roll Morton in the 1920s. Rose and Souchon 1984.

Kirby, John, 92. 1908–52; sb, ldr, performed with Fletcher Henderson and Chick Webb in the 1930s before becoming established as leader of a prominent swing sextet in New York. Kernfeld 1988.

"Kiss My Ass," 28. Bawdy song associated with Kid Ory in the 1910s.

Kyle, Billy, 159. 1914–66; pn; performed with LA and the All Stars from 1953 until 1966. Kyle's career began in the mid-1930s and included stints with the Mills Blue Rhythm Band, the John Kirby Sextet, and Sy Oliver's orchestra. Kernfeld 1988.

Lafayette Theater, 105, 148. Variety theater in New York City, located at 2227 Seventh Avenue. LA performed there fronting Carroll Dickerson's band in 1930. After about fifteen years as a leading jazz venue, the Lafayette was converted to a movie theater in 1935. Kernfeld 1988; Armstrong 1936, 97.

Lake Tahoe, NV, 190.

Lala, Pete, 120. Bar owner in Storyville, New Orleans, from 1908 to 1917. Lala's saloon was located at the corner of Customhouse and Marais streets. Rose and Souchon 1984; Armstrong 1954, 95; Armstrong 1936, 36.

Las Vegas, NV, 159, 163, 190.

"The Last Time," 134. Song by Ewing and Martin, recorded by LA and His Hot Five, September 1927.

"Laughin' Louie," 108. Song composed by Clarence Gaskill and recorded by LA and His Orchestra, April 1933.

Lawrence, MA, 93.

Lax, Mr., 70. First mate on the SS *Sidney*, 1919.

"Lazy River," 148. Song composed by Hoagy Carmichael and Sidney Arodin, 1931. Recorded by LA and the All Stars, December 1956.

Library of Congress, 24.

Lincoln Gardens, 29, 49, 52–54, 57–59, 62–64, 66, 72, 75, 85, 87, 92, 130, 183. Dance hall in Chicago, located at East 31st Street and South Cottage Grove Avenue. Open from the early years of the century, this spacious venue was known as the Royal Gardens until 1921, when the name was changed to Lincoln Gardens. Joe Oliver's band performed there from June 1922 until February 1924. A gangster-style bombing in 1927 caused the hall, then known as the Cafe de Paris, to be closed. Kenney 1993; Kernfeld 1988; Armstrong 1954, 231; Armstrong 1936, 69.

Lindsay, Johnny, 108. 1894–1950; sb, tbn; bassist with LA's touring orchestra in 1931–32. Lindsey played trombone in New Orleans until 1925, when he relocated in Chicago and concentrated mainly on string bass. He recorded with Jelly Roll Morton in 1926 and with LA in 1931. Rose and Souchon 1984; Kernfeld 1988; Armstrong 1936, 95.

Little Mack, 125. Brass band drummer, childhood friend, and member of LA's vocal quartet, c. 1913. Armstrong 1954, 34.

Lomax, Alan, 4.

Lombardo, Guy, 164, 166. 1902–77; prominent orchestra leader. He formed a dance orchestra called Guy Lombardo and the Royal Canadians in Ontario in the early 1920s and achieved national popularity operating out of Chicago and New York until the mid-1960s. Conservative in style, his music was billed as "the sweetest sound this side of Heaven." Kenney 1993.

"The Lonesome Road," 108. Song with words by Gene Austin and music by Nathaniel Shilkret, 1928. Recorded by LA and His Orchestra, November 1931.

Los Angeles, CA, 78, 106, 111, 117, 160, 163.

Los Angeles Dodgers, 163.

Louis Armstrong and the All Stars, 129, 142, 152, 154, 190. Touring and recording band led by LA from 1947 until the end of his life. The late 1940s personnel included Jack Teagarden, tb; Barney Bigard, cl; Earl Hines, pn; Arvell Shaw, sb; and Sid Catlett, dr.

Louis Armstrong & His Savoy Ballroom Five, 135. Recording band, including Earl Hines, pn; Mancy Carr, bjo; Jimmie Strong, cl; and Fred Robinson, tbn; 1928.

Louis Armstrong Archives, Queens College, New York, 47.

Lyons, Bob, 134. C. 1868–c. 1949; sb; performed in New Orleans with Buddy Bolden and Frank Duson in the early part of the century, and with Kid Ory in the mid-1910s. Rose and Souchon 1984; Armstrong 1954, 23.

Lyric Theater, 31. Nightclub in New Orleans, located at 201 Burgundy Street; open from the 1910s until 1927, when it was destroyed by fire.

Madison, WI, 63.

Magnolia [Brass] Band, 38. Dance orchestra and affiliated brass band active in New Orleans from about 1909 to 1914, led by Emile Bigard (vln) and Joe Oliver. Rose and Souchon 1984; Armstrong 1936, 16.

Major, Mrs. [Majors, Florence], 49, 54. Owner of the Lincoln Gardens dance hall from 1921 to 1924. Kenney 1993; Armstrong 1954, 136.

Mahogany Hall, 135. Brothel in Storyville, New Orleans, located at 235 Basin Street and operated in the early part of the century by Lulu White, the "Octoroon Queen." Rose and Souchon 1984; Armstrong 1954, 147.

Mahoney, Will, 62. 1894–1967; vaudeville entertainer known in the 1930s for his ability to play the xylophone with mallets attached to his feet.

Manetta, Manuel, 148. 1889–1969; piano and various other instruments, ldr; performed with Joe Oliver and Kid Ory in New Orleans in the 1910s and later became known as a music teacher. Rose and Souchon 1984; Kernfeld 1988.

Mangel, Ira, 182. LA's road manager, 1960s.

Manone, Wingy, 33, 108, 166. 1900–82; c, ldr; well known white cornetist of the 1920s-40s. Manone's career began in New Orleans and included periods in Chicago, New York, Hollywood, and Las Vegas. His popular recording of "Isle of Capri" brought national attention in 1935. Rose and Souchon 1984; Kenney 1993; Kernfeld 1988; Armstrong 1936, 14.

"Maple Leaf Rag," 149. Piano rag composed by Scott Joplin, 1899.

Marable, Fate, 51 70, 83. 1890–1947; pn, ldr; bandleader aboard Mississippi riverboats from the 1910s to the 1930s. Marable began performing aboard the steamers in 1907, and led orchestras by the late 1910s. He recruited young musicians from New Orleans, and his group became known as "the floating conservatory." LA, Henry "Red" Allen, and Warren "Baby" Dodds were among his notable personnel. Rose and Souchon 1984; Kernfeld 1988; Armstrong 1954, 181; Armstrong 1936, 36.

Mares, Paul, 33. 1900–1949; c, tpt, ldr; notable white cornetist and leader of the New Orleans Rhythm Kings. Mares moved from New Orleans to Chicago in 1919. In 1922–23 his group made a series of influential recordings, including "Tin Roof Blues" and "Farewell Blues." He performed only occasionally after 1925. Rose and Souchon 1984; Kenney 1993; Kernfeld 1988.

Marshall, Kaiser, 93, 126. 1899–1948; d; performed with Fletcher Henderson from 1924 to 1930, and recorded with LA both under Henderson (1924–25) and with a small group in 1929. His later career included stints with Duke Ellington, Cab Calloway, and Bunk Johnson. Kernfeld 1988.

Martin, Henry, 28, 122, 125, 134. C. 1895–c. 1932; d; performed in New Orleans with the dance orchestras of Joe Oliver and Kid Ory in the early 1910s and also played bass drum with the Onward Brass Band. Rose and Souchon 1984; Armstrong 1954, 30.

Martin, Mrs., and family, 89, 122–23. Childhood friends of LA. Armstrong 1954, 30.

Martin, Wilhelmina, 123–24. Sister of Henry Martin. Armstrong 1954, 31.

Mathews [Matthews], Bill, 69. 1899–1964; tbn, dr; performed in New Orleans with the Excelsior Brass Band in the 1910s. Matthews toured with Jelly Roll Morton in the 1920s and later performed mainly with Papa Celestin. Rose and Souchon 1984.

MCA [Music Corporation of America], 63, 72. Music publishing firm and booking agency in New York City.

McKendricks, Mike, 108. Banjo; performed with LA in Chicago, 1931. Armstrong 1936, 95.

Melody Maker, The, 21. British periodical devoted to jazz and popular music, first issued in 1926.

"Memories of You," 148. Song with words by Andy Razaf and music by Eubie Blake, 1930. Recorded by LA and His New Sebastian Cotton Club Orchestra, October 1930. Armstrong 1936, 95.

Merrill, Robert, 159. Born 1919; opera singer active with the Metropolitan Opera of New York from the 1940s to the 1980s.

Metoyer, Arnold, 28. C. 1876–1935; c, tpt; performed in New Orleans with various dance bands, including that of Luis Russell in the early 1920s, and toured the South with tent shows. Rose and Souchon 1984.

Metronome, ix, 164. American periodical devoted to current music, in publication from 1885 to 1961.

Mezzrow, Mezz, 111. 1899–1972; cl; white clarinetist and recording producer. Mezzrow performed in Chicago in the 1920s and later in New York, where he organized some of the first interracial recording sessions. Kenney 1993; Kernfeld 1988.

Middleton, Velma, 141–42, 154. 1917–61; vcl; a nightclub singer in the 1930s, Middleton toured intermittently with LA from 1942

Middleton, Velma *(continued)* on, and the two often sang comic-romantic duets, such as "Baby, It's Cold Outside." Middleton died while touring Africa with LA and the All Stars. Kernfeld 1988.

Miles, Flora, 88. Cousin of LA, natural mother of Clarence Armstrong. Armstrong 1954, 18.

Miles, Ike, 16. Uncle of LA. Armstrong 1954, 18.

Miller, Dempsey, "Deecie," 65, 89. Mother of Lil Hardin Armstrong.

Millender [Millinder], Lucky, 108. 1900–66; ldr, dancer-entertainer. Known for his acrobatic showmanship, Millinder came to prominence in Chicago in 1931, then moved to New York, where he led the Mills Blue Rhythm Band from 1934–38.In the 1940s he led a popular band at the Savoy Ballroom and appeared in a number of motion pictures. Kernfeld 1988.

Mills Blue Rhythm Band, 106. Well known big band in New York, 1930–38. Formed and first led by drummer Willie Lynch, it accompanied LA on several recordings in 1930. The ensemble was named for its manager, Irving Mills, and was led after 1934 by Lucky Millinder. Kernfeld 1988.

"Minnetonka." *See* "By the Waters of Minnetonka."

Mississippi, 154.

Montreal, Canada, 159.

Moret, George "Old Man," 174. C. 1860–1924; c; ldr; a reading cornetist and leader of the Excelsior Brass Band in New Orleans from 1905 to 1922. Rose and Souchon 1984; Armstrong 1954, 180.

Morton, Jelly Roll [Ferdinand "Jelly Roll" Morton], 4, 24, 135. 1890–1941; pn; ldr, composer; the first great composer of jazz. Morton began playing solo piano in the bordellos of Storyville by 1902 and cultivated a career through the mid-1910s as an itinerant pianist, gambler, and dandy. He retained a base in New Orleans until settling in Los Angeles in 1917. After five successful years there, he moved to Chicago and entered the music publishing and recording fields. His recordings with his band, the Red Hot Peppers, of such original works as "Grandpa's Spells" and "Black Bottom Stomp," mark a high point in early jazz in terms of the integration of composition and improvisation. Morton later moved to New York and then Washington, DC, but by the mid-1930s his music was considered antiquated. Rose and Souchon 1984; Kenney 1993; Kernfeld 1988; Armstrong 1954, 99.

Mosby, Curtis, 117–18. Drummer in Los Angeles, c. 1930.

Moulin Rouge Hotel, Las Vegas, NV, 157–58, 163.

"Muskrat Ramble," 129–30. Song with words by Ray Gilbert and music by Edward "Kid" Ory, 1926. Recorded by LA and His Hot Five, February 1926.

My Cellar, 108. Nightclub in Chicago, 1920s, also known as The Cellar, located at 222 North State Street. Kenney 1993; Kernfeld 1988.

NBC Radio, 147.

Nenest. *See* Trepagnier, Ernest "Ninesse."

New Iberia, LA, 149, 152.

New Orleans, LA, 5–35, 38, 40–42, 51, 57–60, 62, 66, 68–70, 72–74, 82–85, 88–90, 96, 112–13, 116, 120–25, 130, 133–35, 148, 150–54, 170, 174–75, 180, 189. Rose and Souchon 1984; Kernfeld 1988; Armstrong 1954; Armstrong 1936.

New Orleans *Item*, 151, 156.

New Orleans Rhythm Kings, 33. White jazz band active in Chicago in the early 1920s. Its three principal members were Paul Mares (c), George Brunis (tbn), and Leon Roppolo (cl). Its recordings from 1922–23 showed considerable originality as well as a clear influence from Joe Oliver's Creole Jazz Band. Rose and Souchon, 1984; Kernfeld 1988.

New York City, 71, 92–94, 103–6, 109–10, 112, 116, 125–26, 139–40, 144, 148, 185. Kernfeld 1988; Armstrong 1936.

Niagara Falls, NY, 104.

Nicholas, Albert, 92. 1900–1973; cl; respected clarinet soloist. Nicholas led a band in New Orleans at Tom Anderson's saloon in 1923. The following year he moved to Chicago to join Joe Oliver's Creole Band. Until his death he toured widely and performed with leading figures of the New Orleans style, including Sidney Bechet, LA, and Jelly Roll Morton. Rose and Souchon 1984; Kernfeld 1988; Armstrong 1954, 220.

Noone, Jimmie, 33, 101, 134. 1895–1944; cl, ldr; prominent clarinet soloist of the 1920s-30s. Noone migrated from New Orleans to Chicago in 1918 and performed there with Joe Oliver and Doc Cook. From 1926 to 1928 he led a group at the Apex Club and established himself as a leading jazz soloist. He spent his last years on the West Coast, touring and recording with Kid Ory's band. Kenney 1993; Rose and Souchon 1984; Armstrong 1954, 96.

Nootsy, xvii, xviii, xx, 59–60. Consort of LA in New Orleans, c. 1917.

Norvo, Red, 165. 1908–99; xylophone, vibraphone, ldr; performed with Paul Whiteman and Charlie Barnet before joining Benny Goodman's sextet in 1944. An outstanding swing improviser, he was able to adapt to the complexity of bebop for later work with Charlie Parker, Woody Herman, and Billie Holiday. Kernfeld 1988; Armstrong 1936, 107.

Odd Fellows Club, 8, 120. Armstrong 1954, 29.

OKeh Recording Company, 103, 127, 130, 132, 135–36. Record label established in New York in 1916 and absorbed by the Columbia label in 1926. Active in New York and Chicago, OKeh produced an important catalog of jazz, including recordings by Joe Oliver's Creole Band, and LA's Hot Five and Hot Seven. Kenney 1993; Kernfeld 1988; Armstrong 1936, 96.

"Ol' Man Mose," 148. Song composed by Louis Armstrong and Zilner Randolph, and recorded by LA and His Orchestra in November 1935.

Oliver, Joe "King," xviii, 14, 26, 28–29, 33, 37–40, 42–43, 47–55, 57–59, 61–68, 71–72, 75, 82, 84–87, 92, 94, 98, 116, 120, 122, 128–30, 134, 136, 154, 173–75, 183, 189. 1885–1938; c, ldr; leading cornetist of early jazz and mentor of LA. Oliver performed with dance bands and brass bands in New Orleans from about 1907 until 1918, when he moved to Chicago. From 1920 to 1927 he led groups in Chicago and made a series of influential recordings. LA played second cornet in Oliver's Creole Jazz Band from 1922 to 1924 and recorded with the band in 1923. Oliver moved to New York in 1927, but was unable to sustain his earlier level of success. He toured the South and Midwest as a leader from 1930 to 1936, but seldom performed on cornet, in part because of severe dental problems. His last recording was in 1931. Rose and Souchon 1984; Kenney 1993; Kernfeld 1988; Armstrong 1954, 24; Armstrong 1936, 13.

Oliver, Stella, 85. Wife of Joe Oliver. Armstrong 1954, 99; Armstrong 1936, 70.

One Eye Bud, 73. Childhood friend of LA. Armstrong 1954, 17.

Onward Brass Band, 26–27, 31, 38, 42, 174. New Orleans brass band active from 1885 to 1930. Led from 1903 by Creole cornetist Manuel Perez, it was considered by contemporaries to be the most consistent and exciting of the early brass bands. Its instrumentation usually consisted of three cornets, two trombones, two clarinets, alto horn, baritone horn, tuba, snare drum, and bass drum. Members of the band at various times included Isidore Barbarin and Joe Oliver. Rose and Souchon 1984; Kernfeld 1988; Armstrong 1954, 90; Armstrong 1936, 15.

Original Creole Band, 52. Touring jazz band composed primarily of musicians from New Orleans, active from c. 1908 to 1918. Organized by bassist Bill Johnson, the Creole Jazz Band was among the first jazz

Original Creole Band *(continued)* bands to perform on the West Coast, and it also played long term engagements in Chicago, New York, and Boston. Its personnel included at various times Freddie Keppard, c; George Baquet, cl; and George Filhe, tb. Rose and Souchon 1984; Kernfeld 1988.

Original Dixieland Jazz Band, 33. White jazz band active in the 1910s and early 1920s, the first jazz band to make phonograph recordings. The original members were Nick LaRocca (c), Larry Shields (cl), Eddie Edwards (tbn), Henry Ragas (pn), and Tony Sbarbaro (dr), all New Orleans natives. Formed for nightclub work in Chicago, the ODJB moved to New York in 1917 and recorded a number of popular titles, including "Livery Stable Blues" and "Tiger Rag." Rose and Souchon 1984; Kernfeld 1988; Armstrong 1954, 161; Armstrong 1936, 10.

Orpheum Theater, New Orleans, 125.

Ory, Edward "Kid," 28, 31, 38, 69, 125, 128, 130, 132–33, 135–36, 144, 174. C. 1890–1973; tbn, ldr; prominent trombonist of early jazz. Ory led a popular band in New Orleans from 1912 to 1919, when he moved to Los Angeles. There he led several groups and recorded in 1922 with Spike's Seven Pods of Pepper. In 1925 Ory traveled to Chicago, where he recorded with LA, Joe Oliver, and Jelly Roll Morton. He resumed his career on the West Coast and, except for a nine-year hiatus from music during the Great Depression, remained active as a popular figure of traditional jazz until the mid-1960s. Rose and Souchon 1984; Kenney 1993; Kernfeld 1988; Armstrong 1954, 30; Armstrong 1936, 25.

"Ory's Creole Trombone," 133. Song composed by Edward "Kid" Ory, c. 1922. Recorded by LA and His Hot Five, September 1927.

Palmer, Roy, 69. 1892–1964; tbn; performed in New Orleans before moving to Chicago in 1917; active with Lawrence Duhé, Joe Oliver, and Jelly Roll Morton in the 1920s. Rose and Souchon 1984; Kernfeld 1988; Armstrong 1954, 92.

Panassié, Hugues, 153–54. 1912–74; French author and jazz critic, editor of *Jazz Hot* and founder of the Hot Club de France. Kernfeld 1988; Armstrong 1936, 103.

"Panama," 38. Staple of the New Orleans brass band repertory, composed by William H. Tyers, 1911. Recorded by LA and the All Stars, April 1950. Armstrong 1954, 143.

Panico, Louis, 50, 109. Prominent white cornetist in Chicago, 1920s, soloist with Isham Jones's orchestra and self-professed admirer of Joe Oliver. Kenney 1993; Armstrong 1954, 237.

Paris, France, 154.

Paul, Elliott, 147.

Pelican Dance Hall, 128. Dance hall in New Orleans, 1910s-1920s, located at the corner of Gravier and Rampart streets.

Pennies from Heaven, x, 147. 1936 motion picture starring Bing Crosby and featuring LA and His Orchestra.

Perez, Emanuel [Manuel], 26, 38, 42, 66. 1871–1946; c, ldr; prominent brass band cornetist in New Orleans. Except for a stint from 1916 to 1918 as a bandleader in Chicago, Perez led the Onward Brass Band from 1903 to 1930 and performed with various dance bands. An excellent sightreader, he was admired for a clear attack and beautiful tone. Rose and Souchon 1984; Kenney 1993; Kernfeld 1988; Armstrong 1954, 90; Armstrong 1936, 15.

Petit, Joe, 69, 133. C. 1880–1946; tbn; brass band musician and stepfather of Buddy Petit. Rose and Souchon 1984; Armstrong 1954, 100.

Petit, Joseph "Buddy," 31, 69. C. 1897–1931; c, tpt, ldr; respected jazz soloist in New Orleans. Petit performed in New Orleans and surrounding areas with various dance bands from c. 1917; his career included brief associations with Jimmie Noone, Frank Duson, and Jelly Roll Morton, but he was never recorded. Rose and Souchon 1984; Kernfeld 1988; Armstrong 1954, 25; Armstrong 1936, 14.

Peyton, Dave, 92. C. 1885–1956; pno, ldr; leader of a prominent dance orchestra in Chicago from 1912 until the mid-1930s and author of a regular column on music in the *Chicago Defender* in the late 1920s. Kenney 1993; Kernfeld 1988.

Phipps, Charlie, Mr. And Mrs., 161–62. Friends of LA, 1955.

Picou, Alphonse, 38, 141. 1878–1961; cl; known as a fine reader and competent jazz musician, Picou performed with the Excelsior Brass Band, Tuxedo Brass Band and numerous dance orchestras in a long career in New Orleans. Rose and Souchon 1984; Kernfeld 1988; Armstrong 1954, 220.

Plantation Cafe, 92, 94, 129. Nightclub in Chicago, 1924-c. 1934, located at 338 East 35th Street. Joe Oliver's Dixie Syncopators performed there from 1925 to 1927. Kenney 1993; Kernfeld 1988.

Plymouth, England, 21.

Pollack, Ben, 106. 1903–71; dr, ldr; prominent white bandleader of the late 1920s based in Chicago and California; his personnel at times included Benny Goodman, Glenn Miller, Harry James, and Jack Teagarden. Kenney 1993; Kernfeld 1988.

"Potato Head Blues," 128. Jazz instrumental composed by LA and recorded by LA and His Hot Seven, May 1927.

Powers, Ollie, xix, 54–55, 86. Vocalist, dr, ldr; performed and led bands in Chicago from the mid-1910s through the 1920s, employed LA briefly in 1924. Kenney 1993; Armstrong 1936, 70.

Prat's Restaurant, New Orleans, 83. Armstrong 1954, 189.

Prima, Louis, 34. 1911–78; tpt, vcl, ldr; popular bandleader, singer, and personality in the 1950s-60s. Prima performed in New Orleans until 1935, when he began a residency as a bandleader at the Famous Door nightclub in New York. He led a big band and toured in the 1940s, eventually settling in Las Vegas. His extroverted playing and hoarse singing style were clearly influenced by those of LA. Kernfeld 1988.

Pugh, Doc, 161. LA's valet, 1955.

Randolph, Zilner, 108. 1899–1994; tpt, performed in Chicago in the 1930s with LA, Carroll Dickerson, and his own big band. Kernfeld 1988; Armstrong 1936, 95.

Rappolo [Roppolo], Leon, 33. 1902–43; cl; performed and recorded with the New Orleans Rhythm Kings berfore a nervous breakdown resulted in institutionalization in 1925. Rose and Souchon 1984; Kernfeld 1988; Armstrong 1954, 220.

Record Changer, The, ix, 37, 40. American periodical, first issued in 1942.

'Recou, 148. New Orleans musician.

Red, Bud, 49, 54. Manager of the Lincoln Gardens, 1922. Armstrong 1954, 237.

Red Head Happy. *See* Bolton, Red Head Happy.

Red Light District. *See* Storyville.

Redman, Don, 93, 126. 1900–64; as, composer, important arranger of the early swing period. Redman performed with and arranged for Fletcher Henderson's orchestra during the 1920s. His arrangements complimented the talents of the band's soloists, such as LA and Coleman Hawkins and were noted for their sophisticated integration of written passages with improvised solos. In the 1940s and 1950s he became active in radio and television scoring. Kernfeld 1988.

Regal Theater, 107–8. Variety theater in Chicago, located at 4719 South Parkway Boulevard. LA performed in this 3500 seat venue in the 1930s. Kenney 1993; Kernfeld 1988.

Rena, Henry "Kid," 133. 1898–1949; c, tpt; respected jazz soloist in New Orleans, known for his ability to play in the upper register. Rena succeeded LA in Kid Ory's band in 1919, performed with his own Dixie Jazz Band and the Tuxedo Brass Band in the 1920s, and led various other

Rena, Henry "Kid" *(continued)* groups until retiring from music in 1947. Rose and Souchon 1984; Kernfeld 1988.

Reno, NV, 151, 155, 171, 190.

Riverside Hotel, Reno, NV, 151, 155.

Robertson, Alvin, "Zue," 29, 69. 1891–1943, tbn; performed in the bands of Manuel Perez and John Robichaux before leaving New Orleans for Chicago in 1917. In the mid-1920s he worked with Jelly Roll Morton, Joe Oliver, and Dave Peyton. After 1930 he gave up the trombone to play piano and bass for the remainder of his life. Rose and Souchon 1984; Kernfeld 1988; Armstrong 1954, 96.

Robichaux, John, 31, 42, 125. 1866–1939; vln, d, ldr; performed with the Excelsior Brass Band in the 1890s, and from 1893 to 1939 led a highly successful dance orchestra in New Orleans. Conservative in style, with a repertory of stock written arrangements, his band held forth at the Lyric Theater from 1918 to 1927. Rose and Souchon 1984; Kernfeld 1988; Armstrong 1954, 216.

Robinson, Bill "Bojangles," xix, 27–28, 62, 179, 183–86. 1878–1949; dancer, entertainer; tap dance pioneer who toured on the TOBA and RKO circuits in first quarter of the century. Robinson appeared on Broadway and in films in the 1930s and '40s. Kernfeld 1988; Armstrong 1936, 81.

Robinson, Fred, 101, 104, 135. 1901–84; tbn; performed alongside LA in Carroll Dickerson's band in Chicago in 1928 and took part in LA's Hot Five recordings from June to December that year. Later work included stints with Fletcher Henderson, Andy Kirk, and Cab Calloway. Kenney 1993; Kernfeld 1988; Armstrong 1936, 87.

Robinson, Zoo. *See* Robertson, Alvin "Zue."

Rockwell, Tommy, 103–6, 108–9. Recording executive and promoter in New York City, manager of LA, 1929–31. Rockwell billed LA as a solo act and arranged for him to appear in Broadway shows. Kenney 1993; Armstrong 1936, 89.

Roseland Ballroom, 93, 112, 125. Famous dance hall in New York City, open from 1919 to 1956 and located at 1658 Broadway. LA joined Fletcher Henderson's orchestra at the Roseland Ballroom in 1924. The hall hosted most of the major swing bands in the 1930s and 1940s. Kernfeld 1988; Armstrong 1936, 80.

Ross, Ally, 106. Bandleader in New York City, 1929.

"Royal Garden Blues," 127. Song with words and music by Clarence Williams and Spencer Williams, 1919.

Royal Palm Gardens. *See* Lincoln Gardens.

Russell Luis, 92, 140, 142, 185. 1902–63; pn, ldr; performed with Joe Oliver from 1925 to 1927 and then led his own band in New York until 1948, when he retired from music. From 1935 to 1943 his band provided backing for LA. Rose and Souchon 1984; Kenney 1993; Kernfeld 1988; Armstrong 1936, 94.

Russell, William, xxii, 127. Jazz historian, author.

St. Cyr, Johnny, 128, 130, 132–33, 135. 1890–1966; bjo, gtr; performed in New Orleans with various dance bands, including Fate Marable's riverboat orchestra, until 1923, when he moved to Chicago. St. Cyr recorded with LA and the Hot Five and Hot Seven, and also with Jelly Roll Morton and Joe Oliver. He returned to New Orleans in 1930 and remained active on a part-time basis for the rest of his life. Rose and Souchon 1984; Kenney 1993; Kernfeld 1988; Armstrong 1954, 186.

St. Katherine's Hall, 133. Dance hall in New Orleans, 1910s, located at 1509 Tulane Avenue. Rose and Souchon 1984; Kernfeld 1988.

St. Louis, MO, 70–71, 83–84, 101, 140–42. Armstrong 1954, 185; Armstrong 1936, 50.

St. Paul, SS, 70, 83. Streckfus Line riverboat, 1911–39. Rose and Souchon 1984; Kernfeld 1988; Armstrong 1954, 189.

Salle Pleyel Concert Hall, Paris, 154. Kernfeld 1988; Armstrong 1954, 114.

Sands Hotel, Las Vegas, NV, 159.

San Francisco, CA, 121, 163.

Savoy Ballroom, 100–101, 103–4, 131. Dance hall in Chicago, 1927–47, located at South Parkway Boulevard and East 47th Street. Music for dancing was offered seven nights a week, and among the first bands to perform there was Carroll Dickerson's orchestra, led by LA. Kenney 1993; Kernfeld 1988.

Scandinavia, 190.

Schiff, Dr. Alexander, 159, 182. Tour physician for LA and the All Stars.

Scott, Bud, 134. 1890–1949; bjo, gtr, vcl; performed in New Orleans until 1913, then traveled widely, eventually settling in California. Scott recorded with Joe Oliver, Jelly Roll Morton, and Johnny Dodds. In 1947 he appeared with LA in the motion picture *New Orleans*. Rose and Souchon 1984; Kernfeld 1988.

Scott, Howard, 93, 126. Trumpet; a member of Fletcher Henderson's orchestra in 1924.

Sebastian, Frank, 106, 115. Owner of Frank Sebastian's New Cotton Club, Culver City, CA, c. 1930.

Shaw, Arvell, 129, 142, 190. Born 1923; sb; performed with Fate Marable on Mississippi riverboats, 1942, and served in Navy bands before joining LA's big band in 1945. Shaw was the primary bassist for LA and the All Stars from 1947 until the late 1960s. Kernfeld 1988.

Shields, Larry, 33. 1893–1953; cl; clarinetist of the Original Dixieland Jazz Band. Shields performed in New Orleans before moving to Chicago in 1915, where he joined forces with cornetist Nick LaRocca. Composer of "Livery Stable Blues," he left the ODJB in 1921, remaining active in New Orleans and California until his death. Rose and Souchon 1984; Kernfeld 1988; Armstrong 1936, 10.

Showboat Club, 108–10. Speakeasy in Chicago, located on North Clark Street. LA appeared there in 1931. Armstrong 1954, 96.

Sidney, SS, 70, 83. Streckfus Line riverboat, 1911–21. LA performed on this ship, in Fate Marable's orchestra, in the summer of 1919. Rose and Souchon 1984; Kernfeld 1988; Armstrong 1954, 181.

Sinatra, Frank, 164. 1915–1998; vcl, ldr; emerged as a star vocalist with the big bands of Harry James (1939) and Tommy Dorsey (1940–42), and enjoyed a consistently successful career in music and motion pictures into the 1990s. Sinatra is admired among jazz musicians for his relaxed, understated sense of swing. Kernfeld 1988.

Singleton, Arthur "Zutty," 99–106, 116, 125, 131, 164. 1898–1975; dr; performed with Papa Celestin and Fate Marable's riverboat orchestra before leaving New Orleans in 1925. Singleton worked with Jimmie Noone in Chicago in the late 1920s and recorded with LA (1928) and Jelly Roll Morton (1929). He remained active in various traditional and mainstream settings until suffering a stroke in 1970. Rose and Souchon 1984; Kernfeld 1988; Armstrong 1954, 217; Armstrong 1936, 35.

"Skid-Dat-de-Dat," 133. Song composed by Lil Hardin Armstrong and recorded by LA's Hot Five, November 1926.

"Sleepy Time Down South." *See* "When It's Sleepy time Down South."

Small's Paradise, 94. Nightclub in New York City, located at 135th Street and 7th Avenue.

Smiley, Bob, 186. Chauffeur, friend of LA, 1930s.

Smith, Florence, 96–98, 108. Mother of Alpha Smith Armstrong.

Smith, Gunboat, 31. Prizefighter.

Smith, Joe, 93. 1902–37; tpt; brother of Russell Smith; soloist with the Fletcher Henderson orchestra, 1925–28, known for his lyrical tone and use of the plunger mute. Kernfeld 1988.

Smith, Leroy, 147. Orchestra conductor, Hudson Theater, New York City, 1929.

Smith, Russell, 93. 1890–1966; tpt; brother of Joe Smith; played first trumpet with the Fletcher Henderson orchestra from 1925 to 1941 and later worked with the bands of Cab Calloway and Noble Sissle. Kernfeld 1988.

Smith, Sugar Johnny, 50. C. 1880–1918; c; performed with various bands in New Orleans from c. 1902 until 1917, when he moved to Chicago for work with Lawrence Duhé at the Deluxe Café. Rose and Souchon 1984; Armstrong 1954, 99.

Smith, Willie "The Lion," 185. 1897–1973; pn, composer; illustrious exponent of the Harlem stride piano style, active as a soloist in New York from the late 1910s. Kernfeld 1988.

Soldier Boy. *See* Gafford, Luther.

Sousa, John Philip, 36. 1854–1932; composer, conductor; known as the "March King." Sousa conducted the U.S. Marine Band from 1880 to 1892, and then formed his own civilian concert band, which he led on annual tours of North America. He was the composer of numerous popular marches, including "Star and Stripes Forever" (1887), "The Washington Post" (1889), and "Semper Fidelis" (1888). Armstrong 1954, 219.

Spanier, Francis "Muggsy," 103. 1906–67; c; prominent white cornetist, active primarily in Chicago. Spanier performed with the bands of Elmer Schoebel, Ted Lewis, and Ben Pollack in the 1920s and '30s, and then led Dixieland groups during the revival period of the postwar era. Kenney 1993; Kernfeld 1988.

"Spanish Shawl," 95. Song with words by Billy Meyers and Walter Melrose, music by Elmer Schoebel, 1925.

Staulz, Lorenzo, 134. 1880–1928, bjo, gtr; performed intermittently with Buddy Bolden, Freddie Keppard, and Kid Ory in New Orleans during the 1900s-10s. Rose and Souchon 1984.

"Stardust" ["Star Dust"], 108. Song with words by Mitchell Parish and music by Hoagy Carmichael, 1929. Recorded by LA and His Orchestra, November 1931.

"Stars and Stripes Forever," 36. March composed by John Philip Sousa, 1887.

"Static Strut," 29. Jazz instrumental by Jack Yellin and Phil Wall, 1926. Recorded by LA with Erskine Tate's orchestra, May 1926.

"Stomp Off [and] Let's Go," 29. Jazz instrumental by Elmer Schoebel, 1926. Recorded by LA with Erskine Tate's orchestra, May 1926.

Storyville, 4, 13–15, 19, 21, 24–25, 27, 30, 32–33, 68, 120, 135. The brothel district of New Orleans from 1898 to 1917, located in a twenty-block square adjacent to the French Quarter and bounded by North Basin, Customhouse, North Robertson, and St. Louis streets. Named for alderman Sidney Story, whose ordinance outlawing prostitution in the rest of the city fixed its limits, the red-light district offered numerous venues to early jazz musicians. Armstrong 1954, 8; Kernfeld 1988.

Streckfus, Captain Joe, and family, 70, 71, 83. Owners of the Streckfus steamer line. Armstrong 1954, 187.

Streckfus steamer line, 47. Passenger steamship line active on the Mississippi River from the 1910s through the 1930s; many of its ships featured entertainment by resident jazz orchestras. Rose and Souchon 1984; Armstrong 1954, 187; Armstrong 1936, 16.

Strong, Jimmy, 101, 106, 135. 1906-after 1940; cl, ts; performed with Carroll Dickerson's orchestra in Chicago, 1926, and recorded with LA and His Savoy Ballroom Five in 1928. Strong led his own groups in Chicago in the 1930s. Kenney 1993; Kernfeld 1988; Armstrong 1954, 87.

"Struttin' with Some Barbecue," 130. Jazz instrumental composed by LA and recorded by his Hot Five, December 1927.

Sugar Johnny. *See* Smith, Sugar Johnny.

Sunset Cafe, 26, 63, 72, 75, 95, 98–99, 116, 129, 132, 184. Nightclub in Chicago, 1921–37, located at 315–17 East 35th Street. LA performed there with Carroll Dickerson's orchestra in 1926–27. Kenney 1993; Kernfeld 1988; Armstrong, 1954, 84.

Sweden, 115.

"Sweethearts on Parade," 166. Song with words by Charles Newman and music by Carmen Lombardo, 1928. Recorded by LA and His Orchestra, December 1930.

Sweets, 159–61. Consort of LA, c. 1954.

"Swing That Music," 148. Song composed by Horace Gerlach and LA, 1936, and recorded by LA and His Orchestra, May 1936. Armstrong 1954, 118; Armstrong 1936.

Tate, Erskine, xix, 29, 95–96, 127, 184. 1895–1978; vln; prominent orchestra leader in Chicago in the 1920s and '30s. His group enjoyed long residencies at the Vendome Theater (1919–1928) and the Savoy Ballroom (1931–38). LA joined Tate's orchestra after returning to Chicago from New York in November 1925. Kenney 1993; Kernfeld 1988; Armstrong 1936, 84.

Taylor, Mr. And Mrs., 96. Employers of Alpha Smith Armstrong, 1925.

Teagarden, Jack, 126, 129, 142, 165, 190. 1905–64; tbn, vcl; prominent traditional jazz soloist and featured member of LA and His All Stars from 1947 to 1951. Teagarden began performing in the Southwest in the early 1920s. After moving to New York in 1927 he found work with Ben Pollack and then Paul Whiteman, and began to record with other musicians such as LA, Red Nichols, and Eddie Condon. In the 1940s he led his own groups until the formation of the All Stars. Kernfeld 1988; Armstrong 1954, 188; Armstrong 1936, 107.

"That's When I'll Come Back to You," 134–35. Song composed by Lil Hardin Armstrong and recorded by LA's Hot Seven in May 1927.

Thomas, John, 135. 1902–71; tbn; active in Chicago with Erskine Tate, Dave Peyton, and Freddie Keppard in the 1920s. Kernfeld 1988.

"Tiger Rag," 107. Song with words by Harry de Costa and music by the Original Dixieland Jazz Band, 1917. Recorded by LA and His Orchestra, May 1930.

Time magazine, 155.

"Tin Roof Blues," 33. Song with words by Walter Melrose and music by Paul Mares, George Brunis, Leon Roppolo, Mel Stitzel, and Ben Pollack, 1923. Recorded by LA and the All Stars, April 1955.

Toledo, OH, 104.

Tom Anderson's New Cabaret, 83. Nightclub in New Orleans 1910s-20s located at 122–26 North Rampart Street. Kernfeld 1988; Rose and Souchon 1984; Armstrong 1954, 215; Armstrong 1936, 68.

Trepagnier, Ernest "Ninesse," 42–43. C. 1885–1968; dr; played bass drum with the Tuxedo Brass Band from 1916 to 1928. Rose and Souchon 1984.

Trianon Ballroom, 78. Dance hall in Los Angeles, located on Firestone Boulevard. Kernfeld 1988.

Tristano, Lennie, 164. 1919–78; pn; blind pianist and teacher, associated with the bebop movement in the 1940s and known for an original and virtuosic style of improvisation. Kernfeld 1988.

Trumbauer, Frank, 142. 1901–56; s; respected white jazz soloist of the 1920s-30s, active in Chicago and New York and associated with Bix Beiderbecke and Paul Whiteman. Kernfeld 1988; Armstrong 1936, 107.

Tucker, Sophie, 125. 1887–1966. Vaudeville and RKO entertainer and singer active in the 1910s-20s.

Tune Town Ballroom, 142. Dance hall in St. Louis, 1920s-60s, located at 3515 Olive Street.

Tuxedo Brass Band, 42. New Orleans brass band active from 1917 through the 1920s. Formed by Papa Celestin (c) and William "Bébé Ridgley (tbn), it served as a training

Tuxedo Brass Band *(continued)* ground for a number of young musicians, including LA, Sidney Desvigne (c), and Louis Barbarin (d). Rose and Souchon 1984; Kernfeld 1988; Armstrong 1954, 143; Armstrong 1936, 16.

"Twelfth Street Rag," 128. Jazz instrumental recorded by LA's Hot Seven, May 1927.

Twenty-Five Club [Big 25 Club], 120, 123. Nightclub in Storyville, New Orleans, 1902–1950s, located on Franklin Street near Iberville.

Vendome Theater, 63, 95–99, 127–28, 184. Variety theater in Chicago, 1909–49, located at 3145 South State Street. LA performed there with Erskine Tate's orchestra in 1925–26. Kenney 1993; Kernfeld 1988; Armstrong 1936, 84.

Vietnam, 169.

Villec, L/Cpl., viii, xiv, 169–72.

Vincent [Vinson], Eddie, 69. Born c. 1885; tbn; performed in New Orleans with the Olympia Orchestra and Excelsior Brass Band until 1914, when he toured with Bill Johnson's Original Creole Orchestra. Rose and Souchon 1984.

Vocalion Recording Company, 95. Record company and label based in New York City and active from 1916 until 1930, when it was absorbed by Warner Brothers. Kenney 1993; Kernfeld 1988.

Wade, Clerk, 121. New Orleans hustler, c. 1918.

Waller, Thomas "Fats," 185. 1904–43; pn, vcl, ldr, composer; influential jazz soloist and composer of numerous jazz standards, including "Ain't Misbehavin' " and "Honeysuckle Rose." Waller began performing in New York as a solo pianist c. 1919. In the 1920s he composed and recorded, and by the end of the decade was collaborating with lyricists to supply music for musical shows, such as *Hot Chocolates*, featuring LA. His later career included tours as a bandleader, appearances in films, and continued composing for stage shows. Kernfeld 1988; Armstrong 1936, 107.

Washington, Al, 108. Clarinet, ts; member of LA's orchestra in Chicago, 1931. Armstrong 1936, 95.

Washington, George, 146. Born 1907; tbn, arranger; performed with Fletcher Henderson in the mid-1930s and with LA's orchestra from 1937 to 1943. Washington later led his own bands on the West Coast. Kernfeld 1988.

Watson, Ham, 102. Member of Carroll Dickerson's orchestra in Chicago, 1926.

"Weary Blues," 135. Jazz instrumental recorded by LA's Hot Seven, May 1927.

Weatherford, Teddy, 29. 1903–45; pn; moved from New Orleans to Chicago by 1922 and performed with Erskine Tate's orchestra in 1925–26. Weatherford left the United States in 1926 and spent most of the remainder of his career as a bandleader in the Far East. Kernfeld 1988.

Welles, Orson, 77. 1916–85; radio broadcaster, actor, and motion picture director, 1930-60s.

"West End Blues," 148. Song with words by Clarence Williams and music by Joe Oliver, copyright 1928. Recorded by LA's Hot Five (with Earl Hines on piano), June 1927.

Wethington, Crawford, 101–2. Alto sax; a member of Carroll Dickerson's orchestra in Chicago, 1926. Armstrong 1936, 87.

"What Will I Do," 55. Possibly "What'll I Do?," song composed by Irving Berlin, 1924.

"When It's Sleepy Time Down South," 108. Song composed by Leon Rene, Otis Rene, and Clarence Muse, 1931. Recorded by LA and His Orchestra, April 1931.

"When the Saints Go Marching In," 125, 171. Traditional hymn and jazz standard, first recorded by LA and His Orchestra, September 1938.

"When Your Lover Has Gone," 108. Song composed by E. A. Swan, 1931. Recorded by LA and His Orchestra, April 1931. Armstrong 1936, 96.

"When You're Smiling," 184. Song composed by Mark Fisher, Joe Goodwin, and Larry Shay, 1928. Recorded by LA and His Orchestra, September 1929.

White, Lulu, 24, 83, 135. C. 1865–c. 1940. Well-known madam of Mahogany Hall, a brothel in Storyville, New Orleans. Rose and Souchon 1984; Armstrong 1954, 147.

Williams, Bert, 27, 54. 1874–1922; prominent black vaudeville comedian.

Williams, Black Benny, viii, 31, 121, 125, 157, 159–60. C. 1890–1924; New Orleans hustler and brass band drummer, performed with the Tuxedo Brass Band in the 1910s. Rose and Souchon 1984; Armstrong 1954, 75.

Williams, Bobby, 75–76. Died 1920s; tpt; member of Carroll Dickerson's orchestra in Chicago, 1920s.

Wills, Harry, 31. Prizefighter.

Woods, Mr., 97–98. Husband of Florence Smith.

"World on a String." *See* "I've Got the World on a String."

"Wrap Your Troubles in Dreams," 108. Song with words by Ted Koehler and Billy Moll, music by Harry Barris, 1931.

"Yes, I'm in the Barrel," 132. Jazz instrumental composed by LA and recorded by LA's Hot Five, November 1925.

"You'll Never Walk Alone," 169, 171–72. Song with words by Oscar Hammerstein II and music by Richard Rodgers, 1945.

Youmans, Vincent, 103. Composer of music for stage shows in New York City, 1920s–30s, including *Great Day* (1929), which he also produced.

Zeno, Henry, 27, 120–21, 125. C. 1880–1918; dr; performed with brass bands of Buddy Bolden, Manuel Manetta, Joe Oliver, and others in New Orleans from c. 1900 to 1918. Rose and Souchon 1984; Armstrong 1954, 23.

Ziegfeld, Florenz, 186. 1867–1932; prominent vaudeville producer, creator in 1907 of *The Ziegfeld Follies*, a long-running annual revue.

Zucker, Dr. Gary, 3, 6, 179–81. LA's physician at Beth Israel Hospital, 1969–70.

Zulu Social Aid and Pleasure Club, 150–55. Prominent black social club and Mardi Gras krewe in New Orleans. Armstrong 1954, 126.

Zuttie. *See* Singleton, Arthur "Zutty."